Chinese Research Perspectives on Society, Volume 7

Chinese Research Perspectives on Society

International Advisory Board

Yanjie Bian (*University of Minnesota*)
Nan Lin (*Duke University*)
Xueguang Zhou (*Stanford University*)

VOLUME 7

BEIJING

The titles published in this series are listed at *brill.com/crso*

Chinese Research Perspectives on Society, Volume 7

Analysis and Forecast of China's Social Conditions (2018)

Chief Editors

Li Peilin
Chen Guangjin
Zhang Yi

Associate Editors

Li Wei
Fan Lei
Tian Feng

BRILL

LEIDEN | BOSTON

This book is a result of the co-publication agreement between Social Sciences Academic Press and Koninklijke Brill NV. These articles were selected and translated into English from the original 《2018年中国社会形势分析与预测》 (2018 *nian Zhongguo shehui xingshi fenxi yu yuce*) with financial support from the Innovation Program of the Chinese Academy of Social Sciences.

Library of Congress Cataloging-in-Publication Data

Names: Li, Peilin, 1955– editor. | Chen, Guangjin, editor. | Zhang, Yi, 1964– editor.
Title: Analysis and forecast of China's social conditions (2018) / Peilin Li, Guangjin Chen, Yi Zhang.
Other titles: 2018 nian Zhongguo she hui xing shi fen xi yu yu ce. English
Description: Leiden ; Boston : Brill, [2022] | Series: CRP-CRSO - Chinese research perspectives on society, 2212-747X ; Vol. 07 | Includes index.
Identifiers: LCCN 2021040088 (print) | LCCN 2021040089 (ebook) | ISBN 9789004500716 (hardback) | ISBN 9789004500723 (ebook)
Subjects: LCSH: China—Social conditions—2000– | China—Social policy. | Social change—China.
Classification: LCC HN733.5 .A543 2022 (print) | LCC HN733.5 (ebook) | DDC 361.6/10951090512—dc23/eng/20211007
LC record available at https://lccn.loc.gov/2021040088
LC ebook record available at https://lccn.loc.gov/2021040089

Typeface for the Latin, Greek, and Cyrillic scripts: "Brill". See and download: brill.com/brill-typeface.

ISSN 2212-747X
ISBN 978-90-04-50071-6 (hardback)
ISBN 978-90-04-50072-3 (e-book)

Copyright 2022 by Koninklijke Brill NV, Leiden, The Netherlands.
Koninklijke Brill NV incorporates the imprints Brill, Brill Nijhoff, Brill Hotei, Brill Schöningh, Brill Fink, Brill mentis, Vandenhoeck & Ruprecht, Böhlau Verlag and V&R Unipress.
All rights reserved. No part of this publication may be reproduced, translated, stored in a retrieval system, or transmitted in any form or by any means, electronic, mechanical, photocopying, recording or otherwise, without prior written permission from the publisher. Requests for re-use and/or translations must be addressed to Koninklijke Brill NV via brill.com or copyright.com.

This book is printed on acid-free paper and produced in a sustainable manner.

Contents

List of Figures and Tables VII

1   China's Social Development in a New Era: Analysis and Forecast of China's Social Conditions in 2017–2018
The Research Group for Social Conditions Analysis and Forecast, the Chinese Academy of Social Sciences   1
Zhang Yi and Fan Lei

2   Report on Income and Spending among China's Urban and Rural Households in 2017   33
Lyu Qingzhe

3   Report on the Situation and Quality of Employment for College Graduates in 2017   46
Mo Rong, Chen Yun, and Wang Xinyu

4   Report on the Reform and Development of China's Social Security System in 2017   71
Lyu Xuejing and Wang Yongmei

5   Report on the Reform and Development of China's Education System in 2017   94
Li Tao, Zhang Wenting, and Fang Chen

6   Report on the Development of China's Health Care in 2017   115
Fang Lijie

7   Report on China's Public Safety Situation in 2017   132
Zhou Yandong and Gong Zhigang

8   Survey Report on the Quality of Social Development in China in a New Era   151
Cui Yan

9   Survey Report on the Development of the Sharing Economy and Its Social Impact in China: An Analysis of Data from Seven Cities   179
Lu Yangxu, He Guangxi, and Zhao Yandong

10   Survey Report on Chinese College Students' Philosophy of Life and
      Social Attitudes: An Analysis of Data from a Longitudinal Survey
      of Students from Twelve Colleges and Universities   193
      Liu Baozhong

11   Survey Report on the Living Conditions of the New White-Collar
      Urban Workers: A Study of Shanghai in 2017   213
      Sun Xiulin and Shi Runhua

12   Survey Report on Internet Use among Senior Citizens in China   240
      Zhu Di, Gao Wenjun, and Zhu Yanqiao

13   Survey Report on the Conditions of Urban and Rural Residents Living
      under Economic and Material Hardship   269
      Jiang Zhiqiang, Wang Jing, and Tian Feng

14   Analytical Report on Online Public Opinion in China in 2017   296
      Zhu Huaxin, Liao Canliang, and Pan Yufeng

15   Analytical Report on China's Food and Drug Safety Situation
      in 2017   320
      Luo Jie and Tian Ming

16   Analytical Report on Environmental Protection in China in 2017   334
      Jia Feng, Yang Ke, Tian Shuo, Huang Jingyi, and Zhou Liantong

17   Analytical Report on China's Industrial Labor Force in 2017   364
      Qiao Jian and Liu Xiaoqian

18   Analytical Report on Rural Household Development in China
      in 2017   386
      Peng Chao and Zhang Xiaorong

19   Analytical Report on Newly Established Small and Micro-Enterprises
      in China in 2017   406
      Zhang Jiurong, Lyu Peng, and Jin Zhaohui

20   A Statistical Overview of China's Social Development in 2017   422
      Zhang Liping

      Index   437

Figures and Tables

Figures

2.1 Structure of the Per Capita Income of Residents in 2012 and 2016   35

2.2 The Gini Coefficient of China's Resident Income, 2002–2016   36

2.3 The Urban-Rural Income Ratio, 2000–2016   37

2.4 Structure of Resident Spending in 2012 and 2016   39

3.1 Newly Employed People in Urban Areas in Different Quarters   48

3.2 Registered Urban Unemployment Rates   49

3.3 Changes in the Ratio of Job Vacancies to Job Seekers in the HR Market   50

3.4 Changes in the PMI and Employee Index in Manufacturing   51

3.5 Number of Current College Graduates   52

3.6 Employment Index for Graduates, 2011–2015   56

3.7 Actual Employment Rate for Graduates, 2011–2015   57

3.8 Percentage of Graduates Starting Up Independent Businesses, 2011–2015   58

3.9 The Rate of Enrollment for Graduates, 2011–2015   59

3.10 Employment Quality Index for Graduates, 2011–2015   60

3.11 Graduates' Satisfaction with Their Employment, 2011–2015   61

3.12 The Stability of Graduates' Employment, 2011–2015   62

3.13 Rate of Flexible Employment among Graduates, 2011–2015, with a Comparison between Junior College Graduates and Undergraduates   62

4.1 Total Expenditure on Social Assistance since 2014 (first three quarters)   78

4.2 Changes in Expenditures on Subsistence Allowances in Urban and Rural Areas and the Number of People Receiving Subsistence Allowances in the Past Five Years (first three quarters)   79

4.3 Per Capita Subsistence Allowances in Urban and Rural Areas in the Past Five Years (first three quarters)   80

4.4 Expenditure on Medical Assistance and the Number of People Receiving Medical Assistance in the Past Five Years (first three quarters)   82

4.5 Basic Conditions of Expenditure on Disaster Relief in the Past Five Years (first three quarters)   83

4.6 Expenditure on Temporary Assistance in the Past Five Years (first three quarters)   84

4.7 Expenditure on Preferential Treatment and the Number of Preferential Treatment Objects in the Past Five Years (first three quarters)   85

4.8 Expenditure on Social Welfare in the Past Five Years (first three quarters)   86

4.9 Basic Conditions of the Development of Undertakings Related to the Elderly and the Disabled in the Past Five Years (first three quarters)   88

4.10	Basic Conditions of Adoption and Assistance Services Provided for Children in the Past Five Years (first three quarters) 89
4.11	Basic Conditions of Services Provided to Mentally Handicapped People and to Patients with Mental Disorders in the Past Five Years (first three quarters) 90
6.1	Total Health Expenditures per Annum 118
7.1	Number of Injury, Homicide, Robbery, and Fraud Cases Recorded by Public Security Organs, 2010–2016 134
7.2	Number of Cases of Smuggling Filed by Public Security Organs, 2010–2016 135
7.3	Number of Cases Regarding Public Safety Recorded by Public Security Organs, 2010–2016 136
7.4	Number of Cases of Dispute Mediation, 2010–2016 137
7.5	Number of Cases Requiring Mediation in Housing and Homestead Disputes, 2010–2016 137
7.6	Number of Typical Terrorist Attacks in China, 2012–2017 139
7.7	Sites and Frequencies of Typical Terrorist Attacks in China, 2012–2017 141
8.1	Comparisons between Interviewees in 2015 and in 2017 in Terms of Their Sense of Social Fairness 167
9.1	Public Awareness of the Services of a Sharing Economy in Different Fields 183
9.2	Proportions of the Sharing Economy Services Obtained by the Public 185
9.3	Willingness of the Public to Use Sharing Economy Services 186
9.4	Review of Users' Comments and Willingness to Use Sharing Economy Services 188
9.5	Relationship between Degree of Social Trust and Experiences with Sharing Economy Services 189
10.1	Employers Chosen as Ideal by College Students 195
10.2	Employment Locations Chosen as Ideal by College Students 196
10.3	College Students' Confidence in Finding Employment 197
10.4	Major Business-Starting Motivations for College Students 199
10.5	The Best Time to Start a Business according to College Students 200
10.6	College Students' Motivations in Buying Mobile Phones 201
10.7	Usage of Microblogs among College Students 206
10.8	Usage of WeChat among College Students 206
10.9	Degree of College Students' Trust in Different Government Organs (2015) 210
10.10	College Students' Feelings about Social Conflicts 211
11.1	Sample Distribution and Topic Design of SUNS 217
11.2	Origins of the New White-Collar Urban Workers 217
11.3	Industries in Which the New White-Collar Urban Workers Work 218
11.4	Employers of the New White-Collar Urban Workers 219

FIGURES AND TABLES

11.5   Employers and Gender Distribution of the New White-Collar Urban Workers   219

11.6   Employers and Educational Background of the New White-Collar Urban Workers   220

11.7   Employers and Household Registers of the New White-Collar Urban Workers   220

11.8   Working Hours of the New White-Collar Urban Workers in Units of a Different Nature   221

11.9   Monthly Salaries of the New White-Collar Urban Workers in Units of a Different Nature   222

11.10   Working Hours of the New White-Collar Urban Workers with Different Household Registers   223

11.11   Monthly Salaries of the New White-Collar Urban Workers with Different Household Registers   223

11.12   Gender Comparison of Monthly Salaries of the New White-Collar Urban Workers   223

11.13   Rates of Participation in Social Insurance of the New White-Collar Urban Workers in Units of a Different Nature   224

11.14   Gender Comparison of the Social Security of the New White-Collar Urban Workers   224

11.15   Social Security among New White-Collar Urban Workers with Different Household Registers   225

11.16   Types of Residence among the New White-Collar Urban Workers   226

11.17   Living Areas of the New White-Collar Urban Workers   227

11.18   Place of Residence and Daily Commuting Time of the New White-Collar Urban Workers   227

11.19   Physical Exercise in the Past Three Months   227

11.20   Feeling of Refreshment in the Morning   228

11.21   Common Diseases among the New White-Collar Urban Workers   229

11.22   Composition of the Circles of Friends of the New White-Collar Urban Workers   229

11.23   Proportion of Fellow Townsmen among the Friends of New White-Collar Urban Worker from Other Places   230

11.24   Feelings of Job Satisfaction among the New White-Collar Urban Workers in Shanghai   231

11.25   Job Satisfaction and Intention to Change Jobs among the New White-Collar Urban Workers in Shanghai   231

11.26   Satisfaction of the New White-Collar Urban Workers with Their Residences   232

X FIGURES AND TABLES

11.27 Vulnerable Group or Not 233
11.28 Opinions on Fairness of Current Income 233
11.29 Attitudes of the New White-Collar Urban Workers toward Shanghai Natives 234
11.30 Social Distance between the New White-Collar Urban Workers and the Natives 234
11.31 Self-Identity of the New White-Collar Urban Workers 235
11.32 Willingness to Trust Neighbors to Receive Express Packages 236
11.33 Participation of the New White-Collar Urban Workers in Community Activities 237
11.34 Community Identity of the New White-Collar Urban Workers 237
12.1 Relationship between Smartphone Payment and Bank Card Connection among Senior Citizens 249
12.2 Relationship between Perception of Safety and the Use of Smartphone Payment by Senior Citizens 250
12.3 Basic Conditions for Male and Female Senior Citizens in Participating in Group Activities 252
12.4 Relationship between the Social Participation of Senior Citizens and Their Means of Communication 252
12.5 Sources of Online Information Trusted by Senior Citizens 257
12.6 Channels of Cheating Experienced by Senior Citizens 258
12.7 Types of Cheating Messages Received by Senior Citizens 258
12.8 Sources of Help Sought by Senior Citizens after Incidents of Internet Fraud 259
12.9 Degree of Literacy Regarding Internet Safety of Senior Citizens with Different Educational Backgrounds 261
12.10 Degree of Literacy Regarding Internet Safety of Senior Citizens with Different Jobs at Present or before Retirement 262
12.11 Degree of Literacy Regarding Internet Safety of Senior Citizens with Different Incomes 262
12.12 Concerns of Senior Citizens about Smartphone Use 264
12.13 Relationship between Concern about Smartphones and Experiences of Internet Fraud 266
13.1 Changing Tendency of the Per Capita Income of Poor Urban and Rural Households, 2014–2016 277
13.2 Changing Tendency of the Per Capita Expenditure of Poor Urban and Rural Households, 2014–2016 278
13.3 Changing Tendency of the Engel Coefficients of Poor Urban and Rural Households, 2014–2016 278

FIGURES AND TABLES

13.4 Changing Tendency of the Causes of Poverty in Poor Urban and Rural Households, 2014–2016 281

13.5 Changing Tendency of the Major Disease Expenditures of Poor Urban and Rural Households, 2014–2016 283

13.6 Changing Tendency in the Size of Poor Urban and Rural Households, 2012–2016 289

16.1 Proportion of Indicators in Different Concentration Ranges in 338 Cities at the Prefecture Level and Above in 2016 341

16.2 Water Quality in the Seven Major River Basins, the Zhejiang–Fujian Rivers, the Northwestern Rivers, and the Southwestern Rivers in 2016 343

16.3 Ratios of Average Levels of the Quality of the Daytime Acoustic Environment in Cities Nationwide, 2015–2016 346

16.4 Ratios of Average Levels of the Quality of the Daytime Traffic Acoustic Environment in Cities Nationwide, 2015–2016 347

18.1 Householder Age Distribution 388

18.2 Educational Background of Householders 388

18.3 Family Characteristics of Rural Households 389

18.4 Distribution of Farmland Area of Rural Households 389

18.5 Local Working Time 390

18.6 Working Time in Other Places 390

18.7 Proportion of Total Expenditures Spent on Necessities 391

18.8 Age Structure of Rural Householders according to Type 393

18.9 Educational Background of Rural Householders according to Type 394

18.10 Status of the Members of Rural Households 394

18.11 Number of Permanent Residents and Laborers in Rural Households 395

18.12 Religious Belief in Rural Households 396

18.13 Annual Household Income 397

18.14 Government Subsidies 397

18.15 Total Household Expenditures 397

18.16 Proportion of Total Household Expenditures Spent on Necessities of Life 398

18.17 Proportion of Total Household Expenditures Spent on Food 399

18.18 Proportions of Expenditures on Life's Necessities 400

18.19 Farmland Distribution of Rural Households 401

18.20 Land Lots Operated by Rural Households 401

18.21 Types of Housing for Rural Households 402

18.22 Main Grain Crops Planted by Rural Households 403

18.23 Average Yields of Main Grain Crops 403

19.1 Number of New Private Enterprises and Individual Businesses Nationwide (2013–First Half of 2017) 408

XII FIGURES AND TABLES

19.2 Proportions of New Small and Micro-Enterprises with Different Degrees of Vitality in the Third Quarter of 2016   411

19.3 Activity Indexes of New Small and Micro-Enterprises in Each Quarter since the Second Quarter of 2014   412

19.4 Rates on the Anniversary of the Opening of New Small and Micro-Enterprises in Each Quarter since the Second Quarter of 2014   412

19.5 Profits and Losses among New Small and Micro-Enterprises That Had Opened by the Third Quarter of 2016   414

19.6 Proportions of Types of Employees of New Small and Micro-Enterprises in the Third Quarter of 2016   415

19.7 Relationship between the Scale of an Enterprise and Its Factor of Difficulty   417

20.1 Growth of the GDP since 1990   423

20.2 Total Retail Sales of Consumer Goods since 2010   423

20.3 Total Retail Sales of Consumer Goods and Growth Rates in Different Regions in 2016   424

20.4 Online Retail Sales by Region in 2016   424

20.5 Total Population and Natural Growth, 1978–2016   425

20.6 Population Age Structure and Dependency Ratio, 1990–2016   426

20.7 Marriages and Divorces, 1990–2016   426

20.8 Changes in Average Household Size, 1990–2016   427

20.9 Members of the Population Constantly in Motion and Those Whose Registered Residence Did Not Match Their Actual Residence, 2010–2016   427

20.10 Urban and Rural Structure and Industrial Structure of the Employed Population, 2000–2016   428

20.11 Newly Employed Population and Unemployment since 2006   428

20.12 Changes in the Income and Expenditures of Urban and Rural Residents, 2006–2016   429

20.13 Per Capita Disposable Income of Residents, 2013–2016   430

20.14 Per Capita Expenditures of Residents, 2013–2016   430

20.15 Impoverished Population and Poverty Incidence, 1978–2016   431

20.16 Inputs in Research and Development (R&D), 2010–2016   432

20.17 Total Health Care Expenditures, 1990–2016   432

20.18 Number of Medical Personnel for Each 1,000 People, 2005–2016   433

20.19 Number of Medical Personnel for Each 1,000 People in 2016, by Region   433

20.20 Participants in Social Insurances, 2000–2016   434

20.21 Fund Income and Expenditures of Social Insurances, 2000–2016   434

20.22 Social Assistance, 2007–2016   435

20.23 Community Service Organizations, 2005–2016   435

20.24 Changes in the Number of Village Committees and Neighborhood Committees, 1995–2016   436

Tables

2.1 Residents' Per Capita Disposable Income and Growth, 2010–2016   34
6.1 Medical Services Provided by Health Care Organizations in the First Half of 2017   117
6.2 Service Fees of Public Hospitals Per Annum   118
6.3 Service Fees of Grassroots Medical Institutions Per Annum   119
6.4 The Cost of Drugs in Previous Years   120
7.1 List of Typical International Terrorist Attacks in 2017   140
8.1 Classification of Interviewed Households by Per Capita Annual Income   153
8.2 Attitudes of Interviewees toward the System of Social Security   155
8.3 The Sense of Employment Equity Expressed by Interviewees   156
8.4 Degrees of Interpersonal Trust among Interviewees   160
8.5 Degrees of Trust in Organizations and Institutions Expressed by Interviewees   162
8.6 Degrees of Social Acceptance Expressed by Interviewees   164
8.7 Opinions of Interviewees on Degrees of Social Discrimination   165
8.8 Interviewees' Sense of Fairness   166
8.9 Opinions of Interviewees Regarding the Work of Government Departments   168
8.10 Participation of Interviewees in Social Groups   170
8.11 Social Participation and Political Participation among Interviewees   172
8.12 Interviewees' Sense of Political Efficiency   175
9.1 Proportions of Sharing Economy Services in the Broad and Narrow Sense within Public Services   185
9.2 Usage of Sharing Economy Services by Different Groups   190
10.1 Proportions of College Students Born after 1980, 1990, and 1995 Who Choose to Go Dutch for Restaurant Meals   201
10.2 Differences among College Students Born after 1980, 1990, and 1995 in Concepts of Housing and Housing Purchases   203
10.3 Frequency of Social Network Activities of College Students   204
10.4 College Students' Opinions of WeChat   207
10.5 College Students' Addiction to Smartphones   208
12.1 Basic Population Characteristics of the Survey Subjects   242
12.2 Performance Requirements of Senior Citizens Regarding Smartphones   243
12.3 Use of Internet Functions by Senior Citizens   244
12.4 Analysis of the Top 20 Topics Browsed by Senior Citizens (N = 35.76 Million)   246
12.5 Types of Audio Files Listened to and Ranking of Topics Searched for by Senior Citizens (N = 20970)   247
12.6 Balances on Bank Cards Connected by Senior Citizens (N = 316)   249

12.7	Experiences of Senior Citizens in Using Smartphone Payment	251
12.8	Types of Articles Favored by Senior Citizens on WeChat	253
12.9	Types of Articles Liked by Senior Citizens Who Also Like Articles Regarding the Maintenance of Health	255
12.10	Anxiety of Senior Citizens over Birth, Aging, Disease, and Death	255
12.11	Relationship between Mental Mechanisms and the Reading Preferences of Senior Citizens	256
12.12	Senior Citizens' Degree of Literacy Regarding Internet Safety	261
12.13	Influence of Senior Citizen's Image of the Internet on Smartphone Use	265
12.14	Relationship between the View That "The Internet Is Something for Youth and Senior Citizens Cannot Use It Fluently" and Degree of Literacy Regarding Internet Safety	267
12.15	Relationship between the View That "Only Those with Higher Educational Backgrounds Can Use Smartphones Well" and Degree of Literacy Regarding Internet Safety	267
13.1	Types and Proportions of Poor Urban and Rural Households in the 2017 Survey	271
13.2	Population Structure of Poor Urban and Rural Households	272
13.3	Health Conditions of the Members of Poor Urban and Rural Households Based on Self-Evaluation	273
13.4	Educational Backgrounds of the Members of Poor Urban and Rural Households	274
13.5	Employment and Schooling of the Members of Poor Urban and Rural Households	275
13.6	Employers of the Members of Poor Urban and Rural Households	276
13.7	The Structure of Income of Poor Urban and Rural Households in 2016	279
13.8	Structure of the Expenditures of Poor Urban and Rural Households in 2016	280
13.9	Problems Faced by Poor Households in 2016	282
13.10	Expenditures on Disease in Poor Urban and Rural Households as a Proportion of Household Expenditures, 2014–2016	283
13.11	Education Expenditures of Poor Urban and Rural Households in Different Educational Stages, 2014–2016	285
13.12	Expenditures on College Education in Poor Urban and Rural Households as a Proportion of Household Expenditures, 2014–2016	286
13.13	Dwelling Structures of Poor Urban and Rural Households in 2016	287
13.14	Proportion of Poor Urban and Rural Households in Dilapidated Buildings, 2014–2016	287
13.15	Size and Proportion of the Subsistence Allowance and Extremely Impoverished Populations in China, 2012–2016	289

FIGURES AND TABLES

13.16 Size, Incidence, and Growth Rate of the Rural Impoverished Population, 2012–2016 290

13.17 Ratios of Coverage under the Social Security Policies for Poor Urban and Rural Households in 2016 291

13.18 The Changing Tendency in Different Assistance Policies for Poor Urban and Rural Households, 2014–2016 292

13.19 Proportion of Households Receiving Subsistence Allowances and Other Preferential Policies, 2014–2016 292

13.20 Health Care Insurance Reimbursements for Chronic and Major Diseases for Poor Urban and Rural Households, 2014–2016 293

13.21 Ratio of Health Care Insurance Reimbursement for Chronic and Major Diseases among Poor Urban and Rural Households, 2014–2016 294

14.1 Top 20 Hot-Button Issues in 2017 298

14.2 Index of the Pressure in Different Public Opinion Areas, 2015–2017 301

14.3 Index of the Pressure Due to the Focus on Social Contradictions, 2015–2017 301

14.4 Gender, Region, and Age of Internet Users Concerned about Hot-Button Issues 310

14.5 Educational Background of Internet Users Concerned about Hot-Button Issues 312

14.6 Transmission Data of Overseas Social Platforms Linked to Mainstream Media in China 317

15.1 Results of a Random Check on Various Food Products in the First Quarter of 2017 323

15.2 Drug Inspections Completed in 2016 325

16.1 Inorganic Soil Pollutant Over-Limits in China 345

16.2 Organic Soil Pollutant Over-Limits in China 345

18.1 Classification of Rural Households 392

19.1 Number of New Enterprises per 10,000 People Nationwide and Year-on-Year Growth Rates of New Private Enterprises by Province (2016) 410

19.2 Important Indicators 411

19.3 Reasons for the Failure to Open or the Suspension of New Small and Micro-Enterprises in the Third Quarter of 2016, by Percentage 413

19.4 Proportions of Operation Difficulties Reported by Small and Micro-Enterprises in the Third Quarter of 2016 416

19.5 Perception of Costs by Enterprises in the Third Quarter of 2017 418

19.6 Opinions of Enterprises on Basic Public Services in the Business Environment in the Third Quarter of 2017 418

CHAPTER 1

China's Social Development in a New Era: Analysis and Forecast of China's Social Conditions in 2017–2018

The Research Group for Social Conditions Analysis and Forecast, the Chinese Academy of Social Sciences

Zhang Yi[1] and Fan Lei[2]

Abstract

The year 2017 immediately preceded the fortieth anniversary of China's adoption of the reform and opening-up policy. The successfully concluded 19th National Congress of the Communist Party of China charted a grand blueprint for turning a society moderately prosperous in all respects into a new modern great power. Since the start of reform and opening-up, especially since the 18th National Congress of the Communist Party of China, China has made remarkable achievements in economic and social development. In 2017, China witnessed overall progress in economic and social development, with outstanding advances in some areas. The national economy grew steadily, and the supply-side structural reform delivered preliminary results; spending on livelihood continued to increase, and urban and rural residents enjoyed a sustained growth in income; social security coverage was expanded, and significant achievements were made in targeted poverty alleviation. As socialism with Chinese characteristics has entered a new era, the principal contradiction facing Chinese society has evolved: what we face now is the contradiction between unbalanced and inadequate development and the people's ever-growing needs for a better life. Therefore, the main task for China in its future development is that the country needs to proceed from this starting point in the new historical period to vigorously improve the quality and effect of its development, promote social fairness and justice, and better meet the people's increasing needs in the economic, political, cultural, social, and ecological fields.

---

1 Zhang Yi, Director, research fellow at the Institute of Social Development Strategy, Chinese Academy of Social Sciences.
2 Fan Lei, associate research fellow at the Institute of Sociology, Chinese Academy of Social Sciences.

© KONINKLIJKE BRILL NV, LEIDEN, 2022 | DOI:10.1163/9789004500723_002

Keywords

new era – social development – social fairness

For China, the year 2017 will certainly be prominent forever thanks to its epoch-making nature. China will soon usher in the fortieth anniversary of reform and opening-up, a cause initiated in 1978. As we review the course of trials and hardships over forty years at an important historical juncture, we find that China has undergone significant transformation from a planned economy to a market economy, from an agricultural society to an industrial society, from a closed society to an open society, from widespread poverty to being well-off in all respects, from a unitized society to a community-oriented society, and from a society with an adult population to a society with an aging population. In just under forty years, China's economic aggregate soared, the people's standard of living improved markedly, its capacity for scientific and technological innovation and its comprehensive national strength were on the rise, and China's international influence became increasingly significant. The year 2017 marked the twentieth anniversary of the passing of comrade Deng Xiaoping. As China's cause of reform and opening-up will soon enter a new historical period, we immeasurably cherish the memory of the great man who called for emancipating the mind and seeking truth from facts, and who laid a solid foundation for the great rejuvenation of the Chinese nation and pinpointed the correct direction.

In 2017, the 19th National Congress of the Communist Party of China was convened. Based on practical innovations, the report delivered at the 19th National Congress of the Communist Party of China presented systematic theoretical innovations and stressed that the principal contradiction in China in the new era is the contradiction between unbalanced and inadequate development and the people's ever-growing need for a better life. The 19th National Congress of the Communist Party of China also made significant arrangements, which feature top-level design for China's future development, and it developed a new two-step developmental strategy. According to the goal set by the 19th National Congress of the Communist Party of China, we will, after finishing the building of a moderately prosperous society in all respects by 2020, have basically achieved modernization by 2035, and we will have developed China into a great modern socialist country that is prosperous, strong, democratic, culturally advanced, harmonious, and beautiful by 2050. Finishing building a moderately prosperous society in all respects and carrying out the new developmental strategy is bound to continue the transformation of Chinese society, raise per capita disposable income, expand middle-income groups, promote new-type urbanization, enable urban-rural integration, boost the implementation of the rural revitalization strategy, and help realize the Chinese Dream of national rejuvenation amid efforts at resolving the new principal contradiction.

1 The Overall State of Economic and Social Development in China in 2017

In 2017, China witnessed all-around sound economic and social development with various highlights. On the economic front, China presented a sound operational pattern characterized by medium-high growth, low inflation, and a low unemployment rate; the growth of urban and rural residents' income continued to be faster than economic growth; social consumption remained the main driving force; the real economy developed steadily and showed signs of improvement; the strategy of innovation-driven development was implemented effectively; regional development was promoted in a more coordinated way; and great improvement was shown in market confidence and expectations. On the social front, fiscal expenditure continued to favor livelihood and social development; social security provided more coverage and showed a steady improvement in benefits; the quality of education improved steadily, and great progress was made in promoting equal access to education; China generally joined the middle-high-income countries in its level of resident health; China made enormous achievements in poverty alleviation, drawing wide attention from the international community; and the state of public security continued to improve. In the meantime, the capacity for national governance and governance modernization further improved. With the aim of guaranteeing steady development in national economy and livelihood, overall arrangements were made and targeted measures were taken; there were policy innovations within departments and coordination among departments; policies were introduced in light of local conditions, and inter-regional interaction was also achieved; and relevant policies were strengthened to effectively guard against and defuse systemic risks in the financial, real estate, and other fields, thus fostering a good economic and social atmosphere for successfully convening the 19th National Congress of the Communist Party of China and for the subsequent implementation of the guiding principles adopted at that Congress.

1.1 The National Economy Grew Steadily, and Supply-Side Structural Reform Delivered Notable Results

At present, the international economy generally continues to recover, and China's sustained and steady economic growth has played a crucial role in this process. According to statistics from the National Bureau of Statistics, China's GDP grew annually by 7.2% on average during the period 2013–2016, which was higher than the average growth levels in the world and among the developing economies in the same period, which were 2.6% and 4%, respectively. In 2016, China contributed an average of 30% to the world's economic growth, making China number one in the world and surpassing the combined rate of contribution made by the United States, the Eurozone, and Japan. During the period 2013–2016, the CPI rose by an average of 2.0%, the surveyed urban unemployment rate in 31 large cities basically stood at about 5%, and China's economy generally featured medium-high growth, low inflation, and a low unemployment rate. Furthermore, economic structure was optimized gradually, new drivers of economic development emerged, and the quality of economic development improved. The added value of China's tertiary industry accounted for 51.6% of the GDP in 2016, up 6.3 percentage points over 2012; during the period 2013–2016, China's final consumption annually contributed an average of 55% to economic growth, and domestic demand became the main driving force of China's economic growth. The booming online retail industry and the flourishing sharing economy became the new highlights in China's economic development.

Since 2017, China's economy has continued to maintain a good developmental momentum. Based on comparable prices, the GDP increased by 6.9% in the first three quarters, up 0.2 percentage points over the same period in the previous year. The added value of the primary, secondary, and tertiary industries increased by 3.7%, 6.3%, and 7.8% in the first three quarters; tertiary industry continued to lead the way in the growth of added value. Final consumption contributed 64.5% to economic growth in the first three quarters, up 2.8 percentage points over the same period in the previous year; final consumption still played an irreplaceable, important driving role. During the period of January—August, the CPI rose by 1.5% and remained at a low level; in September, the surveyed urban unemployment rate in 31 large cities was 4.83%, the lowest level since 2012;[3] in 2017, the GDP growth rate will certainly be higher than the target 6.5%, thus laying a solid foundation for building a moderately prosperous society in all respects in the future.

---

3 Guo Tongxin, "Four Major Macro Indicators Were Better Than Expected, Sustained and Stable Development Was Achieved," http://www.stats.gov.cn/tjsj/zxfb/201710/t20171030_1547428.html.

1.2 *There Was a Sustained Decrease in the "Three Public Expenses" and a Continuous Increase in Spending on Improving People's Lives*

China's sustained, steady, and coordinated economic development provided strong material conditions for a decent living standard for all citizens. In the first three quarters of 2017, the nation's general public budget revenue surpassed the 13 trillion yuan mark, reaching 13.4 trillion yuan, up 9.7% over the same period the year before. In the meantime, fiscal expenditure grew rapidly; the nation's general public budget expenditure was about 15.2 trillion yuan, up 11.4%.

In early April 2017, the budgets of central government departments and the budgets of the "three public expenses" were released in quick succession, generating considerable media attention. This time the budgets of central government departments were released earlier, a greater number of central government departments released their budgets, and more details were released. The public platform was used to release budgets in a centralized way for the first time. The budgets of the "three public expenses" at the central level declined by 31 million yuan over 2016, and the State Council continued to carry out its three-point decision on curbing government spending, making sure that only a decrease occurred. In the public opinion, this showed that the government was determined to promote reform and standardization through information disclosure and thereby to become a clean, fiscally disciplined, and efficient government; this practice adopted by the government was well received in the society.

In recent years, the tension between fiscal revenue and expenditure caused by the economic slowdown has been acute, but improving people's living standards and quality of life has always been a priority. In particular, fiscal support has grown for science, technology, education, medical service and health, labor and employment, social security, and other areas closely related to quality of life. As indicated by the main items of expenditure in the first three quarters of 2017, spending on education was 2,231.2 billion yuan, up 13.3%; spending on science and technology was 466 billion yuan, up 17%; spending on technology research and development grew by 31.5%; spending on culture, sports, and media was 208.1 billion yuan, up 10.7%; spending on social security and employment was 1,994.6 billion yuan, up 20%; and spending on medical service, health, and family planning was 1,183.4 yuan, up 14.6%.[4] More prominently, spending on poverty alleviation grew by 52%, an indication of the importance of the issue to the Party and the government. As spending on economic development issues increased, further progress was made in

---

4 "Press Conference on Fiscal Revenue and Expenditure in the First Three Quarters of 2017 Held by the Ministry of Finance," https://www.sohu.com/a/198334330_173240.

addressing the tension between unbalanced and inadequate development and the people's need for a better life.

1.3 *People's Income Grew and Their Lives Improved*

Achieving shared prosperity for the entire population is one of the basic starting points for governance by the Communist Party of China. With respect to the income of urban and rural residents, the 18th National Congress of the Communist Party of China set the goal of doubling, by 2020, the 2010 average income of urban and rural residents. Since 2012, Chinese urban and rural residents have seen a steady growth in income. The per capita disposable income of Chinese urban and rural residents was 23,821 yuan in 2016, up 33.3% in real terms over 2012, an average annual increase of 7.4% in real terms. The income gap narrowed continually amid income growth. The Gini coefficient among the residents across China in terms of per capita disposable income was 0.465 in 2016, down 0.009 compared with 0.474 in 2012.

In the first three quarters of 2017, the income of urban and rural residents continued to grow steadily. The nation's per capita disposable income was 19,342 yuan, up 7.5% in real terms, 1.2 percentage points higher than in the same period in the previous year. The per capita disposable income of urban residents was 27,430 yuan, up 6.6% in real terms; the per capita disposable income of rural residents was 9,778 yuan, up 7.5% in real terms. The gap between the per capita income of urban and rural residents was a factor of 2.81, down 0.01 compared with the same period in the previous year. The increasing income of urban and rural residents effectively expanded the scale of middle-income groups. According to data from the National Bureau of Statistics, middle-income groups accounted for about 24.03% in China in 2013 as compared with 34.79% in 2016; that proportion will rise to 45.01% by 2020, showing a trend of rapid growth.[5]

Resident income increased rapidly, laying a solid foundation for realizing the Income Doubling Program. According to estimates from the National Bureau of Statistics, in the next four years, as long as resident income grows at an average annual rate above 5.3% in real terms, the resident income achieved in 2010 can be doubled by 2020.[6]

Further deepening the reform of the system of income distribution amid economic development, improvement of labor productivity and expansion of

---

5 "The Income Distribution Reform for Increasing the Income Level of Low-Income Groups and Expanding the Scale of Middle-Income Groups Was Accelerated Again," http://finance .ifeng.com/a/20171101/15758560_0.shtml.

6 The National Bureau of Statistics, "Resident Income Will Annually Grow by More Than 5.3% on Average in the Next 4 Years," http://news.sina.com.cn/c/nd/2017-07-06/doc-ifyh wefp0140035.shtml.

the scale of middle-income groups is also an important part of the efforts to achieve common prosperity for the entire population. In 2017, the National Development and Reform Commission issued *Priority Areas in Deepening the Income Distribution System Reform in 2017*. According to the document, with regard to primary distribution, the income distribution system has been improved for multiple groups including skilled talent, scientific research personnel, enterprise operation management personnel, and new-type professional farmers, so as to arouse the enthusiasm of key groups; with respect to redistribution, the income tax system and the social insurance system have improved, the capability for ensuring that the basic needs are met has been enhanced, and solid work is being carried out in poverty alleviation; and in conjunction with efforts to promote equality of opportunity in the educational, employment, and other fields and guarantee social fairness, actions are being taken to curb excessive speculation in various types of assets and to stabilize expectations. The 19th National Congress of the Communist Party of China vowed to make sure that income grew at rates comparable to the economic growth rate, and that earnings increases kept up with productivity increases. This means that building a sound income distribution mechanism and managing people's expectations will be of particular importance in future reform.

The improvement in the people's sense of fulfillment and satisfaction during reform is directly related to the residents' level of consumption and the speed with which it improves. The nation's per capita consumption expenditure of residents was 13,162 yuan in the first three quarters of 2017, up 5.9% in real terms. In terms of permanent residents, the per capita consumption expenditure of urban residents was 17,846 yuan, up 4.5% in real terms; the per capita consumption expenditure of rural residents was 7,623 yuan, up 7.4% in real terms. The real growth rate of the per capita consumption expenditure of rural residents was 2.9 percentage points higher than that of urban residents. This suggests that the gap in per capita consumption between urban and rural residents is narrowing.

With the intensification of supply-side structural reform and steady economic growth, the structure of urban and rural residents' consumption was gradually optimized. Resident expenditures on the necessities of life, including food and clothing, were on the decrease. The nation's per capita resident expenditure on food, tobacco, and alcohol was 3,847 yuan in the first three quarters of 2017, up 5.0%, accounting for 29.2% of the per capita consumption expenditure, down 0.7 percentage points over the same period in the previous year. With the impact of decreases in the prices of pork, vegetables, poultry, and eggs, the nation's per capita resident expenditure on food grew at a relatively low rate (3.3%)—expenditure on meats grew by 2.9%, while that on vegetables and eggs decreased by 2.6% and 5.0%, respectively. The per capita expenditure on clothing grew by 2.6%, accounting for 6.8%

of the per capita expenditure, down 0.3 percentage points over the same period in the previous year.

The decline in expenditures on food, clothing, and so on will certainly increase the proportion of resident spending on services. The nation's resident spending on housing, education, culture, entertainment, and other services grew rapidly, at the rates of 9.0%, 8.9%, and 12.2%, respectively, in the first three quarters of 2017, accounting for 22.1%, 11.2%, and 2.6% of the per capita consumption expenditure, up 0.3, 0.2, and 0.2 percentage points compared with the same period in 2016. Moreover, in the first three quarters of 2017, the nation's per capita resident expenditure on cosmetics and other personal items grew by 13.1%; the per capita spending on tourism, entrance tickets to scenic spots, fitness, and other areas grew by 13.4%, 13.5% and 17.3%, respectively; the per capita expenditure on hotel accommodation, hairdressing, and beauty and bath grew by 18.9% and 10.4%; the per capita consumption expenditure on household services grew by 12.2%.[7]

At present, the contribution from consumption to economic growth has reached 64.5%. The Engel coefficient among urban and rural residents continued to decline; in 2016, the nation's Engel coefficient among residents decreased to 30.1%, while the Engel coefficient among urban and rural residents fell to 29.3% and 32.2%, respectively.[8] In the first three quarters of 2017, the nation's Engel coefficient among residents further decreased to 29.2%.[9]

1.4 *The Employment Situation Was Stable, and Entrepreneurship Contributed Significantly to Job Creation*

Employment is absolutely key to improving living standards and quality of life. Since 2012, amid an economic slowdown and supply-side structural reform, China's employment has continued to improve and has become the brightest spot in the nation's economic and social development in recent years. In five years in urban China, more than 65 million people entering the job market for the first time found employment, and more than 27.90 million laid-off workers and more than 8.80 million unemployed found jobs. The rates of employment either according to surveys or according to official unemployment claims were at relatively low levels. A total of 10.97 million people were newly employed in urban areas across the country in the first three quarters of 2017, an increase of

---

7 Wang Pingping, "Resident Income Continued to Grow Rapidly, the Consumption Structure Was Optimized and Upgraded Continuously," http://www.stats.gov.cn/tjsj/sjjd/201710/t20171020_1544404.html.

8 "The Engel Coefficient among Chinese Residents Was 30.1% in 2016, Close to the Standard of Affluence," http://news.ifeng.com/a/20171010/52548221_0.shtml.

9 "Resident Income and Consumption Expenditure in the First Three Quarters of 2017," http://www.stats.gov.cn/tjsj/zxfb/201710/t20171019_1543840.html.

300,000 people. If the increase in the fourth quarter is considered, the annual target of adding 11 million jobs in urban areas will certainly be achieved. Since 2017, the nation's registered urban unemployment rate has been kept under 4%, and it was 3.95% at the end of the third quarter; the surveyed urban unemployment rate in 31 large cities was lower than 5% for seven consecutive months, standing at 4.83% at the end of the third quarter; and both the registered urban unemployment rate and the surveyed urban unemployment rate dropped to their lowest levels in the past five years.

This achievement is attributable to sustained and steady economic development as well as strong growth in tertiary industry; to the government's efforts in streamlining administration, delegating powers, and improving regulation and services; and to business system reform and the promotion of innovation. A total of 4.51 million new businesses were registered nationwide in the first three quarters of 2017, up 12.5%, a daily average increase of 16,500 enterprises; 14,146,000 new market entities were registered nationwide, up 16.7%, a daily average increase of 51,800 market entities. China has entered a golden age of entrepreneurship and innovation. The rapid growth of the sharing economy against this general backdrop was a particularly notable development in 2017. According to the *2016 Annual Report on the Development of the Entrepreneurship and Innovation Initiative in China*, released by the National Development and Reform Commission, in 2016 the market scale of the Internet sharing economy alone hit two trillion yuan and more than 50 million people took part in providing related services, accounting for 5.5% of the total working population. In 2016, the labor demand in such fields as special vehicle sharing, education, entertainment, medical services, and health care grew at a double-digit rate. China's push for entrepreneurship and innovation has been praised by the international community. The United Nations has included the idea in its official documents, calling on countries around the world to counter economic downturn through greater innovation. A broad agreement has emerged around the world that, as China continues to make great strides in its push for more entrepreneurship and innovations, we will be witnessing the robust growth of a new economy that is driven by technology, the Internet, and the consumption choices of 415 million "millennials."

Since enrollment expansion in higher education, the number of university graduates has been on the increase. Their number reached 7.56 million in 2016 and hit a record high of 7.95 million in 2017. Given part-time education, including self-taught examinations, the number of graduates from junior college, undergraduate, and graduate education throughout the year will be much larger than expected. However, the state of university student employment throughout the year is unchanged, and the task of their employment has been basically completed. Some provincial capitals in the central and western regions have also introduced a number of preferential policies for attracting talent; for instance, such cities as Xi'an, Wuhan, and Changsha have sought to attract university students by means of housing-related preferential policies. Previously, large cities focused development efforts on attracting investment; however, since 2017, the provincial capitals that have been deemed to be new first-tier cities and that have a population of more than 5 million have placed more emphasis on talent attraction, while still paying attention to investment attraction.

Unlike in previous years, the number of rural migrant workers working and doing business outside their home villages increased modestly in the first three quarters of 2017. The growth of rural migrant workers declined from the period 2011–2016—their growth rates were 3.4%, 3.0%, 1.7%, 1.3%, 0.4%, and 0.3% in 2011, 2012, 2013, 2014, 2015, and 2016, respectively. The number of rural migrant workers decreased by 2.1% in the first quarter of 2017, but that percentage rose to a certain degree in the second quarter, and continued to grow in the third quarter.

As rural migrant workers competed on the labor market, the trend of localization and temporary employment was strengthened. The number of local rural migrant workers who no longer carried out farming but did not leave their native land was on the rise. In 2016, 112.37 million out of more than 280 million rural migrant workers were local rural migrant workers, up 3.4% over the previous year, with the growth rate being 0.7 percentage points higher than that in the previous year; this increment accounted for 88.2% of the number of newly increased rural migrant workers. However, according to a relevant survey on manufacturing enterprises in coastal areas, with regard to rural migrant workers working outside, the turnover rate of rural migrant workers on production lines annually reached 7% or 8%. In some enterprises, the turnover rate of front-line workers even exceeded 50% in the first three quarters of 2017. The trend of temporary employment of rural migrant workers was due to competition among enterprises and production instability caused by enterprise shutdown, migration, and relocation, which could be related to seasonal closure of a business, suspension of a business, or layoffs. The interaction between enterprises and rural migrant workers affected each other's employment policy. However, temporary employment may lead to an interruption of payment for social insurance relating to rural migrant workers. This is an important issue that deserves urgent attention.

1.5 Strengthening the Education System and Improving Higher Education

Education is the largest livelihood project and the foundation for national revival. China's educational undertaking has developed steadily since the 18th National Congress of the Communist Party of China. In 2016, the national fiscal educational fund exceeded 3 trillion yuan for the first time and reached

3,139,625 million yuan; it accounted for 4.22% of the GDP,[10] and its proportion of the GDP has surpassed 4% for five consecutive years since 2012. The fiscal educational fund favored compulsory education, the central and western regions, and teachers' salaries and student aid, thus effectively ensuring equal access to education. With increasing educational input, educational opportunities were on the increase. The national gross enrollment rate in various phases of study increased to some extent in 2016 over 2012. The enrollment rate in three-year preschool education rose from 64.5% to 77.4%, while the enrollment rates at primary schools, junior middle schools, senior middle schools, and higher education stages increased from 104.3%, 102.1%, 85.0%, and 30.0% to 104.4%, 104.0%, 87.5%, and 42.7%, respectively.[11] The enrollment rates in three-year preschool education and higher education exceeded the average levels in middle and high-income countries, and the extent to which nine-year compulsory education became universal exceeded the average level in high-income countries. With the development of the educational undertaking, equal access to education has increasingly become the focus of social attention. In recent years, the governments and administrative departments for education at various levels have given first priority to ensuring equal access to education in the development of the educational undertaking, with relevant work targeted at key areas and key groups. The reform toward urban-rural integration in compulsory education was promoted in a coordinated way to narrow the urban-rural gap in education; intensified efforts were made to support education in the central and western regions in order to noticeably increase the educational level in those regions; high-quality educational supply was increased, and the layout was optimized to guarantee the sharing of high-grade educational resources; the basic conditions of the schools with weak compulsory education in poor areas were improved to create the material conditions for enhancing their educational quality; more policy assistance was provided to students with financial difficulties, students migrating to other areas together with their parents, and left-behind children so that they can successfully attend and finish school; and the overall level of special education was raised to safeguard the rights and interests of the handicapped.

For a long time, China was a significant world player only in elementary and secondary education. However, in this new era, the country is quickly become a formidable force in higher education. According to statistics, there were 2,880 institutions of higher learning nationwide in 2016, an increase of

---

10　Statistical Communiqué of the Ministry of Education, the National Bureau of Statistics, and the Ministry of Finance on the National Execution of Educational Funds in 2016, http://www.moe.gov.cn/srcsite/A05/s3040/201710/t20171025_317429.html.

11　Statistical Communiqué on National Educational Development in 2016, http://www.moe .gov.cn/jyb_sjzl/sjzl_fztjgb/201707/t20170710_309042.html.

90 institutions over 2012, including 2,596 regular institutions of higher learning. There were 36.99 million students at institutions of higher learning, an increase of 3,738,000 students or 11.2% over 2012. Students at institutions of higher learning accounted for 20% of the total scale of higher education in the world, so the gross enrollment rate in higher education reached 42.7% in China. In 2017, the number of students enrolled by general universities was on the rise; the number of newly enrolled junior college and university students exceeded 7.50 million. The enrollment expansion in higher education has provided strong human capital support for the development of middle-income groups and has also prepared a technical force for the transformation and upgrading of Chinese enterprises. Therefore, after China becomes the number one major country of higher education in the world, it will enjoy greater potential for future economic and social development.

Another great event in higher education in 2017 was the smooth progress in building world-class universities and disciplines. According to the *Circular Concerning the Release of the Candidate List of World-Class Universities and Academic Disciplines with World-Class Research Capacity* issued by the Ministry of Education, the Ministry of Finance, and the National Development and Reform Commission in September, 36 Category A universities and 6 Category B universities were included in the list of universities to be built into world-class universities, and related disciplines at 96 institutions of higher learning were included in the list of disciplines to be built into world-class disciplines. The orderly building of world-class universities and disciplines will certainly, to a large extent, change the pattern of teaching and scientific research in China and other great education powers in the world and will contribute to building China into a great modern country and achieving great rejuvenation of the Chinese nation by the mid-21st century. However, even as we build world-class universities and disciplines with world-class research capacity, we still need to address the development imbalance among different universities and make sure that those not included in the "world-class" list do not end up hemorrhaging top talents as a result.

1.6 *Steady Improvements in Social Security and Health*

Social security is the security net for livelihood and the stabilizer in a society. Since the 18th National Congress of the Communist Party of China, China has established a social security system covering the largest population in the world. As of late 2016, 888 million, 181 million, 219 million, and 185 million people were covered by basic endowment insurance, unemployment insurance, work-related injury insurance, and maternity insurance, up 99.80 million, 28.64 million, 28.79 million, and 30.22 million people over late 2012, respectively. More than 1.3 billion people have been covered by basic medical insurance; indeed, basically everyone has been covered by medical insurance. The social security level increased steadily while the coverage of social security was expanded. The minimum standard of basic pension funds from basic endowment insurance for urban and rural residents was raised from 55 yuan/(person·month) to 70 yuan/(person·month); the per capita pension level was about 120 yuan. The national monthly basic pension for enterprise retirees was increased from 1,686 yuan in 2012 to 2,362 yuan in 2016, an average annual increase of 8.8%.[12] The subsidy standard for basic medical insurance for urban and rural residents was raised from 240 yuan in 2012 to 420 yuan in 2016. The maximum payment limits for workers' medical insurance and residents' medical insurance were six times the average annual wage of local workers and the annual per capita disposable income of local residents, respectively, while the fund payment ratios for hospitalization expenses within the policy scope were about 80% and 70%. More than one billion urban and rural residents were covered by serious disease insurance, and the payment ratio specified by policies was not lower than 50%. The national monthly unemployment insurance level was 1,051 yuan in 2016, up 344 yuan over 2012, an average annual increase of 10.4%; the one-time subsidy standard for work-related death reached 624,000 yuan, up 188,000 yuan; the maternity insurance benefit level reached 15,385 yuan per capita, up 4,098 yuan. The reform in social security was intensified. As of October 31, 2017, all provincial-level non-local medical treatment settlement systems and all areas within the scope of fund pooling across the country have been connected to the national non-local medical treatment settlement system.

In the first three quarters of 2017, social security coverage continued to be expanded. As of late September, 905 million, 1,129 million, 186 million, 224 million, and 190 million people were covered by basic endowment insurance, basic medical insurance, unemployment insurance, work-related injury insurance, and maternity insurance nationwide, respectively. The social security level continued to rise. In 2017, the subsidy standard concerning basic medical insurance for urban and rural residents was increased to 450 yuan.[13] The pension for enterprise workers was adjusted for the thirteenth consecutive time; the national monthly basic pension for enterprise retirees was further increased by 5.5% on average, benefiting 100 million retirees.

Health is the source of the people's happiness and the foundation for making the country prosperous and strong. Since the 18th National Congress of the Communist Party of China, the Party and the government have attached great

---

12 Wei Yuping, "Five Years of Social Security: Establishing a Social Security System Covering the Largest Population in the World," http://finance.sina.com.cn/roll/2017-10-17/doc-ifymvuyt2093351.shtml.

13 "Press Conference of the Ministry of Human Resources and Social Security on the Progress in the Work on Human Resources and Social Security in the First Three Quarters of 2017," http://www.china.com.cn/zhibo/2017-11/01/content_41820919.htm.

importance to the development of the medical and healthcare undertaking. In October 2016, the Central Committee of the Communist Party of China and the State Council unveiled the *Plan for a Healthy China 2030*, specifying the principle of "giving priority to health," strategically identifying health as a priority in development and incorporating the philosophy of promoting health into the whole process of making and implementing public policies with a view to achieving sound and coordinated health, economic, and social development. It is the first medium and long-term strategic plan developed at the national level for the health field since 1949. According to the plan, in 2015, China's per capita life expectancy reached 76.34, while the infant mortality rate, the mortality of children below the age of 5, and maternal mortality rate decreased to 8.1‰, 10.7‰, and 20.1/100,000, respectively; residents' health level in China was generally higher than the average level in middle and high-income countries. The plan specifies the following developmental goals: China will be at the forefront of middle and high-income countries in the main health indicators concerning residents by 2020; China will join the high-income countries in the main health indicators concerning residents by 2030, and China will become a healthy country commensurate with a modern socialist country by 2050. An important vision for a healthy China is that by 2030, the national per capita life expectancy will reach 79 and even hit 80, while the infant mortality rate and the maternal mortality rate will decrease to 6‰ and 12/100,000.[14]

1.7 *Targeted Poverty Alleviation Measures Helped Lift Many Out of Poverty*

Lifting a poverty-stricken population out of poverty is the key factor for China in finishing the building of a moderately prosperous society in all respects by 2020. The Central Committee of the Communist Party of China has vowed to combat poverty since the 18th National Congress of the Communist Party of China. In an effort to fight poverty, the governments at various levels have accurately identified the support targets, arranged poverty alleviation projects, and utilized special poverty alleviation funds in a targeted way; they have assigned 188,000 first secretaries and more than 2.70 million cadres to 133,000 poor villages, thus making sure that poverty alleviation work is carried out in a targeted manner. With unremitting efforts for five years, more than 60 million poor people were lifted out of poverty, and the poverty rate dropped from 10.2% to less than 4%. During the period 2013–2016, the per capita disposable income of rural residents in poor areas grew annually by an average of 10.7% in real terms, up 2.7 percentage points compared with the national growth rate

---

14   "The Nation's Maternal Mortality Rate Declined to 19.9/100,000 in 2016," https://www .sohu.com/a/125023957_387204.

of rural resident income; the growth of farmers' income in poor areas outpaced national growth. In 2017, 28 poor counties passed special national evaluation and inspection; they will exit the status of poor counties with the approval of the provincial people's governments. Counties climbing out of poverty were removed from the list of poor counties in a centralized way for the first time since the fight against poverty was launched; the number of poor counties showed a net decrease for the first time in 31 years since China identified the poor counties.

Based on the rural poverty standard of 2,300 yuan net income per capita per annum (constant price in 2010), the rural poor population decreased to 43.35 million nationwide in 2016, down 12.40 million over 2015. In 2017, increased support was provided to contiguous destitute areas, old revolutionary base areas, areas inhabited by ethnic groups, and border areas. Preferential policies were introduced for the construction of infrastructure and basic public services. If the annual poverty alleviation task specified for 2017 can be finished, China can further lift more than 10 million poor people out of poverty, causing China's poor population to drop to about 30 million.

China's work on poverty alleviation has been highly praised by the global community. It is internationally acknowledged that lifting an immense poor population out of poverty in a short time is an unprecedented achievement in China's of poverty reduction and even in human history; it offers Chinese wisdom and a Chinese approach to solving the problems facing mankind.

2 The Challenges and Difficulties in China's Economic and Social Development in 2017

In 2017, as a number of strategic arrangements were effectively put into practice, and all-around positive changes took place in China's economic and social development. The present and future tasks are formidable, and China will also face huge challenges. On the one hand, the GDP is no longer the core goal among the macro developmental goals, but maintaining a medium-high rate of economic growth is still an important prerequisite. On the other hand, the tremendous achievements made in the social and livelihood fields in the past five years have put huge pressure on future rapid development; maintaining the current momentum of development is the biggest challenge.

2.1 *The Risk of Economic Downturn Persists, and Developmental Imbalance Must Be Addressed*

As shown by the economic growth rate in the first three quarters of 2017, new growth drivers were intensified to some extent, and the role of spending on stimulating economic growth gradually emerged. However, the role of consumption became evident mainly because investments and exports declined. In the process of intensifying the new growth drivers, the old growth drivers still play an extremely important role. Therefore, some difficulties in economic and social development are unavoidable and need to be solved.

First, regional development was unbalanced. Some provinces continued their previous growth rates, some provinces speeded up adjustment, and some provinces faced a great risk of downward development. According to the data released regarding the first three quarters of 2017, the GDP growth rates in Chongqing and Guizhou were 10% and 10.1%, and they were at the forefront nationwide. However, GDP growth rate in Gansu, a province in the western region, was only 3.6%, the gap was very large. Some eastern coastal provinces showed a good momentum of development thanks to economic transformation, but continued efforts should be made to develop Northeastern China—the economic growth rate in Liaoning was only 2.1% in the first half of the year. This suggests that imbalance and inadequacy are still prominent in regional development.

Second, the income level was unbalanced. In the first three quarters of 2017, the per capita disposable income of residents in Shanghai, Beijing, Zhejiang, Tianjin, Jiangsu, and Guangdong was at the forefront nationwide and was 44,360.24 yuan, 42,641.17 yuan, 32,413.77 yuan, 29,448.10 yuan, 26,529.72 yuan, and 26,054.75 yuan, respectively. However, the per capita disposable income of residents was relatively low in the provinces in the western region; for instance, that in Guizhou, Gansu, and Tibet was only 11,948.62 yuan, 11,476.91 yuan, and 10,573.54 yuan, respectively, in the first three quarters of 2017. Income has a direct impact on consumption, so it is hard to upgrade spending on the western region.

Third, the proportion of land finance was too large. Land finance and real estate development still played a big role in economic growth. In some second-tier cities, land transfer income made up a very high proportion of the fiscal revenue; it even exceeded 80 percent in some cities. Even in cities with a relatively low proportion of land transfer income, the proportion was larger than 30 percent. Therefore, as the pressure on real estate adjustment is mounting, the urban fiscal revenue structure needs to be adjusted.

Fourth, the prices of agricultural products declined and the growth of farmers' income was hindered. The price of pork has always been low. The rural households that were induced by the rising price of pork to engage in the cultivation industry in 2016 suffered a loss for a long time in 2017. The price of live pigs was between 6.5 yuan per jin and 7.5 yuan per jin (one jin = 1/2 kilogram) for a long time. In October, 2017, the price of pork was 7.2 yuan per jin, down 1.2% over the previous period. In 2017, the price of corn was also low and stood

CHINA'S SOCIAL DEVELOPMENT IN A NEW ERA

at about 0.8 yuan per jin. In the farmers' net income, the proportion of income from farming and cultivation was on the decrease, while that of income from work and transfer was on the increase. For the rural households whose plantation and cultivation income made up a large proportion, the decline in the prices of grain and pork and the rise in the prices of agricultural material products severely affected the improvement of their life.

2.2 Some Cities Showed Rising Housing Prices, and the Urban Cost of Living Increased

In the second half of 2016 and early 2017, housing prices jumped nationwide. Shenzhen, Shanghai, Beijing, and Guangzhou, among the first-tier cities, experienced surging commercial housing prices. The prices of new commercial housing soared by 35.7%, 45.6%, 48.1%, and 36% in Beijing, Shanghai, Shenzhen, and Guangzhou in March 2017 compared to March 2015, respectively. The increases may have been greater in some second-tier cities. The prices of the new commercial housing in Hefei, Xiamen, and Nanjing surged by 48.7%, 50.7% and 47.9% in March 2017 compared to March 2015, respectively.[15]

After strict control in March 2017, the hike in housing prices was curbed to a certain degree; there was a slight decline in some areas, but decreases were very small considering that the prices were exorbitantly high. According to data from September 2017, prices of new commercial housing and secondhand housing declined by 0.2% in first-tier cities over the previous period. In second-tier cities, the prices of new commercial housing rose by 0.2% over the previous period, while the price of secondhand housing increased by 0.2% over the previous period, the increase was down 0.1 percentage point over the previous month. In third-tier cities, prices of new commercial housing and secondhand housing rose by 0.2% and 0.3% over the previous period; the increases were down 0.2 and 0.1 percentage points over August.

The increase in housing prices makes it more difficult for rural migrant workers to purchase houses in cities; the increase also largely drives up house rent and raises the proportion of tenants' expenditure on rent in their total consumption expenditures. According to statistics, the ratio of rural migrant workers' rent expenditure to total consumption expenditure has reached about 35%; rural migrant workers employed in megacities and megalopolises see a higher proportion of rent expenditure in total expenditure. The increasing proportion of rent expenditure will reduce the cash savings rate among wage

---

15   "In March, Housing Prices Generally Rose, Increases in the Prices of Secondhand Housing Continued to Expand in 70 Third-tier Cities," http://house.ifeng.com/detail/ 2017_04_24/51065459_0.shtml.

earners and largely suppress the speed of consumption upgrading among the employed workers.

2.3 Key Progress Was Made in Pollution Prevention and Control, but Continued Efforts Are Still Needed to Prevent Pollution from Reoccurring or Worsening

Guarding against and defusing significant risks, preventing and controlling pollution, and conducting targeted poverty alleviation are considered by the media to be three crucial initiatives for building a moderately prosperous society in all respects. Since the 18th National Congress of the Communist Party of China, China has made outstanding achievements in environmental protection and environmental governance. The forest coverage rate increased from 21.38% in 2012 to 22.3% in 2016. Air quality improved continually, and the average concentration of PM2.5 in Beijing, Tianjin, Hebei, the Yangtze River Delta, and the Pearl River Delta marked a decrease of more than 30% in 2016 over 2013, drawing widespread attention. Water quality generally remained stable. In 2016, cross-sections with Category I–III water quality accounted for 67.8% of the cross-sections controlling surface water across the country, up 1.8 percentage points and surpassing the annual target (66.5%) set in the *Action Plan for Prevention and Control of Water Pollution*. Cross-sections with Category V water quality (inferior quality) accounted for 8.6%, down 1.1 percentage points and surpassing the annual target (9.2%) set in the *Action Plan for Prevention and Control of Water Pollution*. In 2017, the water in the Yellow River became clear, which became the focus of social attention. In 2016, a central environmental inspection mechanism was initiated, providing an important guarantee for achieving crucial success in pollution prevention and control. Central environmental inspection rapidly covered 31 provinces within two years, and more than 17,000 people were held accountable; 135,000 cases were accepted for handling, and 98% of these cases were handled. The environmental quality improved significantly amid economic slowdown in China, proving that synchronizing ecological development with economic development is feasible and that it can also play a huge role in promoting social development.

However, China still faces great challenges in environmental protection. First, unbalanced regional development in environmental protection is prominent. In August, 2017, the Ministry of Environmental Protection reported the state of the water environment in the first half of the year. This was the first time that the Ministry of Environmental Protection reported to the general public the annual water quality targets and performance in the "mid-term examination" of water quality in 31 provinces (autonomous regions, municipalities). According to the report, the quality of surface water across the country generally improved in the first half of 2017; the proportion of good water bodies increased by 1.2 percentage points, while that of unusable water bodies decreased by 1.7 percentage points. However, the amount of progress was not identical across the provinces (autonomous regions, municipalities); in some areas, it is very hard to achieve the target for water quality that was set for 2017. The proportion of good bodies of bodies declined to varying degrees in 8 provinces (autonomous regions, municipalities), including Hebei, Jilin, Fujian, Jiangxi, Guangxi, Chongqing, Guizhou, and Shaanxi. Second, there is pressure to prevent pollution from reoccurring or worsening. In November 2017, some cities, including Beijing, Tianjin, and the cities in Hebei, Shanxi, Shandong and Henan, gave out an orange alert concerning heavy air pollution, and a joint emergency response was made by Beijing, Tianjin, Hebei, and the surrounding areas; in Beijing alone, the local environmental protection departments found 83 violations of laws, and 693 enterprises were ordered to halt or limit production. This shows that the task of promoting and strengthening environmental protection cannot be finished overnight. Pollution prevention and control is a crucial and long war.

2.4 The Task of Targeted Poverty Alleviation Is Arduous, and Comprehensive Policies Need to Be Devised for Completely Lifting Poor People Out of Poverty

China has made enormous achievements in poverty alleviation, but the work still faces bigger challenges in the future. As of late 2016, there were more than 43 million poor people in rural areas nationwide. In the past five years, China helped more than 10 million people overcome poverty each year on average, this is a remarkable achievement. However, the efforts to maintain this speed in the next three years are subject to severe tests. Most of the remaining people in abject poverty live under extremely severe geographical and ecological conditions, and they also face extreme difficulties in themselves and their families and can hardly get access to social security and public services. They are also a population that is highly prone to falling back into poverty after overcoming it.

For the groups in abject poverty, on the one hand, it is necessary to continue adopting comprehensive means, including living relief, relocation, ecological compensation, and social security, to help them break away from abject poverty. On the other hand, priority is given to increasing the sustainability of shaking off poverty; more attention is paid to rational and effective allocation of such factors as capital, land, and labor in overcoming poverty, and to the role of education in empowerment, so as to enhance skills and eliminate the root causes of poverty. As shown by the previous experience in combating poverty, it is extremely easy for groups in abject poverty to rely highly on the government's support policies and poverty alleviation measures, and to have a continued demand for resettlement, credit, compensation, and work policies relating to poverty alleviation. To a certain extent, this makes it hard for groups in abject poverty to develop the ability for independent development in a short time. Therefore, in an effort to help groups in abject poverty overcome it, it is essential to strengthen administrative means to get instant results as well as to value the roles of the market and the society, leveraging the influence of market forces and social forces to fundamentally solve the problems in the endeavor to lift the groups in abject poverty of out poverty.

2.5 *The Problem of Population Aging Is Severe, and the Family Planning Policy Needs to Be Further Reformed*

China's problem of population aging is very grim. In late 2016, the elderly population aged 65 and above accounted for 10.8% of the total population, and the elderly population aged 60 and above accounted for 16.7% of the total population on the Chinese Mainland. The average life expectancy of the Chinese population has been extended to about 76.5 years.

In order to change the structure of the population, on January 5, 2017, the State Council unveiled the *National Plan for Population Development (2016–2030)*, specifying the following goals: the total fertility rate will increase to some extent and become stable at an appropriate level, and the population will reach 1.42 billion by 2020 and 1.45 billion by 2030. Based on a population of 1,382 million in 2016, only if the population increases by 38 million during the period 2017–2020 can the population reach 1.42 billion by 2020. If the deaths each year in this period are considered (based on 9.77 million deaths in 2016), it is necessary to annually increase the population by 19.20 million on average during the three-year period of 2017–2020. However, in reality, changes in population size are not fully consistent with the expectations.

According to the *Population and Family Planning Law of the People's Republic of China*, revised on December 27, 2015, China advocates that a couple should have two children. This is another major reform in the family planning system after the selective two-child policy was initiated in 2013. With the impact of the new system, in late 2016 the newly-born population was 17.86 million, and the birth rate, death rate, and natural growth rate were 12.95‰, 7.09‰, and 5.86‰ on the Chinese Mainland. Population growth was mainly driven by an increase in the proportion of births of a second child. According to statistics from the National Bureau of Statistics and the health and family planning department, birth of a second child accounted for about 30% of the annual newly-born population before 2013. The proportion increased significantly in 2014 and 2015. In 2016, birth of a second child or more accounted for more than 45% of the newly-born population. Such compensatory growth will gradually mitigate amidst those marriages in which both husband and wife come from a single-child family and in which either the husband or the wife comes from a single-child family or a release of dividends from the universal two-child policy. In such a circumstance, if the current family planning policy is not changed, it is likely that a slight growth and then a decrease will occur in the near future.

After the relevant policy is introduced to relax control on births, the fertility rate does not fully reach policy expectations mainly because rising living costs restrict the willingness of new couples to give birth. If it is hard to build and improve the supporting system for family development, the birth rate will continue to decline in the near future. According to the experiences of developed countries in encouraging births, family development, economic support, housing improvement, care for female employment, the improvement of maternity leave, nursery and kindergarten services, and equal access to educational resources exert a significant impact on increasing the fertility rate. However, it is very difficult to make these basic public goods fully available in a short time. Therefore, with rapid population aging, it is necessary to promptly study continued improvement of the family planning policy or a full removal of restrictions from the family planning policy. An important issue that must be addressed at present is how to build a population structure fit for implementing the strategy of the great rejuvenation of the Chinese nation and to continue to give play to the role of population in supporting socialism with Chinese characteristics under the long-term goals of basically achieving modernization by 2035 and turning China into a great modern country by 2050.

Furthermore, in parallel to further improving the social security system of old-age care and the service system of basic old-age care as well as fostering a good social atmosphere of respecting, loving, and helping elderly people, the institutional design related to the retirement postponement policy is being carried out to mitigate such objective dilemmas as a shortage of working population and an excessively high dependency ratio. The basic endowment insurance replacement rate decreased from 70.79% in 1997 to 45% in 2014, so it is difficult for the single basic endowment insurance system to meet the growing needs of elderly people in life; the labor participation rate involving the elderly population has increased to some extent in China in recent years. According to the *2016 Survey Report on the Chinese Resident Retirement Readiness Index*, jointly released by Tsinghua University and Aegon THTF Life

Insurance, the Chinese Resident Retirement Readiness Index was 6.0 in 2016, noticeably lower than the figure of 6.51 in 2015; the index declined for the first time in four years. Only 15.3% of respondents believed that they had made full preparations for their retirement, the lowest in three years; the proportion of those who believed that retirement preparations were not enough to support their life after retirement increased by 10% over 2015.[16] With respect to the labor participation rates involving elderly people between the ages of 60 and 64 and 65 and 69, they were 62.90% and 41.44% in Japan, and 55.80% and 31.56% in the United States. The reemployment of elderly people has become widespread in an aging society. However, in order to promote the reemployment of elderly people, it is still necessary for China to make greater efforts to improve the laws and regulations relating to their reemployment, broaden the channels for their reemployment, encourage employers to employ them, and provide consulting, training, management, and other services concerning reemployment.

3 China's Social Development and Important Tasks in 2018

The year 2018 marks the fortieth anniversary of China's reform and opening-up. In the meantime, the last decisive stage for finishing the building of a moderately prosperous society in all respects by 2020 has begun. According to the report delivered at the 19th National Congress of the Communist Party of China, as socialism with Chinese characteristics has entered a new era, the principal contradiction facing Chinese society has evolved. What we now face is the contradiction between unbalanced and inadequate development and the people's ever-growing needs for a better life. Therefore, the main task for China in future development is that the country needs to proceed from its starting point in a new historical period to vigorously improve the quality and effect of development, promote social fairness and justice, and better meet the people's increasing needs in the economic, political, cultural, social, and ecological fields. The pressing task for social development lies in further narrowing rural-urban disparity, both the income gap and the regional gap; promoting employment, education, and the development of other key livelihood fields; and encouraging private enterprises and social organizations to develop, thus vitalizing the society.

---

16   Fu Yang, "Release of the Survey Report on the 2016 Chinese Resident Retirement Readiness Index," *Beijing Evening News*, December 19, 2016.

3.1 *Urbanization Should Be Steadily Pushed Forward, but the Long-Term Mechanism for Regulating Housing Prices Needs to Be Improved*

In late 2017, China's urbanization rate exceeded 58%. China's urbanization rate is expected to reach 60% by 2020. According to the international record of urbanization, urbanization increases rapidly for a period before it reaches 70%. Therefore, China's urbanization rate will rise rapidly in the next decade. According to data from the National Bureau of Statistics, the total population was 1,382.71 million in China in late 2016, including an urban permanent resident population of 792.98 million; about 180 million people need to migrate from rural areas to urban areas during rapid urbanization. The report delivered at the 19th National Congress of the Communist Party of China calls for carrying out the rural revitalization strategy and for better promoting rural development amid rapid urbanization, thus further narrowing urban-rural disparity.

Improving urban governance amid efforts to boost urbanization and the citizenization of the agricultural migrant population is an important task. As shown by international experiences of urbanization, when the urbanization rate reaches about 50%, urban areas are vulnerable to many social problems, thus certain social risks occur. With the increasingly prominent population aggregation in large cities and megacities in recent years, many urban diseases have loomed large in these cities, including disorderly and excessive population growth, exorbitantly high housing prices, traffic jams, poor social security, severe environmental pollution, and undersupply of excellent public services. Therefore, rationally planning the urban layout, optimizing the urban spatial structure, increasing the level of basic urban public services, and innovating urban social governance become important aspects of the effort to promote urban development; they are also essential for enhancing the quality of urbanization and truly embodying a people-oriented kind of urbanization.

As China steadily pushes urbanization forward, the country should place emphasis on preventing the unemployment of rural migrant workers whose agricultural land has been circulated to others. At present, 170 million rural migrant workers have left their native places to work outside, accounting for nearly one-fourth of the employed population across the country. Some of them have fully circulated their land to others. According to statistics, in late 2016, the area of circulated agricultural land across the country accounted for more than 35% of all agricultural land. If the rural migrant workers working and doing business in urban areas cannot better integrate themselves into urban society, or if it is hard for them to find jobs due to economic fluctuation, it will be difficult for them to return home in the period during which their land is possessed by others through circulation. Thus, it is necessary to intensify employment training among rural migrant workers, making these workers worry-free.

Moreover, great fluctuation in urban housing prices should be avoided amid the endeavor to promote urbanization. At present, particular attention should be paid to preventing housing prices from further rising or rebounding. The hikes in housing prices across the country increase the costs of purchasing houses during urbanization, making it more difficult for wage earners to purchase houses, and they also curb the speed of consumption upgrading in the whole society. According to data from multiple sources, the migrant population's expenditure on house rents in cities has increased with housing prices: their house rent expenditure makes up an increasing proportion in the total amount of their consumption, and that proportion has approached one-half for some groups in some cities. With strict regulation during the period 2016–2017, the rate of increase in housing prices in first-tier and second-tier cities declined or remained unchanged (housing prices dropped slightly in some areas), but rapid increase continued in third-tier and fourth-tier cities. Housing prices were controlled to some extent and their increase slowed at the end of the third quarter of 2017, but the trend of investing in real estate to preserve or increase its value and earn profits was not reversed. Once control was relaxed, housing prices would rebound vehemently. Under strict control, the selling price of new housing was much lower than that of secondhand housing in many areas, so selling new housing as secondhand housing can generate a great price difference in a short time. For society overall, if the increase in per capita disposable income is lower than that of housing prices, an implicit real estate bubble may become an explicit bubble. In many towns and county-level cities, the housing vacancy rate increased with the reduction of excess inventory, such that house rent was much lower than bank mortgages in the same period. Therefore, relevant government departments should continue to monitor the trend in the change in housing prices and study and introduce a long-term mechanism for the regulation of housing prices, so as to enhance the people's sense of fulfillment, happiness, and security.

3.2 *The Income Gap Should Be Narrowed and the Middle-Income Groups Should Be Expanded*

Since the reform and opening-up, with rapid economic and social development in China, there have been basic consensuses on expanding middle-income groups and building a middle-class-dominated social structure to boost domestic demand and consumption upgrading, maintain a medium-high rate of economic growth, and safeguard social harmony and stability. In the future, in conjunction with efforts to continue economic development to lay a foundation for expanding middle-income groups, it is necessary to further intensify the reform of income distribution and combine work-based distribution with distribution based on production factors to further reform the remuneration system; to take increasing knowledge and enhancing skills and management capability as value orientation to arouse the enthusiasm of key groups; and to deepen the supply-side structural reform of agriculture in order to increase farmers' income.

The pressing task consists of speeding up the growth of residents' real income. According to the data for 2016 released by the National Bureau of Statistics in April 2017, the average monthly income of rural migrant workers was 3,275 yuan, up 203 yuan or 6.6% over the previous year, but the growth rate decreased by 0.6 percentage points over the previous year. From the sectoral perspective, the income in the manufacturing sector showed a certain increase in its growth rate in 2015; growth rates in the resident service, repair, and other service sectors were the same as that in the previous year, but the growth rates in the average monthly income of rural migrant workers in the construction sector; the wholesale and retail sector; the transportation, warehousing, and postal sector; and the lodging and catering sector declined by 1.5, 1.9, 1.5, and 0.7 percentage points, respectively. In the meantime, growth in the disposable income of urban residents slowed down. In 2016, the national per capita disposable income of residents showed a decreasing growth rate compared with that during the period 2013–2015. In terms of permanent residence, the per capita disposable income of urban residents was 33,616 yuan, up 5.6% in real terms over the previous year, while the per capita disposable income of rural residents was 12,363 yuan, up 6.2% in real terms over the previous year. The per capita disposable income of urban residents increased to some extent in the first three quarters of 2017, but it is worth noting that although the average level increased, the median growth rate dropped from 8.1% in 2016 to 7.1% in 2017. This suggests that the income gap had widened to a certain degree.

3.3 The Regional Gap Should Be Further Narrowed, and Regional Development Should Be Promoted in a More Coordinated Way

The large gap in regional development has always been an important issue affecting China's economic and social development. Since the 18th National Congress of the Communist Party of China, the Central Committee of the Communist Party of China has, in light of the domestic and foreign development landscape, put forward and intensively carried out the Belt and Road Initiative; the strategy of coordinated development of Beijing, Tianjin, and

Hebei Provinces; and the strategy of developing the Yangtze River Economic Belt, making significant achievements. The report delivered at the 19th National Congress of the Communist Party of China placed more emphasis on coordinated regional development, presented the strategy of coordinated regional development, and called for intensifying efforts to speed up the development of the old revolutionary base areas, the areas inhabited by ethnic groups, border areas, and poverty-stricken areas. Other goals included strengthening measures to reach a new stage in the large-scale development of the western region, intensifying reforms to more rapidly revitalize the old industrial bases in the northeast and other parts of the country, helping the central region rise by tapping into local strengths, supporting the eastern region in taking the lead in pursuing optimal development through innovation, and establishing a new, more effective mechanism for coordinated regional development. The new strategy of coordinated regional development starts with solving the main problems in the development of different areas and proceeds from the developmental advantages of different areas; it also offers a plan based on the national overall developmental layout, and accurately and objectively pinpoints the directions for the future development of different areas. In particular, with a focus on the strategic goal of finishing the building of a moderately prosperous society in all respects, it combines coordinated regional development with efforts at poverty alleviation, and it breaks the past convention of establishing the regional strategy of development merely on the basis of areas; instead, it gives first priority to developing those areas in which poverty is most concentrated during poverty alleviation, and it highlights the interconnection and synergy among the various parts of the national overall strategy of development.

As city groups are the growth poles for stimulating regional economic and social development, the building of city groups is of great significance in the coordinated strategy of regional development. The original three major city groups—Beijing—Tianjin—Hebei, the Yangtze River Delta, and the Pearl River Delta—still play a significant role as engines and growth poles. The national city groups approved in recent years—including the Central Plains City Group, the city group in the middle reaches of the Yangtze River, the Chengdu—Chongqing City Group, the Harbin—Changchun City Group, the Mid-Southern Liaoning City Group, the Shandong Peninsula City Group, the city group on the west coast of the Taiwan Straits, the Beibu Gulf City Group, and the Guanzhong City Group—have also developed rapidly, and they have become an important support for national or regional economic and social development. In the future, the building of city groups should be promoted by strengthening overall arrangements in urban planning, industrial layout, transportation networking, and urban function orientation, and by rationally allocating local resources, valuing the balanced development of the ecological environment and population size, and adapting to the economic and social bearing capacity of cities. In April 2017, the Central Committee of the Communist Party of China and the State Council decided to establish a national-level new area in Xiong'an in Hebei Province. It is an additional national new area following the Shenzhen Special Economic Zone and the Pudong New Area of Shanghai. This new national area is of great realistic and far-reaching historical significance for mitigating the non-capital functions of Beijing in a centralized way; optimizing the urban layout and spatial structure of Beijing, Tianjin, and Hebei Province; and cultivating new engines for innovation-driven development, so it is hailed as a project of vital and lasting importance.

3.4 *The Strategy of Giving Priority to Employment Should Be Adopted to Achieve Fuller Employment with a Higher-Quality Workforce*

According to a report delivered at the 19th National Congress of the Communist Party of China, it is essential to implement the strategy of giving priority to employment and the policy of active employment so as to bring about fuller employment with a better equipped labor force. As the total size of the working-age population has been decreasing for years, the aggregate employment contradiction characterized by oversupply that has affected the Chinese labor market for a long time has been mitigated preliminarily, and employment pressure has eased to some extent. However, the structural contradiction in employment remains acute, the mismatch between supply and demand makes it difficult to effectively solve the problem concerning the employment of university graduates in a short time, and the shortage of highly skilled workers is still salient. Against the background of an economic slowdown and an intensified supply-side structural reform, the employment problem in particular areas and certain industries will become prominent, and the contradiction featuring local oversupply on the labor market will remain apparent. Therefore, overcoming the employment problem in a quantitative respect will remain the baseline for the government in determining the economic growth rate for some period of time.

We should attach importance to the quality of employees and the realization of higher-quality employee training while stressing the quantity of employment and fuller employment. Currently some problems exist in the quality of employment. First, the stability of employment needs to be further improved. According to data over the years from the Chinese Social Survey (css) conducted by the Institute of Sociology at the Chinese Academy of

Social Sciences, with respect to the possibility of unemployment in the next six months, more and more non-agricultural employed people held that it was entirely possible or possible, and their proportion was 21.2%, 23.3%, and 26.0% in 2013, 2015, and 2017, respectively. Second, the level of safeguarding the rights and interests of workers needs to be further increased in an all-around way. With the government's efforts at standardizing the behavior of market-oriented employment and safeguarding the legitimate rights and interests of workers, the proportion of workers signing labor contracts in various types of enterprises has increased steadily. According to data over the years from CSS, enterprise workers signing labor contracts accounted for 56.5%, 61.3%, and 82.2% in 2013, 2015, and 2017, respectively. However, the workers and staff signing labor contracts in private enterprises, villagers' committees and neighborhood committees, or individual businesses accounted for 52.1%, 44.2%, and 16.1% in 2017, respectively. Therefore, it is necessary to further standardize the employment behaviors of the above units in the future so that the level of safeguarding the rights and interests of workers can be fully increased. Third, overtime work is severe among workers. Reasonable working time is conducive to the physical and mental health of workers, and it is also beneficial for workers to strike a balance between work and family life. As shown by data over the years from CSS, 45.1% of non-agricultural workers worked for more than 8 hours each day in 2013, while that proportion was 44.2% and 41.9% in 2015 and 2017. Overall, overtime work improved slightly but was still severe among non-agricultural workers, which reduced the quality of workers' employment to a certain extent. Therefore, besides upholding the strategy of giving priority to employment and promoting an active employment policy to ensure continuous improvement in the state of employment in China in the future, it is also imperative to further improve the operational mechanism on the labor market and to establish a mechanism for enabling a rational flow of labor forces, to fully standardize the employment behaviors in various types of employers to safeguard the rights and interests of workers, to strengthen skills training among workers to constantly enhance the quality of workers, and to reinforce the structure of the labor market service system to provide a good guarantee for workers.

3.5 The Quality of Education Should Be Further Improved, and It Is Necessary to Make High School and Secondary Vocational Education Universal

According to the report delivered at the 19th National Congress of the Communist Party of China, the building of an educationally strong country is a basic project for the great rejuvenation of the Chinese nation and calls for giving priority to the educational undertaking. In recent years, China's educational undertaking has developed rapidly, but there is still room for making education satisfactory for the people. The gross enrollment rate in the three-year preschool education reached 77.4%, higher than the average level (73.7%) in middle and high-income countries. The number of full-time teachers in preschool education rose by 50.9%, from 1,479,000 in 2012 to 2,232,000 in 2016; the teachers at and above the junior college level increased by 11%, but the problem concerning the number of preschool teachers, especially their quality, remains the bottleneck hindering the development of preschool education. Besides ensuring access to preschool education, it is also necessary to place more emphasis on safeguarding and promoting the physical and mental health of children. For compulsory education, it is essential to continue implementing the principle of ensuring equal access to education, to boost urban-rural integration in compulsory education, and to highly value rural compulsory education. The balanced development of schools for compulsory education should be fostered by rationally adjusting the school layout, further renovating the underdeveloped schools, and more rapidly standardizing the construction of schools for compulsory education. For higher education, the accelerated building of world-class universities and disciplines presents new requirements and new opportunities for the development of higher education in China. More attention should be paid to intensive development, and the quality of education should be improved constantly; high-caliber innovative talents should be cultivated to serve national economic and social development and to lead the development of higher education in the central and western regions as well as local high-level university development, and to accomplish the important mission of building world-class universities and disciplines.

With the popularization and consolidation of nine-year compulsory education in China, making high school and secondary vocational education universal is the key to increasing the overall national level of education. China is close to reaching the internationally accepted full popularization standard, namely, that that the gross enrollment rate in high school and secondary vocational education should reach 90%, but achieving this goal in rural areas, especially the poor areas in the central and western regions, the areas inhabited by ethnic groups, remote areas, and the old revolutionary base areas is still the greatest difficulty. For a long time, China's rural areas have been subject to a number of dilemmas in high school and secondary vocational education, including a lack of teachers, a loss of students, insufficiency of funds, and a low admission rate to the institutions of higher learning. In April 2017, the Ministry of Education released the *Plan for Making High School and Secondary Vocational Education Universal (2017–2020)*, calling for making high school and secondary vocational education universal nationwide in order to meet the need among junior middle school graduates to receive a good high school and secondary vocational education by 2020. The plan specifies five goals: the gross enrollment rate will exceed 90% nationwide in different provinces (autonomous regions, municipalities), and the gross enrollment rate in poor areas in the central and western regions will increase significantly. According to the plan, much energy will be dedicated to the poor areas in the central and western regions, the areas inhabited by ethnic groups, remote areas, and the old revolutionary base areas, as well as to students from families with financial difficulties, handicapped students, and students migrating to urban areas together with their parents. Efforts will also be made to solve three prominent problems: the proportion of large classes in regular senior high schools is high, the enrollment ratio in vocational education is on the decrease, and there are difficulties in school operations. With the gradual implementation of the plan, the overall quality of nationals and the competitiveness of workers in China will further improve in the future.

3.6 The Development of Private Enterprises and Social Organizations Should Be Encouraged, and Various Social Forces Conducive to National Rejuvenation Should Be Pooled Together

In order to realize the great rejuvenation of the Chinese nation, it is necessary to stimulate social vitality and gather strength from the whole society. Rapid economic and social development in China since reform and opening-up could not have been achieved without the extensive participation of the private economy and social organizations. The enormous social vitality aroused by reform and opening-up has tremendously promoted the cause of building socialism with Chinese characteristics.

During the initial stage of reform and opening-up, China held that the private economy was a beneficial supplement to the public sector of the economy; in the 1990s, China stressed that the private economy was an important part of a socialist market economy; and at the beginning of the 21st century, China vowed to unswervingly encourage, support, and guide the development of the non-public sectors of the economy. The 3rd Plenary Session of the 18th Central Committee of the Communist Party of China vowed to ensure equal rights, equal opportunities, and equal rules for the economy with various types of ownership, thus China's private economy has enjoyed unprecedented opportunities for development. At present, the private economy achieves 80% employment, provides 60% of the GDP, and pays 50% of the taxes; it has become an important force in China's economic development. In September 2017, the

Central Committee of the Communist Party of China and the State Council issued *Opinions on Fostering an Environment Conducive to the Healthy Growth of Entrepreneurs, Carrying Forward the Excellent Entrepreneurial Spirit, and Better Giving Scope to the Role of Entrepreneurs*, specifying the overall requirements and concrete measures for protecting the legitimate rights and interests of entrepreneurs according to law and for arousing an excellent entrepreneurial spirit. These steps have been well received by private entrepreneurs. For the first time, the document calls for encouraging innovation, tolerating failure, and arousing the entrepreneurial and innovative vitality of entrepreneurs; this is hailed by the general public as a symbol that China is ushering in a new era of private economy. However, with the impact of international economic fluctuation, China's private economy is still facing many challenges in development. The growth of private fixed-asset investments markedly slowed down in 2016; it increased to some extent in 2017, but there were certain decreases in the proportion of private fixed-asset investments in the total fixed-asset investments and in the growth rate of private fixed-asset investments in the first three quarters of 2017. In the past five years, the proportion of private fixed-asset investments in the total amount of fixed-asset investments exceeded 60% and peaked at 65.4%, while it dropped to 60.5% in the first three quarters of 2017. Private fixed-asset investments grew by 7.7% in the first quarter of 2017; afterward, their growth rate declined; their growth rate stood at 6.0% in the first three quarters of 2017.

Since the reform and opening-up, social organizations have developed rapidly in China. They have played an important role in innovating social governance, preventing and resolving social contradictions, and helping the government transform its functions. Since the 18th National Congress of the Communist Party of China, China has seen a swift development of social organizations. There were more than 499,000 social organizations of various kinds nationwide in 2012, while their number increased to 702,000 in 2016; social organizations have made important contributions to mobilizing and organizing social resources, improving livelihood, promoting economic development, innovating social management, and boosting social harmony. However, China still faces many problems in social organizations, including an insufficient number of them and the fact that they are underdeveloped. The dilemmas in resources, talents, and even institutions remain the main obstacles to the further development of social organizations. There is still room for expanding the participation of social organizations in social affairs and social services in the future.

References

The National Bureau of Statistics. "The Resident Income and Consumption Expenditure in the First Three Quarters of 2017." http://www.stats.gov.cn/tjsj/zxfb/201710/t20171019_1543840.html.

Press Conference on "Meeting the People's New Expectations, Ensuring and Improving the People's Wellbeing." http://www.xinhuanet.com/politics/19cpcnc/zb/zb10/index.htm?isnm=1.

Wang Pingping. "The Resident Income Continued to Grow Rapidly, the Consumption Structure Was Optimized and Upgraded Continuously." http://www.stats.gov.cn/tjsj/sjjd/201710/t20171020_1544404.html.

Wei Yuping. "Five Years of Social Security: Establishing a Social Security System Covering the Largest Population in the World." http://finance.sina.com.cn/roll/2017-10-17/doc-ifymvuyt2093351.shtml.

CHAPTER 2

Report on Income and Spending among China's Urban and Rural Households in 2017

Lyu Qingzhe[1]

Abstract

In 2017, China witnessed a steady growth in its resident income, a gradual reduction in the income gap, and continuous improvement in the level of consumption and standard of living. According to an estimate, in 2018, the Chinese economy was able to maintain a stable yet positive tendency at a growth rate of about 6.5%. To continuously increase the incomes and consumptions of rural and urban residents, we recommend the government and related departments to do the following: improve the income of rural and urban residents by promoting employment; encourage residents to increase their income by making innovations and starting up businesses based on the strengthened policy supports; increase the property benefits of the residents by guiding investments; improve the social security system based on a targeted poverty reduction policy; stimulate the consumption potential of residents by increasing the supply of innovative services; and create a good environment for consumption by reinforcing standardized policy guidance.

Keywords

resident income – resident consumption – quality of life

1 Resident Income Grew Continuously and the Income Gap Gradually Narrowed

1.1 *Resident Income Grew Continuously*

From 2010 to 2016, the per capita disposable income of national residents increased from 12,522.2 yuan to 23,821.0 yuan, with a rate of increase of 90.2% and an actual average annual growth rate (AAGR) of 8.4% in terms of comparable prices. To be more precise, the per capita disposable income of urban

---

1 Lyu Qingzhe, Ph.D., senior statistician at the Institute of Statistical Science, National Bureau of Statistics.

© KONINKLIJKE BRILL NV, LEIDEN, 2022 | DOI:10.1163/9789004500723_003

TABLE 2.1   Residents' Per Capita Disposable Income and Growth, 2010–2016

Year	National residents		Urban residents		Rural residents	
	Absolute number (yuan)	Indicator (= 100 in the previous year)	Absolute number (yuan)	Indicator (= 100 in the previous year)	Absolute number (yuan)	Indicator (= 100 in the previous year)
2010	12522.2	—	18779.1	—	6271.3	—
2011	14550.8	10.3	21426.9	8.4	7393.9	11.4
2012	16509.6	10.6	24126.7	9.6	8389.3	10.7
2013	18310.7	8.1	26467.0	7.0	9429.6	9.3
2014	20167.0	8.0	28844.0	6.8	10489.0	9.2
2015	21966.2	7.4	31194.8	6.6	11421.7	7.5
2016	23821.0	6.3	33616.0	5.6	12363.0	6.2

SOURCE: DEPARTMENT OF HOUSEHOLD SURVEYS OF THE NATIONAL BUREAU OF STATISTICS, *CHINA YEARBOOK OF HOUSEHOLD SURVEYS 2017*, CHINA STATISTICS PRESS, 2017

residents increased from 18,779.1 yuan to 33,616.0 yuan, increasing by 79.0% and with an actual AAGR of 7.3% in terms of comparable prices. The per capita net income of rural households increased from 6,271.3 yuan to 12,363.0 yuan, with an increase of 97.1% and an actual AAGR of 9.0% in terms of comparable prices. The income of rural residents grew faster than that of urban residents (see Table 2.1).

In the first three quarters of 2017, the per capita disposable income of national residents was 19,342 yuan, with a nominal year-on-year growth of 9.1%, and an actual increase of 7.5% after adjusting for inflation. Among them, the per capita disposable income of urban residents was 27,430 yuan, with a nominal year-on-year growth of 8.3%, and an actual increase of 6.6% after adjusting for inflation; and the per capita disposable income of rural residents was 9,778 yuan, with a nominal year-on-year growth of 8.7%, and an actual increase of 7.5% after adjusting for inflation. Rural residents had an even faster income growth than urban residents.

1.2   *The Proportions of Net Transfer Income and Net Asset Income Increased*

In 2016, the ratio of per capita national net transfer income to per capita disposable income increased from 16.5% in 2012 to 17.9% in 2016, with an increase of 1.4 percentage points; the ratio of per capita net asset income to

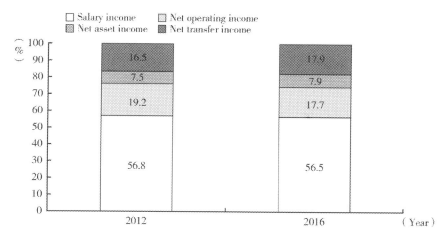

FIGURE 2.1 Structure of the Per Capita Income of Residents in 2012 and 2016

per capita disposable income increased from 7.5% in 2012 to 7.9% in 2016, with an increase of 0.4 percentage points (see Figure 2.1). In the first three quarters of 2017, the ratio of per capita net transfer income and net asset income of national residents to per capita disposable income witnessed a continuous increase, reaching 18.3% and 8.1%, respectively.

Regarding transfer income, in recent years, on the one hand, the social pension guarantees such as retirement pensions and old-age pensions have increased year by year. In 2012, the average basic old-age pension for retirees of enterprises was 1,686 yuan/month, which increased to 2,362 yuan/month in 2016, an increase of 8.8%. At the same time, the minimum level for the fundamental pension of the basic pension insurance for rural and urban residents has increased from 55 yuan to 70 yuan per month, and the per capita pension reached about 120 yuan. In addition, subsidies of medical insurance for urban residents and subsistence allowances for the aged have also witnessed increases year by year. On the other hand, policies aiming at improving agriculture, benefiting farmers, and helping rural areas to flourish have been implemented. In 2014, the fund for benefiting farmers in China totaled 1.4 trillion yuan, which increased to 1.6 trillion yuan in 2015 and 1.8 trillion yuan in 2016, maintaining a rate of increase of about 15% per year. All these measures have effectively ensured a stable increase in the transfer income of rural and urban residents.

Regarding asset income, the Report to the 17th CPC National Congress stated for the first time that "conditions will be created to enable the public to own asset income," and the Report to the 18th CPC National Congress further declared the aim to "increase the asset income of residents via multiple channels." In recent years, we have deepened the reforms of state-owned enterprises and lands in rural areas to enable the people to share the benefits

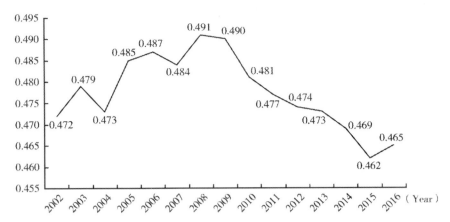

FIGURE 2.2 The Gini Coefficient of China's Resident Income, 2002–2016
SOURCE: HOUSEHOLD SURVEY DATA FROM THE NATIONAL BUREAU OF STATISTICS

from the development of enterprises and the appreciation of the land; we have strengthened financial reform and expanded investment channels for rural and urban households to enable the people to obtain financial benefits in a diversified and safe way; and we have actively forged, promoted, and standardized the development of the house leasing market to create more opportunities for rural and urban residents to increase their asset income, all of which measures have effectively increased the asset income of rural and urban households.

1.3   The Income Gap Gradually Narrowed

1.3.1   The Gini Coefficient Dropped to Some Extent

Since the 18th National Congress of CPC, the growth rate of the income of rural and urban residents has been higher than the economic growth rate for years, and the size of the middle class has been increasing. In 2013, the proportion of the middle class in China was 24.03%, which increased to 34.79% in 2016 and will reach 45.01% by 2020, showing a rapid increase. The expanding middle class has significantly improved the distribution of the income of urban and rural residents, narrowed the income gap, and effectively reduced the Gini coefficient. In 2008, the Gini coefficient of resident income in China peaked at 0.491, then began to diminish and reached 0.465 in 2016 (see Figure 2.2). In addition, we have also seen that the slight increase in the Gini coefficient in 2016 over 2015 indicated that it was a tough task to further reduce the income gap when the macro-economy had not improved fundamentally; to be sure, this was only a fluctuation in the reduction of the Gini coefficient.

INCOME & SPENDING AMONG CHINA'S URBAN & RURAL HOUSEHOLDS

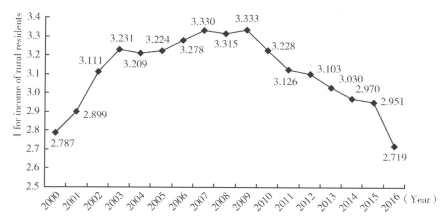

FIGURE 2.3   The Urban-Rural Income Ratio, 2000–2016
SOURCE: *CHINA STATISTICAL YEARBOOK 2017*

1.3.2   The Urban-Rural Gap Declined Continuously

With the rapid growth of the income of rural residents, the urban-rural gap was decreasing gradually. The ratio of urban-rural incomes decreased from 3.333:1 in 2009 to 2.719:1 in 2016 (see Figure 2.3). Since 2002, China's urban-rural income gap has increased to some extent. In 2001, that ratio was 2.899:1, which has been higher than 3:1 for 12 consecutive years since 2002. The ratio reached a peak of 3.333:1 in 2009, following the implementation of the policy of reform and opening-up. In recent years, to improve the income of rural residents, the government has implemented various measures, such as accelerating the new urbanization; developing moderate scale management; developing large-scale projects for irrigation and water conservation infrastructure; promoting the integration of the primary, secondary, and tertiary industries in rural areas; speeding up the reform of the pricing mechanism for agricultural products; and narrowing the gap in providing public services in rural and urban areas, effectively reversing the expanding income gap between urban and rural residents. Since 2010, the growth rate of the income of rural residents has been higher than that of urban residents for many years. In 2014, the urban-rural income ratio fell below 3:1 again, to 2.970:1. Under the Countryside Promotion Strategy proposed at the 19th National Congress of the CPC, the urban-rural income gap may be further reduced in the future.

1.3.3   The Inter-Regional Income Gap Decreased Continuously

Since the reform and opening-up, the coastal regions in East China have been developed first, laying a solid foundation and accumulating experience for the rapid development of China's economy for more than 40 years. With the implementation of regional developmental strategies such as the China Western Development Strategy, the Rise of Central China Strategy, and the Revitalization of Northeast China Strategy, overall development based on the reform and opening-up of China has been realized. Factors such as talents, funds, and technologies are flowing to the central, western, and northeastern regions of China, effectively balancing the inter-regional differences. Since the implementation of the Belt and Road Initiative and the two regional strategies for the coordinated development of Beijing, Tianjin, and Hebei and the development of the Yangtze River Economic Belt, the coordination of regional development of China has been further improved, realizing cooperation among regions based on their geological and resource advantages, promoting the economic and social development of the regions, and narrowing the income gap among the various regions. From 2012 to 2016, the per capita disposable income of the residents in the west of China increased at an annual rate of 10.3%, which is higher than those in central China, eastern China, and northeastern China by 0.4 percentage points, 0.9 percentage points, and 1.8 percentage points, respectively. From 2012 to 2016, the ratios of per capita income in eastern China, central China, and northeastern China to that in the west of China (with the resident income in the west of China as 1) decreased from 1.73, 1.11, and 1.29 to 1.67, 1.09, and 1.21, respectively.

2 The Consumption Level of Residents Continued to Increase and Their Living Standard Improved Significantly

2.1 *The Level of Consumption Continued to Increase and the Consumption of Services Improved Rapidly*

2.1.1 The Level of Consumption Continued to Increase

In 2016, the per capita consumption expenditure of residents throughout China was 17,111 yuan, increasing by 33.1% over 2012 with an annual average nominal growth of 7.4%. Whereas the per capita consumption expenditure of urban residents was 23,079 yuan, an increase of 26.2% over 2012, and the average annual nominal growth rate was 6.0%, the per capita consumption expenditure of rural residents was 10,130 yuan, with an increase of 43.4% over 2012, and the average annual nominal growth rate was 9.4%. Rural residents had a faster per capita growth in consumption expenditure than that of urban residents.

In the first three quarters of 2017, the per capita consumption expenditure of all the residents of China was 13,162 yuan, with a nominal growth of 7.5% over the same period in 2016, where the per capita consumption expenditure of urban residents was 17,846 yuan with a year-on-year nominal growth of 6.2%; and the per capita consumption expenditure of rural residents was 7,623

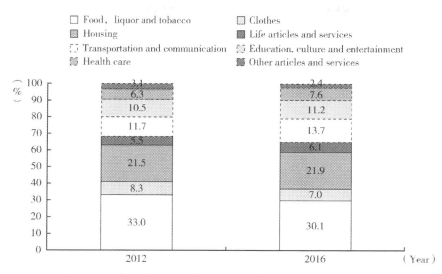

FIGURE 2.4 Structure of Resident Spending in 2012 and 2016

yuan with a year-on-year nominal growth of 8.6%. In recent years, while economic growth has been slowing down, internal demand has become the major driving force behind the economic growth of China. The rising e-commerce platforms of China have made a great contribution to the growth of consumption throughout the world. On November 11, 2017, the volume of transactions at T-Mall reached 168.2 billion yuan in a single day, covering 225 countries and regions all over the globe, making it a shopping carnival for the world.

2.1.2   The Engel Coefficient Continued to Decline

In 2016, the per capita consumption expenditure of residents on food, liquor, and tobacco throughout China was 5,151 yuan, increasing by 21.2% over 2012, with an average annual growth of 4.9%. The proportion of expenditure on food, liquor, and tobacco in the consumption expenditure (Engel coefficient) decreased from 33.0% in 2012 to 30.1% in 2014, with a reduction of 2.9 percentage points (see Figure 2.4), while the per capita expenditure of urban residents on food, liquor, and tobacco was 6,762 yuan, with an increase of 17.6% over 2012 and an average annual growth of 4.1%. The Engel coefficient for urban residents decreased from 31.4% in 2012 to 29.3% in 2016, a reduction of 2.1 percentage points (see Figure 2.4). The per capita expenditure of rural residents on food, liquor, and tobacco was 3,266 yuan, with an increase of 23.3% over 2012 and an average annual growth of 5.4%. The Engel coefficient for rural residents decreased from 37.5% in 2012 to 32.2% in 2016, with a reduction of 5.3 percentage points. The reduction of the Engel coefficient for residents indicates the further improvement of the living standard of residents.

2.1.3 Service Consumption Maintained Rapid Growth

In 2016, the per capita expenditure of residents in China on transportation and communication was 2,338 yuan, with an increase of 55.7% over 2012 and an average annual growth of 11.7%, which was higher than the per capita consumption expenditure of residents of China by 4.3 percentage points, accounting for 13.5% of the per capita consumption expenditure, which in turn was higher than that in 2012 by 2.0 percentage points. In 2016, the per capita expenditure of residents in China on education, culture, and entertainment was 1,915 yuan, with an increase of 41.7% over 2012 and an average annual growth of 9.1%, which is higher than the per capita consumption expenditure of residents of China by 1.7 percentage points, accounting for 11.2% of the per capita consumption expenditure, which was higher than that in 2012 by 0.7 percentage points. In 2016, the per capita expenditure of residents in China on healthcare was 1,307 yuan, with an increase of 60.6% over 2012 and an average annual growth of 12.6%, which was higher than the per capita consumption expenditure of residents of China by 5.2 percentage points, accounting for 7.6% of per capita consumption expenditure, which in turn was higher than that in 2012 by 1.3 percentage points. The rapid growth of service consumption benefited from life services provided in a more convenient, professional, and comfortable way and from the comprehensive integration of information technologies. Against the background of the shift in the focus of living from material demands to the desire for a better life, the consumption of services will see another wave of rapid development, and the demand for that consumption, with entertainment and health care at the core, will witness rapid growth.

2.2 *The Quality of Consumption Improved Constantly and the Pace of Updating Accelerated*

2.2.1 More Nutritional and High-Quality Products Were Consumed

In 2016, the per capita edible oil consumption of urban residents was 10.6 kg, with an increase of 1.4 kg or 15.2% over 2012; the per capita consumption of beef and mutton was 4.3 kg with an increase of 0.6 kg or 16.2% over 2012; and the per capita consumption of fresh milk was 16.5 kg, with an increase of 2.6 kg or 18.7% over 2012. Compared with 2012, the quality of the consumption of food for rural residents had fully improved, and the quantities of high-quality food products, such as meat, eggs, milk, and aquatic products improved significantly. In 2016, the per capita consumption of pork for rural residents was 18.7 kg, an increase of 4.3 kg or 29.9% over 2012; the per capita consumption of eggs and egg products was 8.5 kg, an increase of 2.6 kg or 44.1%; the per capita consumption of milk and milk products was 6.6 kg, an increase of 1.3 kg or 24.5%; and the per capita consumption of aquatic products was 7.5 kg, an increase of 2.1 kg or 38.9%.

2.2.2 Consumption Was Constantly Updated

The quantities of durable consumer goods owned by urban and rural residents grew constantly, and the tendency toward increasing consumption among rural residents became more obvious. In 2016, the number of passenger cars per 100 households in rural areas was 17, with an increase of 11 cars or 183.3% over 2012, and automobiles were the durable consumer goods with the highest growth rate for rural residents; the number of air-conditioning machines per 100 households in rural areas was 48, an increase of 22 units or 84.6% over 2012; that of water heaters was 60, an increase of 19 units or 46.3% over 2012; that of refrigerators was 90, an increase of 22 units or 32.4% over 2012; that of personal computers was 28, an increase of 6.6 units or 30.8% over 2012; that of washing machines was 84, an increase of 17 units or 25.4% over 2012; and that of mobile phones was 241, an increase of 43 units or 21.7% over 2012.

2.3 *The Living Environment Conspicuously Improved and Public Services Entered a New Phase*

2.3.1 Living Space Was Expanded and the Quality of Housing Continuously Improved

In 2016, the per capita housing construction area of residents in China was 40.8 square meters, the per capita housing construction area for urban residents was 36.6 square meters, and that for rural residents was 45.8 square meters. The per capita housing construction areas for urban and rural residents increased by 11.1% and 23.3% over 2012, with average annual growth rates of 2.7% and 5.4%, respectively. In 2016, the proportion of reinforced concrete or brick-concrete-structure housings inhabited by rural residents was 64.4%, an increase of 8.8 percentage points over 2013.

2.3.2 The Living Environment Continuously Improved

Almost all of the urban areas were fully covered by roads, electrical power, telephone service, and cable TV, and the coverage of such services in rural areas has been expanding. In 2016, in rural areas, 99.7% of natural villages had road access, an increase of 1.4 percentage points over 2013; 99.7% of natural villages had electrical power, an increase of 0.5 percentage points over 2013; 99.7% of natural villages were covered by telephone service, an increase of 1.1 percentage points over 2013; and 97.1% of natural villages were covered by cable TV, an increase of 7.9 percentage points over 2013.

In 2016, 94.2% of the communities in urban areas had drinking water treated centrally, while the proportion in rural areas was 53.6%, with increases of 2.9 and 8.8 percentage points over 2013, respectively. In 2016, garbage from 97.7% of the communities in urban areas could be treated centrally, an increase of 1.8 percentage points over 2013; and garbage from 66.9% of the natural villages in rural areas could be treated centrally, an increase of 18.2 percentage points over 2013.

2.3.3 Improvements in Health Care, Culture, and Education Services

Regarding health care, health stations were established in 83.6% of the communities in urban areas and 87.4% of the natural villages in rural areas, with increases of 3.9 and 5.8 percentage points over 2013, respectively. Urban areas enjoyed abundant educational resources while rural areas witnessed an improvement in conditions for education. In 2016, 97.8% of the communities in urban areas had convenient access to kindergartens or preschool classes, an increase of 1.1 percentage points over 2013; and 98.1% of the communities had convenient access to primary schools, an increase of 1.3 percentage points over 2013. In 2016, 81.8% of the natural villages in rural areas had convenient access to kindergartens or preschool classes, with an increase of 6.1 percentage points over 2013; and 84.6% of the natural villages had convenient access to primary schools, with an increase of 3.8 percentage points over 2013.

3 Recommendations for Increasing the Income and Consumption of Urban and Rural Residents in 2018

In 2017, under the firm leadership of the Central Committee of the Party, with President Xi Jinping at the core, all regions and departments implemented the new developmental concept, upheld the general working keynote of making progress based on stability, focused on structural reform on the supply side, expanded general demand appropriately, deepened reforms and innovations, promoted physical economy, prevented and reduced risks, and strengthened the guidance of expectations to ensure the general stability of the national economy. It is estimated that the economic growth rate over the whole year would be 6.9%. In 2018, a stable yet positive tendency could be maintained for the Chinese economy at a growth rate of about 6.5%. To promote continued growth in the income and consumption of Chinese urban and rural residents, the following recommendations are made.

3.1 Promote Employment and Increase Income for Urban and Rural Residents

Employment is an effective way to improve the living standard of urban and rural residents. Governments at all levels should strengthen employment guidance to establish more channels for employment and expand new fields for employment in multiple ways; they should organize skill training with specific aims free of charge, devise effective employment policies according to the features of urban and rural residents in order to promote flexible and diversified employment methods, and encourage flexible employment to provide more employment opportunities for rural households. Jobs related to public projects implemented by governments should be offered to rural residents preferentially to guide them and help them to establish a correct outlook on finding jobs, and they should be encouraged to actively participate in various skill training courses, improve their working skills, improve their market competitiveness, and change the passive nature of employment to an active nature.

3.2 Strengthen Policy Support and Encourage Residents to Improve Their Income by Making Innovations and Starting Businesses

In the first three quarters of 2017, the household operations service industry of residents witnessed rapid development, becoming a major force driving the expansion of operating income. We should actively implement several policies, such as Mass Entrepreneurship and Innovation, and make a stronger effort to publicize the policies, strengthen the supporting policies, guide residents to start up new businesses, establish a mechanism for the supervision of policies and measures, provide services for residents to start up new businesses, encourage the participation of residents in the Mass Entrepreneurship and Innovation program, improve economic development, and increase the income of residents.

3.3 Guide Investments to Increase Asset Benefits of Residents

Net asset income is an important part of disposable income. We should increase publicity and education regarding investment and finance so that residents can improve their risk consciousness and financial skills. We should accelerate the transformation of the assets of urban residents into capital to increase asset income, such as benefits from rents, interest, and saving insurance; make more effort to publicize financial knowledge and educate investors about risk to improve the capacities of residents in investment and finance and risk prevention; further increase the asset income of urban residents; and gradually increase the proportion of net asset income. We should deepen reform of the rural collective property rights system; accelerate authentic rights registration and certification for contracted lands, forestry lands, house sites, and houses in rural areas; and implement a system of executing ownership rights, contracting rights, and operational rights of rural lands.

3.4 Improve the Social Security System Based on a Precise Policy for Poverty Reduction

From now to 2020 is a critical period if we are to build a moderately prosperous society in all respects, and the most important quality of the project for the improvement of living standards is to realize targeted poverty reduction. To achieve targeted poverty reduction, we should identify the objects of poverty reduction, analyze the causes of poverty, implement poverty reduction measures, create files based on problems, and learn about the size of the impoverished population and the degrees and causes of poverty. We should use poverty reduction as an opportunity to improve a social security system covering unemployment, pension, health care, work-related injuries, and maternity, as well as to expand the coverage of social security, especially to include the rural population within the scope of social security funded by the central government. We should fully motivate all walks of society to establish a third system or mechanism of distribution in the form of social aid, civil donations, charities, and volunteer actions. Redistribution should be realized effectively through social security to make it possible for the public to share the achievements of economic and social development.

3.5 *Increase the Provision of Innovation Services and Stimulate the Consumption Potential of Residents*

In recent years, residents' demand for living services has been increasing, and the increase in overseas consumption and the outflow of purchasing power could reflect the fact that the quality and convenience of individualized goods and services in China might not meet the new needs resulting from the updating of the consumption structure of residents. Huge consumption spaces and great potentials for living services can be identified, from physical needs to mental health at all ages. Given the rapid increase in the consumption of services regarding food, health care, education, and cultural entertainment, the supply of innovative services should be increased, and service branding should be strengthened to encourage spending on fields related to the elderly— geriatric nursing, health care, and housekeeping—to release the residents' potential for consumption.

3.6 *Strengthen Policy Guidance and Create a Good Environment for Consumption*

We should provide residents with healthy, safe, and better goods and services in real terms; promote the concepts of health consumption, green consumption, and safe consumption; and create a good market environment for consumption. To achieve this, we need to improve the management system for the quality of goods and services; improve the support of policies and guidance in terms of taxation, finance, and pricing; and accelerate the construction of infrastructures, especially efforts in support of the development and expansion of rural markets for consumption. Policy guidance and support should be further improved to guarantee the consumption of residents; enable more households to benefit from handy services for the public, such as online shopping, catering, and entertainment; and create an environment for spending in which residents can spend their money in whichever way they want.

References

China Economic Climate Monitoring Center of the National Bureau of Statistics. *China Monthly Economic Indicators*, 2017(10).

Department of Household Surveys of the National Bureau of Statistics. *China Yearbook of Household Surveys 2017*. China Statistics Press, 2017.

Li Peilin, Chen Guangjin, and Zhang Yi. *Analysis and Forecast of China's Social Conditions (2017)*. Social Sciences Academic Press (China), 2015.

National Bureau of Statistics. *China Development Report 2017*. China Statistics Press, 2017.

National Bureau of Statistics. *China Statistical Yearbook 2017*. China Statistics Press, 2017.

CHAPTER 3

Report on the Situation and Quality of Employment for College Graduates in 2017

Mo Rong,[1] Chen Yun,[2] and Wang Xinyu[3]

Abstract

In 2017, China witnessed a generally stable employment situation with a year-on-year increase in new employment in urban areas, low unemployment, a dynamic balance between market supply and demand, and a basically stable enterprise workforce. In 2018, a generally stable yet growing pattern was maintained for employment, but attention should also be paid to some outstanding issues, such as the weakening supply and demand in the labor market, the risks of local unemployment, and the difficulties of some groups in looking for jobs. At the 19th National Congress of the CPC, the government put forward a requirement of "realizing more sufficient employment with a higher quality." In this article, we use data to analyze the current situation of the employment of college graduates, and we propose some policy suggestions to improve the quality of employment.

Keywords

situation of employment – college graduates – quality of employment

---

1 Mo Rong, deputy director, research fellow, and doctoral advisor of the Chinese Academy of Labor and Social Security, the Ministry of Human Resources and Social Security of the People's Republic of China, and an expert on China's employment issue, is mainly engaged in the study of labor and employment, the management of human resources, vocational training, international labor security and big data, etc.
2 Chen Yun, deputy director of the Employment and Business-Starting Research Laboratory of the Chinese Academy of Labor and Social Security, the Ministry of Human Resources and Social Security of the People's Republic of China, is mainly engaged in the study of employment and business-starting.
3 Wang Xinyu, director and professor of the Human Resources Management Institute of Beijing Union University, mainly studies the employment issues of college graduates and migrant workers.

© KONINKLIJKE BRILL NV, LEIDEN, 2022 | DOI:10.1163/9789004500723_004

1 The General Situation of Employment Was Stable and Became Better

In recent years, the Chinese economy has been operating under a "new normal" characterized by slower but steady growth rates. In 2016, the GDP growth rate was 6.7%. According to an initial calculation, the GDP over the first three quarters of 2017 was 59,328.8 billion yuan, with a year-on-year growth of 6.9% in terms of comparable prices. The growth rate was the same as that of the first half of the year and higher than that in the same period in 2016 by 0.2 percentage points. The economy was maintained within a reasonable scope. The economic structure was optimized continuously, and the service-industry-led orientation became more obvious. In 2016, the added value of tertiary industry accounted for 51.6% of the GDP, with an increase of 1.4 percentage points over that of 2015. In the first three quarters of 2017, the added value of primary industry was 4,122.9 billion yuan, with a year-on-year increase of 3.7%; that of secondary industry was 23,810.9 billion yuan, with a year-on-year increase of 6.3%; and that of tertiary industry was 31,395.1 billion yuan, with a year-on-year increase of 7.8%. The rate of contribution of the service sector to economic growth reached 5.8%, with a year-on-year increase of 0.3 percentage points over 2016.

Emerging industries were growing rapidly. In the first three quarters of 2017, strategic emerging industries witnessed a year-on-year increase of 11.3%, faster than that of scaled industries by 4.6 percentage points. In the service industry, the index growth rates of the service sector for information transmission, software, and information technologies and the service sector for businesses reached 29.4% and 11.4%, respectively.[4] New business patterns and models were flourishing; the digital economy, the platform economy, and the sharing economy were permeating the economy widely, and new services appeared continuously. Innovative business start-ups provided more support to development. The policy of Mass Entrepreneurship and Innovation advanced steadily. In 2016, 5.53 million new enterprises were registered throughout the country, at a rate of 15,000 new enterprises registered per day. From January to July 2017, 3.454 million new enterprises were registered throughout the country, or 16,000 every day. A group of new entrepreneurship and innovation demonstration bases were established with approval, and nearly 5,000 popular innovative spaces and entrepreneurship and innovation platforms of state-owned enterprises were built, driving employment forward in a more outstanding way.

---

4 The macroeconomic data were prepared according to the statistical bulletin and news press information of the National Bureau of Statistics, using materials from the official website of the National Bureau of Statistics.

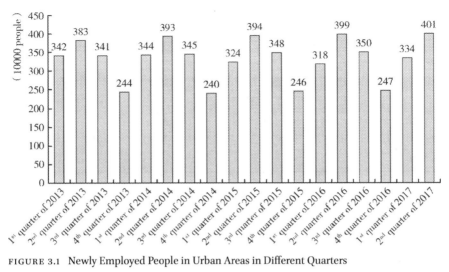

FIGURE 3.1 Newly Employed People in Urban Areas in Different Quarters

Against such a macroeconomic background, the current rate of employment was growing stably. Especially since 2017, with the return of the macro-economy, the good developmental tendency and active factors for employment have been further realized, and various employment indicators have improved, making this process a highlight in social and economic development.

1.1   The Scale of Employment Expanded Continuously and the Number of New Workers in Urban Areas Constantly Increased

From 2012 to 2016, the number of new workers in urban areas initially surpassed 13 million and reached 65.24 million over five years. The total number of employed persons throughout the country grew by 2.25 million, reaching 776 million by the end of 2016. In 2017, urban areas were off to a good start in the number of newly employed people, with 3.34 million newly employed people in the first quarter and 4.01 million in the second quarter (see Figure 3.1), which was a record high for a single season since 2004. From January to September, the accumulated number of newly employed people reached 10.97 million, with a year-on-year increase of 300,000 people,[5] making a historical record in the same period.

1.2   The Unemployment Rate Was Maintained at a Low Level

The two unemployment rates were reduced to their lowest points in years, and they were also at a low level compared to the major economies in the world.

---

5 The data about newly employed people in urban areas, the urban registered unemployment rate, and HR market supply and demand are from the Ministry of Human Resources and Social Security.

REPORT ON THE SITUATION AND QUALITY OF EMPLOYMENT 49

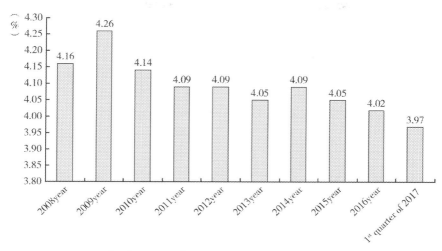

FIGURE 3.2 Registered Urban Unemployment Rates

Since 2012, the national urban registered unemployment rate has been maintained at 4.1% and below, maintaining stable operation at a low level. At the end of the fourth quarter of 2016, the national urban registered unemployment rate was 4.02%, and the number for the first three quarters in 2017 was lower than 4.0%. The registered unemployment rate in the second quarter was reduced to lower than 4.0% again and was maintained at 3.95% at the end of the third quarter, with a reduction of 0.09 percentage points year on year. This was the lowest level since the financial crisis in 2008 (see Figure 3.2). According to the Statistics Bureau, the unemployment rate of the urban survey witnessed a rise before it decreased, showing a tendency to decline with fluctuations. In the first nine months of 2017, the unemployment rates in a survey of 31 major cities were lower than those in the same period in 2016, which was 4.83% in September, reduced by 0.14 percentage points over the same period in the previous year, and reaching the lowest point since 2012. The national unemployment rate of the urban survey was also maintained at a low level. That rate in September 2017 was lower than what it was in the same period in 2016 by 0.12 percentage points.[6]

1.3   *The Supply-Demand Relationship in the HR Market Has Improved and Shows Ever-Increasing Vitality*

The Ministry of Human Resources and Social Security indicated that, according to the market supply and demand data provided by public employment

---

6 The rate of surveyed unemployment is from the press conference materials of the National Bureau of Statistics. See the official website of the National Bureau of Statistics.

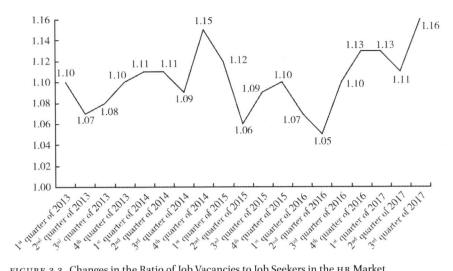

FIGURE 3.3 Changes in the Ratio of Job Vacancies to Job Seekers in the HR Market

service agencies in 100 cities, the vitality of the HR market has been increasing. In 2016, both the number of jobs and the number of people looking for jobs on the HR market decreased in the first half of the year. The job vacancies-to-seekers ratio remained low, but it rose again in the third quarter and reached 1.13 in the fourth quarter, which was the second-highest level in the past five years. In 2017, with an economy that was stabilizing and recovering, enterprise employment witnessed an improvement. According to the analysis of HR supply and demand in 100 cities, the number of people to be recruited and the number of people looking for jobs saw a year-on-year increase for three consecutive quarters, showing a dual-increase tendency instead of the dual-decline tendency of recent years. The job-vacancies-to-seekers ratio remained at 1.1 and above and reached 1.16 in the third quarter of 2017, increasing by 0.05 over the previous quarter and by 0.06 over the same period in 2016, which was the highest value this statistic reached since it was first recorded in 2001 (see Figure 3.3). At the same time, according to survey and monitoring data, enterprise employment is stable at the moment. According to the Ministry of Human Resources and Social Security, in 2017, the number of enterprise jobs witnessed a continuous increase from February to April. Despite a fluctuation in May, the number returned to the range of increase in June. Seven of the first nine months of 2017 saw an increase in the number of jobs, marking the end of a decline in enterprise employment over several years. According to the PMI indicator issued by the National Bureau of Statistics, enterprise employment displayed a stable and good tendency. The employee index for each month of the first two quarters of 2017 was maintained at 49.0 and above, which was

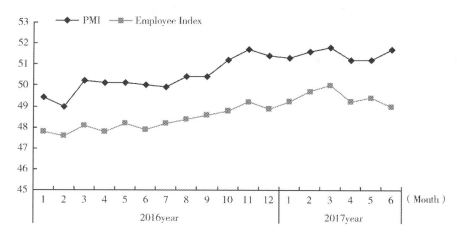

FIGURE 3.4 Changes in the PMI and Employee Index in Manufacturing

higher than that in the same period in 2016 (see Figure 3.4). This indicates that although employment in the manufacturing industry was shrinking, the pace of that shrinkage was decreasing and becoming more stable. Likewise, the employee index of non-manufacturing industries was also maintained at more than 49.0, which was better than the previous two years overall.

1.4 Employment among Key Groups Remained Stable, and the Employment Situation in Key Regions Improved

First of all, the employment of college graduates remained stable in the face of a huge amount of pressure. In recent years, due to the expansion of enrollment in higher education, the number of college graduates has set new records many times. In 2017, the number of college graduates reached a historical high of 7.95 million, increasing by 300,000 over 2016's total (see Figure 3.5). Sustained by efforts from all walks of society, the general employment rate of college graduates held stable despite enormous pressure. At the end of the year, the general employment rate of college graduates was maintained at more than 90%, realizing a double increase in the number of graduates starting businesses or finding jobs. According to the statistics of the Ministry of Education, as of July 1, 2017, the hiring rate of college graduates in 2017 upon graduation increased by 0.7 percentage points over the same period in the previous year, and the hiring rate has witnessed a rare year-on-year increase in recent years. As of September 1, the initial employment rate of college graduates increased by 0.5 percentage points over the same period in the previous year. Second, the employment of migrant workers remained stable. The number of rural laborers looking for jobs in other sectors continuously increased, while the unemployment rate was stabilized at a low level. The total number of migrant workers increased from 263 million in

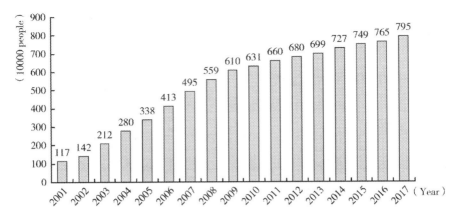

FIGURE 3.5 Number of Current College Graduates

2012 to 282 million in 2016. According to monitoring data, at present, the number of rural laborers looking for jobs in cities is still increasing. At the end of the third quarter of 2017, rural laborers working in cities totaled 179.69 million, increasing by 3.2 million or 1.8% over the same period in 2016. According to a survey by the Statistics Bureau, the unemployment rate in the survey of the agricultural household population in urban areas remained at a low level, below the national average. According to the front-line survey of the observation program of the Ministry of Human Resources and Social Security, the recruitment, payroll, job stability, and employment expectations of migrant workers were basically stable, without any obvious changes or fluctuations. All of these facts indicate that the employment of migrant workers remained generally stable. Third, the resettlement of staff who were cut due to overcapacity progressed with minimal difficulty. The task of resettling staff who were cut due to overcapacity in the iron and coal industries was burdensome, but efforts from various quarters ensured that the resettlement of that staff went smoothly. Fourth, greater efforts were made to reemploy laid-off workers and to secure employment assistance for people with difficulties in finding jobs, turning the employment situation into a good one. From 2012 to 2016, 27.9 million laid-off workers and 8.81 million people with difficulties in finding jobs were employed. Since 2013, the laid-off workers and people with difficulties in finding jobs have met more difficulties when seeking employment, as the number of employed people in these two groups decreased slightly year on year. In 2017, however, this situation changed. The situation of employment thus improved to some extent. From January to September, 4.27 million laid-off workers in urban areas found new jobs, with a year-on-year increase of 10,000 people, while 1.33 million people with difficulties in employment found jobs, with a year-on-year increase of 80,000 people. While the employment of key groups was

REPORT ON THE SITUATION AND QUALITY OF EMPLOYMENT   53

stabilizing, employment in some key regions was also changing for the better. In the past two years, the situation of employment in Northeastern China has been worsening and the unemployment rate in this region reached new highs. In the first three quarters of 2017, the economic development of Northeastern China followed a stable and good path and the industry grew by 1.6%, reversing a negative development trend for the first time in years. With the revitalization of Northeastern China and the constant efforts made to aid those areas with difficulties in employment, the unemployment rate in Northeastern China gradually decreased and the gap between this area and the whole country has been narrowing. At the same time, the number of newly employed workers in urban areas increased again after falling. In the first half of 2017, the year-on-year increase in this aspect reached 4.8%, and Northeastern China ranked first among the four major areas.

1.5 *The Employment Situation Has Been Stable and Has Improved in 2018, but Attention Should Also Be Paid to Existing Risks*

In general, with the stable recovery of economic growth and the implementation of the preferential employment strategy and active employment policy, a stable and good employment trend was maintained in 2018. However, we should also recognize that there were still some outstanding conflicts and problems in the economy, such as the conflict between overcapacity and the updating of the structure of demand, insufficient internal motivation for economic growth, and increasing difficulties in some areas. All of these problems would negatively influence our employment situation, and some difficulties should not be neglected.

First of all, market instability has increased, which may lead to a higher risk of unemployment for workers. At present, the economy of China is in a critical period featuring a transformation from old to new motivations, a more intensified structural adjustment, and accelerated technical advances. The economic uncertainties and instability of the labor market have increased, leading to more risks of unemployment for workers. According to statistics, in the past two years, fluctuations in the rate of surveyed unemployment and registered urban unemployment have become more obvious. The surveyed rates of unemployment in some areas have stayed at a high level. A lot of jobs in the traditional manufacturing industry and the accommodation industry have been continuously disappearing. The poor sustainability and unstable employment practices of new business patterns and platforms may lead to higher unemployment risks for workers.

Second, the pressure on SMEs (small- and medium-sized enterprises) to stabilize their jobs has increased. With the economy's general tendency of stable growth, under the influence of a reduced pace of investment in fixed assets and an increase in the price of raw materials, the operational difficulties faced by SMEs did not change fundamentally and the pressure on them to stabilize jobs would further increase. The general growth rate of social fixed assets was reduced for five consecutive months. Private fixed-asset investment witnessed a constant decline in terms of growth rate, while the growth rate of secondary industry remained low. Some infrastructure projects and manufacturing projects were suspended or even canceled, which had a significant influence on jobs in production on the front line. At the same time, with the increasing prices of raw materials for industry, such as iron, steel, coal, non-ferrous metals, and chemical industry materials, SMEs in the middle and lower reaches have seen higher costs and lower profits, and this has reduced their willingness and capacity in terms of employment while making it more difficult for them to stabilize jobs and recruit more workers. Furthermore, with the implementation of the green developmental concept and environmental protection supervisory work, some SMEs without sufficient input in environmental protection would be shut down according to the compulsory environmental protection requirements, and in that case some workers may face unemployment.

Third, resource-oriented regions may face higher employment pressure, and the unemployment rates in some regions may increase. Despite the generally stable employment situation in China, some old industrial bases and resource-oriented areas such as the three provinces in northeastern China—Hebei Province, Shanxi Province, and Inner Mongolia—were facing high employment pressure. In some cities with exhausted resources and independent industrial and mining areas, energy and resource industries were highly concentrated, with a proportion of traditional heavy industry and mining industry, and this led to a heavy burden in cutting overcapacity, problems in workplace safety and environmental protection, complicated issues due to the reform of stated-owned enterprises, and poor transformation from old to new motivation. Given the few industries in such areas, there were few channels for employment. Furthermore, the wide funding gap and the fact that laid-off workers were not a good fit for the market in terms of skills and thoughts led to a narrow employment space. Therefore, the regional risk of unemployment should not be overlooked.

Fourth, college graduates have continuously seen a high amount of pressure in finding employment. Despite the general stability in the employment of college graduates, the number of college graduates has been increasing and may surpass 8 million in 2018. Pressure in finding employment has continued to be high. The difficulty in finding employment for college graduates was a hot issue then. Some college graduates suffering from long-term unemployment may encounter more difficulties in finding jobs. In addition to the employment difficulties faced by some graduates, it was also difficult for them to find suitable or "good" jobs. More and more college graduates have chosen flexible employment, slow employment, or even no employment. Therefore, some college graduates or their parents were still unsatisfied despite the generally stable employment situation of the college graduates.

Fifth, the quality of the employment of some workers was poor. Jobs generated through an economic structure dominated by low-end industries could not meet the expectations of workers, especially the new generation of laborers who were born in the 1980s and 1990s. On the labor market, some workers are vulnerable groups with unstable jobs, low incomes, and no guarantee for employment benefits. A few workers were even owed back pay. For the employees of some SMEs, the rate of participation in the social security system was low, the basis for contribution was small, and the suspension of contributions of the social security fee increased, which damaged their social security benefits. At the same time, employment stability and occupational development were insufficient. Migrant workers and those looking for job opportunities in big cities have been flowing and changing jobs frequently between rural and urban areas, as well as between different regions, industries, and enterprises. They have had a flexible employment status for a long time, leading to low employment stability, narrow occupational developmental space, reduced quality of employment, and increased employment insecurity.

2 The Situation of Employment for College Graduates Has Improved While the Quality of Employment Should Be Improved

A comprehensive arrangement was made in the Report to the 19th CPC National Congress on employment, and a target was set to "realize better and more sufficient employment." However, we should not only focus on the quantity of jobs, or the realization of the target of sufficient employment, but we should also ensure the quality of employment. To accurately describe the changes in the quality and quantity of the employment of college graduates, we have established an employment index system, using data from the systematic survey conducted by MyCOS for college graduates for five to six consecutive years, to analyze the employment of undergraduates and college graduates from 2011 to 2015. The employment index has two dimensions, namely, the realization of employment and the quality of that employment. In this index, the realization of employment is represented by the employment rate, which reflects the percentage of graduates employed within six months after graduation. The quality of employment is represented by a salary ratio (reflecting the relative level of salary), employment satisfaction, and employment stability, which reflects the quality of employment of the graduates. The weighted average of the four indicators is used to calculate the employment index of the graduates, which reflects the overall employment of the graduates. At the same time, other related statistical indexes, such as the employment rate, the rate of hiring for employment, the flexible employment rate, the rate of independent business start-ups, and the rate of enrollment, are used to enhance the description of the employment and changes of graduates.[7]

2.1 The Employment Index of Graduates[8] Has Been on the Increase, with Some Fluctuations, and the Situation of Employment Has Been Stable in General

From 2011 to 2015, the employment index of graduates rose slightly from 76.64 in 2011 to 79.19 in 2015, an increase of 2.55, showing a good tendency with a slight fluctuation. The employment index for graduates in 2014 was the highest one, 79.83, and although the number in 2015 witnessed a slight decrease, it was still higher than those of graduates in other years, indicating the stability of the overall employment situation of graduates under the "new normal" economic conditions, with middle- and high-growth rates (see Figure 3.6).

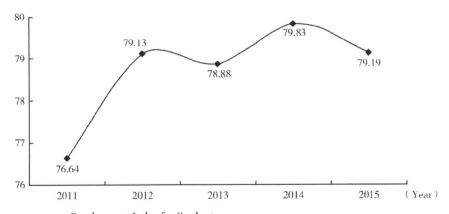

FIGURE 3.6 Employment Index for Graduates, 2011–2015

---

7   This study is the result of the think-tank research program of the HR Management Research Center of Beijing University of Chemical Technology, and is a part of the "Research on the Employment of College Graduates under Industrial Transformation and Updating" (approval number: 14ZDA068), a major project of the National Social Science Foundation in which the center participates. The person responsible for the topic is the research fellow Mo Rong. The research has been supported with a great amount of data provided by MyCOS. The research group hereby expresses its great gratitude to MyCOS.
8   The range of the employment index calculated in this report is from 0 to 100%, and a value of 80% or above is good.

2.2 In Terms of the Quantity of Employment, a High Employment Rate Is Key to the Stable Improvement of the Employment Index, but It Carries a Certain Number of Risks

At present, the actual employment rate of graduates[9] has been increasing year by year and has maintained a high level, which has been significantly supported by the rate of independent start-ups and the enrollment rate.

First of all, the actual employment rate of graduates has generally been increasing year by year and has been more than 90% for years. From 2011 to 2015, the actual employment rate of graduates showed an obvious tendency to increase, rising from 90.2% in 2011 to 91.7% in 2015, with an increase of 1.5 percentage points, and it has been maintained at more than 90% for these years.[10] The actual employment rate of graduates in 2014 was the highest, at 92.1%, and although the number in 2015 witnessed a slight decrease, it was still higher than those of the other years (see Figure 3.7).

Second, the rapidly increasing rate of independent start-ups has contributed to the growth of the employment rate of graduates. The proportion of graduates who started up independent businesses increased from 1.6% in 2010 to 3.3% in 2015, an increase of 1.7 percentage points (see Figure 3.8); the proportion of graduates who started up independent businesses was the highest

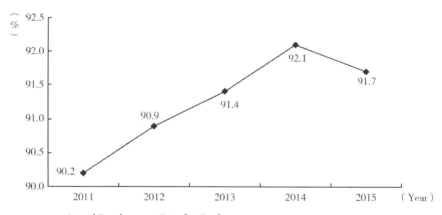

FIGURE 3.7 Actual Employment Rate for Graduates, 2011–2015

---

9   Actual employment rate = number of employed graduates (not including the number of those enrolled in higher education) / number of graduates with employment plans × 100%. The actual employment rate is the statistic indicator designed for this report, which is used to display the proportion of employed graduates to the graduates planning employment; the numerator and denominator do not include the enrolled graduates.
10 This is the survey data from MyCOS, which shows a difference of 3 percentage points from the employment rate issued by the government.

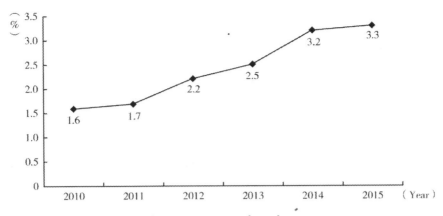

FIGURE 3.8 Percentage of Graduates Starting Up Independent Businesses, 2011–2015

in 2014, similar to that in 2015, indicating the active response of college graduates to the challenge of founding independent businesses. This has relieved, to some extent, the pressure on graduates to find employment and has provided a driving force to stimulate the market economy and the labor market.

It is worth noting, however, that upon graduation, graduates are not well prepared in terms of knowledge, skills, and experience, which may significantly influence the level at which they start a business, their survival rate in business, and their efficiency in starting up a business. According to a survey conducted by MyCOS on the survival rate of businesses started by graduates, the survival rate of businesses started by undergraduates was 48.6%[11] and that of junior college graduates was 47.5%. Therefore, given the rapid growth in businesses started by graduates, we should pay more attention to the quality of such businesses, so as to improve the overall efficiency of starting a business.

Third, the ever-increasing rate of enrollment of graduates over the years has greatly assisted in relieving employment pressure. From 2011 to 2015, the enrollment rate of graduates increased from 7.0% to 10.1%, an increase of 3.1 percentage points, showing rapid growth (see Figure 3.9). Take the year of 2015, for instance: the number of graduates in 2015 increased by 222,200 over that in 2014. According to the calculation of the rate of enrollment based on the survey by MyCOS, out of all graduates, about 688,400 people would pursue higher educational degrees, reducing the number of graduates looking for jobs. Thus,

---

11 The business-starting survival rate of graduates means the ratio of the graduates who are still in the business-starting phase to the graduates who started their own businesses in the longitudinal survey within three years after graduation.

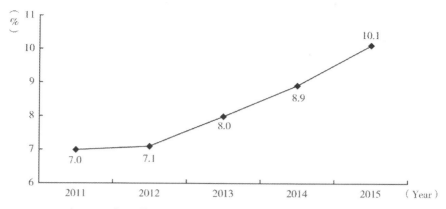

FIGURE 3.9 The Rate of Enrollment for Graduates, 2011–2015

we can see that the growth of the rate of enrollment has played an active role in reducing the pressure on graduates to find employment.

However, we still need to see the risks behind the high employment rate and the high employment pressure faced by college graduates. First, the rate of hiring of graduates saw a slight decrease, which may negatively influence the employment stability and employment quality of graduates to some extent. Second, the proportion of graduates still looking for jobs among unemployed graduates was diminishing, revealing a slow rate of employment among graduates. At the same time, the proportion of graduates who chose to stop looking for jobs and had no other plans was on the increase.

2.3 *The General Quality of Employment among College Graduates Has Been Improving but Is Not Yet Good Enough*

2.3.1   Despite a Slight Increase and Overall Stability, the Employment Quality Index[12] for Graduates Witnessed a Decrease in 2015, Directly Reflecting the High Pressure for Employment

The employment quality index of graduates was calculated using the weighted average of the salary ratio, employment satisfaction, and employment stability for graduates. According to the quality of employment for graduates from 2010 to 2015, except for the low quality of employment in 2011, the indexes for the other years were between 66% and 68%, with a slight increase in general. The overall level of quality of employment remained stable. The quality of employment for graduates in 2015 went down slightly. The relatively high

---

12   The range of employment quality is from 0 to 100%, and a value of 80% or above is good.

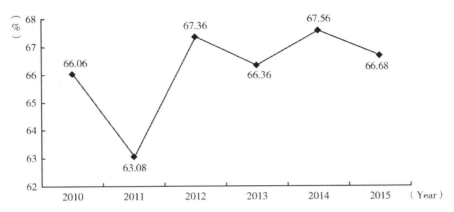
FIGURE 3.10   Employment Quality Index for Graduates, 2011–2015

degree of employment pressure for current graduates could be reflected in the quality of employment (see Figure 3.10).

2.3.2   The Conspicuous Growth, by Stages, of College Graduates' Satisfaction with Their Employment[13]

From 2010 to 2015, graduates' satisfaction with their employment increased from 47% to 62%—an increase of 15 percentage points. The change in their satisfaction with their jobs can be divided into three stages. Their satisfaction with their employment in both of the years 2010 and 2011 was 47%, which means that the number of graduates who were satisfied with their jobs accounted for 47% of the total number of graduates. Their satisfaction with their employment in both of the years 2012 and 2013 was similar, that is 55% and 56%, respectively, with increases of 8 and 9 percentage points over 2010 and 2011, respectively. Their satisfaction with their employment in the years 2014 and 2015 was also close, that is, 61% and 62%, increasing by 6–7 percentage points over 2012 and 2013 (see Figure 3.11).

MyCOS investigated the reasons for the graduates' low degree of satisfaction with their employment in 2013 and 2014, and they found that the major reason was low income. In addition, insufficient opportunities for development, bad working atmosphere, poor working conditions, too much overtime work, high pressure due to low competence, and poor performance in the eyes of leaders also negatively influenced the graduates' degree of satisfaction with their employment.

---

13   Satisfaction with employment is the proportion of the graduates who are satisfied with their jobs, and the value is between 0 and 100%.

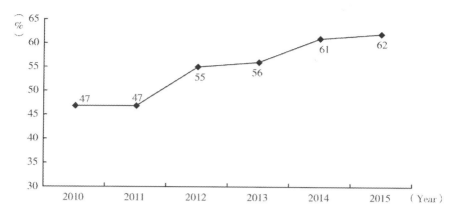

FIGURE 3.11   Graduates' Satisfaction with Their Employment, 2011–2015

2.3.3 The Stability of Graduates' Employment Did Not Change Too Much

Except for the year 2011, the stability of graduates' employment[14] remained at between 66% to 67%, which means that the number of graduates who did not change their jobs within six months after graduation accounted for 66% to 67% of the total number of graduates (see Figure 3.12).

According to the MyCOS survey, 98% of the graduates in 2015 who resigned within six months resigned actively for the top three reasons for resignation: "insufficient personal space for development," "low salary and benefits," and "desire to change job or industry."

In addition, among the employment options, full-time jobs, as the most traditional form of employment, were still dominant, but the proportion of such jobs has been decreasing year by year. The number of graduates taking part-time jobs and starting their own businesses has been increasing. The rate of flexible employment among graduates increased from 2.7% in 2010 to 5.0% in 2015, increasing by 2.3 percentage points. The rate of flexible employment among junior college graduates was much higher than that among undergraduates. For example, in 2015, the rate of flexible employment among junior college graduates was 6.2%, while the rate for undergraduates was only 3.7% (see Figure 3.13). Such diversified employment tendencies for graduates is good for releasing employment pressure and improving the structure of employment, but it would increase the instability of the graduates' employment.

---

14   Employment stability is used in this report to measure the employment stability of graduates, which means the proportion of graduates who have not changed their jobs within six months after being employed, and the value is between 0 and 100%.

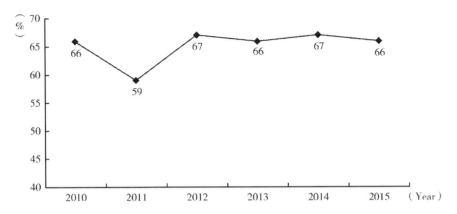

FIGURE 3.12   The Stability of Graduates' Employment, 2011–2015

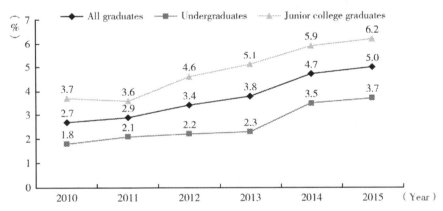

FIGURE 3.13   Rate of Flexible Employment among Graduates, 2011–2015, with a Comparison between Junior College Graduates and Undergraduates

2.3.4   The Relative Level of Graduates' Salaries[15] Witnessed a Rapid Decrease, Becoming the Major Force Leading to the Risk of a Decrease in the Quality of Employment

According to the level of salaries in the MyCOS survey of college graduates six months after graduation, the nominal salaries for graduates from 2011 to 2015 six months after graduation increased significantly from 2,766 yuan in 2011 to

---

15   The relative level of salary is calculated based on the average monthly income of graduates and that of employed workers in urban areas, which is reflected in the salary ratio in this report. Salary ratio = average monthly income of graduates in six months after graduation / the monthly average salary of workers in urban areas in the year of graduation.

3,726 yuan in 2015, but the year-on-year growth rate was in decline, with some fluctuation. The growth rate of salaries for graduates in 2012 was 10.2%, and it decreased to 6.9% for the graduates in 2015. The absolute average monthly salary of workers in urban areas was higher than the salary of graduates six months after graduation, and the growth rate of the salary of workers was also higher than that of graduates. The growth rate of graduates' salaries in 2015 was lower than that of workers in urban areas by 3.4 percentage points.

There are three major causes of the continuous decrease in the relative salary of graduates. First, the rapid increase in the number of college graduates is the direct cause of the reduction in graduates' relative salaries. According to survey data on urban households from 1992 to 2009 from the National Bureau of Statistics, since 2002, the proportion of the salary of college graduates under 25 years of age with respect to the average salary of workers in urban areas in that year had clearly been declining. In 2002, the students who had enrolled in universities and colleges under the plan for enrollment increase in 1999 began to graduate. Since then, the number of college graduates has been increasing rapidly year by year. The increase in the number of college graduates has increased the talent resources on the labor market, but it also changed the labor supply-demand relationship for college graduates, reducing their relative advantages on the labor market. In recent years, the number of graduates kept reaching new highs. Under the pressure of the economic downturn, the relative stability of the rate of employment for graduates came at the price of reducing the relative income of the graduates. Therefore, the quality of employment of graduates decreased. Second, the economic structural adjustment and the transformation and updating of the industrial structure in China have changed the demand structure of the labor market for talent, but the development of talent at universities and colleges could not meet the market needs, leading to a mismatch between talent supply and demand and causing difficulties for students seeking jobs and for employers recruiting talents. The knowledge, skills, and qualities of graduates could not meet the needs of the market, reducing the expectations of employers and their evaluation of graduates, which was eventually reflected in a low salary. Third, after the expansion of college enrollment, a huge number of graduates entered the labor market, weakening the effect of their high degree of education. Employers could hardly identify the strengths of employees based on their college diplomas, and so they tended to use low salaries to reduce the losses caused by misjudgment.[16]

16   Yao Xianguo, Fang Xin, and Qian Xueya, "The Interference of Enrollment Expansion of Colleges on the Salaries of College Graduates," *Population & Economics*, 2014(1).

3 Policy Suggestions

Although the general situation of employment for college graduates was stable, with a constantly increasing total number of graduates and the continuing pressure of the economic downturn, labor demand among enterprises has been diminishing, and the conflict between total supply and demand has constantly increased the pressure for employment for graduates. Faced with that pressure, governments at all levels should still pay close attention to the employment of college graduates.

3.1 *Monitor the Quality of the Employment of College Graduates*

In light of the general stability in the employment rate of college graduates, greater attention should be paid to the quality of employment of graduates to prevent a further decline in the quality of employment. To this end, a uniform system for assessing the quality of employment of college graduates should be established. Such a system should be established on the principles of systematic soundness, effectiveness, stability, dynamics, operability, and quantifiability by choosing typical, representative indicators to objectively reflect the actual quality of graduates' employment and to compare them horizontally and vertically in a simple way.

At the same time, an official statistical system should be established to survey college graduates to collect accurate and comprehensive employment data. On the one hand, such a system will enable us to handle more accurately the current situation and dynamics of the employment of graduates and to conduct real-time monitoring of the quality of employment of college graduates based on the assessment system. On the other hand, we can focus on key groups (those who have difficulty in finding jobs or no confidence that they will find a job) and key employment problems (such as the conditions of the employment of graduates and the causes of unemployment) to provide a scientific, objective, and true basis for implementing specific policies.

3.2 *Establish a Mechanism for Determining the Level of Salaries for College Graduates*

The level of salaries is mainly adjusted on the basis of the talent supply-demand relationship in the labor market, which could reflect the effects of the market mechanism. The level of the salaries of college graduates at the beginning of employment should also follow this principle. The decrease in the relative level of salaries for graduates discussed in this study was influenced by a change in the supply-demand relationship on the market. However, we should keep in mind that most laborers in China have only received a secondary education with an average duration of 9.28 years (2014 data[17]), which is a relatively low level of education. Nationwide, the number of college graduates has not surpassed the demand. Therefore, the rapid reduction in the relative level of salaries of graduates was unusual. The distribution of college graduates was imbalanced. Too many graduates entered developed areas and advantageous industries, leading to fierce local competition for employment. Under the joint influence of the market and man-made factors, the relative level of the salaries of graduates declined, and some negative attitudes spread within society, such as "college graduates are inferior to migrant workers" or "it's useless to go to universities." Therefore, a guidance mechanism regarding the level of salaries, with market adjustment as the major force, should be established for college graduates in order to provide authoritative guidance for graduates, employers, and the public by regularly issuing the recommended salaries of graduates, so as to ensure that graduates receive fair salaries at the beginning of their employment, maintain a reasonable growth rate in their salaries, realize a reasonable return on their investment in higher education, and prevent negative attitudes and beliefs from further expanding within society.

3.3 *Provide College Graduates with More Effective and Flexible Services for Starting a Business*

In recent years, the rate of flexible employment among graduates has seen an obvious increase; in particular, the proportion of graduates who started up an independent business increased greatly. Flexible forms of employment would play an active role in relieving employment pressure, but they may also reflect the high pressure faced by graduates on the job market. At present, the rate of starting an independent business among junior college graduates is higher than that among undergraduates, and the rate of starting up an independent business among graduates from higher vocational colleges and non-211 universities is higher than that among graduates from 211 universities. Although graduates' educational background and level of university or college could not completely predict the quality and efficiency of an independent business started by graduates, they could to some extent reflect the overall quality of the graduates. For this purpose, although we are encouraging college graduates to start their own businesses, we should also pay attention to the cultivation of college graduates in the field of business, strengthen education about starting a business and create training courses for graduates, and provide more policy support and convenient services for graduates who start

---

17   The data are from the official website of the Ministry of Education, http://www.moe.edu .cn/jyb_xwfb/s5147/201512/t20151207_223334.html.

businesses, so as to improve the survival rate of the businesses independently started up by college graduates.

First of all, we should improve the awareness of college graduates regarding policies for starting up a business. According to statistics, college graduates are not very familiar with the policies for starting up a business provided by governments, and many college graduates were not able to obtain support in this matter. Therefore, more efforts need to be made to publicize business-starting policies and services on campuses in order to actively introduce college graduates to the support networks and services for starting up a business and to provide them with contact information for related departments, so as to provide services, assistance, and guidance in the future.

Second, we should improve surveys of the business-starting needs of college graduates. Through surveys, we can learn about the difficulties and needs of college graduates who are starting their own businesses. Only when the needs of college graduates for business-starting services are understood can we provide specific services and improve their efficiency.

Third, we should further enrich the content and forms of business-starting services for college graduates. Business-starting services should be provided throughout the process in a comprehensive way, including guidance on project selection before starting the business, assistance while starting up the business, and tracking, assessment, and feedback after starting the business. Assessment of the business-starting practices of many college graduates shows that most college graduates do not have sufficient experience and funds to set up a business. The relevant government departments need to focus on the content of their services in order to provide graduates' businesses with effective guidance and sufficient funds. In terms of the delivery of services, the Internet and mobile media devices should be fully utilized to provide college graduates with convenient and high-quality services.

Fourth, we should establish a business-starting guidance system integrating business-starting consciousness education, development of the capacity for starting up a business, and good business-starting practices. We should also encourage local governments, higher educational institutions, and teachers and students to jointly establish a business-starting service system and a business-starting information market system that will closely connect business R&D, promotion, incubation, and industrialization. Then we should improve and implement a business-starting policy system that will enable college graduates to raise business-starting funds, promote business-starting development, and realize the multiplication effect of business-starting in driving employment.

3.4 Improve the Collection of Statistics and the Assessment of Talent to Better Match Talent Development with Market Demand

The most outstanding conflict in the employment of college graduates is the structural imbalance between supply and demand, which could be reflected by mismatching between qualities, skills, concepts, and desires, on the one hand, and on the other hand the demands of the labor market. To adjust the methods for talent development in universities and colleges, improve the quality of that development, and enhance matching between talent development and market demand are not new topics. However, in the face of a new economic tendency, the demand for talents for industrial transformation and the optimization of the industrial structure has also changed. To effectively connect higher education with the demands of the labor market, work on the following aspects should be considered.

First of all, we should improve estimates of the development of industries and occupations in order to estimate the demand of the labor market for college graduates, and provide a scientific reference for adjusting the talent development and course organization of universities and colleges. For this purpose, specific organs should use the statistics from the relevant departments.

Second, in correspondence with the features and tendency of the demand for talent, we should encourage universities and colleges with different features and at different levels to establish different developmental levels and targets. At present, the employability profiles of graduates from universities and colleges of different levels and types vary, with many overlaps and conflicts. To solve this problem, we need to improve the special characteristics of universities and colleges to meet the market's diversified demand for talents.

Third, we should strengthen education and training in innovation and starting businesses, in order to improve the capacities of college graduates in these two areas. At present, innovation and start-up education in China is still at an early stage. Compared to college graduates in foreign countries, most college graduates in China do not have a sufficiently innovative consciousness and ability, which hinders the promotion of innovation and business-starting among new graduates. Therefore, on the one hand, universities and colleges should establish specific departments to actively work with enterprises to introduce quality innovation and start-up resources and to jointly launch innovation and start-up education for college graduates. On the other hand, the relevant government departments should provide college graduates with quality innovation and start-up training periods through subordinate bodies or government purchasing.

3.5 Create a Fair Employment Environment to Improve Policy Support in the Areas in Need of Talent

First of all, fierce market competition would lead to improper competition, unreasonable employment, and unfair employment issues, which could harm the employment prospects of graduates. Therefore, we need to motivate all walks of society in order to guide the whole society to form correct public opinions and employment concepts through various publicity methods. Especially, we need to guide employers to establish a fair recruitment concept; strengthen market supervision and control in order to standardize the recruitment and employment activities of employees and reduce discrimination in schools on the basis of gender, native place, ethnic group, and age; and strengthen legal education for graduates to encourage them to protect their benefits during employment.

Second, the imbalanced distribution of employment resources is a major cause of the concentrated flow of graduates. To direct graduates to those areas in need of talent, we need to improve the advertisement of employment opportunities and guide public opinion to encourage graduates to look for jobs in small cities, middle and western China, and grassroots units; to guide them to establish correct opinions on working in private enterprises; and to build a correct concept of employment. On the other hand, we need to improve policy to attract graduates to the areas in need of talent, such as providing more support in terms of labor protection and employment subsidies, in order to reduce the mental differences felt by the graduates in different areas, industries, and occupations, and to promote the reasonable distribution of the resources of graduates.

3.6 Improve Legal Systems to Protect Flexible Employment among College Graduates

First, we should improve the laws and regulations that govern the flexible employment of college graduates. In this way, we can protect the benefits of employees and enterprises on a fundamental level and promote the improvement and development of the flexible service system.

Second, we should improve the facilities supporting the flexible employment of college graduates. An information service system should be established for the flexible employment of college graduates. We need to promote communication and sharing of information and resources as well as the establishment and development of a supporting service system for flexible employment groups in colleges. At the same time, we need to establish a system of supervision and a system of assessment for the flexible employment of college graduates.

Third, we should improve the system of guaranteed benefits for the flexible employment of college graduates. At present, the social security system of China is still improving and developing. At the same time, given the flexibility of the employment of college graduates in terms of form, place, and time, there is a greater risk of harming the interests of these graduates, so a complete social security system must be established to protect the legal benefits of graduates with flexible employment.

References

He Yiming. "Empirical Analysis of the Change in the Rate of Return to Education under Educational Expansion." *Chinese Journal of Population Science*, 2009(4).

Mo Rong. "The Employment Issue for College Students Is a Responsibility." *Human Resources and Social Security of China*, 2015(4).

Mo Rong. "Employment Policy 4.0: Make Entrepreneurship Become an Engine." Report on Current Events, College Students Edition, "Situation and Policy" lecture, first semester of the 2016–2017 academic year.

Mo Rong. "Entrepreneurship Driving Employment." *Economic Daily*, June 17, 2014.

Mo Rong. "Why Employment Has Better Performance than Expected under the New Normal. Report on Current Events, College Students Edition, second semester of the 2015–2016 academic year.

Mo Rong and Wang Xinyu. "Analysis and Thinking on the Employment Issue of College Students." Report on Current Events, College Students Edition, "Situation and Policy" lecture, first semester of the 2014–2015 academic year.

Mo Rong and Zhou Xiao. "The Industrial Transformation and Updating of China Promote High Quality Employment: Take Chengdu as an Instance." In Wu Jiang, *Report on the Human Resources Development of China (2013)*, Social Sciences Academic Press (China), 2013.

Mo Rong, Zhou Xiao, and Meng Xuduo. "Employment Tendency Analysis: Industrial Transformation and Employment." *China Labor*, 2014(1).

MyCOS Institute. *Report on the Employment of College Students in China in 2014, Report on the Employment of Undergraduates in China in 2015*, and *Report on the Employment of College Students in China in 2016*. Social Sciences Academic Press (China), 2014, 2015 and 2016.

Wang Xinyu. "Structure and Level of the Capacity of Employment of College Students in the Perspective of Job Demands—Survey Based on Beijing." *Human Resources Development of China*, 2014(9).

Xing Chunbing and Li Shi. "Enrollment Expansion, Educational Opportunities, and the Employment of College Graduates." *China Economic Quarterly*, 2014(3).

Yao Xianguo, Fang Xin, and Qian Xueya. "The Interference of the Expansion of Enrollment in Colleges on the Salaries of College Graduates." *Population & Economics*, 2014(1).

yuan Huiguang and Xie Zuoshi. "Testing Research on the Employment and Relative Salary Adjustment of College Students after the Enrollment Expansion of Universities and Colleges." *Journal of Education Research*, 2012(3).

Yue Changjun and Zhou Liping. "New Economic Normal Conditions and Features of the Employment of College Grauates—Empirical Analysis of the Sampling Survey Data of College Graduates in China in 2015." *Peking University Education Review*, 2016(2).

CHAPTER 4

Report on the Reform and Development of China's Social Security System in 2017

Lyu Xuejing[1] and Wang Yongmei[2]

Abstract

China's social security undertakings shifted from the experimental stage to maturity with a generally stable pattern of development and basically balanced income and expenditures. Social assistance work became more accurate and precise poverty-reduction undertakings advanced significantly. Social welfare and charity undertakings became more mature. Welfare undertakings for the aged and the disabled have been promoted day by day. A grand pattern of development for charity undertakings was formed. Volunteer services entered an age of legislation. The important stipulation in the Report to the 19th CPC National Congress about strengthening the construction of the social security system indicated the direction for the development of China's social security undertakings, which have entered a new age.

Keywords

social security – investment fund operations – social assistance – social charity

In 2017, China's social security undertakings shifted from the experimental stage to maturity with a generally stable pattern of development and basically balanced income and expenditures. Social assistance work became more accurate and precise poverty-reduction undertakings advanced significantly. Social welfare and charity undertakings became more mature. Welfare undertakings for the aged and the disabled have been promoted day by day. A grand pattern of development for charity undertakings was formed. The volunteer services entered an age of legislation. Upon the successful conclusion of the 19th National Congress

---

1　Lyu Xuejing, professor at the Labor and Economics School of the Capital University of Economics and Business.
2　Wang Yongmei, lecturer and postdoctoral candidate at the Labor and Economics School of the Capital University of Economics and Business.

© KONINKLIJKE BRILL NV, LEIDEN, 2022 | DOI:10.1163/9789004500723_005

of the CPC, the government proposed, under the stated goal of "strengthening the construction of social security system," to comprehensively establish a sustainable social security system at all levels by covering the whole population with urban and rural integration, clear credibility, and moderate guarantees based on the requirements of ensuring a bottom line, forming a network, and building a mechanism. This strategy indicates the direction for the future development of China's social security undertakings, which have entered a new age.

1 Social Security Undertakings Developed Stably

1.1 *Coverage Was Further Enlarged*

According to the statistics of the Ministry of Human Resources and Social Security, as of the end of September 2017, the numbers of participants in basic pension insurance, basic health care insurance, unemployment insurance, work-related injury insurance, and maternity insurance were 905 million, 1,129 million, 186 million, 224 million, and 190 million, respectively, increasing by 17.23 million, 385 million, 5.11 million, 5.11 million, and 5.49 million over the end of 2016, respectively. The number of participants in basic health care insurance increased by about 51%, showing significant growth. The rate of participation in the new rural cooperative medical system (NCMS) was nearly 99%, covering nearly all of the people that should be insured.[3] At the same time, the long-term nursing insurance system, which grew out of a pilot program initiated in June 2016, achieved stable operations, and by the end of September 2017 the number of participants had surpassed 38 million.[4]

1.2 *Income and Expenditures Were Basically Balanced*

From January to August 2017, the total incoming funds of the five major social insurances reached 4.12 trillion yuan, with a year-on-year increase of 27.78%; the income of basic pension insurance, basic health care insurance, unemployment insurance, work-related injury insurance, and maternity insurance amounted to 2,786.4 billion yuan, 1,171 billion yuan, 65.5 billion yuan, 53 billion yuan, and 40.1 billion yuan, with year-on-year increases of 23.80%, 43.82%, -15.03%, 13.48%, and 23.95%, respectively. From January to August 2017, the total expenditures of the five major social insurances reached 3.47 trillion

---

3 "Press Conference of the 3rd Quarter of 2017 Held by the Ministry of Human Resources and Social Security," http://www.mohrss.gov.cn/SYrlzyhshbzb/dongtaixinwen/fbh/lxxwfbh/2017 11/t20171101_280424.html.

4 Ministry of Human Resources and Social Security, "Number of Participants in Long-term Nursing Insurance Surpassed 38 Million, Showing an Initial Effect," http://www.sohu.com/a/201599767_118392.

yuan, with a year-on-year increase of 28.9%; the expenditures of basic pension insurance, basic health care insurance, unemployment insurance, work-related injury insurance, and maternity insurance were 2,473.3 billion yuan, 852.7 billion yuan, 51.2 billion yuan, 41.1 billion yuan, and 50.5 billion yuan, with year-on-year increases of 28.31%, 32.10%, -1.05%, 8.32%, and 79.01%, respectively. It was the first time that the current income of social security funds was slightly lower than the expenditures. The growth of income from the unemployment insurance fund was lower than the growth of its expenditures. The expenditures of maternity insurance witnessed a significant amount of growth, which was closely related to the Second Child policy implemented on January 1, 2016.

1.3   *Treatment Improved Constantly*

The pension was improved continuously. As of the end of September 2017, the number of residents receiving a pension in urban and rural areas reached 150.77 million, an increase of 2.77 million over 2016, which was higher than the growth rate of those enrolled in the insurance. The level of the pension was increased by 5.5%, and the basic pension standards for urban and rural residents improved in 14 provinces. The pensions of retirees from enterprises improved by 277 yuan per month, which was the highest rate in history. After the increase, the per capita pension per month improved from 2,773 yuan to 3,050 yuan, passing the threshold of 3,000 yuan for the first time.[5]

The allowance for health care insurance improved. In April 2017, the Ministry of Human Resources and Social Security issued the *Notice on Doing the Work for Basic Health Care Insurance for Urban Residents in 2017*, indicating that the standard of per capita allowance for health care insurance for urban residents should be increased by 30 yuan over what it had been in 2016, to a total of 450 yuan per person per year. The central financial department was to provide allowances to the western and central regions at ratios of 80% and 60%, respectively, and to provide allowances to the provinces in eastern China according to certain ratios.

The standard of unemployment insurance benefits increased. In September 2017, the Ministry of Human Resources and Social Security and the Ministry of Finance jointly issued the *Guiding Opinions on Adjusting the Standard of Unemployment Insurance Benefits*, which called for adjusting the standard of unemployment insurance benefits on the basis of ensuring a living standard and promoting employment step by step to increase the standard unemployment insurance benefits to 90% of the minimum salary standard. For example, after the adjustment, standard unemployment insurance benefits in Inner Mongolia increased by 7.3% over the previous year, and unemployment

---

5   "Pension Standard for Enterprise Retirees Increased in 2017! Per Capita Increase of 277 yuan Each Month!" http://www.sohu.com/a/133237550_132269.

insurance benefits would be issued according to the newly adjusted standard beginning on August 1, 2017.[6] In Shandong Province, the three levels of unemployment insurance benefits increased by 80 yuan, from 1,080 yuan, 1,030 yuan, and 980 yuan to 1,030 yuan on average, with a growth rate of 8.4%.[7]

1.4 New Progress Was Made in Investment Fund Operations

The investment operations of pension insurance were officially launched. For a long time, the preservation of the value of pensions has been a hotspot for the government and for academics, as well as a hard problem to be solved, in order to make sure that all of the elderly will be supported. In 2016, to implement the *Method on Managing Investment with the Funds of the Basic Pension Insurance* issued by the State Council, the Ministry of Human Resources and Social Security established a working team and made related working plans to actively promote the investment operations of local pension insurance funds. As of September 2017, the governments of nine provinces (autonomous regions and municipalities), including Beijing, Shanghai, Henan, Hubei, Guangxi, Yunnan, Shaanxi, and Anhui, signed entrusted investment contracts with the council for the social security fund totaling 430 billion yuan, of which 180 billion yuan have been transferred for investment.[8]

New progress was made in managing the professional annuity fund. To standardize the opening and management of the collection accounts of the professional annuity fund and to ensure the safety of that fund, in August 2017, the General Office of the Ministry of Human Resources and Social Security and the General Office of the Ministry of Finance jointly issued the *Interim Measures for Managing the Collection Accounts of the Professional Annuity Fund* (hereinafter the Method). The Method identified the nature of the specific deposit of the account for the collection asset trusteeship of the professional annuity fund ("the collection account"); indicated that the major functions of the collection account are to temporarily deposit payment income, transfer income, interest income, and other types of income of units and individuals, as well as to transfer and collect account assets; and determined the criteria for establishing collection accounts and the obligations to be performed by the organs responsible for social security and trusteeship banks at all levels.

---

6 "Standard of Unemployment Insurance Benefits Was Increased in the Inner Mongolia Autonomous Region," http://www.mohrss.gov.cn/SYrlzyhshbzb/shehuibaozhang/gzdt/2017 09/t20170921_277800.html.

7 "From November, the Unemployment Insurance Benefit Standard in Shandong Will Be Adjusted and Unemployed People May Receive an Additional 80 yuan Each Month," http://news.qlwb.com.cn/2017/1018/1091944.shtml.

8 "Press Conference of the 3rd Quarter of 2017 Held by the Ministry of Human Resources and Social Security," November 1, 2017.

The issuance of the Method laid a solid foundation for the investment, operations, and management of professional annuities in China.

1.5 A Stable Advance Was Made in the Pilot Program of Long-Term Nursing Insurance

The population aging of China manifests itself in the form of old age and disability. In 2015, the population of over-80-year-olds reached 26 million,[9] and it is estimated that the number will be more than 100 million by 2050, accounting for one-fourth of the total number of elderly. The number of disabled or semi-disabled persons will increase from about 40 million in 2015[10] to about 97.59 million in 2025.[11] The pressure caused by long-term care of the elderly has been increasing. In 2016, the Ministry of Human Resources and Social Security issued the *Guiding Opinions on Launching the Pilot of the System of Long-Term Nursing Insurance*, proposing to launch pilots for long-term nursing insurance in 15 cities, including Chengde in Hebei Province, Changchun in Jilin Province, and Tsitsihar in Heilongjiang Province. At present, 14 cities have issued documents and launched the pilots. As key provinces, Shandong and Jilin have not only steadily promoted long-term nursing insurance in pilot cities, but each of the provincial governments has also issued implementation guidance for the entire province.

As of October 2017, the number of participants in long-term nursing insurance had surpassed 38 million. The operation of the system was stable and its initial effect could be seen. First of all, the insurance reduced the economic and transactional burdens on the elderly and their families. Long-term nursing costs meeting the regulations could generally be reimbursed at the rate of 70%. Second, the comprehensive social function of the system could be fully utilized. The pilots played an active role in driving forward employment and business start-ups, promoting support for the elderly, developing the nursing service industry, and supporting the development of the home service industry.[12] According to the pilots, the system received positive social feedback and was welcomed by all walks of society.

---

9   Calculated based on the 1% population sampling survey data provided by the National Bureau of Statistics in 2015.

10   Wu Yushao and Wang Lili, *Report of Research on the Development of Nursing Institutions for the Elderly in China*, Hualing Press, 2015.

11   General Report Drafting Team, "General Report of Research on the National Strategy in Dealing with Population Aging, *Scientific Research on Aging*, 2015(3).

12   "News Conference of the 3rd Quarter of 2017 Held by the Ministry of Human Resources and Social Security," November 1, 2017.

1.6 The Premium Rate of Unemployment Insurance Was Further Reduced and the Functions of Unemployment Insurance Were Further Expanded

Reducing the premium rate of unemployment insurance hinges on reducing the cost of the five major tasks of structural reform on the supply side. According to incomplete statistics, for more than two years, the social insurance premium was reduced by more than 123 billion yuan in total, accounting for about 10% of the reduced enterprise tax burden annually. The unemployment insurance premium was reduced by 90 billion yuan, showing a significant effect.[13] Since 2015, the Ministry of Human Resources and Social Security and the Ministry of Finance have issued several documents to reduce or adjust the premium rates of unemployment insurance, work-related injury insurance, and maternity insurance. In February 2017, the Ministry of Human Resources and Social Security and the Ministry of Finance issued the *Notice on Issues Related to the Reduction of the Premium Rate of Unemployment Insurance by Stages* to reduce the total premium rate of the provinces (autonomous regions and municipalities) from 1.5% to 1% from January 1, 2017, onward.

The functions of unemployment insurance were further expanded. According to the *Opinions on Further Completing the Work on Employment and on the Starting Up of a Business under the New Situation* issued by the State Council in 2015, the policy of using unemployment insurance to enable enterprises to stabilize their jobs was expanded from three types of enterprises to include all enterprises meeting the criteria. To date, the job stabilization allowance of 42.4 billion yuan has been distributed among nearly 640,000 enterprises, benefiting 79.26 million workers. Despite the effectivity of this action, many issues remained to be addressed, such as imbalanced regional progress, insufficient services in this undertaking, and insufficient implementation of the policy. Against this background, the Ministry of Human Resources and Social Security issued the *Notice on Implementing the Escorting Action for the Job Stabilization of Enterprises with Unemployment Insurance*, and decided to launch the Escorting Action throughout the country from 2018 to 2020.[14] This is an important measure for using unemployment insurance to assist enterprises in overcoming developmental difficulties and in stabilizing jobs under the "new normal" economic conditions, and it has become the service brand for unemployment insurance in assisting the work of job stabilization at enterprises.

---

13   Zheng Bingwen, "Outstanding Achievement of the Reform on Social Security in China," *People's Daily*, October 24, 2017.

14   "Interpretation of the Notice on Implementing the Escorting Action for the Job Stabilization of Enterprises with Unemployment Insurance by the Ministry of Human Resources and Social Security," www.ccoalnews.com.

1.7 A Pilot Program Was Established for the Combination of Maternity Insurance and Basic Health Care Insurance for Employees

To leverage the mutual aid capacities of funds, improve the effectiveness of comprehensive management, and reduce the cost of management and operations, in the *13th Five-Year Plan for National Economic and Social Development*, the government devised a plan to combine maternity insurance with basic health care insurance for employees. In January 2017, the General Office of the State Council issued the *Plan on Piloting the Combination of Maternity Insurance and Basic Health Care Insurance for Employees*, with the intent of launching pilot programs combining the two insurances in 12 cities throughout the country. In the pilot plan, the principle of maintaining insurance types, ensuring treatment, conducting uniform management, and reducing costs was proposed to promote the combination of the two insurances. The contents of the pilot plan included unifying participant registrations, collection and management of funds, medical service management, and undertaking and information services, while leaving the treatment of maternity insurance during the childbearing period unchanged. Afterward, the general offices of the Ministry of Human Resources and Social Security, the Ministry of Finance, and the Population and the Family Planning Commission issued specific notices to ensure that the pilot plan combining the two insurances could be officially launched in June 2017 for a period of about one year.

The initial effects of the combination of the two insurances have already been observed. Employers in Kunming City are making contributions to the basic health care insurance for employees at the premium rate of 9.9%, and the employees do not need to pay the premiums for maternity insurance personally. The personal contribution ratio of the health care insurance premium was also 2%. The number of participants in maternity insurance increased from 860,000 to 1,050,000.[15] After the combination of the two insurances in Handan City, people under the flexible employment system who could not receive maternity insurance benefits were directly covered by maternity insurance and received full coverage under the maternity insurance benefits. The fixed allowance for natural childbirth was increased from 3,000 yuan to 4,000 yuan.[16]

2 Undertaking Social Assistance Became More Accurate

The social assistance system is a social security system in which the national government and society are to provide financial and physical assistance through

---

15   http://rsj.km.gov.cn/c/2017-06-28/1897469.shtml.

16   http://www.handannews.com.cn/news/handan/c/2017-10/13/content_345645.htm.

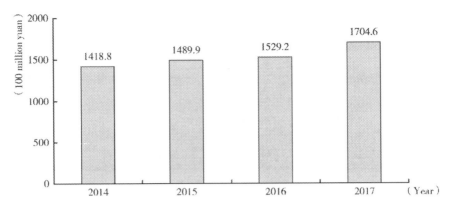

FIGURE 4.1   Total Expenditure on Social Assistance since 2014 (first three quarters)
SOURCE: THREE-QUARTER SOCIAL SERVICE STATISTICS OF THE MINISTRY OF CIVIL AFFAIRS

legislation to those who cannot maintain a minimum living standard to meet their minimum needs. In recent years, a series of social-assistance measures represented by targeted poverty reduction, subsistence allowances, and medical assistance have played a vital role in ensuring social stability and harmony.

In the first three quarters of 2017, total expenditures on social assistance reached 170.46 billion yuan, with a year-on-year increase of 11.47% (see Figure 4.1). Expenditure on subsistence allowances totaled 46.34 billion yuan in urban areas and 76.52 billion yuan in rural areas. The total expenditure on medical assistance (including medical assistance certified by civil affairs departments and implemented by related departments) was 20.63 billion yuan. Expenditures on temporary assistance reached 4.64 billion yuan. Expenditures on living assistance due to natural disasters totaled 5.12 billion yuan.[17]

2.1   *Subsistence Allowances*

Subsistence allowances are the major form of aid in the social assistance system. In October 2016, the General Office of the State Council issued the *Notice on Further Strengthening the Subsistence Allowances for Urban Residents* to explain the tasks, measures, and methods of the system of subsistence allowances in China under the new situation. In the same year, the General Office of the State Council forwarded the *Notice on Implementing the Guiding Opinions on the Effective Connection between the System of Subsistence Allowance in Rural Areas and the Poverty Reduction Development Policy,* issued by the Ministry of Civil Affairs and the Poverty Reduction Office of the State Council, to connect

---

17   Ministry of Civil Affairs, "National Social Service Statistics in March 2017," November 2, 2017.

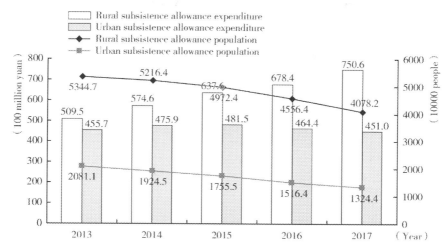

FIGURE 4.2 Changes in Expenditures on Subsistence Allowances in Urban and Rural Areas and the Number of People Receiving Subsistence Allowances in the Past Five Years (first three quarters)
SOURCE: THREE-QUARTER SOCIAL SERVICE STATISTICS OF THE MINISTRY OF CIVIL AFFAIRS

the system of subsistence allowances and the measures of targeted poverty reduction, which was of important significance as a guide in the fight against poverty in the new age.

Figure 4.2 displays the changes in expenditures on subsistence allowances in urban and rural areas and the number of people receiving subsistence allowances in the past five years. Since 2013, expenditures on subsistence allowances in urban areas have not changed too much, and have even witnessed a tendency to decrease. However, in rural areas, expenditures have been increasing at the rate of 9.46% every year. Expenditures on subsistence allowances in rural areas in the first three quarters of 2017 reached 75.06 billion yuan, which was closely related to the increased efforts we made in recent years in reducing poverty in rural areas. At the same time, the number of people receiving subsistence allowances in both rural and urban areas was diminishing. This number decreased significantly especially in rural areas, a direct result of the targeted poverty reduction measures implemented by the national government that were focused on those who really needed the subsistence allowances.

It can easily be seen that, while expenditures on subsistence allowances in rural areas were increasing, the number of people receiving subsistence allowances was decreasing. Therefore, the amount of the per capita subsistence allowance has been increasing. As shown in Figure 4.3, per capita subsistence allowances in rural areas increased at the annual rate of 14.65%, while in

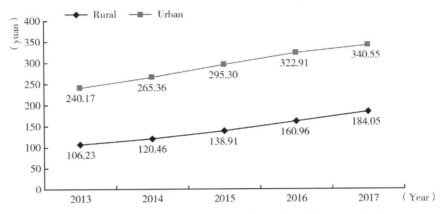

FIGURE 4.3 Per Capita Subsistence Allowances in Urban and Rural Areas in the Past Five Years (first three quarters)
SOURCE: CALCULATION BASED ON FIGURE 4.2

urban areas this number was 8.36%. The subsistence allowances have played a more and more important role in improving the living conditions of the impoverished population in particular.

2.2   *Assistance for Extremely Impoverished People*

Ensuring the basic living conditions of extremely impoverished people in urban and rural areas is an important measure to improve the system of social assistance and establish an intensified safety network to guarantee the quality of people's lives. In February 2016, the State Council issued the *Opinions on Further Improving the System of Assistance to and Support for Extremely Impoverished People*, requiring that the supporting system for extremely impoverished people should be established in such a way as to uphold bottom-line support, territorial management, urban-rural integration, a moderate guarantee, and social participation. The elderly, the disabled, and those below 16 years of age who have no work abilities, income sources, or legal supporting agents, or whose legal supporting agents are unable to perform their obligations, could be covered by the system of assistance set up to support extremely impoverished people. Then in October 2016, the Ministry of Civil Affairs issued the *Method of Identifying Extremely Impoverished People* to further define the identification criteria, procedures, and methods for assessing extremely impoverished people, and the criteria for terminating assistance.

According to the social service statistics collected by the Ministry of Civil Affairs for all provinces in the first three quarters of 2016 and 2017, the total expenditure on assistance and support for extremely impoverished people in rural areas in the first three quarters of 2017 was 19.06 billion yuan, with a year-on-year increase of 14% over 2016. The number of extremely impoverished people receiving assistance in rural areas was 4.743 million, which was reduced by 5.86% over 2016 year on year. This means that the amount of assistance received by extremely impoverished people increased, indicating the improvement in precision in providing assistance to extremely impoverished people in China.

Upon the successful conclusion of the 19th National Congress of the CPC, the Ministry of Civil Affairs held forums on the social reform of the supporting service organs for extremely impoverished people in rural areas in some provinces[18] to explore ideas and measures to strengthen the network of supporting services in rural areas under the new situation. We should ensure four goals: to make sure that the mission of such organs of serving extremely impoverished people will not change; to ensure that the legislative rights of the extremely impoverished people will be protected; to make sure that ownership of the supporting organs will not change; and to ensure that the quality of services provided by supporting organs will be steadily improved. These four goals reflect the attention of the national government to extremely impoverished people, and the government's determination in not leaving anyone behind during the construction of a moderately prosperous society in all respects.

2.3 *Medical Assistance*

Medical assistance means providing assistance and support to those citizens who are unable to have their diseases treated due to poverty. In 2015, the General Office of the State Council forwarded the *Notice of the Opinions on Further Improving the System of Medical Assistance to Comprehensively Conduct Assistance Work for Major and Serious Diseases* in order to provide medical assistance in such a way as to focus on the bottom line, integration and connection, openness and justice, and efficiency and convenience. Since 2016, a uniform system of urban and rural medical assistance has been established. Figure 4.4 shows the expenditure on medical assistance in China and the number of people receiving assistance in the past five years. Direct medical assistance tended to increase year by year, and rose from 11.02 billion yuan in the first three quarters of 2013 to 15.03 billion yuan in the first three quarters of 2017. During the same period of time, the expenditure on assistance for basic health care insurance was increased from 2.22 billion yuan to 3.44 billion yuan. From Figure 4.4 we can also see changes in the objects and forms of medical assistance in China. The number of participants in basic health care insurance receiving assistance has been decreasing, but the number of people receiving direct medical assistance has witnessed a significant increase. The difference between the two numbers has been narrowed by 1.6 times. This

---

18   http://www.mca.gov.cn/article/zwgk/mzyw/201711/20171100006618.shtml.

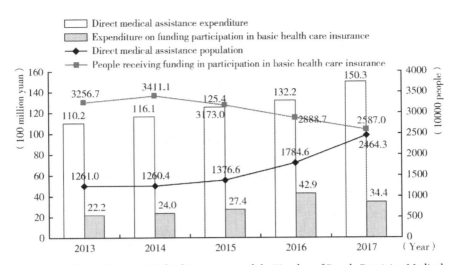

FIGURE 4.4 Expenditure on Medical Assistance and the Number of People Receiving Medical Assistance in the Past Five Years (first three quarters)
SOURCE: THREE-QUARTER SOCIAL SERVICE STATISTICS OF THE MINISTRY OF CIVIL AFFAIRS

fully reflects that the social security of our country has started to change from providing funds to guaranteeing services, which can meet the developmental principle of the modern system of social benefits in which a social security system focusing on economic guarantees is updated to a modern system of social services focusing on service guarantees.[19] We need to note that in the statistics for 2017, the direct objects of medical assistance were divided into the key objects and the major and serious disease objects under basic medical assistance. The key assistance objects accounted for 26% of the direct medical assistance objects, and the major and serious disease objects under basic medical assistance accounted for 2.1%, further highlighting the accuracy of medical assistance.

2.4   Other Assistance

2.4.1   Disaster Assistance

China's existing disaster assistance was implemented mainly based on the *Disaster Alleviation Rules of the People's Republic of China* issued in 1997. In

---

[19] Du Peng and Wang Yongmei, "A Well-Off Society in an All-Around Way and Long-Term Nursing: Problems and Countermeasures," *China Civil Affairs*, 2016(17); Liu Jitong, "Outline on the Establishment of the Modern Social Service System in China," *Social Construction*, 2016(1).

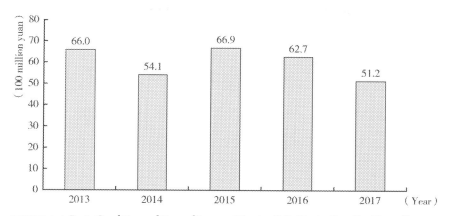

FIGURE 4.5 Basic Conditions of Expenditure on Disaster Relief in the Past Five Years (first three quarters)
SOURCE: THREE-QUARTER SOCIAL SERVICE STATISTICS OF THE MINISTRY OF CIVIL AFFAIRS

the past five years, expenditure on disaster relief has fluctuated between 5 and 7 billion yuan per year. The expenditure on disaster relief in the first three quarters of 2017 was 5.12 billion yuan, reduced by about one-fifth over 2016 year on year (see Figure 4.5). The expenditure was basically determined by the disasters that occurred during each year.

2.4.2   Temporary Assistance

Temporary assistance is the emergency and transmission assistance provided to those who cannot maintain the basic living standard due to emergencies, accidents, major diseases, or other special causes that are not covered by the other systems of social assistance.[20]

In the past five years, the expenditure on temporary assistance in 2013 was as high as 18.95 billion yuan. Expenditures in other years were between 3 and 7.4 billion yuan (see Figure 4.6). In 2017, expenditure on temporary assistance witnessed a rapid increase compared to that in 2016, which was related to the 4.65 billion yuan spent on other temporary assistance expenditures in the statistics of 2017. Before 2017, the objects of temporary assistance were those receiving subsistence allowances. With the improvement in the system of subsistence allowances and the promotion of the targeted poverty reduction policy, a greater amount of temporary assistance may cover the other

20   Wang Degao, *Social Security Science*, Wuhan University Press, 2010.

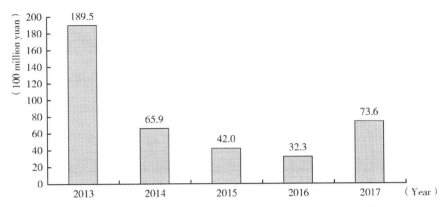

FIGURE 4.6 Expenditure on Temporary Assistance in the Past Five Years (first three quarters)
SOURCE: THREE-QUARTER SOCIAL SERVICE STATISTICS OF THE MINISTRY OF CIVIL AFFAIRS

conditions that have not been considered under the system, fully reflecting the flexibility of the system of temporary assistance.

2.4.3   Preferential Treatment

The system of preferential treatment is a social security system providing those who accept special jobs and their families, such as soldiers and their relatives, with special treatment, compensation, and settlements. In 2017, the Ministry of Civil Affairs and the Ministry of Finance issued the *Notice on Adjusting the Compensation and Living Allowance Standards for Some Preferential Treatment Objects* to further improve the treatment for those objects. In the past five years, expenditures on preferential treatment in China witnessed a constant increase from 30.54 billion yuan in 2013 to 45.1 billion yuan in 2017. The number of preferential treatment objects decreased slightly from 9.517 million in 2013 to 8.603 million in 2017. The per capita amount of preferential treatment has been increasing (see Figure 4.7).

2.4.4   Employment Assistance

According to the *Interim Measures for Social Assistance*, employment assistance should be given to unemployed people who are able to work in households receiving subsistence allowance in the form of loans with discounted interest, social security subsidies, job subsidies, training subsidies, cost reduction and exemption, and placement in public welfare positions. As of the end of 2017, 5.53 million registered impoverished people in China had found jobs, showing the excellent effect of poverty-reduction efforts. However, among the 5 million

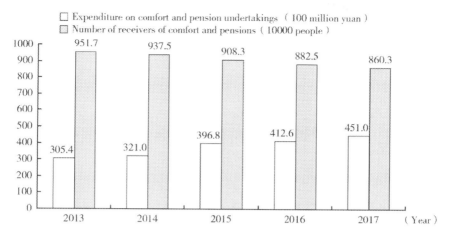

FIGURE 4.7 Expenditure on Preferential Treatment and the Number of Preferential Treatment Objects in the Past Five Years (first three quarters)
SOURCE: THREE-QUARTER SOCIAL SERVICE STATISTICS OF THE MINISTRY OF CIVIL AFFAIRS

employed impoverished laborers, only 10% were employed by enterprises, and those who selected flexible employment or other employment forms accounted for 80%, leading to a low degree of employment stability. The leaders of the Ministry of Human Resources and Social Security pointed out that special employment poverty-reduction policies could be implemented in the extremely impoverished places.[21]

2.4.5   Education Assistance

According to the *Interim Measures for Social Assistance* in 2014, the government would provide education assistance to members of households receiving subsistence allowances and to extremely impoverished people who are supporting others and still receiving compulsory education. In 2017, the General Office of the State Council paid closer attention to educational poverty-reduction issues in the *Notice on Further Strengthening Control over Dropouts to Improve the Consolidation Level of Compulsory Education*, identifying students in registered impoverished households as major recipients of assistance to reduce poverty and considering disabled children, children of disabled people, minor children of people serving sentences, left-behind children, and children of school age in the ethnic groups that are directly entering socialism as the top priority for

---

21   http://news.xinhuanet.com/2017-11/09/c_1121931986.htm.

preferential assistance and targeted poverty reduction. Educational assistance has become one of the core measures in preventing the intergenerational transmission of poverty.

3 Social Welfare and Charity Undertakings Have Become More Mature

Social welfare means the task of providing social care and services to children, the elderly, the disabled, and chronic mental patients with low capacities for earning a living. Since the 18th National Congress of the CPC, China's social welfare undertakings have witnessed significant progress. From Figure 4.8 we can see that, since 2013, expenditure on social welfare in China has been increasing significantly. In the first three quarters of 2017, the total social welfare expenditure reached 17.19 billion yuan, with a year-on-year increase of about 51% over 2016.

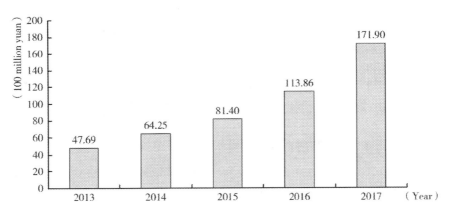

FIGURE 4.8 Expenditure on Social Welfare in the Past Five Years (first three quarters)
SOURCE: THREE-QUARTER SOCIAL SERVICE STATISTICS OF THE MINISTRY OF CIVIL AFFAIRS

3.1 *Social Welfare Undertakings for the Elderly and the Disabled Were Maturing*

In light of the aging of the population, we have paid closer attention to the development of welfare undertakings for the elderly. In the *13th Five-Year Plan for National Economic and Social Development* in 2016, the government proposed to establish a social-service system for the elderly with their homes as the foundation, communities as the basis, and organs as the supplementary units. In December 2016, the General Office of the State Council issued *Several Opinions on Fully Opening the Elderly Service Market and Improving the Quality of Services for the Elderly* to lead the development of the undertaking of services for the elderly into a new stage.

At present, there are 85 million disabled people in our country and 30 million of them have disability certificates, a situation that directly influences 270 million households.[22] In 2008, the government mentioned in the *Law on the Protection of Rights and Interests of the Disabled* that the national government should encourage and support social forces to establish organizations in support of the disabled and to help raise them. In the *Opinions on Accelerating the Development of Services to Help Raise the Disabled in 2012* and the *13th Five-Year Plan for Promoting Equitable Access to Basic Public Services* issued in 2017, closer attention was given to services to help improve the conditions of the disabled and of rehabilitation services for them.

In 2017, the national government issued several policy documents for the elderly and the disabled in an effort to pay closer attention to the development of undertakings related to these groups. For example, in April 2017, the Ministry of Civil Affairs and the Ministry of Finance jointly launched the first pilot programs on reforming home and community elderly services supported by central finance. In October, after the first pilot programs for the reform of public elderly service organizations launched in 2013, the Ministry of Civil Affairs launched the second round of pilot programs for the reform of public elderly service organizations to further promote the development of services for the elderly. In February 2017, the related departments issued the *Regulations on Disability Prevention and Rehabilitation* to prevent the occurrence of disabilities, reduce the degree of disabilities, help the disabled to recover, promote the equality of the disabled, ensure their full participation in social life, and develop disability prevention and rehabilitation undertakings.

Figure 4.9 displays the basic conditions of the development of undertakings related to the elderly and the disabled in the past five years. The number of beds used to provide services for these groups of people has increased from 4.338 million in 2013 to 7 million now. The number of beds used to provide services to the elderly in communities was also increasing rapidly, from about 300,000 in 2013 to 3.253 million now. These conditions were closely related to national policies encouraging the development of services for the elderly in communities. However, the number of people providing services to these groups has been decreasing.

---

22   http://finance.people.com.cn/n/2015/0128/c1004-26461253.html.

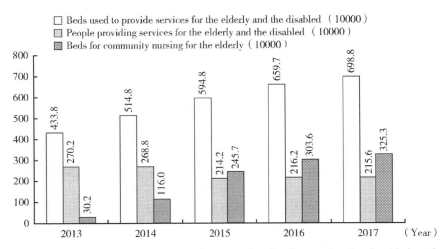

FIGURE 4.9 Basic Conditions of the Development of Undertakings Related to the Elderly and the Disabled in the Past Five Years (first three quarters)
SOURCE: THREE-QUARTER SOCIAL SERVICE STATISTICS OF THE MINISTRY OF CIVIL AFFAIRS

3.2 *Children's Welfare Services Saw Steady Development*

In 2016, the State Council issued the *Opinions on Strengthening the Guarantee for Children in Trouble*, making it necessary to ensure basic living standards and basic health care for children in trouble, and to strengthen the guarantee of their education, implement supervision accountability, and improve welfare services for disabled children based on the principle of home accountability, government guidance, social participation, and classification guarantee. In 2016, the State Council also issued the *Opinions on Strengthening the Caring for and Protection of Left-behind Children in Rural Areas* to fully establish a caring and protection system for left-behind children in rural areas with the efforts of their homes, governments, and schools and the active participation of all walks of society, so as to ensure the effective operations of the caring and protection mechanisms for left-behind children in rural areas, such as compulsory reporting, emergency treatment, assessment and assistance, and monitoring intervention, and to effectively prevent events harming the rights and interests of left-behind children from happening. In 2017, the Ministry of Civil Affairs issued the *Guiding Opinions on Giving Full Play to the Role of Professional Social Work Talents in Caring for and Protecting Left-behind Children in Rural Areas*, laying a solid foundation for the emerging forces, enabling professional social workers to participate in psychological services, and promoting the healthy growth of left-behind children in rural areas.

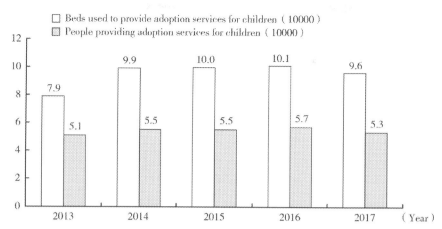

FIGURE 4.10   Basic Conditions of Adoption and Assistance Services Provided for Children in the Past Five Years (first three quarters)
SOURCE: THREE-QUARTER SOCIAL SERVICE STATISTICS OF THE MINISTRY OF CIVIL AFFAIRS

According to the statistics of the Ministry of Civil Affairs, over the past five years, the number of beds used to provide care for children ranged from about 79,000 to 101,000 each year, and the number of people providing adoption services and care to children was about 50,000 to 60,000 every year (see Figure 4.10).

3.3   Welfare Undertakings for Mentally Handicapped and Disabled People Witnessed Good Development

In the *Planning Outline for Accelerating the Construction of A Well-Off Society for the Disabled under the 13th Five-Year Plan* issued in 2016, the State Council pointed out that medical assistance should be provided preferentially to patients with mental disorders who still have difficulties after paying medical expenditures through basic health care insurance, or who cannot pay for medical treatment expenses through basic health care insurance; that timely assistance should be given to homeless disabled people; that a system guaranteeing return to a home should be improved for homeless disabled people; and that proper care and arrangements should be provided for those homeless disabled people who have stayed homeless for a long time or whose identities cannot be confirmed.

Figure 4.11 is about the basic conditions of the services provided to mentally handicapped people and patients with mental disorders based on

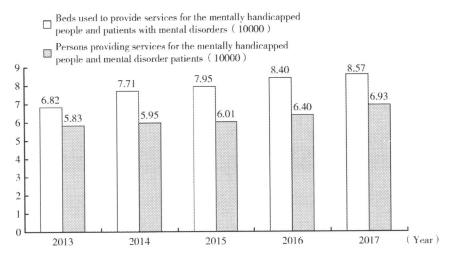

FIGURE 4.11 Basic Conditions of Services Provided to Mentally Handicapped People and to Patients with Mental Disorders in the Past Five Years (first three quarters)
SOURCE: THREE-QUARTER SOCIAL SERVICE STATISTICS OF THE MINISTRY OF CIVIL AFFAIRS

statistics from the Ministry of Civil Affairs. From the figure, we can see that the number of beds used to provide services for mentally handicapped people and patients with mental disorders has increased year by year, and that the number increased by 25.7% in 2017 over that in 2016. The number of people providing services to mentally handicapped people and patients with mental disorders was also increasing, and the number in 2017 was higher than that in 2016 by 18.9%.

3.4 *The Grand Pattern of the Development of Charity Undertakings Has Taken Form*

Charity is one of the traditional virtues of the Chinese nation, and charity undertakings are an important part of the undertaking of socialism with Chinese characteristics and the social security system of China. Since the 18th National Congress of the CPC, the grand pattern of charity undertakings with Chinese characteristics featuring government promotion, civil operations, social participation, and multiple-party cooperation has gradually taken form. Especially since the promulgation of the *Charity Law* in 2016, the charity undertakings of our country have entered into a period of rapid development.

First of all, charity organizations have developed prosperously. In recent years, the contributions made by charity organizations to society have been increasing, and they are becoming an active force in building a moderately prosperous society in all respects. As of October 2017, the total number of social organizations throughout the country reached 756,000, including 2,429 recognized and registered charity organizations, to which 606 public donation-raising qualification certificates have been issued. Second, there have been many forms of charity events. The campaigns of the public good have witnessed rapid development, gradually expanding from traditional disaster relief, poverty reduction, assistance for the disabled, and caring for the elderly and children in various fields such as education, science and technology, culture, health care, environmental protection, and physical education. In addition, charity events have taken more and more forms covering more and more fields. Third, online donations have become a new charity mode. According to incomplete statistics, during the one year since the implementation of the *Charity Law*, the number of online donations has surpassed 1 billion, with the amount of revenue exceeding 2 billion yuan. In some charity organizations, donations from the Internet have accounted for more than 80% of all donations. The age-old pattern with enterprises as major donors has changed. Fourth, public availability of charity information has been strengthened. As of October 2017, 1,676 charity programs and 1,219 public donation-raising plans were made public through platforms, making charity undertakings more public and transparent, improving their social credibility, and stimulating the passion of the public to participate in charity undertakings.[23]

3.5 *Volunteer Services Have Entered into an Age of Legislation*

Volunteer service is an important sign indicating the advancement of modern social civilization. With the modernization of the governance of our country, volunteer services have also witnessed a flourishing development. According to data from the volunteer service information system of China, as of the end of 2016, the proportion of registered volunteers in the total population was 2.56%, and the proportions in 10 provinces were higher than the average level. As of June 2017, the number of volunteer service groups throughout the country increased to 342,065. Volunteer services have become a lifestyle for some people. In the activities conducted by volunteer service organizations, the proportion supporting services for the aged was the highest among all the services—82.19%. Disabled assistance services ranked second, at 68.85%. In

---

23   "Grand Pattern of Charity Undertakings with Chinese Characteristics Gradually Takes Form," *Charity and Public Benefit Newspaper*, October 18, 2017.

addition, community resident services and environmental protection volunteer services were fields with a lot of volunteer activity.[24]

In August 2017, in order to protect the legislative rights and interests of volunteers, volunteer service organizations, and volunteer service objects, and to encourage and standardize volunteer services, develop volunteer service undertakings, forge and implement the core values of socialism, and promote social progress, the central government officially issued the *Regulations on Volunteer Services*, marking a new starting point and a new stage of development for volunteer service undertakings in our country.

4 Outlook on the Development of Social Security Undertakings in 2018

The Report to the 19th CPC National Congress pointed out that socialism with Chinese characteristics has entered a new age, and that the major social conflict has become the conflict between the ever-increasing desires of the people for a better life and the imbalanced and insufficient state of development, marking the fact that China has transformed from a subsistence rights society into a developmental rights society. Developmental thought, with the people at its center and a desire for the comprehensive development of the people and the common wealth of the entire population, would be the starting point and final destination of further reform. The social-security undertakings of our country have become mature following an experimental stage.

In 2018, the situation of social security funds was not optimistic. The level of treatment was not even increased; it was only the carryover effect of the adjustment of the level of the basic pension and other treatments that would generate a huge pressure on the fund for payment. The number of provinces encountering a gap between expenditures and income in funds from pension insurance and health care insurance would increase. Fortunately, more and more pension funds have been put into investment, which may release the pressure caused by such an imbalance. The significant increase in payments from the fund of maternity insurance due to the adjustment of the universal two-child policy would be maintained, leading to enormous pressure on the maternity insurance fund. Financial departments at all levels should adjust their expenditure structures to adapt to this change.

---

24 China Volunteer Service Federation, *Annual Report on the Development of Voluntary Services in China* (2017), Social Sciences Academic Press (China), 2017.

In 2018, the nationwide integration of pensions would be a hot topic. The Report to the 19th CPC National Congress indicated that the nationwide integration of pensions should be realized as soon as possible. This would be a long-term measure to deal with interregional imbalance and a huge difference in degrees of aging. In 2018, the first step would be taken to implement a central regulation system for basic pensions in order to balance the burdens on pension insurance. However, at present, a nationwide integration plan for pensions has not been formulated, and the provinces with a surplus in pension insurance have not been fully motivated. We need to further explore how to implement that integration.

In 2018, education for all children and support for all weak groups will be the focus of policies and practices. In the Report to the 19th CPC National Congress, the five tasks for the improvement of the quality of people's lives were expanded to include education for all children and support for all vulnerable groups, which are to become key points in the undertakings of social welfare and social assistance. In 2018, the relevant departments will issue related policies and measures in these two aspects.

References

China Volunteer Service Federation. *Annual Report on the Development of Voluntary Services in China* (2017). Social Sciences Academic Press (China), 2017.

Du Peng and Wang Yongmei. "A Well-Off Society in An All-around Way and Long-term Nursing: Problems and Countermeasures." *China Civil Affairs*, 2016(17).

"Grand Pattern of Charity Undertakings with Chinese Characteristics Gradually Takes Form." *Charity and Public Benefit Newspaper*, October 18, 2017.

Liu Jitong. "Outline on the Establishment of a Modern System of Social Services in China." *Social Construction*, 2016(1).

Ministry of Civil Affairs. National social service statistics in March 2017. Official website of the Ministry of Civil Affairs, November 2, 2017.

Ministry of Human Resources and Social Security. "Number of Participants of Long-term Nursing Insurance Surpassed 38 Million, Showing an Initial Effect." http://www.sohu.com/a/201599767_11839.

"Press Conference of the 3rd Quarter of 2017 Held by the Ministry of Human Resources and Social Security." Official website of the Ministry of Human Resources and Social Security, November 1, 2017.

Report to the 19th CPC National Congress, October 2017.

Wang Degao. *Social Security Science*. Wuhan University Press, 2010.

CHAPTER 5

Report on the Reform and Development of China's Education System in 2017

Li Tao,[1] Zhang Wenting,[2] and Fang Chen[3]

Abstract

The year 2017 was a critical year for the construction of socialism with Chinese characteristics in the new age. It was especially important for us to uphold the strategy of developing education preferentially and accelerating the modernization of education. In 2017, the general level of the development of education in China entered the middle and upper range of the world. The qualities of education at all levels and of different kinds witnessed steady improvement. Investment in education expenditures continued to increase. The reform of the educational system and its mechanisms was further deepened, mainly in the areas of education management, separation of management, organization and assessment, the system of examination and recruitment, private schools, and talent development mechanisms. In 2017, the Chinese government made greater efforts to establish the ideological and political educational system for colleges, middle schools, and primary schools; screen and build Dual Leading universities and colleges; ensure the balanced development of compulsory education in county territories; and launch the Belt and Road Initiative Education Action. In terms of promoting services for improving the quality of people's lives, the government conducted many core tasks, such as targeted poverty reduction for education, recruitment of teacher teams, development of the education industry, and attention to weak groups. In addition, school bullying, equal rights for home tenants and owners, and child enrollment and the prevention of college students from joining pyramid selling were the most popular topics in education in 2017.

---

1 Li Tao, distinguished professor at the China Research Institute for the Development of Rural Education of Northeast Normal University of the Humanistic and Social Science Focused Research Base of the Ministry of Education, and post-doctoral fellow at the Institute of Sociology of the Chinese Academy of Social Sciences.
2 Zhang Wenting, head of the China Research Institute for the Development of Rural Education of Northeast Normal University.
3 Fang Chen, head of the China Research Institute for the Development of Rural Education of Northeast Normal University. Dai Si, Yang Qianying, and Zhang Zongqian, postgraduates in the Educational Science Department of Northeast Normal University, participated in the preparation, document analysis, and compilation of this report.

© KONINKLIJKE BRILL NV, LEIDEN, 2022 | DOI:10.1163/9789004500723_006

Keywords

education development – educational reform – education equality

Since the 18th National Congress of the CPC, the educational undertaking in China has witnessed comprehensive development. Education in central and western China and rural areas was strengthened significantly. In the new age, greater efforts should be made to provide more equitable education of a higher quality. We should still uphold the principle of putting the development of education first, building a powerful educational country, accelerating the modernization of education, and providing the people with satisfactory education. The year of 2017 was a critical year for implementing the 13th Five-Year Plan. The modernization of education has entered a crucial stage. In January, the State Council issued the *13th Five-Year Plan for the Development of National Educational Undertakings* (hereinafter the 13th Five-Year Plan for Education), which took the overall improvement of education quality as its theme and the structural reform of education as its main line and laid out the requirements for optimizing the structure of the allocation of educational resources, the structure of the system of education, and the structure of personnel training.[4]

1 The General Educational Developmental Level Ranked High in the World

As of the end of 2016, there were 512,000 schools in China with 265 million students, forming the largest teaching system in the world. The reform and development of education at all levels has been deepened. To uphold the strategy of putting education first, the education expenditure in national finances accounted for more than 4% of China's GDP for five consecutive years and surpassed 3 trillion yuan for the first time in 2016. According to a third-party assessment, the general level of the development of education in China ranked high in the world.[5]

---

4 "Time Selection for China's Education," *China Education Newspaper*, October 17, 2017, layout 1.
5 "The Educational Undertakings of Our Country Witnessed Comprehensive Development," *China Education Newspaper*, October 23, 2017, layout 7.

1.1 *Education at All Levels and of All Kinds Has Witnessed a Good Level of Development*

Preschool education saw leapfrog development. The total number of kindergartens throughout the country reached 240,000, increasing by 32.6% over 2012. The number of public kindergartens in urban areas was 17,400 and that in rural areas was 68,200, increasing by 82.3% and 76.8% over the totals in the early period of the 12th Five-Year Plan, respectively. The number of children in kindergartens nationwide was 44.139 million, increasing by 19.8% over 2012. The gross rate of enrollment in the three years before going to school was 77.4%, increasing by 12.9 percentage points over five years. The target of 70% coverage specified in the *Outline of National Long- and Mid-Term Educational Reform and Development Planning* (2010–2020) (hereinafter the Planning Outline) was achieved ahead of schedule, higher than the average level of 73.7% in high- and middle-income countries by 3.7 percentage points. The proportion of new primary school students who received preschool education reached 98.4%, which means that almost all new primary school students have received preschool education for a certain period of time.[6] To solve the problem of weak preschool education in rural areas, from 2011 to 2016 the central finances poured a total of more than 100 billion yuan into the rural areas of central and western China to modify and expand kindergartens in these areas, and to support enterprises, institutions, and groups in establishing kindergartens, in order to provide more children in rural areas with access to kindergartens.

The nine-year compulsory education system covered the whole population. There were 177,600 primary schools in China with 99.13 million students. The net enrollment rate of school-age children reached 99.92%, and the consolidation rate was 93.4%, which was close to the target of 95% by 2020. There were 52,100 middle schools in China with 43.2937 million students. The gross enrollment rate at the junior high school level was 104%, and the promotional rate of junior high school students was 93.7%. Based on the comprehensive coverage of compulsory education, more efforts were made to improve the quality of education and to balance educational resources to create a more balanced compulsory education system benefiting all children. The coverage and level of the nine-year compulsory education program has surpassed the average level of the high-income countries in the world.

Great progress was made in special education undertakings. There were 2,080 special education schools in China, an increase of 27 over the previous year. The number of students in such schools was 491,700, an increase of 49,500 over the

---

6 Introduction by the Ministry of Education, "Development of the Education Reform since the 18th National Congress of the CPC," government portal website of the Ministry of Education of the People's Republic of China, September 28, 2017.

previous year. The number of special students studying in ordinary or special classes in primary schools or junior high schools was 51,800, and the number of students learning at school was 270,800, accounting for 56.60% of the total enrollment of special students and 55.07% of the total number of special students studying at schools. With the steady increase in the quantity of special education schools and the number of students enrolled, more special children will get the opportunity to receive an education. Learning in ordinary or special classes will provide the special children with better studying experiences.

Senior high school education was further popularized. There were 13,400 ordinary senior high schools in China with 23.6665 million students, and 10,900 secondary vocational schools with 15.9901 million students. The gross enrollment rate at the high school and secondary vocational educational stage reached 87.5%, which was higher than the average level of high- and mid-income countries by 5 percentage points, and only one step short of the popularization of senior high school education. The students at schools of secondary vocational education accounted for 40.28% of all students at the high school and secondary vocational education level. The structure of ordinary senior high school education and secondary vocational education was more balanced.

The level of popularization of higher education was higher. There were 2,880 ordinary and adult higher education schools with 36.99 million students in total, including 1,237 ordinary universities and 1,359 higher vocational colleges. The gross enrollment rate of higher education was 42.7%, which was close to the popularization of higher education.[7]

1.2   *National Financial Expenditure on Education Accounted for More than 4% of the GDP for Five Consecutive Years*

In May 2017, the Ministry of Education issued a bulletin of educational fund statistics, indicating that the total amount of education funds expended was 3,888.839 billion yuan, an increase of 7.64% over the previous year. The national financial educational expenditure reached 3,139.625 billion yuan, surpassing 3 trillion yuan for the first time, with an increase of 7.44% over the previous year. The proportion of the national financial educational expenditure in the GDP was 4.22%, surpassing 4% for five consecutive years. The proportion of national public financial education expenditure within the total of public financial expenditures also increased over the previous year, meaning that China had made another step toward becoming a powerful educational country. Education expenditures at different stages witnessed increases. The preschool education expenditure of China reached 280.2 billion yuan, an

---

7   "Statistical Bulletin of the Development of National Educational Undertakings in 2016," government portal website of the Ministry of Education of the People's Republic of China.

increase of 15.48% over the previous year. The total expenditure input in compulsory education throughout the country was 1,760.3 billion yuan, an increase of 9.76% over the previous year. In terms of average educational expenditure, the kindergartens had the highest growth, at a rate of 15.97% over the previous year. The amount of average educational expenditure on students in ordinary higher education schools was the highest, at 30,457 yuan.[8]

2 Fully Deepen the Reform of the System and Mechanism and Stimulate the Vitality of Educational Development

Fully deepening the reform is an important way to develop the educational undertaking, and the reform of the system and mechanisms of education is the key task. In 2017, according to the official targets of development, such as the Planning Outline and the 13th Five-Year Plan for Education, and based on the features and requirements of the development of educational undertakings in China, reforms were made in system simplification, examination enrollment, and opening-up.

2.1 Promoting Reform by Streamlining Administration, Delegating Power, Combining Management and Delegation, and Optimizing Services for Education

In March 2017, the Ministry of Education, the National Development and Reform Commission, the Ministry of Finance, the State Commission Office of the Reform of Public Sectors, and the Ministry of Human Resources and Social Security jointly issued *Several Opinions on Deepening the Reform on Streamlining Administration, Delegating Power, Combining Management and Delegation, and Optimizing Services for Education* (hereinafter the Opinions). The formulation of the Opinions was an important step in improving the modern university system with Chinese characteristics. The major purpose was to provide the colleges and universities with more autonomy in running schools under the necessary monitoring system by reducing burdens and delegating powers to local governments and colleges to stimulate energy for innovation in the colleges, and by providing more space for improving the quality of teaching, cultivating and introducing talents, and developing their advantageous and special disciplines. In the Opinions, related regulations were issued concerning discipline organization,

---

8 "Statistical Report on the Implementation of Education Expenditures in 2016 by the Ministry of Education, the National Bureau of Statistics, and the Ministry of Finance," National Bureau of Statistics of the People's Republic of China.

the system of management of college titles and posts, and the environment of talent introduction and utilization in colleges.

In addition, in terms of salary distribution, the Opinions required a further improvement of distribution that can match the features of modern colleges with Chinese characteristics and improve the system for managing the utilization of expenditures. We should note that during the delegation of power, the monitoring and management of the above items is the important work for the related education administration departments. Local governments and departments should further transform their functions and methods of management and innovate their monitoring and management techniques and methods to disqualify or modify, within certain time frames, those degree programs and disciplines that do not comply with standards or that have other managerial issues.

2.2 Vigorously Promoting the Reform of Separating School Administration, Establishment, and Evaluation

Vigorous promotion of the reform of separating school administration, establishment, and evaluation was one of the major tasks in 2017. In 2017, the reform of national education supervisory organs was basically completed. In 31 provinces (autonomous regions and municipalities), commissions and offices for the supervision of the people's government education were established, forming the basic framework for the reform of supervisory organs responsible for local education. Then, the document *Interim Measures for the Management of School Inspectors* was issued to establish a system for the management of school inspectors. The separation of school administration, establishment, and evaluation could help to form a new pattern of governance in education, and it is one of the important steps in deepening the reform of the system of education. It could form a more professional and service-oriented structure for school management, establishment, and evaluation by identifying the responsibilities of the subjects. Of course, we should still acknowledge that, given the influence of ideas from the planned economy and the incomplete nature of systems and mechanisms during the social transition, the government still needs to solve many issues that arise from changing functions and methods of management, so as to promote the reform.

2.3 Promoting Reform of the System of Examination Enrollment

The year 2017 is called the First Year of the New College Entrance Examination. Since the issuance of the *Implementation Opinions of the State Council on Deepening the Reform of the Examination Enrollment System* was implemented, new methods for enrollment in examinations have been explored in many places. As the sites of the first pilot programs, Zhejiang Province and Shanghai City completed the enrollment work of that year smoothly, setting the standard for the reform of the college entrance examination. The new college entrance examination reform was launched in Beijing, Tianjin, Shandong, and Hainan in September. During the new round of the reform of college entrance examinations, administrators could use the experiences of Zhejiang and Shanghai to improve their enrollment examination systems and accumulate experience for the promotion of the reform of enrollment examinations nationwide.

The ultimate starting point and target of college entrance examination reform was to expand the students' right of choice. The detailed contents of the reform included implementing the 3 + 3 subject combination examination, eliminating the segregation of the arts and sciences, instituting several examinations in English, canceling the examination bonus, and in general canceling the batches of enrollment.

Some new issues were identified during the summarization of the new college entrance examination and enrollment procedure. In actual teaching, not all course combinations could be offered to students. In addition, an optional class system had to be used, since the choice of examination subjects was expanded. Therefore, higher requirements were established for teaching management, teacher quantity, and the quantity of sites. The method of selecting examinations eliminated the disadvantage of the college entrance examination as the final word for admissions, but the new students from the senior high school would encounter promotion pressure too early. Take Zhejiang as an example: most senior high schools would ask new students to complete eight optional examination courses so that they could focus on fewer subjects for the college entrance examination. In addition, since the optional examination subjects were classified based on percentages, many students preferred not to compete with good students, and so they would avoid the difficult physics exam. Instead, they would select good colleges based on their examination scores instead of pursuing good disciplines. This would have an adverse effect on the cultivation of natural science talents in colleges and universities.

2.4   *Promoting the Reform of the System of Running Private Schools*

In the reform of the system of school administration, private education is the priority. In September 2017, the *Private Education Promotion Law of the People's Republic of China* was promulgated to resolve outstanding conflicts and key problems concerning the attributes of a legal person, ownership, supporting policies, and equal status from the perspective of law. Resolving these issues would further encourage social forces to establish schools and promote the healthy development of private education. This is of great importance to promoting the development of educational undertakings, deepening comprehensive reform in the field of education, and establishing a pattern of joint development of public education and private education. In terms of promoting the development of private education, the policy supports affirmed the legality of the profitability of private education, encouraging more social forces to participate in private education. Various private education units, such as preschool, senior high school, and higher and non-diploma education, could meet people's diversified needs for education. It is worth noting that, to reflect the will of our country, the government required that no for-profit private school should be established for compulsory education. As for the social supervision of private education, a system of information publicity and credit filing was established for private schools.

2.5 Deepening the Reform of Talent Cultivation Modes

The Made in China 2025 program is an important step for China as it transforms from a large manufacturing country to a powerful manufacturing country. During this process, the reform of education regarding innovation and business-starting and the manner of cultivating innovation talents in colleges and universities is an important concern. To enact the *Implementation Opinions of the General Office of the State Council on Deepening the Reform of Education Regarding Innovation and Business-starting in Higher Educational Institutions*, by 2017, three Internet + innovation and business-starting competitions for college students were held. The competitions attracted millions of students from more than 2,000 colleges and universities and involved more than 26,000 full-time teachers who delivered education on innovation and start-ups and more than 76,000 part-time teachers. Nearly 14,000 practice platforms for innovation and start-up education were established, and 7.04 billion yuan was budgeted for education regarding innovation and start-ups as well as more than 260,000 educational projects for students regarding innovation and starting businesses.[9] The reform of education related to innovation and start-ups nationwide demonstrated a satisfactory pattern, featuring multiple breakthroughs and a deeper level of development.

Regarding the construction of higher educational institutions, the government guided some ordinary universities as they transformed themselves into application-type higher educational institutions and also implemented the *Guiding Opinions on Guiding Some Local Ordinary Universities to Transform into Application-Type Higher Educational Institutions*, with the goal of enabling higher educational institutions to participate in regional economic development and to develop talents and provide scientific services based on major initiatives/strategies, such as the Belt and Road Initiative; the coordinated development of Beijing, Tianjin, and Hebei; the construction of the Yangtze River Economic Belt; and the transformation and updating of regional specific

---

9 "New Change in Higher Education, 'Three Highs, Three News and Two Strengths,'" China .com.cn, September 28, 2017.

and advantageous industries. A platform should be established to encourage cooperation between industries and enterprises to improve the requirements for practical abilities during talent cultivation, and to allow schools, local governments, and enterprises to jointly run and govern schools. The construction of a team of teachers with good professional knowledge and skills and teaching and practical abilities shall be strengthened to provide flexible measures to recruit special talents and elites in industries, as well as to establish a green channel to attract outstanding professional technical talents and management talents from enterprises to higher educational institutions. In this way, good examples can be provided for students during the cultivation of talents in order to expand their views. During the cultivation of talents for occupational education, the government has been promoting the mode of production-teaching integration and school-enterprise cooperation. The disciplines are determined based on the demands of the market, and appropriate enterprises are selected for deep cooperation in order to productively integrate study with work and implement a modern apprenticeship system.

3   Undertaking Key Construction and Overall Planning for the Development of Education

In February 2017, the National Development and Reform Commission, the Ministry of Education, and the Ministry of Human Resources and Social Security jointly issued the *Implementation Plan for the Program for the Promotion of the Modernization of Education*, defining five major construction tasks, including the construction of compulsory education schools and the construction of world-class universities and first-class disciplines. These construction targets and the developmental targets specified in the Outline of the Plan and the 13th Five-Year Plan for Education are the key points for reform and construction in the field of education in 2017.

3.1   *Establishing an Ideological and Political Education System for Colleges, Middle Schools, and Primary Schools by Strengthening Moral Education and Cultivating Civic Virtues*

The Third Plenary Session of the 18th Central Committee of the Communist Party of China clearly pointed out the fundamental task of strengthening moral education and cultivating civic virtues for education. Afterward, the Ministry of Education issued the *Opinions on Fully Deepening the Reform of the Curriculum and Implementing the Fundamental Task of Strengthening Moral Education and Cultivating Civic Virtues*. In January 2017, the State Council issued the 13th Five-Year Plan for Education to make the implementation of the task of strengthening moral education and cultivating civic virtues the fundamental mission, indicating that we need to focus on ideological and political educational work in higher education institutions as well as strengthening and improvement in various schools at all levels, including moral education, so as to integrate ideological and political work into the whole process of education and teaching. In July, the State Council issued its decision on establishing the national commission on teaching materials to guide and plan the work regarding teaching materials throughout the country; implement the major policies made by the Party and the national government for teaching materials; research and review the plans for creating teaching materials and the annual working plans; consider and resolve the major issues in the creation of teaching materials; guide, organize, and coordinate the tasks related to teaching materials in different regions and departments; review the organization of the teaching curriculum and curriculum standards; and review the national planned teaching materials with outstanding ideological attributes.[10]

To establish an overall moral educational system for colleges, middle schools, and primary schools, we need to use the targets, contents, ways, methods, management, and assessment of moral education as a basis, with moral education for primary schools, junior high schools, senior high schools (secondary vocational schools), and universities and colleges (higher vocational schools) as targets, so as to establish a school moral educational system featuring Chinese characteristics, representing the orientation of advanced cultures and meeting the requirements for comprehensive quality education.[11] The leading party group of the Ministry of Education defined 2017 as the Year of Quality of Ideological and Political Teaching in Higher Educational Institutions to strengthen the leadership of the party over higher educational institutions, improve the party's system of leadership management, strengthen the ideological and political work of teachers and the ideological and political education of college students, implement the fundamental task of strengthening moral education and cultivating civic virtues, and strive to improve the quality and level of ideological and political courses in higher educational institutions. Active efforts have been made in different places to strengthen the construction of ideological and political courses according to actual conditions, and to constantly improve the desirability and pertinence of ideological and political courses.

---

10   "Notice of the General Office of the State Council on Establishing a National Commission for Teaching Materials," portal website of the Central People's Government of the People's Republic of China.

11   "Establishing an Overall Moral Education System for Colleges, Middle Schools, and Primary Schools," *Guangming Daily*, March 16, 2017, Layout 14.

3.2 Lists of World-Class Universities and First-Class Disciplines Were Defined

The overall construction of world-class universities and first-class disciplines is a historical breakthrough for China as it transforms from a large higher educational country to a powerful one, and one of the important steps in the modernization of China's education. In January 2017, the Ministry of Education, the Ministry of Finance, and the NDRC jointly issued the *Implementation Method for the Overall Promotion of the Construction of World-Class Universities and First-Class Disciplines* (*Interim*) (hereinafter the Implementation Method) to define in detail the screening of world-class universities and first-class disciplines. In September, the lists of world-class universities and first-class disciplines were defined. The lists were made with the disciplines as funding subjects, and should be adjusted every five years. This time, the lists included 42 world-class university construction colleges (36 class A colleges and 6 class B colleges) and 95 first-class discipline construction colleges.[12] The lists of world-class universities and first-class disciplines were determined by taking the 985 Program and the 211 Program universities and colleges as the logical starting point and inherent basis. At the same time, the lists were not limited by the previous key higher educational institutions; also taken into consideration were the strategic layout of the higher education of the country as well as the potential contribution of special discipline construction to higher educational institutions in the country and the developmental target of developing world-class disciplines in a rapid and efficient way. From the beginning of the construction of world-class universities and first-class disciplines, the self-positioning and developmental vision of the universities and colleges will be more clearly defined. The policy of adjusting the lists every five years will make the universities and colleges more confident. The existing world-class universities and first-class disciplines may not actually be world-class, however, and the effect should be verified in the future.

3.3 Conducting Supervision, Guidance, and Assessment of the Quality and Balanced Development of Compulsory Education in Counties

China has fully popularized its nine-year compulsory education. The compulsory education work is moving forward to meet the challenges in balance, general benefit, and high quality. Compulsory education will experience a transformation from a basic balance to a quality balance. In order to consolidate the achievements of the basic balance development of compulsory education and guide the improvement of the balance development of

---

12 "Lists of World-Class Universities and First-Class Disciplines Were Published," Xinhuanet .com.

compulsory education to a higher level in different places, in April 2017 the Ministry of Education issued the *Method of Supervising, Guiding, and Assessing the Quality and Balanced Development of Compulsory Education in Counties* (hereinafter the Method) to supervise, guide, assess, and certify the counties (county-level cities and districts) that have started to address the quality and balanced development of compulsory education, indicating that compulsory education has entered a quality developmental stage. The Method mainly defined the purpose, reference, object, principles, basic conditions, contents and standards, procedures, and results of supervision, guidance, and assessment. This method features newer and improved indicators, higher standards, more scientific and effective methods, more attention to education quality and social recognition, and strengthened results. As of the end of 2016, 1,824 counties (county-level cities and districts) had achieved national certification for the basic supervisory assessment of balanced development for compulsory education, and 62.4% of the administrative units at the county level realized the target in terms of the basic balanced development of compulsory education. In 2017, about 500 counties (county-level cities and districts) accepted the national supervisory assessment, and the total number of such counties would reach 2,300, accounting for nearly 80% of those in China.[13]

3.4 Jointly Promoting the Development of the Belt and Road Initiative Education Action

The *Outline of the Plan for the National Long- and Mid-Term Educational Reform and Development (2010–2020)* made it necessary to continue to expand and improve the opening-up of education to foreign countries and to promote the international influence of China. In August 2016, the Ministry of Education issued the *Promotion of the Belt and Road Initiative Education Action* (hereinafter the Education Action). In this document, the Ministry of Education requested that educational development and economic cooperation be promoted at the same time to fully take advantage of the soft power of education to improve the efficiency of the construction of the Belt and Road Initiative.

Since its implementation, the Education Action has basically served the major node provinces by implementing leading programs such as the Chinese Government Scholarship. Students from countries along the route of the Belt and Road Initiative accounted for 61% of the scholarship winners. As of the end of 2016, the number of students studying in China from such countries had reached 200,000. In 2016, 75,000 Chinese students were studying in countries along the route of the Belt and Road Initiative, an increase of 38.6% over 2012.

---

13   "Improvement in the Quality of the Lives of Chinese People Regarding the Aspect of Education," *China Education Newspaper,* October 15, 2017, Layout 1.

In recent years, the Ministry of Education has actively strengthened communication on education with the countries and regions along the route of the Belt and Road Initiative. As of May 2017, the Ministry of Education signed mutual recognition agreements regarding educational background and academic degrees with 46 countries and regions, including 24 Belt and Road Initiative countries. The number of approved teaching programs involving cooperation between China and foreign countries reached 2,539, including 1,248 programs at or above the undergraduate level, and 928 programs at the higher vocational education level. A group of demonstrative cooperative teaching programs with high levels have been established, providing an international exchange platform for Chinese universities and colleges and for developing international talents in the Belt and Road Initiative countries.[14]

4 Promoting Equity and Making Education Serve the Quality of People's Lives

As of the spring semester of 2017, all students at the compulsory education stage from all public and private schools in rural and urban areas were no longer required to pay tuition or textbook fees, and living subsidies were also provided to resident students from impoverished families. In addition, achievements have also been made in terms of reform on the supply side of education, support for rural educational undertakings, the adjustment of the structure of talent cultivation, further improvement in the system of enrollment for examinations, and promotion of the development of the education industry, in order to make sure that education can develop in a fair way and maintain a good quality, and that the educational undertaking can better enrich the quality of people's lives.

4.1 Targeted Poverty Reduction for Education Provides Hope for Students' Families

Targeted poverty reduction is an important measure for building a moderately prosperous society in all respects. We should not only focus on targeted poverty reduction, but also on the combination of poverty reduction and support for building confidence and knowledge. We should see education as the foundation of people's quality of life in order to develop talents at different levels for impoverished areas through education, and to put a stop to the intergenerational transmission of poverty by reducing educational poverty. In recent years, given that education in different poverty-stricken areas is lagging behind and poverty

---

14　"The Belt and Road Initiative Education Action (Education Eye)," *People's Daily*, May 11, 2017, Layout 18.

with respect to educational quality is prominent, the Ministry of Education has given full play to the advantages of departments and industries and has adopted a series of policies and measures in line with local conditions. It has achieved remarkable results in eliminating poverty through education in old revolutionary areas, Western Yunnan, ethnic minority areas, and frontier areas.

To address the problem of dropouts, in July 2017 the General Office of the State Council issued the *Notice on Further Strengthening Control over Dropouts to Improve the Consolidation Level of Compulsory Education* to guide local governments to improve their working systems and take a series of specific measures, in line with actual conditions, that respond to the reasons why students become dropouts, so as to prevent them from dropping out due to learning difficulties, poverty, or having to travel long distances to attend school, and thus to fully perform the obligations of governments and all parts of society in controlling dropouts.[15] In some regions, attention has been paid to voluntary dropouts. In addition to improving the appeal of going to school and the consolidation rate of compulsory education, we also need to publicize the long-term importance of education in developing a life plan.

Another strategy for improving education by improving quality of life is to provide additional meals to students in impoverished areas. From the end of 2011 to June 2017, the central finance bureau budgeted 159.1 billion yuan to implement a plan to improve nutrition for students in compulsory education in rural areas. In addition to Beijing, Tianjin, and Shandong, which have independent student meal programs, nutrition improvement plans have been implemented in 1,590 counties in 29 provinces, covering 134,000 schools, benefiting more than 36 million students, and significantly improving the physical conditions of those students.

Experience has shown that vocational education is the most effective way to reduce poverty. All public secondary vocational schools have eliminated tuition fees for students from rural areas, students in agricultural disciplines, and students from impoverished families. These schools will also provide such students with a national learning-support fund of 2,000 yuan per person per year. In higher-level vocational schools, a multi-level funding system has been established and offers scholarships and subsidies covering 30% and 25% of students, respectively. At the same time, the Poverty Reduction Office of the State Council would provide each registered impoverished student with a subsidy of about 3,000 yuan per year.[16] China has gradually extended vocational education

---

15 "Build More Good Schools near Our Homes (People's Eye: Balanced Development of Compulsory Education)," People.cn, September 29, 2017.

16 "A Relatively Complete System of Vocational Education for Poverty Reduction Has Been Established in China," www.xinhuanet.com, October 9, 2017.

funding to cover all registered impoverished students and has basically established a complete poverty reduction system through vocational education.

4.2 *Strengthen the Construction of Teaching Teams*

During the five years after the conclusion of the 18th National Congress of the CPC, the main framework for thoroughly reforming the teaching team was established, significantly improving the configuration of teachers, optimizing the teaching team, and enhancing the quality of teachers. According to statistics, as of 2016, the number of full-time teachers in various schools at all levels throughout China was 15.78 million, an increase of 1.16 million over 2012. The teacher ratio for primary school students was reduced from 17.71:1 to 17.12:1; the ratio for junior high school students was reduced from 13.59:1 to 12.41:1; and that of ordinary senior high school students was reduced from 15.47:1 to 13.65:1. Most teachers are young and middle-aged, and the proportion of teachers with a high educational background has increased. The ratio of full-time teachers with qualifying educational backgrounds in primary schools, junior high schools, ordinary senior high schools, and ordinary universities reached 99.94%, 99.76%, 97.91%, and 98.78%, respectively.[17]

It is important and critical to construct a teaching team for rural areas. The difficulties include low income and profits, small developmental spaces, and difficulties in recruiting rural teachers. In 2015, the Central Committee of the Party and the State Council issued the *Rural Teacher Supporting Plan (2015–2020)*, which will provide more benefits to rural teachers and improve the above conditions. The detailed contents of the policy include implementing room and board subsidies for rural teachers, strengthening the cultivation and supply of rural teachers, reforming and implementing the national cultivation plan, unifying staff arrangement for teachers in urban and rural areas, and establishing an honor system for rural teachers, to make rural teachers feel at ease in teaching in rural areas and to encourage more rural students go back to school.

Support for higher educational institutions includes great efforts to introduce foreign talents. Since the 18th National Congress of the CPC, we have launched the Discipline Innovation and Talent Introduction Program for Higher Educational Institutions ("the 111 Program"), the Key Supporting Program for Introducing High-End Overseas Scientific and Teaching Experts, and the High-End Foreign Expert Program. As of February 2017, 136 talent introduction bases under the 111 Program had been built, and 359 talent introduction bases covering 80 central higher educational institutions had been established.

---

17   "Creating the Builders of the Dream Team of the Chinese Nation—General Introduction to the Comprehensive Strengthening of the Construction of Teaching Teams since the 18th National Congress of the CPC," Xinhua News Agency, September 9, 2017.

The talent introduction bases of higher education institutions have made great efforts in building up their talent teams by improving policies and mechanisms and expanding the channels for the introduction of overseas talents. Each year, more than 50,000 foreign experts will come to China to work through the foreign expert programs, showing the great benefit of talent agglomeration. The talents introduced have become a valuable think tank and sources of innovation for the improvement of quality in developing high-end talents for science and teaching, as well as for the capacity for carrying out innovation and a high level of scientific research.

4.3   The Development of the Education Industry Entered a New Stage

With the improvement of the standard of living, people's requirements for quality education have also been increasing, and educational needs have also witnessed diversified development. In recent years, as an emerging industry, the education industry has witnessed rapid development in the market economy. From the perspective of scale and market vitality, the education industry in China is still in the expansion stage. It is estimated that the total volume of the industry in 2020 will be twice what it was in 2015, or that it will have increased from 1.6 trillion yuan in 2015 to 3 trillion yuan in 2020, with an annual compound growth rate of 12.7%.[18] In addition, with support from educational policies, the improvement of information technologies, and the innovation of management concepts, the education industry is becoming stronger day by day.

The revised *Private Education Promotion Law* has clearly defined the profit-making and non-profit-making natures of private education, further affirming the legal rights and economic benefits of for-profit private schools, which may attract a great number of educational investors to enter the education industry. The integration of education and a market economy has driven the expansion of the education industry. The three driving forces, namely, investment, mergers, and IPOs, have been driving the rapid development of the whole education industry. Under the influence of related policies, the year 2015 witnessed an explosive development of the education industry, and a rapid developmental tendency was maintained for the next two years. In 2016, 340 educational investment events occurred, with an investment of 18 billion yuan, even though the amount in 2014 was only 2.12 billion yuan.[19] With respect to the asset securitization of the education industry, the new *Private Education*

---

18   "The Volume of the Education Industry of China Will Double within 5 Years," *Shanghai Financial News*, May 31, 2016, A15.

19   Education Industry Research, "Review and Outlook on the Investment and Merger of the Education Industry in 2016," data from Bright Century Shareholding.

Promotion Law in 2017 provided great benefits to organizations offering non-diploma training, and the asset securitization of the education industry would be accelerated constantly. In general, in an environment with good policies, a stable market, and expanding service needs, the education industry is developing in a direction featuring refinement, individuality, information, and services. In the future, the "cake" of the education industry will become bigger and bigger.

4.4 Paying Attention to Marginalized Groups' Right to Receive an Education

In July 2017, the *Second Special Education Promotion Plan* (2017–2020) was issued, and that plan was officially launched. By 2020, the enrollment rate for disabled children in compulsory education should reach more than 95%; the volume of special education other than compulsory education should be further expanded; and the popularization and level of special education at different levels should have improved comprehensively.[20] Each special child should be registered to implement an accurate "One Person One File" policy implementation method. Each district (county) should establish an account to collect information on special children to help and support each special child specifically, so as to help special children of school age receive compulsory education. At the same time, we should also accelerate the development of preschool, senior high school, and senior special education to improve the educational background of the disabled. At present, the enrollment methods for disabled children are limited, and the number of special schools is far from enough. Only a few special children are reading in classes in ordinary schools. Compared with developed countries, the proportion of integrated education in China is still low. All places should further increase the ratio of special children learning in ordinary classes, not only by increasing the number of schools receiving special children but also by improving the qualities of special education teachers, classrooms, and barrier-free facilities.

In recent years, the issues caused by left-behind children have attracted more and more attention from society. Several ministries and offices, such as the Ministry of Civil Affairs, the Central Government Office of Integrated Governance, and the Ministry of Education, jointly issued a notice to implement a special action to jointly protect and accompany left-behind children in rural areas from November 2016 to the end of 2017. Education departments

---

20   "The Second Special Education Promotion Plan (2017–2020) Was Launched," portal website of the Ministry of Education of the People's Republic of China.

at all levels have also made many efforts to help more than 10,000 left-behind children who had dropped out of school in rural areas to return to school. Public security organs at all levels have completed the household registers for 13,000 left-behind children without household registers in rural areas.

5 Surveying Public Opinion on Education

Education is closely related to all families. The media, supported by information technologies, could rapidly transmit relevant educational news and transform such information into opinions with which the whole society should be concerned in a short period of time. Public opinions regarding education are often concentrated on education policies and on periods when educational programs are undergoing changes, and they always aim at the typical events that harm social order and violate the laws regarding education. In such cases, the public voice would be used to express the concerns of the public to benefit education. Therefore, public opinion on education could highlight educational conflicts. Concern, reflection, and action on public opinion regarding education could promote the improvement of the ecological environment of education.

5.1 *Eliminating School Bullying and Violence*
In recent years, many cases related to school bullying and violence have been reported, such as extorting money, beating classmates, verbal insults, and the abuse of children by kindergarten teachers. All these cases are the bane of education and society and should attract wide attention from society in a rapid way. However, similar cases have not been totally eliminated. In April 2017, the General Office of the State Council issued the *Opinions on Strengthening the Construction of the System of Safety Risk Prevention and Control for Kindergartens, Primary Schools, and Middle Schools*, requiring the relevant departments at all levels to work with kindergartens, primary schools, and middle schools to identify and solve any campus safety issues. The Ministry of Education has worked with the high court, the high procuratorate, and the Ministry of Public Security to control bullying at school. Conditions have been improved, but the problem has not been totally eliminated. In the future, campus safety protection mechanisms should be further improved. Audits and inspections should also be conducted by third parties to summarize the control experiences based on the developmental features of students, the features of school bullying incidents, and the introduction of effective measures from other countries and regions. School violence is a crime, and anyone who

commits school violence should be subject to severe punishment according to the *Criminal Law*, in order to respond to the concerns of students, teachers, and parents regarding school safety.

5.2   *Equal Rights for Renters and Homeowners and Child Enrollment*

In 2017, Beijing and Nanjing as well as Guangzhou, Foshan, Wuhan, and Jinan issued regulations on the reform of the administration of housing leasing, and the era of equal rights for home tenants and owners is imminent. The implementation of equal rights for home tenants and owners responded to the call made by President Xi Jinping that houses are used for living in, but not for speculation, which has improved the house leasing market and means that qualified workers from rural areas to cities could send their children to nearby schools as homeowners do, even if they are renting houses. This could ensure the legislative rights of the house tenants, guarantee their children's right to receive education in public schools, and reduce the number of children who have to stay at home due to barriers to enrollment. In the past ten years, the price of school district housing has always reached sky-high levels from time to time, due to the educational rights attached to the ownership of that housing. However, the implementation of the policy of equal rights for home tenants and owners may relieve the sky-high prices of school district housing to some extent.

Of course, we should also recognize that the problem of school district housing cannot be fundamentally reversed with this policy, and that the policy of equal rights for home tenants and owners cannot completely ensure fair enrollment for all. A constant increase in educational resources is the key to solving the fundamental problem.

5.3   *Preventing College Students from Joining Pyramid Selling Schemes*

In the summer of 2017, the deaths of several college students after joining pyramid selling organizations caused a great disturbance in society, raising great concern among countless graduates and their parents. Pyramid selling organizations would send invitations to college students who were looking for jobs. Given their limited social experience, college students would easily become the targets of pyramid selling organizations, and increasing pressure for employment could make it easier for students to be trapped in such schemes due to their lack of critical judgment.

In August 2017, the State Administration for Industry and Commerce, the Ministry of Education, the Ministry of Public Security, and the Ministry of Human Resources and Social Security issued a notice on launching a special action to control pyramid selling activities in the name of recruitment and to introduce jobs. The four departments implemented a three-month measure to strike at pyramid selling activities and destroy pyramid selling bases.[21] To totally protect college students from pyramid schemes, we need to strengthen employment and business-starting guidance for college students, on the one hand, to help them make their career plans and improve their consciousness about jobs. On the other hand, we need to depend on social governance to strike at pyramid schemes in terms of legislation, administration, and justice, since pyramid schemes have been a social problem for decades.

6 Outlook on the Future of the Development of the Education Industry

The 19th National Congress of the CPC pointed out that the construction of socialism with Chinese characteristics has entered a new age, and this is the latest historical orientation of the social development of China. In the new age, the major social conflict in China is between the desire of the people for a better life, on the one hand, and imbalance and insufficient development, on the other hand. It is part of a better life to provide people with satisfactory working-class education, which is also our expectation for the development of education undertakings in the future.

By 2020, an education information system matching the national government's target of the modernization of education could be established to enable everyone to learn at any place and any time.[22] We should further improve educational fairness to narrow the educational gaps among different groups and different regions in order to provide people with opportunities to receive various quality educational services at all levels. At the same time, we should improve the level of labor capital and consider this an important task to eliminate the shortage in the structural reform on the supply side, so as to strive to build an innovative country. According to the new target for the modernization of education by 2035, educators should focus on the core social values regarding education proposed at the 19th National Congress of the CPC, the modernization of education in two stages, the strengthening of moral

---

21 "Notice of the State Administration for Industry and Commerce, the Ministry of Education, the Ministry of Public Security, and the Ministry of Human Resources and Social Security on Launching the Specific Action to Strike at Pyramid Selling Activities in the Name of Recruitment or Job Introduction," portal website of the State Administration for Industry and Commerce of the People's Republic of China, August 14, 2017.

22 "The 13th Five-Year Plan for the Informatization of Education Issued," *China Education Newspaper*, June 24, 2016.

education and the cultivation of civic virtues, the construction of world-class universities and first-class disciplines, and the construction of the learning society, so as to change their methods of research and further promote the plan of establishing national education think tanks with Chinese characteristics.

At the beginning of 2017, the relevant UN departments held the 2030 Educational Seminar in Beijing, aiming at promoting and implementing the *2030 Sustainable Development Agenda* of the UN and the *2030 Education Action Framework* of UNESCO. Dankert Vedeler, the chairman of the drafting commission of the 2030 UNESCO Education Action Framework, mentioned that China should make more efforts to ensure the right to quality education for marginalized groups;[23] to provide the disabled, people in remote areas, and the children of populations that move around with fair education; and to render the benefit of a fair education to the vulnerable groups. These are the things that have been done by China for its educational undertakings and are important directions for future efforts. China has already made remarkable achievements in education in the world and the experiences of China in the development of education could be capitalized on by other countries, especially the developing countries, for their educational undertakings.

References

"Creating the Builders of the Dream Team of the Chinese Nation—General Introduction to the Comprehensive Strengthening of the Construction of Teaching Teams since the 18th National Congress of the CPC." Xinhua News Agency, September 9, 2017.

"Establishing an Overall Moral Educational System for Colleges, Middle Schools, and Primary Schools." *Guangming Daily*, March 16, 2017, Layout 14.

"Time Selection for China's Education." *China Education Newspaper*, October 17, 2017, Layout 1.

"The Volume of the Education Industry of China Would Be Doubled within 5 Years." *Shanghai Financial News*, May 31, 2016, A15.

23 "Special Interview with Dankert Vedeler, the Chairman of the Drafting Commission of the 2030 Education Action Framework: Global Cooperation and Chinese Participation in Education 2030," *Journal of World Education*, 2016(1).

CHAPTER 6

Report on the Development of China's Health Care in 2017

Fang Lijie[1]

Abstract

In this report, we first review the data and policy implementation for health care reform from 2016 to 2017. According to our review, the new reform of health care is still moving forward along a systematic route of development that was established in 2016. Given the short duration of that systematic development, no significant change can be seen in terms of data. During that period, some innovative measures were taken by local governments, but the effects need to be further verified. According to an estimate, the data in 2017 should not see any great changes. The breakthrough in systematic reform depends on the fundamental function of health care insurance in linking the reform of health care insurance, the reform of the system of health care, and the reform of the circulation of drugs. The report also analyzes three major shortcomings affecting people's livelihood in the field of health: poverty caused by illness, the health problems of a floating population, and the health literacy of the population. Although corresponding countermeasures have been established for these three problems, the effects of such countermeasures were not as successful as expected. Therefore, great attention should be given to these problems during the period of the 13th Five-Year Plan, and the existing ideas on policy must be changed.

Keywords

interlink of reforms on health care insurance, health care system and system of drug circulation – poverty caused by diseases – health risks for a population in constant movement – health literacy

According to the 19th National Congress of the CPC, we must strive to generate benefits, resolve concerns, and eliminate shortcomings to improve the lives of

---

1 Fang Lijie, associate research fellow of the Institute of Sociology, the Chinese Academy of Social Sciences.

© KONINKLIJKE BRILL NV, LEIDEN, 2022 | DOI:10.1163/9789004500723_007

people and promote social fairness and justice. New progress should be made in educating all children, teaching all students, benefiting all workers, treating all patients, supporting all senior citizens, providing housing to all those in need, and helping vulnerable groups. We should implement the Healthy China Strategy.

Based on the shortcomings in the health care industry at present, as well as the spirit of the 19th CPC National Congress, during the period of the 13th Five-Year Plan, the core problem to be resolved is to select an appropriate road for the reform of China's health care. In addition, in the documents issued by the Central Government and the National Health and Family Planning Commission, we can see three other issues regarding shortages that have been emphasized. Therefore, our report has not only focused on the progress of health care reform, but it has also expanded our view of the above two kinds of issues.

1 Progress of the Reform of the New Health Care from 2016 to 2017

1.1 Health Care Resources and Services from 2016 to 2017[2]

According to the 2015 data provided in the Report on the Development of Health Care in the *Blue Book of China's Society* in 2016, the growth of personal health expenditure was lower than that of the per capita net income of urban and rural residents. The ratio of personal health expenditure to total health expenditure decreased to lower than 30%. The issue of the high cost of medical treatment was relieved to some extent. However, the growth of the amount of services provided by grassroots medical institutions was still lower than that of hospitals. Most patients would like to seek treatment in large hospitals, leading to a shortage of beds in such hospitals. According to the data from 2016 to 2017, that tendency has not changed.

In terms of services, according to the conditions of the first half of 2017 as shown in Table 6.1, first of all, based on the comparison between hospitals and grassroots medical institutions, the growth of the amount of services provided by hospitals was still higher than that of grassroots medical institutions. In particular, services in clinics provided by grassroots medical institutions did not see any growth, indicating that the goal of having the initial diagnosis done at the grassroots medical institutions was not realized. Second, according to the classes of hospitals, the growth of the amount of services provided by class 3 hospitals was obviously higher than those of class 1 and class 2 hospitals, and so were the services in clinics, which means that large hospitals were still siphoning patients. The growth of the amount of services in class 2 hospitals

---

2 Unless otherwise specified, all data in this report are from the *China Health Statistics Yearbook* and the *China Health and Family Planning Statistical Digest 2017*.

REPORT ON THE DEVELOPMENT OF CHINA'S HEALTH CARE IN 2017

TABLE 6.1 Medical Services Provided by Health Care Organizations in the First Half of 2017

Type	Number of patients receiving diagnosis and treatment (10,000)		Growth in the number of patients receiving diagnosis and treatment (%)	Number of discharged patients (10,000)		Growth in the number of discharged patients (%)
	Jan.–June, 2016	Jan.–June, 2017		Jan.–June, 2016	Jan.–June, 2017	
Total number of medical institutions Hospitals	384569.5	391698.5	1.9	10878.5	11474.1	5.5
Hospital by class	156870.4	163468.0	4.2	8379.4	8932.7	6.6
Class 3 hospitals	76306.6	80991.8	6.1	3565.3	3915.9	9.8
Class 2 hospitals	60313.2	61787.3	2.4	3755.6	3878.9	3.3
Class 1 hospitals	10052.3	10452.9	4.0	473.4	517.2	9.2
Unclassified hospitals	10198.3	10236.0	0.4	584.7	620.7	6.2
Grassroots medical institutions	213877.6	213786.5	0.0	2019.1	2032.8	0.7
Community health care service centers	32925.9	34215.9	3.9	170.2	157.8	−7.3
Township health centers	50993.2	50371.5	−1.2	1830.4	48.5	1.0
Clinics (medical rooms)	29600	30520.0	3.1	—	—	—
Village medical rooms	94990	92590.0	−2.5	—	—	—
Other organizations	13821.5	14444.0	4.5	480.0	508.7	6.0

SOURCE: NATIONAL MEDICAL SERVICES FROM JANUARY TO JUNE 2017, INFORMATION DISCLOSURE WEBSITE OF THE NATIONAL HEALTH AND FAMILY PLANNING COMMISSION, HTTP://WWW.NHFPC .GOV.CN/MOHWSBWSTJXXZX/S7967/201708/D3E339644E394863AC6511BEA41C7456.SHTML

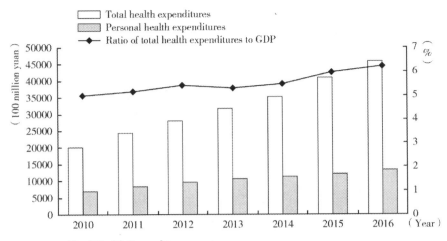

FIGURE 6.1 Total Health Expenditures per Annum

TABLE 6.2 Service Fees of Public Hospitals Per Annum

Year	One-time use fee for clinics		Per capita hospitalization expenses	
	Amount (yuan)	Proportion of the cost of drugs (%)	Amount (yuan)	Proportion of the cost of drugs (%)
2010	167.3	48.5	6415.9	43.4
2011	180.2	51.5	6909.9	42.2
2012	193.4	51.3	7325.1	41.3
2013	207.9	50.2	7860.2	39.7
2014	221.6	49.3	8290.5	38.4
2015	235.2	48.3	8833.0	36.9
2016	246.5	46.7	9229.7	34.6

was the lowest, indicating that the amount of services at specialized hospitals and rehabilitation hospitals saw limited growth; this was in conflict with the service needs caused by the aging population of our country and needs to be focused on. Finally, as seen from the internal conditions of grassroots medical institutions, the amount of services in clinics in rural areas decreased, as did the amount of hospitalization services in urban areas, showing that access to medical treatment and hospitalization services in rural areas was decreasing.

According to the total health expenditures, as can be seen in Figure 6.1, in 2016, the proportion of personal health expenditures in the total health

REPORT ON THE DEVELOPMENT OF CHINA'S HEALTH CARE IN 2017

TABLE 6.3   Service Fees of Grassroots Medical Institutions Per Annum

Year	Community health care service centers				Township health centers			
	One-time use fee for clinics (yuan)	Proportion of the cost of drugs (%)	Per capita hospital-ization expense (yuan)	Proportion of the cost of drugs (%)	One-time use fee for clinics (yuan)	Proportion of the cost of drugs (%)	Per capita hospital-ization expense (yuan)	Proportion of the cost of drugs (%)
2010	82.8	70.9	2357.6	49.3	47.5	60.4	1004.6	52.9
2011	81.5	67.4	2315.1	45.8	47.5	53.3	1051.3	46.8
2012	84.6	69.1	2417.9	46.5	49.2	54.8	1140.7	48.2
2013	86.5	68.7	2482.7	45.5	52.7	54.5	1267.0	46.8
2014	92.3	68.7	2635.2	44.1	56.9	54.3	1382.9	45.8
2015	97.7	68.9	2760.6	43.1	60.1	54.2	1487.4	45.4
2016	107.2	69.6	2872.4	41.8	63.0	54.8	1616.8	44.0

expenditures in 2016 decreased slightly, from 29.2% in 2015 to 28.9% in 2016. From 2015 to 2016, the growth of personal health expenditures was 10.5%. According to the data from the *Statistical Bulletin for the National Economic and Social Development of the People's Republic of China in 2016*, the per capita net income of urban and rural residents in 2016 grew by 8.4%, which was slightly lower than the growth of personal health expenditures. Therefore, health expenditures should be controlled in a more effective way.

In terms of the costs of medical institutions, the proportion of the cost of drugs in public hospitals has been decreasing in a slightly different manner from reductions in previous years (see Table 6.2). The cost of drugs at grassroots medical institutions did not change much. This tendency was basically the same as that in the past three years (see Table 6.3).

Compared to drug costs in previous years, the proportion of drug costs in the total amount of expenditures on health in 2015 was slightly lower than that in 2014 (see Table 6.4). According to the composition of the drug costs, despite the reduction of the proportion of the drug costs of medical institutions in the total amount of expenditures on health, the costs of drug stores increased significantly, which was related to the reform of the medical organization in separating drugs from hospitals, indicating that the motivation for doctors to prescribe drugs had decreased and patients had more options. However, there was a possibility that the drugs in medical institutions would not meet the needs of patients. It is worth noting that, compared to other data, the statistics

TABLE 6.4   The Cost of Drugs in Previous Years

Type \ Year	2010	2011	2012	2013	2014	2015
Total cost of drugs (100 million yuan)	8835.9	9826.2	11860.5	13307.7	13925.0	16166.3
Per capita cost of drugs (yuan)	658.9	729.3	875.9	978.0	1018.0	1176.1
Proportion of cost of drugs in total health expenditures (%)	41.6	38.4	40.4	39.8	37.8	37.7

on the cost of drugs were lacking to some extent. The other data reflected the conditions of the reform in 2016, while the latest statistics on the cost of drugs reflected the conditions in 2015, but not the latest progress of the new reform of health care. In particular, the effects of the reform route of the public hospitals in making room, adjusting the structure, and ensuring linkage since 2016 was not demonstrated by the data regarding the cost of drugs.

1.2 *Progress of the Reform on the Central Level in 2017*
At the end of 2016, the General Office of the CPC Central Committee and the General Office of the State Council forwarded the *Several Opinions of the Leading Group for Deepening the Reform of the Health Care System of the State Council on Further Promoting and Deepening the Experiences in the Reform of the Health Care System*. This document could be considered the second important opinion of the Central Committee and the State Council since the launching of the new reform of health care in 2009, and it signifies a new stage of the new reform of health care. The core of the document is to emphasize the working mechanism of the linkage among health care, health care insurance and drugs, and a systematic reform and interlock.

Under the overall plan described in the above document, in 2017, the General Office of the State Council issued four documents to promote four major tasks. The four documents were as follows: *Several Opinions on Further Reforming and Improving Policies Regarding the Production, Circulation, and Utilization of Drugs*; *Guiding Opinions on Promoting the Construction and Development of a Health Care Consortium*; *Guiding Opinions on Establishing a Modern Hospital Management System*; and *Guiding Opinions on Further Deepening the Reform of the Payment Method of Basic Health Care Insurance*.

In improving the production, circulation, and utilization of drugs, which are the basic links of making room, adjusting the structure, and ensuring linkage and the Interlink of Reforms on Health Care Insurance, the Health Care System, and the System for the Circulation of Drugs, this part of the reform was the priority in 2017. The General Office of the State Council issued related documents to emphasize the reform of the two-invoice system again, requiring that the two-invoice system should be implemented in all public pilot cities and fully implemented by 2018 throughout the country. At the same time, the documents emphasized strict control over the unreasonable increase in health care costs; it restated that control of those costs should be related to financial subsidies, outstanding employee evaluation, performance bonus assessment, and the promotion of directors for public hospitals; and it also required strengthening the function of the health care insurance standardization actions and cost control; upholding the interlock of health care, health care insurance, and drugs; promoting the cancellation of additions to the price of drugs; adjusting medical service prices; and encouraging patients to buy drugs in drug stores.

In terms of the construction of a medical consortium, our working target is to basically establish the system framework of a medical consortium and fully implement the construction of pilot medical consortiums in various forms by 2017, and to fully promote the construction of medical consortiums based on experiences from the pilot consortiums and establish a complete medical consortium policy by 2020. In related documents in the past, the focus was on the function of the medical consortium in improving grassroots capacities. However, in the documents issued by the General Office of the State Council in 2017, more attention was paid to the implementation of systems, including responses and corrections for some original issues. For example, the documents required further use of the function of economic leverage of health care insurances, improvement in the system of a personnel guarantee and stimulation, and the establishment of a performance examination system matched with the medical consortium.

The reform of public hospitals was fully implemented in 2017. According to the documents, all governments at the local level should make a plan to implement a comprehensive reform of public hospitals in cities; the comprehensive reform of public hospitals should be fully implemented to cancel all of the additional prices on drugs in all public hospitals (except TCM tablets and liquids); the average growth rate of the medical costs in public hospitals should be controlled at 10% or below; the proportion of the cost of drugs in the total health expenditure of the first four pilot cities should be reduced to lower than 30% (excluding TCM tablets and liquids); the cost of health care materials in the medical income of public hospitals in the first four pilot cities should be reduced to lower than 20 yuan; the number of diseases for which treatment fees are charged according to the disease should be reduced to lower than 100; and the proportion of income from medical services provided by public hospitals at the county level in the total operating income (excluding income from drugs, consumables, inspections, and tests) should be improved.

In terms of the reform on health care insurance payment, the focus was on the leverage function of health care insurance in adjusting the activities of medical institutions and guiding the reasonable distribution of resources for medical services. In the past, reform was mainly driven by administrative orders, but in the documents issued by the General Office of the State Council in 2017, the government recognized that health care insurance could stimulate the standardized activities of medical institutions, control their costs, and ensure the reasonable acceptance and transfer of patients. In the documents, according to the features of different medical services, a multiple-factor and compound method for the payment of health care insurance is required to effectively standardize the diagnosis and treatment activities of different medical institutions. At the same time, health care insurance could be used as a way to distribute the resources of medical services: based on the hierarchical diagnosis and treatment mode and the system of family doctor contracting services, health care insurance could guide the participants to seek medical advice at grassroots clinics, and the qualified family doctor contracting service costs should be included in the coverage of health care insurance.

1.3 Innovative Practices at the Local Level in 2017

In addition to the progress of the reform at the central level, there were a lot of innovative practices at the local level. For example, the author of the report on the reform of health care in 2016 stated that from the documents issued by the central government, we can see that the targets of the reform were made into indicators, representing the determination of the government to promote the reform of health care. These administrative indicators are the source of external pressure for the reform of local health care, and it was the internal motivation of the local government to resolve the issues encountered in the process of reforming health care and to constantly promote that reform. Under the two forces, we could see that a lot of innovative measures were taken in local health care reforms. Similar to the reform logic at the central level, these innovative practices were the correction of the issues encountered during reform in the past and the exploration of a way to systematically promote reform.

Since the remuneration and staff management of grassroots medical institutions were too bureaucratic, medical personnel had insufficient motivation to provide services, which has been a problem since the launching of the new health care reform. According to data from previous years, the growth of the amount of services provided by grassroots medical institutions was lower than that of hospitals. Under pressure from the initial diagnosis at the grassroots level and the inner motivation of relieving the difficulty in seeking medical advice in large hospitals, reform of the performance of grassroots medical institutions has been explored in many regions. For example, in Wuhou District, Chengdu City, the system of grassroots staff management was reformed, and the personnel were no longer managed based on the public institution system. Independent legal person status was implemented for community health centers. At present, the proportion of community medical personnel under the system of public institution staff is only 18.08%, and the proportion of personnel recruited from the society has reached 81.92%. In this way, a flexible staff system has been established. Meanwhile, the system of performance bonuses was reformed. After the reform, the post-performance bonus accounted for 60% of the total income of medical personnel, and their comprehensive performance was evaluated according to the quantity, quality, and satisfaction of their services. At present, the income gap between different organizations has surpassed 20%, and this system of distribution could effectively motivate grassroots medical personnel.

Exploration regarding the medical consortium is one of the key points. For example, as described in the *Blue Book of China's Society* in 2015, attempts in south China regarding the medical consortium were taken as representative, since no actual innovative cases could be found in other regions at that time. However, in the past two years, especially in relation to health care insurance, a lot of outstanding cases occurred. The cases of Luohu of Shenzhen and Tianchang of Anhui were typical. In these two cases, the common factor was that medical institutions at different levels in the same area were combined into a medical group to prepay service fees according to the total amount of health care insurance based on the total population in the area, and the balance of the health care insurance fund would be distributed as performance bonuses. The difference between Luohu and Tianchang was that in Luohu, all medical institutions in the region were combined into a single medical group, but in Tianchang, three medical groups were established under the leadership of a county hospital, a county TCM hospital, and a private hospital, respectively, which may compete with each other. With the health care insurance fund, the operators of the medical groups were motivated to save resources. In this way, internal motivation was generated to transfer patients from the top to the bottom, to use more grassroots medical institutions with lower costs, and to control large prescriptions and excessive treatment plans. At present, given the short duration of the pilot programs in these two cities, we have not collected enough data to evaluate the results. Although these cases have provided an outstanding innovative experience logically, there are still problems and risks in its promotion. For example, there is only one medical group in Luohu, so would such a monopoly on medical services generate discontent against the health care insurance department? Tianchang has three medical groups that may generate competition, but for most regions in central and western China, are the medical institutions at the county level large enough to form more than two medical groups?

Besides the innovative cases, under pressure from administrative targets, the activities of some regions may be differentiated. For example, in the investigation, the author found that in 2017, the central government required that the proportion of the cost of drugs in public hospitals in the pilot cities should be reduced to lower than 30%. However, the unit prices of drugs in some areas did not decrease in real terms. Therefore, the public hospitals have no option but to reduce the prescriptions of drugs to reduce the proportion of the cost of drugs. On the one hand, this situation may of course relieve the problem of excessive drugs. On the other hand, this would lead patients to buy drugs in drug stores with prescriptions. So we can predict that, among the drug data for 2017, although the drug expenditures of medical institutions will diminish, the expenditures for drug stores, especially their proportion, will increase significantly.

1.4　*Summary*

The data in 2016 mainly reflected the implementation of the reform in 2016. As mentioned by the author in the report in the previous year, the key points of the new reform of health care in 2016 were hierarchical diagnosis and treatment and the Comprehensive Reform of Public Hospitals. Hierarchical diagnosis and treatment was an expansion and reinforcement of the policy pursued in 2015, aiming to attract more patients to grassroots medical institutions. The reform of public hospitals was the reinforcement of the reform of the drug system in 2015. Compared to previous years, the above two key points of reform were more detailed and clearer in 2016, and their implementation routes, quantitative targets, and strict evaluation rules have highlighted a powerful driving force for reform. However, according to the data in 2016, services at grassroots medical institutions did not improve, and the proportion of drug expenditures in public hospitals was only reduced to a limited extent.

According to documents from 2017, the working style of 2016 was continued to promote a more systematic reform. The reform of the drug system, the building of a medical consortium, public hospital reform, and the reform of the system of health care insurance payments were the four key points in 2017, which were closely related to each other, according to each document. All of these facts indicate that the new reform of health care was moving on the way toward systematic reform.

The year 2016 was the first year of the systematic reform. The change in data was not significant. Despite the further development in 2017, the effects of the two fundamental reforms were not as good as expected. First of all, in terms of the reform of the drug system, despite the two-invoice system, the unit prices of drugs did not decrease significantly except in few regions, such as Fujian. Second, with respect to the reform of grassroots medical institutions, innovative experiences in 2017 were mainly at a local level, such as the performance reform and the construction of medical groups at grassroots medical institutions mentioned above. Although the directions of such reforms were good, they were not yet fully consolidated and promoted. Hence, we can see that the data in 2017 should not change too much.

In general, the new reform of health care was moving forward in the process of testing mistakes. In the following systematic advancement, the eventual achievement mainly depends on whether health care insurance can standardize the activities of medical institutions and control the prices of drugs.

2 Other Shortcomings in the Health Care Sector and the Policy Response

The purpose of the new reform of health care was to deal with the high costs of medical treatment and difficulties in seeking medical advice, and to respond to changes in the disease spectrum caused by the change in the structure of the population. On the one hand, although the problem of high treatment costs was relieved to some extent in general, disease was the top cause of poverty. On the other hand, the new reform of health care did not consider the factor of population flow, with its attendant special health risks and the external attributes of such risks. Therefore, people suffering from poverty caused by diseases and the health problems of migrant population are the population shortcomings. Furthermore, the health literacy of the whole population is becoming a barrier to the target of a Healthy China. Corresponding policies have been made to address these three problems, indicating the determination of the central government in dealing with the shortcomings of health. But the effects of such policies were not as good as we expected. Therefore, great attention should be given to these problems during the period of the 13th Five-Year Plan, and the existing policy ideas must be revised.

2.1 Poverty Caused by Diseases

Despite the improvements to the social security system and the level of guarantee in our country, medical expenditures in the case of major diseases are still a major course of poverty. According to the Poverty Reduction Office of the State Council, by the end of 2014, the impoverished population of China was 70.71 million, including 2.4 million patients suffering from serious and major diseases and 9.6 million patients suffering from chronic diseases. In 2015, the impoverished population of China was 55.75 million. The number of people suffering from poverty due to diseases was 8.385 million, accounting for 44.1% of the registered impoverished population. In Jiangxi, Sichuan, and Hubei, the ratio of poverty caused by diseases and disabilities was nearly 60%, and diseases have become the number one cause of poverty.[3]

Corresponding policies have been formulated to deal with the vicious circle of poverty, including major disease insurance, medical assistance, and temporary assistance. Based on this, the National Health and Family Planning Commission, the Poverty Reduction Office of the State Council, and the Ministry of Civil Affairs jointly launched the Health Poverty Reduction program and issued the *Guiding Opinions on Implementing the Health Poverty Reduction Program* in 2016. To deal with poverty due to diseases, the major measures undertaken to benefit the impoverished population are to improve the level of guarantees and system integration, classify the impoverished population suffering from major diseases and chronic diseases in rural areas for treatment, and implement a post-payment system for the impoverished population in rural areas at the county level. For impoverished regions, the countermeasure is to strengthen the systems of health care service in those regions, implement one-to-one assistance among the three classes of hospitals and the county-level hospitals in key counties under the national poverty reduction plan, uniformly promote the reform of the drug and health care system in impoverished regions, make greater efforts to control chronic diseases, infectious diseases, and local diseases, and strengthen the work related to the health of children and women in impoverished regions, so as to deepen the patriotic health campaign in those regions.

Under the guidance of this document, in 2017, the *Notice on Conducting the Family Doctor Contracting Services for Chronic Diseases of the Impoverished Population in A Good Way*, the *Notice on Further Improving the Effective Linkage between Medical Assistance and Major Disease Insurances for Urban and Rural Residents*, the *Working Plan for the Post-Payment System for Hospitalized Impoverished Patients in Rural Areas*, and the *Working Plan for the Special Treatment of Major Diseases of the Rural Population* were issued. The contents of these documents were the refined contents of the *Guiding Opinions on Implementing the Program for Health Poverty Reduction*.

---

3 "Special News Press of the National Health and Family Planning Commission for Typical Local Experiences of Health Poverty Reduction," http://www.china.com.cn/zhibo/2017 -05/17/content_40817541.htm.

The above documents have improved the access to medical services to some extent among the impoverished population and areas, but some problems related to the vicious circle of poverty have not yet been resolved. These problems include the following: (1) In terms of the design of the content of health care insurance, the precondition of the guarantee under major disease insurance is within the scope of the policy. Therefore, the costs of the treatment of major diseases that can be reimbursed through insurance only accounts for 40% to 50% of the actual medical expenditures. (2) In terms of reimbursement procedures, although the medical cost could be settled after receiving treatment at the county level, the medical expenditure in different health care insurance regions must also be prepaid by patients, and some serious and complicated diseases cannot be treated at county-level hospitals; therefore, many patients have to borrow money for treatment. (3) The objects of the health poverty reduction program are normally members of the impoverished population, but since most rural people are economically vulnerable, the cost of treating a major disease would confront a normal family with economic difficulties. (4) If any family member developed a major disease, the cost of traveling to cities for treatment, the cost of living during treatment, and the lost income of the other family members taking care of the patient would not be affordable by rural families, which is a major cause of poverty.

Among the above four problems, to resolve the second one, the provincial integration of health care insurance and cross-province settlement have been promoted, and this problem has been relieved to some extent. However, for the other three problems, no further policy has been drawn up. For the three poverty problems, more support could be given to the economically vulnerable groups in terms of social security and a network of social support. First of all, we should further intensify the reform of the reimbursement system of health care insurance so as to establish a nationwide medical assistance circulation fund to prepay expenditures in the treatment of major diseases for members of the impoverished population. Second, we should integrate the fund so that the tasks involved in health poverty reduction can be done more efficiently by supplying the farmers with ordinary incomes to prevent patients' families from becoming poor again before receiving remedies. Finally, we need to establish a network of social support based on communities, and in particular, to deal with the nursing problem for patients suffering from major diseases in the form of government support and mutual assistance in rural areas.

2.2 *Health Problems of the Migrant Population*

Most of the financing responsibilities for health services in China have rested on local governments, and the planning of health service resources often begins with the assumption that the native population is the object of attention. The migrant population is thus unable to access medical guarantees and public health services with the same ease as natives. To deal with the health problems of a population always in movement, under the guidance of the central government's goal to equalize public services, five ministries and commissions, including the National Health and Family Planning Commission, issued the *Guiding Opinions on Providing Basic Health and Family Planning Services for the Population That Is Always in Movement* as early as 2014, requiring that basic public health services in urban areas should cover all of the resident population and that governments should establish a mechanism to ensure equal access to basic public health and family planning services for those members of the population who are always in movement by 2020. In 2016, the *Action Plan of Health Education and Promotion for those Members of the Population Who Are Always in Movement (2016–2020)* was issued. As an extension of the previous document, this plan required that health education be strengthened for three key groups, namely, the new generation of migrant workers (who were born in the 1980s), women, and children who are always in movement. In 2017, the *13th Five-Year Health and Family Planning Service Management Plan for the Population That is Always in Movement* was issued; it continued to emphasize the need to extend coverage for basic public health services over that population.

Based on the implementation performance of the above policies, they were not promoted effectively because local governments did not place great importance on them. However, the more important aspect is not the promotion of these policies, but the fact that basic public health services are designed mainly for the elderly, for pregnant women and new mothers, and for children and patients with mental disorders in order to provide them with health management, which is not a suitable approach to handling the disease risks of most of the population that is always in movement. At present, this portion of the population is made up of migrant workers who are doing physical work. They face risks to their health from two directions.

The first is the risk of occupational diseases. Pneumoconiosis caused by dust pollution is the most hazardous occupational disease. The latest official data available at present is contained in the *National Occupational Disease Report in 2014*, issued by the Chinese Center for Disease Control and Prevention. According to this report, the number of cases of pneumoconiosis reported in 2014 was 27,000, accounting for nearly 90% of all reported occupational diseases. Other prominent risks are chronic occupation toxicity (benzene poisoning) and occupational tumors. These three occupational diseases account for 95% of all occupational diseases. According to estimates by researchers and social organizations in related fields, the actual number is far higher than the number of cases that have been reported.[4] The features common to these three diseases are that they are all chronic occupational diseases, that patients may lose their capacity for working and face long-term heavy burdens, and that it is very difficult to hold employers responsible.

Second, there are infectious diseases related to lifestyles, especially sexually infectious diseases. Among migrant workers, it is common to see temporary couples or one person with several sexual partners. Therefore, the possibility of being infected with a venereal disease is high, and during their movements, migrant workers may bring venereal diseases back to their hometown or other places, leading to an enormous spread of sexually infectious diseases. According to the data in the *China Health and Family Planning Statistical Yearbook 2017*, syphilis and gonorrhea were among the top five infectious diseases in 2016 in terms of rate of incidence. According to developments in previous years, of the type A and type B infectious diseases, infectious diseases related to environmental conditions witnessed a significant reduction; infectious diseases related to lifestyles, such as viral hepatitis, did not see any reduction; and the incidence rates of gonorrhea, syphilis, and AIDS conspicuously increased. This means that sexually infectious diseases are becoming the major infectious diseases, and the increase in the risk of such diseases is closely related to population movement.

In general, the population in motion, especially migrant workers, is a vulnerable group. On the one hand, the overall health system planning is not carried out from the perspective of the flowing population; and on the other hand, we are still focusing on establishing the responsibility of business owners for the occupational diseases of migrant workers, considering it as a labor issue instead of a social issue. Therefore, occupational disease patients may not be able to protect their rights and interests, get the compensation they deserve, or afford expensive medical treatment. Take pneumoconiosis, for instance: at present, most of the treatments for migrant workers suffering from this disease are provided by public service organizations. Such treatments are weak and unstable, and are post-treatments. As the major labor force in their families, once they get pneumoconiosis, migrant workers could lose their ability to work forever, and their families would be trapped by poverty.

In fact, the occupational diseases of migrant workers have been a common social problem for a long time. Surveys on the quantity, treatments, and living conditions of this group are limited, however. In terms of other health issues related to population flow, such as sexually infectious diseases, we still do not have access to detailed and comprehensive surveys and evaluations.

---

4   According to the prevailing data on the Internet, the number of pneumoconiosis patients is 6 million.

To reduce the health risks of the flowing population, we must change our labor perspective to a social perspective and plan medical and health resources based on the permanent resident population, but not the registered population. We should relieve the health issues of the flowing population through various ways, such as medical guarantees, public health programs, and labor protection plans. For example, in addition to improving the medical guarantee for major occupational diseases, we shall consider covering pneumoconiosis, benzene poisoning, and occupational tumors under the major public health program. Meanwhile, we shall consider the flowing population as important objects of intervention for basic public health services to conduct reproductive health management. In addition, we need to supervise the working conditions of migrant workers and improve their living conditions to prevent the breakout of major infectious diseases.

2.3 Health Literacy Issues

In 2016, the Central Committee of the CPC and the State Council issued the *Planning Outline for a Healthy China 2030*, requiring planning from the perspective of overall national health and proposing the strategic topic of the common construction and sharing of the health of the whole population. To establish a healthy China, in addition to reforming the health and medical system on the supply side, we need to improve the health literacy of people on the demand side. Health literacy means the ability of an individual to obtain and understand health information and use such information to maintain and improve personal health. As living standards for urban and rural residents improve, we have paid more and more attention to our health problems. However, at present, the problem is that there is a major conflict between our improved consciousness of the health of the population and low health literacy.

On the one hand, an insufficient amount of knowledge regarding health leads to poor consciousness of prevention, and would directly increase the risk of diseases and influence the health of residents. On the other hand, with an insufficient knowledge of health problems, patients would be more easily seduced by false advertisements. At present, there are a lot of false and extensive advertisements made by some private medical institutions and health product manufacturers for their services and products. These advertisements have been amplified by search engines and have become the major channels for patients seeking medical knowledge. Such a situation may seriously damage the economic benefits of patients, increase their anxiety, delay their treatment, and lead to mistreatment, harm the health of patients, or even endanger their lives. In 2016, the Wei Zexi incident was a typical example in this aspect. In addition, insufficient knowledge about health would further lead patients to have improper expectations from doctors and medical treatment, which is an important factor leading to the worsening relationship between doctors and patients.

To build a healthy China, we must improve the health literacy of the people. However, at present, most policies related to the improvement of the public's knowledge of health are made based on the perspective of health education, which may not have effective methods but only forms. Therefore, we need to identify the causes from other perspectives and respond accordingly.

First of all, from the perspective of family doctors, as the gatekeepers of health, the roles of family doctor teams include the following: (1) Family doctors should provide the contracting families with health education and consultation to help them establish a correct outlook on their health. (2) Family doctors should help the contracting families resolve some basic and common health problems. (3) Family doctors could complete the initial diagnosis of diseases, to ensure an orderly sequence of treatment. Therefore, family doctor teams are the core constructors for the improvement of health literacy among the people. However, just as this author described in reports in the previous years, a competitive family doctor system is far from being established, and family doctors have not worked as the gatekeepers of health; rather, their role in health education has been limited.

Second, supervision of the industry was in chaos and lacked authoritative and effective information disclosure channels. Patients in western countries are able to obtain knowledge regarding their health from the official medical system as well as from various social organizations. Such organizations include patient mutual assistance and support organizations, doctor associations, and various charities and foundations. Independent doctor associations and patient organizations have played an important role in spreading correct knowledge regarding health; on the one hand, doctors' associations could become the most authoritative publishers of knowledge about health publishers, while on the other hand, patient organizations established under professional guidance could become vehicles for people to acquire correct knowledge about health. Furthermore, these organizations are important vehicles for internal and external supervisions, which may significantly improve the efficiency of supervision over the medical industry and make up for insufficient governmental supervision.

References

Zhu Minglai. "Analysis and Thinking of the Accurate Guarantee for Population Suffering from Poverty Due to Diseases." *China Labour and Social Security News*, September 27, 2016.

CHAPTER 7

Report on China's Public Safety Situation in 2017

Zhou Yandong[1] and Gong Zhigang[2]

Abstract

With the continuous improvement in and innovation of the three-dimensional prevention and control system of public safety, the overall situation of public safety in China has remained good. In 2017, the number of terrorist cases was kept at a low level, but the risks of violent terrorism still existed. A satisfactory situation was maintained in terms of personal safety, but property safety witnessed a new development, as the quantity of property crimes decreased but the overall value of the property involved increased. Smuggling crimes have been on the increase for several consecutive years. With the improvement in the prevention and control system of public safety and a mechanism for resolving diversified conflicts, the number of cases of public safety and civil disputes was significantly reduced, showing a reversed U curve. Economic crimes involving a large number of people, illegal criminal activities related to virtual currencies, pyramid selling crimes, and post-unit community safety hazards are the four new major trouble spots for the public safety prevention and control system in the new age. The report recommends improving the operations of public safety and the social order by clamping down on economic crimes involving a large number of people, strictly controlling the investment management of virtual currencies, preventing and controlling pyramid schemes, and improving the capacities for protecting the safety of post-unit communities.

Keywords

public safety – prevention and control system – social order

---

1   Zhou Yandong, lecturer and postgraduate supervisor of the School of Public Security, People's Public Security University of China, and research fellow of the Capital Social Safety Research Base.
2   Gong Zhigang, professor, doctoral supervisor, and dean of the School of Public Security, People's Public Security University of China.

© KONINKLIJKE BRILL NV, LEIDEN, 2022 | DOI:10.1163/9789004500723_008

REPORT ON CHINA'S PUBLIC SAFETY SITUATION IN 2017   133

In[3] 2017, in the Report to the 19th CPC National Congress, President Xi Jinping pointed out that the general aim of fully deepening the reform is to improve and develop socialism with Chinese characteristics, and to promote the modernization of the national governance system and its capacity. We need to create a pattern of social governance with joint construction, governance, and sharing. We should strengthen the construction of the social governance system; improve the social governance mechanism under the leadership of the party committee with government accountability, social cooperation, public participation, and legal guarantees; and improve the socialization, legislation, intelligence, and specialization of social governance. The construction of the prevention and control system of public safety should be accelerated to strike and punish various illegal criminal activities and protect the personal rights, property rights, and personality rights of the people.[4] In recent years, constant innovation and improvement of the three-dimensional prevention and control system of public safety have effectively improved the people's sense of safety, satisfaction, and gains and improved the overall situation of public safety in China. However, in the new age of socialism with Chinese characteristics, the major social conflict has become the conflict between the desire of the people for a better life, on the one hand, and on the other hand, imbalanced and insufficient development. The change in the nature of the social conflict has spawned new troubles and challenges for the public safety of our country.

1   General Conditions and Tendency of Public Safety in 2017

1.1   *A Good Situation Was Maintained in Terms of Personal Safety, and Property Safety Witnessed Reduced Cases and Increased Amounts*

According to the data issued by the National Bureau of Statistics, from 2010 to 2016, the number of the main types of criminal cases involving personal safety, such as killing, injuring, and robbery, that were recorded in public security organs was decreasing (see Figure 7.1). By comparing the data in 2016 with that in 2010, we can see that the number of criminal homicide cases decreased from 13,410 to 8,634, with a reduction of 35.62%; criminal injury cases diminished from 174,990 to 123,818, with a reduction of 29.24%; and criminal robbery

---

3   This article is a funding program: it is the staged achievement of the "Post-Unit Community Safety Crisis and Its Innovation to Governance" of the National Social Science Fund Youth Project (Project No. 16CSH011) and the "Research on Beijing's 'Village-to-Habitat' Community Safety Multi-governing Mechanism" of the Beijing Social Science Fund Youth Project (Project No. 15SHC038).

4   http://www.china.com.cn/cppcc/2017-10/18/content_41752399.htm.

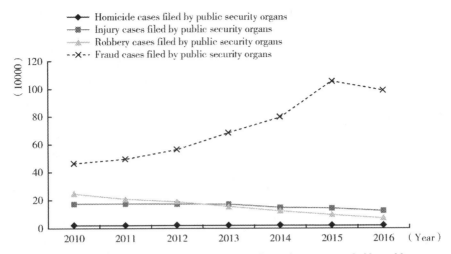

FIGURE 7.1 Number of Injury, Homicide, Robbery, and Fraud Cases Recorded by Public Security Organs, 2010–2016
SOURCE: ANNUAL DATA FROM THE NATIONAL BUREAU OF STATISTICS, HTTP://DATA.STATS.GOV.CN/EASYQUERY.HTM?CN=C01

cases decreased from 237,258 to 61,428, with a reduction of 74.11%. Personal safety is the fundamental kind of safety. The constant reduction of related data indicates that the prevention and control system of public safety has been improving and has achieved much and made a great contribution to protecting the personal safety of the public.

In recent years, the number of cases of fraud witnessed a rapid increase. In 2016, a new turning point occurred and there was a reduction in the number of cases filed for the first time from 1,049,841 in 2015 to 979,956 in 2016, a decrease of 6.66%. According to related statistics from public security organs, the downward trend in 2016 continued in 2017. It is worth noting that, despite the reduction of the number of the cases of fraud that were filed, the amount involved has been increasing. Indeed, the average amount of money involved in some major cases could be higher than 100 million yuan. In other words, cases of fraud displayed new features, such as a reduction in the total number of cases but an increase in the amount of money involved, and a reduction in the number of cases of minor fraud and an increase in the number of serious cases. In February 2017, the amount of money involved in loan frauds with fake gold that were filed in Tongguan, Shaanxi Province, reached more than 10 billion yuan, causing serious damage to the property safety of the public.

In addition, the government and society should pay close attention to the criminal cases of smuggling crimes, which have been increasing in recent years. From 2010 to 2016, the number of cases of smuggling increased from

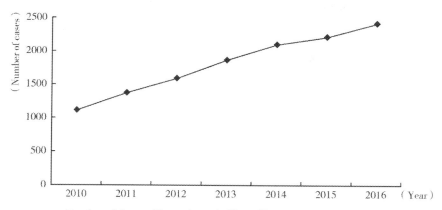

FIGURE 7.2 Number of Cases of Smuggling Filed by Public Security Organs, 2010–2016
SOURCE: ANNUAL DATA FROM THE NATIONAL BUREAU OF STATISTICS,
HTTP://DATA.STATS.GOV.CN/EASYQUERY.HTM?CN=C01

1,105 to 2,407 (see Figure 7.2), an increase of 117.8%. Although the number of cases of smuggling is smaller than other criminal cases, the amounts of money involved in these cases are huge. From January to September 2017, the number of cases of smuggling filed by customs offices nationwide was 2,601, surpassing the total number of those caught smuggling in 2016. The number of cases of smuggling involving taxation was 1,340, including 398 cases of smuggling agricultural products, with a total value of 6.48 billion yuan. The number of cases of smuggling finished oil products was 185, with a total value of 5.74 billion yuan. The number of the cases of smuggling filed for electronic products was 125, with a total value of 2.12 billion yuan.[5] If these smuggled products were to flow into the market and society, social stability and market integrity would be seriously endangered.

According to its analysis, the research group believes that the cases of smuggling that have occurred in our country in recent years display the following new features: (1) The cases were concentrated geographically. Under the influence of geographical environment and economic development, most cases of smuggling occurred in coastal areas. For example, the coastal areas in the east of China have regional features such as large-scale ports, more ships, and outstanding economic development, such as Guangdong, Fujian, and Shanghai. (2) Smuggling activities were well organized. Most smuggling activities have strict structures and a clear labor division, and the participants in such activities cooperate closely while playing their own roles. For

---

5 "In the First 9 Months of 2017, Customs Offices Solved 2,601 Smuggling Cases," *People's Daily*, November 6, 2017.

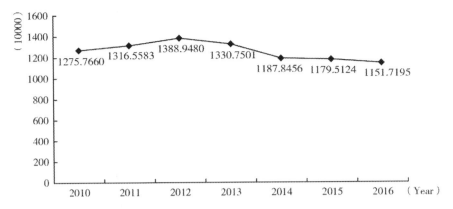

FIGURE 7.3 Number of Cases Regarding Public Safety Recorded by Public Security Organs, 2010–2016
SOURCE: ANNUAL DATA FROM THE NATIONAL BUREAU OF STATISTICS, HTTP://DATA.STATS.GOV.CN/EASYQUERY.HTM?CN=C01

example, in 2017, the Hangzhou Customs Office solved a case of the smuggling of refined oil products valued at 400 million yuan, and more than 20 criminal suspects were caught. Under the leadership of Xu from Wenzhou, the members of the smuggling group cooperated organically in transforming cargo ships into oil ships, purchasing refined oil products in international waters, and unloading and selling the products, showing features of organization. (3) Smuggling activities were well hidden. Rapidly developing network and information technologies have been used in smuggling activities, leading to innovations in criminal methods and effective means of concealment. For example, in the online overseas purchasing agent industry that has developed rapidly in recent years, a great number of purchasing activities are smuggling activities undertaken to avoid tariffs and the control of the customs offices. In such cases, it is very hard for the customs offices to collect evidence to arrest and punish the criminals. Meanwhile, the purchased products are traded through online channels, which helps to conceal the criminals' activity.

1.2 Cases of Public Safety and Dispute Mediation Witnessed Reversed U Curves

On September 19, 2017, during the national commendation conference for the comprehensive governance of public safety, President Xi Jinping issued new instructions and higher standards. He said that we should improve and innovate social governance to better resolve various issues in the society of our country to ensure the vitality and harmony of our society. He also emphasized that innovation is the enduring concern in the comprehensive governance of

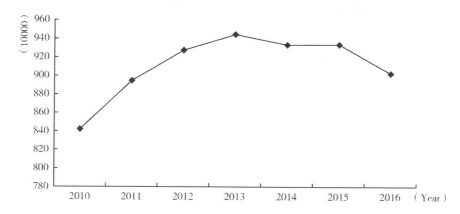

FIGURE 7.4 Number of Cases of Dispute Mediation, 2010–2016
SOURCE: ANNUAL DATA FROM THE NATIONAL BUREAU OF STATISTICS,
HTTP://DATA.STATS.GOV.CN/EASYQUERY.HTM?CN=C01

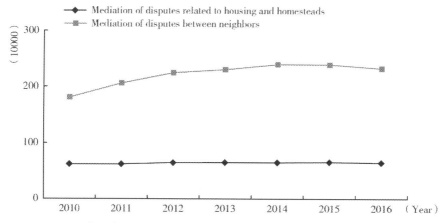

FIGURE 7.5 Number of Cases Requiring Mediation in Housing and Homestead Disputes, 2010–2016
SOURCE: ANNUAL DATA FROM THE NATIONAL BUREAU OF STATISTICS,
HTTP://DATA.STATS.GOV.CN/EASYQUERY.HTM?CN=C01

public safety. According to the statistics of the National Bureau of Statistics, after reaching a peak in 2012, the number of cases regarding public safety recorded by public security organs in our country has been decreasing for several consecutive years. The number in 2016 was reduced by 277,929 over that in 2015, a rate of reduction of 2.36% (see Figure 7.3). This is a notable achievement reached after the proposal of a three-dimensional prevention and control system of public safety made during the 18th CPC National Congress. In recent years, the acceleration and innovation of the construction of the three-dimensional prevention and control system of public safety have played an important role in improving the overall situation of public safety in our country, generally realizing the modernization of social governance and providing a fundamental guarantee for the long-term safety of the country and for the happy and peaceful lives of its people.

According to the National Bureau of Statistics, the number of the cases of dispute mediation also showed a reversed U curve in general (see Figure 7.4), just like that of cases regarding public security. The number of cases of dispute mediation reached a peak in 2013 at 9,439,439. After 2013, the number has decreased in general. In 2016, the number decreased by 312,000 from 2015's total, with a reduction of 3.34%. The number of cases of dispute mediation related to housing and homesteads as well as neighborly relationships, which had been increasing in recent years, witnessed a reduction in 2016 (see Figure 7.5) by 29,000 and 84,000, or 4.44% and 3.54%, respectively. The major reasons for such changes include the following: (1) The thorough intensification of the reform of the mechanism for diversified dispute mediation generated a profound-influence on the people, and the people's recognition of diversified dispute mediation channels has been improving. Besides judicial mediation, those mechanisms for diversified dispute mediation that have not been reflected in the data regarding mediation cases, such as the people's mediation and administrative mediation, played an outstanding role. Specifically, a boom in the various methods of resolving disputes, such as industry mediation, lawyer mediation, business arbitration, labor arbitration, and administrative adjudication, expanded the channels and ways to mediate conflicts and disputes.[6] (2) In recent years, the national government has issued some policies for improving the quality of the lives of the people, such as canceling the charges for applying for future housing fund loans, managing personnel files and transferring housing ownerships, and promoting the parallel development of the purchasing and renting of housing, which have played an important role in reducing the total number of cases of dispute mediation.

1.3 *The Number of Terrorist Cases Was Maintained at a Low Level, but the Risk of Violent Terrorism Remained High*

The *Counterterrorism Law of the People's Republic of China* came into effect on January 1, 2016, and has played an important role in securing national safety, public safety, and the safety of the lives and property of the people and in preventing terrorist activities. As shown in the data and news reports published by

---

6 Long Fei, "A Grand Picture for the Diversified Dispute Mediation Mechanism Is Forming," *People's Court Daily*, October 17, 2017.

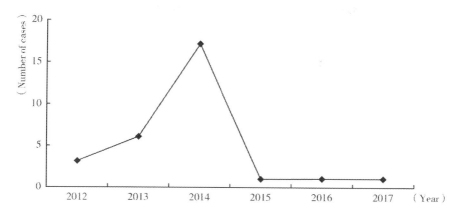

FIGURE 7.6 Number of Typical Terrorist Attacks in China, 2012–2017
SOURCE: THE NEWS REPORTS OF THE FOUR MAJOR PORTALS (SINA, NETEASE, SOHU, AND TENCENT)

the four major portals (Sina, NetEase, Sohu, and Tencent), the number of typical terrorist attacks in the past six years in our country showed an "inverted V" shape (see Figure 7.6). Since 2015, the Party and the government have actively cracked down on violent terrorist crimes to rapidly control the tendency of terrorist attacks, and many violent terrorist groups were brought under control at the beginning, providing a guarantee for the safety of the lives and property of the people. In the past three years (2015, 2016, and 2017), the number of cases of violent terrorism was maintained at one per year.[7] From this we can see that the general situation of anti-terrorism in our country is stable, but we still need to note the serious risk of violent terrorist acts. With the improvement in the three-dimensional prevention and control system of public safety in our country, various forces of control have been combined organically to keep the number of terrorist attacks at a low level.

However, in contrast to the relatively stable anti-terrorist situation in China, many countries in the world have been severely hit by terrorism. In 2017, many places in the world were hit by terrorist attacks and the world was covered by the shadow of terrorism. If 2016 was the International Year of Terrorism, 2017 was the Year of Instability. A lot of terrorist attacks occurred during this year,

---

[7] We need to point out that the blue book *Analysis and Forecast of China's Social Conditions* (*2017*) was published in Beijing on December 21, 2016, and the special report "Report on the Analysis of the Situation of Public Safety in China in 2016" pointed out that no terrorist attack had occurred in 2016 before that date. However, on December 28, 2016, the party committee compound of Moyu County of Xinjiang Province was attacked by terrorists, leading to one death and three injuries. This incident caused serious damage to the lives and property of the country and the people. Therefore, we shall correct the number of terrorist attacks in 2016.

TABLE 7.1   List of Typical International Terrorist Attacks in 2017

Year	Terrorist attack	Place
2017	1.1 Istanbul terrorist attack	Nightclub (entertainment place)
	3.22 London Houses of Parliament terrorist attack	Government
	4.3 St. Petersburg subway terrorist attack	Subway
	4.7 Stockholm truck terrorist attack	Street
	4.9 St. George's Chapel in Cairo and the Basilica of San Marco terrorist attack	Church
	4.20 Terrorist attack on the Champs Élysées in Paris	Business street
	5.22 Manchester stadium terrorist attack	Stadium
	5.31 Exploratory terrorist attack in the embassy region in Kabul in Afghanistan (auto bomb)	Embassy area
	6.5 Melbourne terrorist attack	Apartment
	6.7 Violent terrorist attack in Teheran (Iran's parliament and the Holy Shrine of Imam Khomeini)	Government and graveyard of religious people
	6.18 Finsbury Park terrorist attack in London	Park
	7.14 The Temple Mount terrorist attack in Jerusalem	Religious site
	8.13 Wagadugu terrorist attack	Restaurant
	8.17 Terrorist attack in Catalonian Square in Barcelona	Square
	8.18 Truck attack in Barcelona	Road
	9.18 Violent incident of terrorism in Chaman in Pakistan	National boundary
	9.18 Terrorist attack in Nigeria	Assistance distribution point
	9.21 Terrorist attack in Kashmir, India	Road (government fleet)
	9.21 Terrorist attack in Edmonton, Canada	Road
	10.1 Terrorist attack in Las Vegas, United States	Square
	10.18 Terrorist attack in the eastern region of Afghanistan	Government
	10.22 Terrorist attack in the western region of Egypt	Desert area
	10.31 Terrorist attack in New York, United States	Road
	11.5 Terrorist attack in a church in Texas, United States	Church

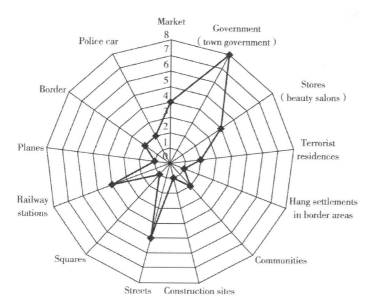

FIGURE 7.7 Sites and Frequencies of Typical Terrorist Attacks in China, 2012–2017
SOURCE: NEWS REPORTS OF THE FOUR MAJOR PORTALS (SINA, NETEASE, SOHU, AND TENCENT)

including the attacks in Istanbul, in the Houses of Parliament in London, and in the subway of St. Petersburg, as well as the truck attack in Stockholm (see Table 7.1), causing many casualties and huge economic losses. These attacks reflected the new features and tendencies of terrorist attacks, such as the expanding scope, increasing methods, and updated techniques. The expansion of international terrorism has posed a serious threat to our national safety.

According to an analysis by a research group of violent terrorist incidents from 2012 to 2016 in the "Report on the Analysis of the Situation of Public Safety in China in 2016," although most terrorist attacks occurred in government areas, police stations, streets, railway stations, markets, and residences of terrorists (see Figure 7.7), other places with a low rate of incidence and weak protection would be subject to terrorist attacks. Accordingly, the research group made an assumption and a forecast: terrorists would attack semi-public areas or private areas with weak protection instead of public areas with strong protection.[8] Unfortunately, our forecast was validated by the terrorist attacks in

---

8   Zhou Yandong and Gong Zhigang, "Report on the Analysis of the Situation of Public Safety in China in 2016," in Li Peilin, Chen Guangjin, and Zhang Yi, *Analysis and Forecast of China's Social Conditions* (2017), Social Sciences Academic Press (China), 2016.

2017. On February 14, 2017, a terrorist attack occurred in a community in Pishan County in Xinjiang Province, in which five innocent people were killed and ten were injured by terrorists with knifes. From the point of view of the location of the crime, this attack indicated a change. In the Report to the 19th CPC National Congress, President Xi Jinping proposed to accelerate the construction of the prevention and control system of public safety. To do this, we need to continue to improve our control over high-risk places (such as governments, police stations, streets, railway stations, markets, and terrorist residences), and further strengthen the construction of the prevention and control systems for semi-public and private areas with weak protection, as well as to conduct and implement specific prevention tactics and arrangements to further reduce the hazards of violent terrorist attacks. In addition, for those sites that have been attacked by terrorists in foreign countries but have not been hit in China (embassy areas, stadiums, and subway stations), the government and public should be very careful, and the related government departments and social organizations should accelerate the construction of the prevention and control system of public safety in those areas. In general, the problem of terrorism is still not a cause of optimism, and this has been manifested in the features of militarization, socialization of members, and internationalization of organizational development. Terrorist attacks have been launched in many forms, such as lone-wolf form, family form, multi-point form, or a combination of group gathering and assassination attack, and violent terrorist activities have become more secret, random, violent, and destructive. Therefore, our country is facing a severe challenge in its anti-terrorism activities.

In addition, according to the analysis, the research group recommended that specific research and analyses should be carried out for the key cities and areas under threat of possible terrorist attacks, and close attention should be paid to following up and investigating the cases in order to ferret out the core people behind those attacks. In this way, we can not only prevent similar terrorist attacks from reoccurring in the same areas, but we can also frighten and strike down other terrorist groups. We should eliminate terrorist attacks in the bud and take the initiative in public safety protection.

2 Four New Trouble Spots for Public Safety in the New Age

With the rapid development of online finances in China, the investment methods of the public have become more diversified, flexible, and convenient, but this situation has led to many new risks and troubles, such as the outstanding problem of social instability caused by economic cases involving huge numbers of people and the increase in the risk of illegal activities related to virtual currencies. In addition, in underdeveloped regions and cities, the three-dimensional prevention and control system of public safety has not been established yet, and the desire on the part of the people for a better life can hardly be met. Therefore, pyramid selling activities and risks of post-unit community safety in cities have become serious hazards to public safety.

2.1 Economic Cases Involving a Large Number of People Have Caused Outstanding Issues of Social Stability

The rapid development of online finance has injected new energy into the economic and social development of our country, and has also led to new financial risks. In recent years, the number of economic crimes involving a large number of people through online financial platforms has witnessed a rapid increase, and those cases often involve an immense area, a large number of people, and a large amount of funds. Once such a crime is exposed, mass disturbances may easily be caused, generating a negative influence on the overall stability of public safety. According to analysis of the data from the Ministry of Public Security in 2017, the number of illegal fund-raising cases has seen a year-on-year decrease, continuing a satisfactory trend from 2016. However, the number of cases to be solved is still large, and some major crimes still occur occasionally. At the same time, most of the illegal fund-raising cases investigated by public security organs have entered into stages of concentrated review and execution, and claims made by the public for their losses in benefits may easily cause social conflicts. Contrary to illegal fund-raising cases, the number of cases of online pyramid selling cases has increased, and some extra-serious cases have occurred, such as the Wuxing Currency Case and the Shanxinhui Case, and vicious incidents like the people involved in containing local governments or in the mass march on Beijing have occurred.

2.2 The Risk of Illegal Activities Related to Virtual Currencies Has Increased

With the development of Internet finance, investment with virtual currencies has become a popular way of investment, and is quite popular among the investors; this has been considered the New World for investment. However, since the transactions and services of investment with virtual currencies are completed online, it is harder for investors to identify the objects of investment. At the same time, since the subjects of investment of virtual currencies are not constrained by time and location during the investment process, it is more difficult for Internet finance supervisors to oversee the transactions, which may easily lead to damaging the legitimate rights and interests of investors.

In crimes related to virtual currencies, financial innovations may be used as stunts and static benefits (currency appreciation) or dynamic benefits (getting benefits by recruiting subordinates) as bait to attract the public to participate. In 2016, 159 such cases were filed in China, involving more than 60 currencies and about 1 million people.[9] In 2017, the virtual currencies represented by Bitcoin attracted great attention from society. Bitcoin uses the Dark Web as a payment tool, but there are many illegal activities on the Dark Web. Such illegal activities include some traditional financial crimes like money laundering and financial frauds, as well as many new crimes with virtual currencies as tools. In some foreign countries, virtual currencies have even been used to provide terrorists with funds.

2.3 New Trouble Caused by Pyramid Selling Activities

Pyramid selling activities have persisted in China ever since they were introduced into China in the 1990s; this has become a crime that may seriously damage the economic order of the market and endanger personal safety in our country. Such cases involve a large number of people and immense areas, and it is difficult to investigate them due to a high degree of concealment. According to the data of the Ministry of Public Security, since 2010, more than 30,000 cases of pyramid selling were solved that involved tens of thousands of people. However, cases of pyramid selling have new features now. In the past, most pyramid selling activities were economic crimes that often led to family break-ups without causing death. However, in recent years, many pyramid selling activities have caused family break-ups and deaths, seriously influencing the safety and stability of society—for example, the Li Wenxing case, which drew much attention from society in 2017. Therefore, the Ministry of Public Security has made more efforts to crack down on those activities. From January to September 2017, the public security organs nationwide filed and investigated 5,983 cases of pyramid selling with a year-on-year increase of 118.5%, involving a total value of 30 billion yuan.[10]

2.4 Post-Unit Community Safety Hazards Continue to Arise

Post-unit communities are those communities for which the original units would not provide management services after bankruptcy during the social and economic transformation; they have features of both traditional units and modern communities. The collapse of the traditional unit mechanism of governance, the weakening or disappearance of governance resources, and the adaptive disorder in obtaining autonomy of the community have caused

---

9   "Public Security Organs Investigated More Than 150 Cases of Pyramid Selling Involving Over 60 Virtual Currencies in 2016," www.huanqiu.com, December 28, 2016.

10   "Public Security Organs Filed 5,983 Cases of Pyramid Selling This Year," www.people.com .cn, September 30, 2017.

post-unit communities to face serious safety dilemmas, and have even posed a threat to the safety and stability of the whole society.

First of all, post-unit communities in China are facing many issues, such as a chaotic community environment, reduced community authority, and a shortage of funds for modern protection and control measures. (1) Post-unit communities often have a poor environment and many illegal structures. (2) A lot of the responsibilities of the original unit communities were transferred to police stations and departments of civil affairs, reducing the dependence of community residents on neighborhood committees and weakening the authority of neighborhood committees in those communities. (3) The combination of unclear definitions of management responsibilities and insufficient funds has led to a serious shortage of modern prevention and control systems in post-unit communities. These issues pose great challenges to the public safety of old communities.

Second, there are still many issues surrounding the safety governance of post-unit communities. President Xi Jinping promoted the community governance to a new level in the Report to the 19th CPC National Congress. He pointed out that we should strengthen the construction of the community governance system, move the focus of community governance to the grassroots, make full use of the function of social organizations, and bring about a positive interaction among governmental governance, community mediation, and resident autonomy.[11] Despite the notable achievements we have reached in community policy practices, there are still problems to be solved. (1) The pattern of making local changes without changing the whole situation has reduced the integration of police work with the grassroots. Moving the focus of social governance to the grassroots is the basic requirement for social governance work in the new age. However, at present, police stations are directed by many superior departments due to the weak system of information sharing, and the repeated heavy workload and disruption of assignments have seriously wasted the energy of the police force and reduced the effects of police work in post-unit communities. (2) The governance subjects and accountability for the safety governance of post-unit communities are not clearly defined. Community police officers, security guards, flowing population managers, and public safety volunteers have not formed a system of governance of community safety with one subject as the leader or point of support, due to their different superiors and financial sources. (3) A separation between community police work and the daily lives of the residents has decreased the level of governance of community safety. Commonly, community police do not have

---

11   Record, "The Report to the 19th CPC National Congress Delivered by President Xi Jinping," www.xinhuanet.com, October 18, 2017.

sufficient ability to provide services to better the lives of the people, and this weakens the residents' appreciation for police work and weakens the connection between community police and the public.

3 Future Prospects

In the new age, the major social conflict of our country has changed. This change in the social conflict is both an opportunity and a challenge for the governance of public safety. Some former public safety issues may be reduced gradually during this process, but imbalance and insufficient development would generate new issues of public safety. For this purpose, we recommend promoting prevention and control work for public safety in the following areas.

3.1 Cracking Down on Economic Crimes Involving a Large Number of People to Ensure Social Stability and Order

Economic crimes involving a large number of people have certain characteristics, such as a broad geographical scope, a huge number of people, and a huge amount of funds, that may generate a negative material influence on the socialist market's economic order and social stability. We need to establish a prevention and control system to prevent such crimes according to actual conditions so as to maintain social stability.

First of all, we need to establish an early warning system for economic crimes involving a large number of people that integrates governments, judicial organs, and financial administrations. Under the early warning system, related departments should devote their attention to the reform and development of the financial market of our country, to identifying the risk of economic crimes involving a large number of people in the financial sector, and to conducting a scientific assessment. Then, plans should be drawn up according to the results of the assessment for related risks, so as to deal with such economic crimes proactively. Second, we should improve the system of supervision and control for the financial market. At present, the private investment sector is developing rapidly. Private investments are often made through online platforms that are beyond traditional supervision, leading to system bugs in financial supervision, including insufficient information disclosure and unclear transaction prices. Given this situation, the People's Bank of China should lead other financial supervisory departments to improve the supervisory system for the financial market and effectively reduce the space for such economic crimes.[12] Third, we should improve the legal framework for financial

---

12   Deng Jianpeng, "Special Control Measures for Internet Finance," *China Finance*, 2016(16).

investment. To fully bring into play the rule of law in the financial investment sector, we need to further summarize and improve the laws and regulations for private investment. In particular, the scope, operation rules, and supervisory subjects of Internet finance should be clearly defined in laws and regulations. Legal guidance should be actively issued for private investments to ensure financial order. Fourth, we should ensure stability and complete the treatment in an appropriate way. If any economic crime involving a large number of people occurs, public security organs should conduct a stable evaluation of that crime and investigate the regions and groups benefiting from the case. After processing the relevant information, a treatment plan should be devised that anticipates the various conditions that may occur and thus ensures that the plan can be executed successfully, so as to solve problems in a legal way.

3.2 Establishing Strict Control over Investments with Virtual Currencies

Virtual currencies have witnessed rapid development throughout the world; they have been recognized by more and more countries, and they have attracted a great number of investors. In recent years, a lot of illegal activities and crimes related to virtual currencies have occurred in our country. Virtual currencies have become a new growth point for crime, posing a serious challenge to the safety of our country's financial system. We need to learn how to manage the current developmental situation of virtual currencies and strengthen supervision and control over crimes related to them.

First of all, we need to strengthen the related legislation. In general, Internet finance in China has been lagging behind developed countries, and thus the legal systems regulating finance are not complete. In the case of virtual currency investment, which is an important part of Internet finance, we are facing the problem of an incomplete system of supervision in China. For this purpose, we have absorbed the experiences of developed countries in controlling virtual currencies. The competent authorities need to understand the risks and challenges in terms of virtual currency investment during the process of supervision, so as to strictly control illegal investments and operations using virtual currencies through laws and regulations. Second, we should strengthen supervision and control over the operations of virtual currencies. To adapt to the rapid development of virtual currencies, supervisors should adjust their supervisory rules and indicators as soon as possible to guide the positive development of investments via virtual currencies under the laws and regulations regarding administrative permission, market access, and operational standards. In this way, the risks related to investments via virtual currencies could be prevented or controlled in advance. At the same time, traditional institutional supervision can hardly keep up with the rapid development of virtual currency finance. Therefore, the departments of financial supervision should change their institutional supervision into business supervision. Third, we should carry out international cooperation to conduct financial anti-terrorism activities in an efficient way. Virtual currencies, represented by Bitcoin, have developed into an international currency. It is easy for criminals to commit crimes using one virtual currency in different countries through the Internet. In recent years, serious terrorist crimes in which virtual currencies were used to finance terrorist activities have occurred throughout the world. This means that it is difficult for any single country to effectively crack down on crimes aided by virtual currencies. We need to strengthen cooperation with the judicial organs and financial management departments of other countries, as well as the international criminal police organization, to jointly crack down on cross-border virtual currency crimes.[13]

3.3 *Prevent and Control Crimes Involving Pyramid Selling*

In recent years, crimes involving pyramid selling have been increasing. They have not only damaged the social and economic order, but they have also threatened the safety of people's lives and property. In July 2017, the Li Wenxing case, which shocked the whole country, occurred. We hereby make the following recommendations according to the causes and features of crimes involving pyramid schemes.

First of all, we need to establish a scientific system of punishment for this type of crime. A scientific system of punishment has an important role to play in cracking down on and preventing illegal activities and crimes. According to the Criminal Law of our country, the punishment for crimes involving pyramid selling is that anyone organizing or leading activities regarding pyramid selling is subject to imprisonment for fewer than five years and a fine, while those who have committed serious crimes of this type are subject to imprisonment for more than five years and a fine. This system of punishment is not able to meet the needs of cracking down on new crimes involving pyramid selling under the new situation in terms of range and types. Therefore, the construction of a system of punishment for activities regarding pyramid selling should be further strengthened.[14] Second, we should improve the connection between administrative law enforcement and criminal justice. The improvement of the connection between administrative law enforcement and criminal justice might make it possible to break down the information asymmetry related to crimes involving pyramid selling, which could provide powerful support

---

13 Li Jing and Li Miaoyan, "Empirical Study on the Actual Development of Virtual Currencies—Survey Report Based on Bitcoin Users," *Henan Social Sciences*, 2017(4).

14 Chen Xuyan, "Research on the Risks Related to Criminal Laws for Internet Crowd Funding," *Study & Exploration*, 2017(9).

in cracking down on such of crimes. Close cooperation between public security organs and administrative departments in cracking down on activities regarding pyramid selling could make full use of the administrative capacities of industry and commerce in collecting leads, and could also take advantage of public security organs in the investigation of crimes involving pyramid selling. A joint force should be created by integrating the law enforcement resources of both parties, establishing a platform for information sharing, standardizing the procedures for transferring clues, and building a regular meeting system for the competent departments and leaders, so as to effectively crack down on crimes involving pyramid selling.[15] Finally, we should create a social atmosphere that will prevent pyramid selling among the people. The activities of pyramid selling are concealed in the daily lives of the people. The public are the victims of those activities, but they are also a source of information enabling public security organs to crack down on those kinds of crimes. Therefore, party committees and governments at all levels should fully motivate the people to crack down on crimes involving pyramid selling and create an atmosphere that will deter people from participating in them, in order to eliminate the space for those activities.

3.4 Improving the Capacity for Prevention to Ensure the Safety of Post-Unit Communities

Regarding the safety risks and trouble faced by post-unit communities, we need to update the governance capacity and innovate the mechanism of governance based on analysis of the composition, governance structure, and practical operations of the communities to ensure their safety and stability.

First of all, we should improve the environment of post-unit communities to establish clean and orderly communities. A clean and tidy community not only helps to improve the sense of happiness among the people and reduce safety hazards, but it also frightens away criminals. To do this, we should (1) set up highly visible signs on the perimeter of the community to make it a safe community; (2) keep the community clean and repair any damaged public facilities promptly; and (3) establish a complete modern security network integrating electric monitoring, a system of access to doors, and a system of patrolling.[16] Second, we should establish an integrated discussion system among the business departments of public security organs. When assigning tasks to grassroots police stations, the business departments should eliminate the business barriers and information chimneys for tasks of the same type in order to prevent

---

15   Chen Xingliang, "Crime of Organizing and Leading Activities of Pyramid Selling: Nature and Boundary," *Tribune of Political Science and Law*, 2016(2).

16   Zhou Yandong, "Image, Power and Relationship: New Framework of Safety Governance for 'Village-to-Habitat' Communities," *Social Construction*, 2017(4).

the duplication of tasks and improve the efficiency of police work, so that community police officers have enough energy and time to complete their work. Furthermore, we should create a pattern of common governance with a different sequence under the leadership of community police officers. We should institute a new pattern of social governance that fosters interaction among official governance, social adjustment, and resident autonomy, and eliminate the dilemma that everyone wants to control the work but no one is able to do it well. We recommend establishing a system in which community police officers guide and evaluate the performance of security guards, the managers of the population that is always in movement, and public safety volunteers in order to fully take on the leading role of community police officers in post-unit community safety management and establish a system of community safety governance with clear responsibilities and multiple participants.[17] At the same time, honors and titles (such as peace guardian and mediation commissioner) should be given to elites and activists in the communities (such as retired cadres, lawyers, and teachers) to improve the people's sense of honor and enable them to participate in the safety governance of post-unit communities. Finally, we should improve the capacity of community police officers to make the lives of residents better. We should integrate the provision of services to improve the lives of people in community police work by setting up space in police work rooms for discussion and communication, providing simple service facilities such as microwave ovens and water heaters, conducting police experience activities and home safety inspections, improving the appeal of community police work to residents, and promoting interaction and communication between the police and the people to identify more sources of information regarding community safety risks, to improve the capacity for safety controls over post-unit communities, and to provide a solid safety net for the construction of world-class cities with harmonious living standards.

17   Zhou Yandong and Cao Lulu, "From Living Community to a New Life Community—Reflection on Community Safety Governance," *Journal of Xiangtan University* (Philosophy and Social Sciences), 2015(6).

CHAPTER 8

Survey Report on the Quality of Social Development in China in a New Era

Cui Yan[1]

Abstract

With China's rapid economic development, we have made notable achievements in the quality of people's lives and significantly improved the level of social security. An active and positive social consciousness has been formed in the public, and the core socialist values have enjoyed popular support from the people. Inclusion in social life has been improving, and the public has highly recognized the values of social fairness and justice. Various forms of social discrimination caused by institutional or non-institutional factors are disappearing. The public's satisfaction with the work of government departments has been significantly improved.

Keywords

social quality – social and economic guarantee – social cohesion – inclusion in social life – social empowerment

In the Report to the 19th CPC National Congress, President Xi Jinping pointed out that the major social conflict or challenge of our country has changed from ensuring material demands to the need for a better life, a change that represents the huge progress we have made since the implementation of the policy of reform and opening-up. The change in the major social conflict may reflect the characteristics of the stages of our country's economic and social development. The transformation of the reform blueprint in the future from economic construction to comprehensive economic and social development has indicated that our country is steadily moving forward toward the vision of a high-quality society. Regarding the topic of the quality of social development, there is wide discussion in the academic field. In the late 1990s, EU scholars

---

1 Cui Yan, assistant research fellow of the Institute of Sociology, Chinese Academy of Social Sciences.

© KONINKLIJKE BRILL NV, LEIDEN, 2022 | DOI:10.1163/9789004500723_009

proposed the theory of social quality, which includes establishing a system of indicators to evaluate social quality, using statistics to measure the social qualities of different countries and carry out an international comparison. In recent years, with the advance of research on social quality, scholars in the field of social development have paid more and more attention to the issue of the quality of development, and the definition of development has been changed from economic growth alone to include comprehensive social development.

To measure the quality of social development in our country at present, from June to November 2017 the Institute of Sociology of the Chinese Academy of Social Sciences carried out the Chinese Social Survey, which specified social quality as the research topic (CSS2017). This survey covered more than 150 counties (county-level cities and districts) and over 600 village (neighborhood) committees in 31 provinces, autonomous regions, and municipalities nationwide. In the survey, the assessment of the quality of social development was conducted in four areas, namely, social and economic guarantees, social cohesion, inclusion in social life, and social empowerment.

1 Social and Economic Guarantees in China

1.1 *The Income of Urban and Rural Residents Has Been Improving Steadily and the Income Gap Has Been Narrowing*

One of the important criteria of evaluation for the construction of a moderately prosperous society in all respects, the basic realization of socialist modernization, and the improvement of the people's sense of earning is the income level of urban and rural residents. According to the results of the survey, the income of urban and rural residents in our country has been improving steadily year by year. Middle- and low-income families in particular have witnessed a notable growth in their income. To be specific, the average annual per capita income of urban and rural residents in 2016 was 16,825.0 yuan. According to data from the past ten years, the per capita income of urban and rural residents has been increasing steadily year by year. Compared to the data ten years ago, or in 2007, the average annual per capita income of urban and rural residents witnessed a nominal growth of 204.5%. If we classify households into five equal groups according to the average annual per capita income of urban and rural residents, then the average annual per capita income of urban and rural residents in low-income households (the bottom 20% of households ranked by income) in 2016 was 1,964.0 yuan, increasing by 138.7% over that for 2007. The average annual per capita income of urban and rural residents of middle- and low-income households was 5,995.9 yuan in 2016, an increase of 120.3% over that in 2007 (see Table 8.1). At the same time, the data also

SURVEY REPORT ON THE QUALITY OF SOCIAL DEVELOPMENT IN CHINA 153

TABLE 8.1   Classification of Interviewed Households by Per Capita Annual Income

Type	2007 per capita annual income (yuan)	2010 per capita annual income (yuan)	2012 per capita annual income (yuan)	2014 per capita annual income (yuan)	2016 per capita annual income (yuan)
Low-income households	822.7871	1345.9	1587.7	1921.5	1964.0
Mid- to low-income households	2721.625	5138.3	5739.5	5884.3	5995.9
Mid-income households	4876.682	8961.7	10172.2	10330.3	10790.2
High- to mid-income households	8395.642	15030.8	16514.7	17141.5	18226.6
High-income households	24454.21	45320.7	43197.5	43485.9	47830.5
Total	8226.067	14629	15558.2	15981.1	16825.0

reflected that, despite the gap between low-income households and high-income households, the gap has been narrowing. For example, ten years ago (in 2007), the ratio of average income in the high-income group to that in the low-income group was 29.72; the proportion declined to 27.21 five years ago (in 2012), and it decreased to 24.35 in 2016. The Report to the 19th CPC National Congress pointed out that we should expand the scale of the middle-income class, increase the income of low-income residents, adjust incomes that are too high, and cancel illegal incomes. We must gradually realize a common measure of wealth for the whole population and further narrow the income gap to improve social fairness and justice, maintain long-term social stability, and improve the quality of social development comprehensively.

1.2   The Housing Conditions of Urban and Rural Residents Improved Further

With the rapid social and economic development and growing urbanization in China, the housing conditions of urban and rural residents have been significantly improved. According to the data in 2017, the rate of homeownership of the interviewed residents was 95.50%, increasing by 0.1 percentage points over 2015 (95.40%). The rate of homeownership of urban residents was 92.06%, increasing by 0.9 percentage points over 2015 (91.2%). 20.8% of the households have more than one house, increasing by 1.1 percentage points over 2015 (19.7%). In 2017, the per capita building area of the interviewed residents was 47.67 square meters. The self-evaluated value of the first property of residents was 378,400 yuan/household in 2017, and the number was 314,000 yuan in 2015. In 2017, the average self-evaluated value of the property of urban residents was 573,600 yuan/household, and it was 467,000 yuan/household in 2015. The number for rural residents was 248,900 yuan/household in 2017, and it was 207,000 yuan/household in 2015.

With the constant regulation of the real estate market and the steady construction of state-supported indemnificatory housing by the national government, as well as the establishment of a long-term mechanism to stabilize the real estate market and restrict the rapid increase of property prices, the real estate market has entered a stage of stable development, the guarantee mechanism in the housing field has been improved gradually, and the multiple-level demands of the people for housing have been gradually met.

1.3 A System of Social Security Covering Urban and Rural Residents Has Been Established, but the Level of Social Security Should Be Further Improved

Since the 18th National Congress of the CPC, the system of social security has been further improved, and a system of social security covering urban and rural residents has been established. According to statistics, in the first three quarters of 2017, social security coverage was expanded constantly and the benefits provided by the system increased steadily. As of the end of September, the participants in the basic pension insurance, basic health care insurance, unemployment insurance, work-related insurance, and maternity insurance numbered 905 million, 1,129 million, 186 million, 224 million, and 190 million, respectively.[2]

As for the attitude of the public toward the system of social security, 73.9% of the interviewees expressed their opinion that the provision of social security is the basic responsibility of the government, and it should not be borne by the public; 63.2% of them thought that the current level of social security was too low to guarantee their benefits; and 46.8% of them were unsatisfied with the social security provided by the government and expressed some negative opinions of the work of the government departments.

To improve the quality of social development, we should make the whole population participate in the system of social security and further improve the

---

2 "An Additional 10.97 Million People Nationwide Found Jobs in Urban Areas from January to September," http://www.gov.cn/shuju/2017-11/02/content_5236287.htm.

SURVEY REPORT ON THE QUALITY OF SOCIAL DEVELOPMENT IN CHINA   155

TABLE 8.2   Attitudes of Interviewees toward the System of Social Security

Type	Completely disagree	Disagree	Agree	Completely agree	It's hard to say
Provision of social security is the responsibility of the government, and it should not be borne by the public	5.1	19.0	36.3	37.6	2.0
The current level of social security is too low to guarantee our benefits	6.5	27.9	37.8	25.4	2.3
The social security provided by the government is so bad that I have some negative opinions on the work of the government	13.7	36.8	30.5	16.3	2.7

system of basic insurance, on the one hand; on the other hand, we should gradually establish a system of social security that can match the level of economic development and meet the demands of the public to make sure that social security is able to provide a bottom-line guarantee in real terms.

1.4   *The Employment Situation Was Basically Stable, but the Quality of Employment Needs to Be Improved*

In 2017, the situation of employment in our country remained basically stable. According to the data published by the National Bureau of Statistics, from January to September 2017, the number of new workers in urban areas nationwide reached 10.97 million, with a year-on-year increase of 300, and the target of 11 million for the whole year was basically achieved. Since 2017, the urban registered unemployment rate of the country has been maintained at 4% and below, and was 3.95% at the end of the 3rd quarter.[3]

---

3   "An Additional 10.97 Million People Nationwide Found Jobs in Urban Areas from January to September," http://www.gov.cn/shuju/2017-11/02/content_5236287.htm.

According to the survey data, when asking about the possibility of being unemployed within the next six months, in 2013, about 21.2% non-agricultural workers said that it was quite possible or possible; in 2015, 23.3% of non-agricultural workers held that opinion; in 2017, the number was 26.0%, with an obvious increase over the previous years. At the same time, 39.50% of the interviewees expressed the opinion that, in the past year, one of the outstanding problems was that their family members had no jobs, were unemployed, or did not have stable work. Meanwhile, according to the data in 2017, 24.54% of the interviewees believed that the issue of unemployment was a major social issue for our country.

Furthermore, in terms of employment contracts, 33.7% of the interviewees had signed fixed-term employment contracts, 10.9% of the interviewees had signed non-fixed-term employment contracts, and 43.7% of the interviewees had not signed any employment contract with employers. From this, we can see that the proportion of interviewees working without a signed employment contract was relatively high.

The data on employment equity indicate that employment equity in China was relatively good, but some interviewees had negative opinions about it. For example, 15.2% of the interviewees expressed the opinion that the distribution of salaries was very unfair or unfair; 12.3% of the interviewees thought that the distribution of the workload was very unfair or unfair; and another 11% of the interviewees said that there were unfair conditions when recruiting or firing employees (see Table 8.3).

TABLE 8.3   The Sense of Employment Equity Expressed by Interviewees

Type	Very unfair	Unfair	Normal	Fair	Very fair	It's hard to say
Is your current unit/company fair in hiring employees?	3.6	7.5	25.3	40.1	18.7	4.8
Is your current unit/company fair in firing employees?	3.9	7.3	20.4	38.2	18.9	11.2
Is your current unit/company fair in assigning jobs?	3.2	6.7	22.8	44.1	17.4	5.8
Is your current unit/company fair in distributing the workload?	4.0	8.3	23.3	42.5	16.9	5.0

TABLE 8.3   The Sense of Employment Equity Expressed by Interviewees (*cont.*)

Type	Very unfair	Unfair	Normal	Fair	Very fair	It's hard to say
Is your current unit/company fair in distributing salaries?	4.9	10.3	22.3	39.6	17.9	5.0
Is your current unit/company fair in promoting or demoting employees?	3.7	6.4	22.7	36.0	14.7	16.5

At the same time, we should note that improvement in the quality of employment was the new target proposed in the 19th CPC National Congress Report, on the grounds that against the background of the economic transformation and updating of our country, we should not only ensure a stable situation of employment but we should also improve the quality of employment, so as to fulfill the desire of the people for a better life through employment and to guarantee and improve the quality of people's lives and maintain the stability and sustainable development of the society through active employment policies.

2   Social Cohesion in China

An important indicator for evaluating the quality of social development is whether a society has a high degree of cohesion. A positive value consensus of the public in terms of values is an important criterion for determining whether a society has cohesion. In the 19th CPC National Congress Report, President Xi Jinping emphasized that we should cultivate and practice the socialist core values and integrate those values into all aspects of social development.[4] Therefore, the establishment of a system of social core values is not only an important part of socialist ideological and ethical progress, but it is also an important part of the system of national governance. The establishment of a system of core values with a powerful emotional appeal is closely related to the improvement of the national capacity for governance.

---

4   http://news.xinhuanet.com/politics/2017-10/18/c_1121820800.htm.

2.1 *The Public Had a Positive Response to Moral and Legal Construction and Fully Accepted the Socialist Core Values*

In this survey, we measured several aspects, including social cohesion and the public acceptance of values. First of all, according to the data in 2017, 60.7% of the interviewees believed that the current level of morals in our society was relatively high or very high. However, in the survey in 2015, this number was 56.7%. By comparison, the number in 2017 increased by 4 percentage points. From this we can see that, with the advancement of cultural construction and the strengthening of the main social theme, the moral level of the public has improved significantly. At the same time, according to the data for 2017, 70.58% of interviewees thought that the level of the public's compliance with the laws of our country was relatively high or very high, increasing by nearly 7 percentage points over that in 2015 (63.7%). Since the 18th National Congress of the CPC, obvious progress has been made in comprehensively promoting the law-based governance of the country, and the legal sense of the public has been improving. With the improvement of laws, regulations, and justice, the construction of a society based on law-abiding behavior has seen leapfrog development.

In the survey, we measured the public's national identity and patriotic enthusiasm. Among the public, 89.1% of interviewees were proud of the achievements made by our country. From this we can see that the public highly recognized the construction achievements made by the country, and that they are highly confident that there is a promising future for a great rejuvenation of the Chinese nation in the new age of socialism with Chinese characteristics. Meanwhile, the public are confident about the Chinese way, wisdom, and plan. The confidence of the public in the Party and the National Government reflected the improvement in the quality of the lives of the people and of social welfare, their expectation that the Chinese society will enter the new age of quality improvement, and the solid social foundations, backed by public opinion, of the realization of the Two Century Goals and the Chinese Dream of the great rejuvenation of the Chinese nation.

Establishing correct values among the public and promoting major social themes are important ways to improve social cohesion and an internal requirement for improving the quality of social development. In the survey, we measured the public's preference for social benefits, honesty, and social norms. According to the data, 62.5% of the interviewees were inclined to accept the values, with a preference for social benefits, and only 37.5% of the interviewees expressed the opinion that personal benefits were more important than social benefits. In the survey in 2015, 40.8% of the interviewees thought that personal benefits were more important than social benefits. By comparison, the number in 2017 decreased by about 3 percentage points. With respect to the values of honesty and a preference for social norms, 72.5% of the interviewees expressed their acceptance. In the survey in 2015, the ratio was 67.4%. By comparison, the number in 2017 increased by 5.1 percentage points. Fundamentally, social development is the comprehensive development of the people. The route toward the improvement of social cohesion was also a route toward the improvement of the positive values of the public. With the constant improvement in the system of socialist core values, the core values have gradually generated a high consensus among the public and have become the criteria for moral judgment for each social member as well as the rules of action for each one. This also means that we have made obvious achievements in improving social morality and cohesion.

2.2 With the Construction of a Credible Society, the Public Has High Interpersonal Trust as Well as Trust in the Governments, Courts, Hospitals, and Banks

Establishing a credible society to improve the public's level of trust is one of the important dimensions in improving the overall quality of social development. In this review, we measured and analyzed the degree of trust in our society in terms of interpersonal trust and trust in various organizations.

First of all, the public has a relatively high degree of trust in other people. For the circle of acquaintances composed of relatives, friends, neighbors, and colleagues, 80% to 90% of the interviewees expressed an attitude of trust. For professional technical personnel, such as teachers and doctors, most interviewees said that they trust them very much or relatively much. A total of 84.8% of the interviewees said that they trust teachers, and 80.4% of them said that they trust doctors. With respect to cadres of the party and government and law enforcement personnel, more than 60% of the interviewees showed their trust, and the ratio of trust in police was as high as 75.2%. However, the data also reflected that the public's degree of trust in enterprise bosses and online store owners was normal; 53.3% of the interviewees said that they trust company bosses but only 38.4% said they trust online store owners. Finally, according to the data, the public's degree of trust in strangers was low: 62.5% of the interviewees said that they did not trust strangers at all, and 28.5% of them said that they did not trust strangers beyond a small degree. The total proportion exceeded 90% (see Table 8.4).

Second, as for the public's trust in organizations and institutions, the public expressed a high degree of trust in government departments. In fact, 90.8%

TABLE 8.4 Degrees of Interpersonal Trust among Interviewees

Type	1. Do not trust at all	2. Very little trust	3. Trust	4. Trust to a high degree	8. It's hard to say
Degree of trust in relatives	0.8	2.4	22.7	73.7	0.4
Degree of trust in friends	1.5	13.4	56.8	26.5	1.8
Degree of trust in neighbors	2.2	15.9	59.1	21.0	1.8
Degree of trust in colleagues	1.6	13.7	63.5	18.6	2.6
Degree of trust in police	5.2	17.0	46.2	29.0	2.6
Degree of trust in judges	5.6	17.2	46.6	26.0	4.5
Degree of trust in cadres of the party and government	9.0	24.4	44.8	18.5	3.4
Degree of trust in enterprise bosses	8.1	33.1	43.2	10.1	5.5
Degree of trust in online store owners	13.3	42.9	33.6	4.8	5.3
Degree of trust in teachers	2.9	10.9	53.6	31.2	1.4
Degree of trust in doctors	3.4	15.0	54.5	25.9	1.3
Degree of trust in strangers	62.5	28.5	6.5	1.1	1.4

of the interviewees expressed their trust in the central government, 73.1% of them said they trust district and county governments, and 66.7% said they trust township governments. From this, we can see that with the improvement in the capacity for national governance, governments at all levels have steadily promoted the construction of a system of governance and the modernization of the capacity for governance, realizing the gradual organic integration of the country, market, and society. The work in terms of balancing economic development and social development, streamlining the relationship between the government and society, understanding the positioning of the government in national governance, and improving the service awareness and capacity of governments has been improved significantly, and a high degree of recognition was obtained from the people.

Meanwhile, we can also see that the public's degree of trust in grassroots governments was significantly lower than that in the central government. In the process of comprehensively deepening the reform, grassroots governments are the executors of the final stage of the implementation of policies and the core of the modernization of the grassroots governance. Despite the obvious improvement in the service capacity of township governments, some grassroots governments still have an insufficient degree of service consciousness, a weak service capacity, and a low service efficiency. Only if the service capacity and system of the grassroots governments is improved in real terms can we actually implement the measures made by the central government to guarantee and improve the quality of the lives of the people, realize the innovation and modernization of social governance, maintain social harmony and stability, and improve the public's degree of trust in the grassroots government departments.

As for the degree of the public's trust in other organizations, 79.8% of the interviewees trusted hospitals, 76.3% of them trusted courts, 70% of them trusted group organizations and units for laborers, youth, and women, 66.8% trusted the news media, 63.8% trusted charity organizations, and only 47.3% trusted the Internet. According to the trust of the public in financial institutions, 88% of the interviewees said that they trust banks, and 57.2% of them trust insurance companies (see Table 8.5).

A high degree of social trust is the precondition for the advancement of social construction and cultural and moral construction. Only by promoting the active recognition and spontaneous internalization of the socialist core values among the public can we create an honest and friendly social atmosphere and improve the quality of social development.

TABLE 8.5   Degrees of Trust in Organizations and Institutions Expressed by Interviewees

Type	1. Do not trust at all	2. Very little trust	3. Trust	4. Trust to a high degree	8. It's hard to say
Degree of trust in the central government	1.9	5.8	34.0	56.8	1.6
Degree of trust in county governments	5.0	19.1	44.1	29.0	2.7
Degree of trust in township governments	8.7	21.9	42.6	24.1	2.8
Degree of trust in group organizations for laborers, youth, and women	5.0	17.2	50.2	19.8	7.8
Degree of trust in working units/ organizations/ companies	3.5	16.5	53.6	16.4	10.1
Degree of trust in charity organizations	6.8	23.7	46.2	17.6	5.7
Degree of trust in the news media	4.4	24.9	49.1	17.7	3.8
Degree of trust in the Internet	8.2	36.2	39.5	7.8	8.4
Degree of trust in banks	1.6	8.5	55.2	32.8	1.9
Degree of trust in insurance companies	9.6	28.5	42.2	15.0	4.8
Degree of trust in hospitals	3.4	15.4	55.1	24.7	1.4
Degree of trust in courts	4.5	14.4	50.9	25.4	4.8

SURVEY REPORT ON THE QUALITY OF SOCIAL DEVELOPMENT IN CHINA   163

3   Social Inclusion in China

A society with high-quality development must have a high degree of inclusion. We should eliminate social exclusion to the largest extent possible by building mutual trust mechanisms among members of society and among social organizations and by reforming discriminatory social systems, and we should reduce misunderstanding among members of society by improving the modernity of the public and social tolerance. Only in this way can we better plan social forces as a whole, balance social benefits, adjust social relationships, standardize social activities, and reduce internal social friction. In the survey, we measured several aspects, such as social discrimination and social tolerance, to assess the degree of social inclusion in our society.

3.1   *At Present, the Public Expressed a Moderate Degree of Social Tolerance, and a Certain Amount of Exclusion toward Some Vulnerable Groups*

One of the important dimensions in evaluating the quality of social development is whether the comprehensive development of the people can be realized, and what comprehensive development of the members of a society means is improvement in the modernity of the citizens. In terms of social inclusion, the modernity of the public can be reflected in its degree of tolerance and acceptance of groups that are different from them, especially the vulnerable groups.

According to the data, the degree of the public's tolerance and acceptance of some groups is moderate. For example, 85.1% of the interviewees could not accept homosexuality; 69.9% of them could not accept AIDS patients; 52.5% of them could not accept premarital cohabitation; 46% of them could not accept beggars; 40.6% of them could not accept convicted criminals who have been released after serving the full term of their sentence; and 39.5% of them could not accept groups with different religious beliefs (see Table 8.6).

A society with inclusive development must be a tolerant and open society. From the data we can see that the Chinese public's degree of tolerance at present is moderate, and the public expressed a strong attitude of exclusion toward some vulnerable groups. To realize inclusive social development, we should further improve the modernity of the citizens and eliminate social misunderstanding of vulnerable groups so that the public accepts those who are different with a more open mind.

TABLE 8.6   Degrees of Social Acceptance Expressed by Interviewees

Type	1. Very unacceptable	2. Unacceptable	3. Acceptable	4. Very acceptable
Premarital cohabitation	28.0	24.5	39.0	8.5
Homosexuality	66.1	19.0	12.1	2.7
Beggars	17.9	28.1	45.6	8.4
Convicted criminals who have been released after serving the full term of a sentence	15.4	25.2	53.1	6.4
People with different religious beliefs	19.7	19.8	48.5	12.0
AIDS patients	47.4	22.5	26.2	4.0

3.2   *At Present, Social Discrimination in Our Country Is Not Prevalent, Thus Laying a Good Foundation for the Inclusive Development of the Society*

To realize inclusive development, institutional and non-institutional social discrimination must be eliminated. The existence of social discrimination will be bound to affect the realization of social fairness and justice. The realization of social fairness and justice is the precondition for the fulfillment of the desire of the people for a better life. According to the actual conditions of our country, various kinds of institutional and non-institutional social discrimination are not so prevalent. Among the interviewees, 9% felt that they were discriminated against due to their family background and social network, 6% felt they were discriminated against due to their age, 5.8% due to their education background, and 4.4% due to their jobs. Only 3% of the interviewees felt they were discriminated against due to their household register. At present, gender discrimination, racial discrimination, and religious discrimination are not outstanding in our society, and the proportions of the interviewees who were discriminated due to the above three factors are 2.4%, 0.9%, and 0.3%, respectively (see Table 8.7). The low degree of social discrimination has provided an excellent social atmosphere and foundation for social inclusion and the inclusive development of the society, representing the achievements made by the Party and government in reforming the system of household registration and the educational system and reflecting the public's recognition of the fair environment at present.

SURVEY REPORT ON THE QUALITY OF SOCIAL DEVELOPMENT IN CHINA

TABLE 8.7 Opinions of Interviewees on Degrees of Social Discrimination

Type	0 No	1 Yes
Received unfair treatment due to age	94.0	6.0
Received unfair treatment due to gender	97.6	2.4
Received unfair treatment due to personality	96.9	3.1
Received unfair treatment due to race/ethnic group	99.1	0.9
Received unfair treatment due to looks and physical condition	97.1	2.9
Received unfair treatment due to household register	97.0	3.0
Received unfair treatment due to religion	99.7	0.3
Received unfair treatment due to educational background	94.2	5.8
Received unfair treatment due to political views	98.3	1.7
Received unfair treatment due to jobs	95.6	4.4
Received unfair treatment due to family background and social network	91.0	9.0

3.3 Great Importance Has Been Attached to Social Fairness and Justice, and the Sense of Social Fairness and Justice Has Been Improving

Finally, a society with inclusive development must have a high degree of fairness. In recent years, the Party and the government have gradually implemented various reform measures, significantly promoting the equalization of the distribution of economic and social resources, and social fairness has seen great improvement. The data also showed that the public's overall sense of fairness in China is strong. In the survey, we analyzed the dimensions of social fairness. According to our data, 70% of the interviewees thought that society was fair or relatively fair in general. At the same time, we analyzed several dimensions of social fairness in detail, including economic fairness, political fairness, educational fairness, and social security fairness. In terms of economic fairness, 59.1% of the interviewees thought that current jobs and employment opportunities were fair or relatively fair; 50.3% of them thought the distribution of wealth and income was fair or relatively fair; and 45.7% of the interviewees thought that rights, interests, and treatments in urban and rural areas were fair or relatively fair. In terms of political fairness, 65.2% of the interviewees thought that the political rights enjoyed by the citizens were fair or relatively fair, and 66.8% of the interviewees thought that the current justice and law enforcement entities were fair or relatively fair. In terms of educational fairness, 76.5% of the interviewees believed that the college entrance examination system was fair or relatively fair. In terms of social security fairness, 73.3%

166   CUI

TABLE 8.8   Interviewees' Sense of Fairness

Type	1. Very unfair	2. Unfair	3. Fair	4. Very fair	8. It's hard to say
Fairness of college entrance examination system	6.5	13.6	49.4	27.1	3.4
Fairness of the political rights enjoyed by citizens	8.2	23.7	49.7	15.5	2.9
Fairness of justice and law enforcement	6.3	22.4	50.7	16.1	4.4
Fairness of the public health care system	5.4	19.5	57.6	15.7	1.9
Fairness of jobs and employment opportunities	7.2	29.1	49.3	9.8	4.6
Fairness of wealth and income distribution	14.0	32.6	41.7	8.6	3.1
Fairness of pensions and other social security benefits	8.5	23.0	52.4	14.4	1.8
Fairness of rights and treatments between urban and rural areas	16.3	35.6	38.7	7.0	2.4
General social fairness	4.4	23.9	61.8	8.2	1.7

of the interviewees thought that the public social health care system at present was fair or relatively fair, and 66.8% of the interviewees thought that social pensions as well as other social guarantee benefits were fair or relatively fair (see Table 8.8).

By comparing the data regarding the public's sense of social fairness in 2017 with that in 2015, we found that the public's sense of fairness in various fields has significantly improved. For example, in the data of 2015, 68% of interviewees thought that the society was fair or relatively fair in general, which was higher than the rate in 2017 by two percentage points. Considering individual fields, the recognition of fairness in the fields of jobs and employment opportunities improved notably by 10 percentage points. In 2017, the recognition of social fairness in terms of wealth and income distribution and justice and law enforcement increased significantly by 9 percentage points. Meanwhile, in terms of social security benefits, such as pensions, and the political rights actually enjoyed by citizens, the public's recognition of fairness also witnessed

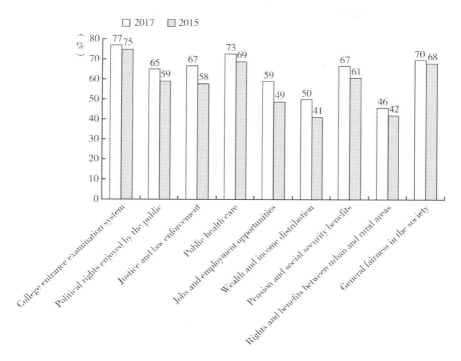

FIGURE 8.1 Comparisons between Interviewees in 2015 and in 2017 in Terms of Their Sense of Social Fairness

a great increase of 6 percentage points (see Figure 8.9). Therefore, with the spread of the reform throughout the society, the social environment has become more fair and just. The achievements of the reform and development can benefit all the people in a more sufficient and fair way. The social fairness perceived by the public has witnessed an obvious increase, and social justice has also increased significantly, providing an excellent social atmosphere for the inclusive development of the society.

4   The Social Empowerment of China

To realize the high degree of development of a society, every member is required to have a sufficient activity that enables participation in social life and political life. At the same time, a high-quality society should be able to provide each and every member with abundant social resources and a wide range of channels of participation in order to improve their activity in participating in the social and political life of the country.

In terms of social empowerment in the survey, we mainly measured the opinions of the public on government departments, the degree of the public's participation in social groups, the degree of participation in social life, the degree of participation in political activities, and the public's efficiency of participation.

4.1 The Public Had a Positive Response to the Work of Local Government Departments

In terms of the overall evaluation of the work of local government departments, 69.1% of the interviewees thought that the work of local governments was done well or relatively well. In terms of individual tasks, 76.2% of the interviewees thought that local governments did well in cracking down on criminals and maintaining public safety; 71.8% of the interviewees thought that local governments did well in providing health and medical services; 68.8% of them thought that local governments did well in providing quality educational resources and ensuring educational equity; and 67.4% of them thought that local governments did well in providing the public with social security (see Table 8.9). Since the 18th National Congress of the CPC, President Xi Jinping proposed a target to improve the public's sense of gain. Governments at all levels have implemented various policies to benefit the people in order to protect the fundamental benefits of the public and improve their living standards, gaining excellent effects. In particular, by deepening the reform, the governments have made the public feel the active changes in terms of public security, health care, education, and social security, and the response to the work of local government departments has improved significantly.

TABLE 8.9 Opinions of Interviewees Regarding the Work of Government Departments

Type	1. Very good	2. Good	3. Bad	4. Very bad	8. I don't know	Rank
Provision of health and medical services	16.2	55.6	20.9	5.1	2.2	2
Provision of social security to the public	13.4	54.0	24.4	5.5	2.8	4
Environmental protection and pollution control	16.0	48.0	25.0	9.7	1.3	6
Guaranteeing political rights of citizens	12.4	54.0	23.0	6.3	4.3	5

SURVEY REPORT ON THE QUALITY OF SOCIAL DEVELOPMENT IN CHINA 169

TABLE 8.9 Opinions of Interviewees Regarding the Work of Government (*cont.*)

Type	1. Very good	2. Good	3. Bad	4. Very bad	8. I don't know	Rank
Cracking down on crimes and maintaining public safety	18.8	57.4	16.7	5.4	1.7	1
To be honest in performing government duties, and fighting against corruption	13.2	42.8	25.8	11.3	6.9	11
Acting according to the law and enforcing the law fairly	13.2	49.6	24.8	7.6	4.7	7
Developing the economy to increase the income of the people	12.9	47.2	29.0	7.7	3.3	8
Improving employment and providing more jobs	11.9	45.3	29.8	7.8	5.2	10
Disclosing government information and improving the transparency of government work	12.6	43.7	27.6	9.6	6.5	9
Promptly responding to the requests of the public	11.5	43.1	29.9	10.6	5.0	12
Providing quality educational resources and ensuring educational equity	14.9	53.9	21.6	6.0	3.7	3
The work of local governments in general	11.4	57.7	23.8	5.6	1.5	

4.2 The Actual Degree of Participation of the Public in Social Groups Was Low, and Willingness to Participate Was Insufficient

According to the data, the degree of participation of the public in social groups was low: 3.8% of the interviewees participated in religious groups; 3.0% of them participated in family clan associations; 5.1% of them participated in associations of natives; 21.3% of them participated in alumni associations (groups); 5.5% of them participated in recreation and sports clubs; 5.0% of them participated in volunteer organizations, owner committees, and environmental protection organizations; and 4.6% of them participated in chambers of commerce, rural cooperative organizations, professional academies, and industrial associations.

The willingness of the public to participate in social groups was not high. Only 4.0% of the interviewees wanted to participate in religious groups; 5.3% of them wanted to participate in family clan associations; 10.4% of them wanted to participate in associations of natives; 19.9% of them wanted to participate in alumni associations (groups); 11.7% of them wanted to participate in recreation and sports clubs; 17.7% of them wanted to participate in volunteer organizations, owner committees, and environmental protection organizations; and 12.2% of them wanted to participate in chambers of commerce, rural cooperative organizations, professional academies, and industrial associations (see Table 8.10).

TABLE 8.10   Participation of Interviewees in Social Groups

In what groups are you participating at present?	Yes	No	In what groups do you want to participate in the future?	Yes	No
Religious groups	3.8	96.2	Religious groups	4.0	96.0
Family clan associations	3.0	97.0	Family clan associations	5.3	74.7
Associations of natives	5.1	94.9	Associations of natives	10.4	89.6
Alumni associations (groups)	21.3	78.7	Alumni associations (groups)	19.9	80.1
Fellowship organizations (recreation and sports groups)	5.5	94.5	Fellowship organizations (recreation and sports groups)	11.7	88.3
Civil associations (volunteer associations, owner committees, environmental protection organizations)	5.0	95.0	Civil associations (volunteer associations, owner committees, environmental protection organizations)	17.7	82.3

SURVEY REPORT ON THE QUALITY OF SOCIAL DEVELOPMENT IN CHINA   171

TABLE 8.10   Participation of Interviewees in Social Groups (*cont.*)

In what groups are you participating at present?	Yes	No	In what groups do you want to participate in the future?	Yes	No
Professional organizations (chambers of commerce, rural cooperative organizations, professional societies, and industrial associations)	4.6	95.4	Professional organizations (chambers of commerce, rural cooperative organizations, professional societies, and industrial associations)	12.2	87.8

Social organizations are an important part of social governance and one of the important indicators in evaluating the quality of social development. However, according to the data, the participation of the public in social organizations in China has been moderate, a situation that may have multiple causes. On the one hand, the capacities of social organizations are insufficient, and the capacity for the arrangement of social resources is weak. This may be why the willingness of the public to participate in social organizations is insufficient. On the other hand, the difference between the willingness to participate and the actual conditions of participation also indicated insufficient channels for participation by the public. Therefore, only by providing resources and spaces for the development of social organizations through policies can we effectively improve the rate of participation and the willingness of the public, and further improve self-management and self-service on the part of society.

4.3   *The Degree of the Public's Actual Social Participation and Political Participation Is Low, but Their Willingness to Do So Is High*

The public's social participation is low. In the past two years, only 7.9% of the interviewees participated in a discussion of major decisions in their villages/communities/companies; 8.5% of them participated in the volunteer activities organized by governments, companies, or schools; and 14.3% of them participated in social activities for the public good, such as cleaning the environment and providing voluntary support to the elderly, the disabled, and hospital patients. Of course, in terms of willingness to participate, a great proportion of the public expressed that they would like to participate in social activities for public welfare. For example, 55.9% of the interviewees declared that they would like to participate in discussing major decisions in their villages, communities, and companies; 61.6% of them would like to participate in the voluntary activities organized by governments, companies, or schools; and 74.4% of them would like to participate in social activities for the public good.

In terms of political participation at present, 33.1% of the interviewees said they participated in the election activities of their village (neighborhood) committees. At the same time, 11.5% of the participants said that they participated in the election of their representatives to the national congress in their districts or counties in the past five years. Besides election activities, other forms of political participation in society were not common. Only 7.1% of the interviewees said that they expressed their opinions to government departments, and 1.3% of the interviewees said they participated in online/offline activities regarding the protection of collective legal rights. Meanwhile, in terms of willingness to take part in political activities, most of the public would like to participate in political life through institutional forms such as elections. For example, 71.1% of the interviewees would like to participate in the election activities of their village (neighborhood) committees, and 65.1% of the interviewees would like to participate in the election of their representatives to the national congress at the district or county level. In addition to participating in elections, 45.4% of the interviewees would like to express their opinions to government departments (see Table 8.11).

TABLE 8.11 Social Participation and Political Participation among Interviewees
Unit: %

Participation	1 Yes	0 No	Willingness to participate	Want to participate	Do not want to participate
Discuss political issues with others	12.5	87.5	Would you like to discuss political issues with others or with online friends?	34.2	65.8
Express their opinions regarding social issues to newspapers, radios, or online forums	2.3	97.7	Would you like to express your opinions regarding social issues to newspapers, radios, or online forums?	34.9	65.1

SURVEY REPORT ON THE QUALITY OF SOCIAL DEVELOPMENT IN CHINA 173

TABLE 8.11 Social Participation and Political Participation among Interviewees (*cont.*)
Unit: %

Participation	1 Yes	0 No	Willingness to participate	Want to participate	Do not want to participate
Express opinions to government departments	7.1	92.9	Would you like to express your opinions to government departments?	45.5	54.6
Participate in the voluntary activities organized by the government/ companies/schools	8.5	91.5	Would you like to participate in the voluntary activities organized by the government/ companies/ schools?	61.6	38.4
Participate in the elections of village (neighborhood) committees	33.1	66.9	Would you like to participate in the elections of your village (neighborhood) committees?	71.1	28.9
Participate in the discussion of major decisions in villages, communities, or companies	7.9	92.1	Would you like to participate in the discussion of major decisions in villages, communities, or companies?	55.9	44.1
Participate in voluntary activities for social welfare, such as voluntary blood donations, voluntary environmental cleaning, and providing voluntary support to the elderly, the disabled, and hospital patients	14.3	85.7	Would you like to participate in voluntary activities for social welfare?	74.4	25.6

174 CUI

TABLE 8.11   Social Participation and Political Participation among Interviewees (*cont.*)
Unit: %

Participation	1 Yes	0 No	Willingness to participate	Want to participate	Do not want to participate
Participate in religious activities	4.2	95.8	Would you like to participate in religious activities?	14.1	85.9
Participate in strikes / merchants' strikes / students' strikes / sit-ins/protests / marches	0.3	99.7	Would you like to participate in strikes / merchants' strikes / students' strikes / sit-ins / protests / marches?	5.0	95.0
Participate in online/ offline actions for the protection of collective rights	1.3	98.7	Would you like to participate in online/offline actions for the protection of collective rights?	36.8	63.2
Participate in elections of representatives to the national congress at the district or county level	11.5	88.5	Would you like to participate in elections of representatives to the national congress at the district or county level?	65.1	34.9

4.4 The Efficiency of Some Members of the Public in Political Participation Was Not High, with a Certain Degree of Political Apathy. However, Most of the Public Have Highly Accepted and Affirmed the National and Social Governance Capacities of the Govern

In terms of the efficiency of political participation, according to the data, the efficiency of the participation of some members of the public is not high at present. 58.5% of the interviewees said that the votes of the voters had no influence on the final results of the elections of village (neighborhood) committees;

SURVEY REPORT ON THE QUALITY OF SOCIAL DEVELOPMENT IN CHINA

51.8% of them said that the village (neighborhood) committees did not care about the voices of ordinary residents at all; and 53.3% of them thought that participation in political activities was useless, as it had no influence on the decisions of government departments. At the same time, a certain degree of political apathy exists among some members of the public, and 52.1% of the interviewees expressed no interest in politics and would not like to spend time on politics. However, most members of the public have accepted and affirmed the national and social governance capacities of government departments at all levels. For example, 67.9% of the interviewees said that the people should follow the instructions of the governments, and that subordinates should follow orders from their superiors; and 56.2% of the interviewees said that national events should be governed by the government, and that ordinary people should not have anything to do with them (see Table 8.12). This shows that the public trusts and accepts the governance capacities of the Party and the government.

TABLE 8.12   Interviewees' Sense of Political Efficiency
Unit: %

Sense of efficiency	1. Completely agree	2. Agree	3. Disagree	4. Completely disagree	8. I don't know
In village (neighborhood) committee elections, the votes of the voters have no influence on the final results	20.7	37.8	26.2	12.2	3.2
The village (neighborhood) committee doesn't care about the opinions of ordinary villagers (residents) like me	16.5	35.3	32.9	11.9	3.3
I have the capacity and knowledge to judge politics and participate in political activities	12.5	36.1	34.6	13.8	3.0

176   CUI

TABLE 8.12   Interviewees' Sense of Political Efficiency (*cont.*)

Unit: %

Sense of efficiency	1. Completely agree	2. Agree	3. Disagree	4. Completely disagree	8. I don't know
I am not interested in politics and would not like to spend my time on this	17.9	34.2	33.3	12.6	1.9
It's useless to participate in political activities, since no influence will be generated on government departments	17.4	35.9	32.7	10.8	3.1
Our freedom of expression would be limited by government departments	10.1	27.8	39.2	19.8	3.0
Ordinary people should follow the lead of the government, and subordinates should follow the orders of their superiors	28.7	39.2	22.7	8.1	1.2
State affairs should be managed by the government, and ordinary people should not worry about those affairs	24.0	32.2	29.8	12.7	1.2

SURVEY REPORT ON THE QUALITY OF SOCIAL DEVELOPMENT IN CHINA 177

5   Consolidating the Achievements in Social and Economic Guarantee, Supplementing Shortcomings in the Improvement of the Quality of People's Lives, and Promoting the Comprehensive Progress of Society

From the data we can see that, with the rapid economic growth of China, the material standard of living of the people has been improved significantly, great achievements have been made in reforming the quality of people's lives, and social security has been promoted to a great extent. Since the 18th National Congress of the CPC, the coverage of and capacity for social security have seen leapfrog development. The speed and efforts in promoting social guarantees have been recognized by the public. Of course, from the data we can still see that social guarantees are insufficient to meet the demands of the public and that we still need to establish a system of social guarantees that can gradually meet the desire of the people for a better life by further deepening the reform and by making more innovations to the system. In terms of social cohesion, an active and positive social consciousness has essentially been formed in the public, the socialist core values have enjoyed popular support from the people, and the public's degree of social trust has been greatly improved. At the same time, social inclusion is thriving and the public has greatly recognized social fairness and justice. Various forms of social discrimination caused by institutional or non-institutional factors have been vanishing. Discrimination due to household registration, origin, and education are no longer barriers to personal development. In terms of social empowerment, on the one hand, the public is satisfied with the work of the government departments; on the other hand, the passion of the public for social and political participation does not match the channels for that participation, to some extent, and we need to further strengthen social construction and political construction, deepen the reform of the political system, improve participation in institutional social and political activities, meet the needs of the public in participating in and discussing political issues, and fully instantiate the activities of the public in social governance.

References

Li Peilin. "New Developmental Concept System Guiding the Realization of the Century-Old Dream of China." In Li Peilin, Chen Guangjin, and Zhang Yi (ed.), *Analysis and Forecast of China's Social Conditions* (2016). Social Sciences Academic Press (China), 2015.

Lin Ka. "Social Quality Theory: A New Perspective for Researching a Harmonious Society." *Journal of Renmin University of China*, 2010(2).

Lin Ka. "Theory on Social Quality and Social Harmony." In Peng Huamin (ed.), *Leading Edge of Social Welfare Theories in Western Countries: On Countries, Society, System and Policy*. China Social Sciences Press, 2009.

Walker, Alan. "A Comparison of Perspectives on Social Quality Research." In Zhang Haidong (ed.), *Social Quality Research: Theory, Methodology and Experience*. Social Sciences Academic Press (China), 2011.

Walker, Alan. "Social Quality Orientation: Bridge Connecting Asia and Europe." Translated by Zhang Haidong. *Jianghai Academic Journal*, 2010(4).

Xi Jinping. "Secure a Decisive Victory in Building a Moderately Prosperous Society in All Respects and Strive for the Great Success of Socialism with Chinese Characteristics for a New Era." Report delivered by President Xi Jinping at the 19th National Congress of the Communist Party of China, 2017.

Zhang Haidong. "Social Quality: A New View on Researching Social Development." *Guangming Daily*, February 16, 2010.

Zhang Haidong. "Social Quality: A Core Issue for Social Development." *Chinese Social Sciences Today*, March 30, 2010.

Zhang Haidong (ed.). *Social Quality Research: Theory, Methodology and Experience*. Social Sciences Academic Press (China), 2011.

Zhang Haidong and Li Zailie (Korean). "Influence of the Financial Crisis in the 1990s on the Society of South Korea." *Society*, 2009(1).

Zhang Haidong, Shi Haibo, and Bi Jingqian. "Social Quality Research and New Progress." *Sociological Studies*, 2012(3).

CHAPTER 9

Survey Report on the Development of the Sharing Economy and Its Social Impact in China: An Analysis of Data from Seven Cities

Lu Yangxu,[1] He Guangxi,[2] and Zhao Yandong[3]

Abstract

In this report, we used the data from the Survey on the Public's Participation in the Sharing Economy in some cities to analyze the development of the sharing economy and its social influence. According to the results of the analysis, the rate of participation and the public's willingness to develop the sharing economy were high. The social foundation of a sharing economy is social trust, and the development of a sharing economy is limited by the degree of social trust. In general, the Chinese sharing economy is an inclusive economic mode that may benefit all walks of society, but it has shown obvious differences among social classes.

Keywords

sharing economy – public – rate of participation - willingness to participate - social trust - differences among social classes

In recent years, the sharing economy has witnessed a prosperous development. In terms of traffic, housing leasing, knowledge service, finance, life service, and manufacturing, the sharing economy has experienced explosive growth. A great number of platform enterprises have emerged, leading to the rapid expansion of

---

1   Lu Yangxu, Ph.D., associate research fellow of the Chinese Academy of Science and Technology for Development, with a research focus on organizational sociology and scientific policies.
2   He Guangxi, master's degree, associate research fellow of the Chinese Academy of Science and Technology for Development, and deputy director of the Technological and Social Development Institute, with a research focus on scientific sociology and scientific policies.
3   Zhao Yandong, Ph.D., research fellow of the Chinese Academy of Science and Technology for Development and director of the Technological and Social Development Institute, with a research focus on social capital and networks, technological and social risks, and innovative social environments.

© KONINKLIJKE BRILL NV, LEIDEN, 2022 | DOI:10.1163/9789004500723_010

the sharing industry and the continuous growth of the market. The sharing economy of our country has witnessed rapid development and has caught up with many developed countries that had begun to develop a sharing economy earlier than China in many fields. According to the data issued by the State Information Center, in 2016, the volume of the market of the sharing economy was nearly 3.5 trillion yuan, with about 60 million service providers and more than 600 million users. In the next few years, the annual growth rate of the sharing economy is projected to be about 40%, and the sharing economy's proportion of the GDP is estimated to be more than 10% and will probably reach 20% by 2025.[4]

Sharing as a social activity has existed since ancient times. The concept of a sharing economy was proposed in 1978 by two social science professors from the University of Texas and the University of Illinois in the United States, respectively, who published an article about collaborative consumption.[5] However, given the limits in terms of the total amount of sharing resources and supply-demand matching technologies, sharing activities throughout history have been limited to small groups or areas. In recent years, as nations have developed a capacity for excess production and an affluent society,[6] and especially with the rapid development and popularization of the Internet, big data, cloud computing, and other information technologies, the sharing economy has become a new economic form and social phenomenon that uses innovations to improve the efficiency of resource distribution and to realize mass participation, mass innovation, and mass benefits. Advocates of the sharing economy believe that it represents the new tendency of economic and social development in the future. For example, Rifkin in his book *The Zero Marginal Cost Society* believes that the sharing of communication, energy, and logistics would allow many products and services to be produced and shared free of charge, and that this would fundamentally change the existing social formation.[7]

1 Questions and Data

1.1 *Questions*
At present, academic analysis of the sharing economy is mainly conducted from the point of view of economics, and few people have focused on its social

---

4 State Information Center, "Development Report on the Sharing Economy of China," February 2017.
5 M. Felson and J. Spaeth, "Community Structure and Collaborative Consumption: A Routine Activity Approach," *American Behavioral Scientist*, 1978, 21(4).
6 John Galbraith, *The Affluent Society*, translated by Zhao Yong, Jiangsu People's Press, 2009.
7 Jeremy Rifkin, *The Zero Marginal Cost Society*, translated by the expert team of the CCID, CITIC Press, 2014.

attributes and influences. In this report, we argue that the economic system and the social system should be matched dynamically and adapted to each other. The emergence and development of a new economic mode requires an appropriate social foundation, and the deepened development of the new economic mode is bound to influence the lifestyles, methods of production, and social structure of the people. In terms of practices, despite the short period of development, the sharing economy has generated obvious influences on the everyday lives of people who participate in it in such areas as food, travel, housing, employment, income, and consumption, and it has led to widespread discussion, which is worth further research.

At present, empirical studies on the sharing economy are mostly based on big data provided by the platform enterprises of a sharing economy. Although these platforms are often large, the available data can limit deep analysis of various issues involving the producers and sellers of the sharing economy, and as a result there is a shortage of information about the social attributes of the social public. In this report, based on the data from a questionnaire survey completed by the public, we try to answer the following questions: (1) What are the attitudes of the public to the sharing economy and how do they participate in it? Does the public know about the sharing economy now? What are the public's rates of participation in the various fields of the sharing economy? Will the public participate in the sharing economy actively in the future? (2) What is the social foundation of the sharing economy? (3) What influences does the development of the sharing economy exert on the social structure? Have differences in social class already given rise to any differences in the operation of a sharing economy?

1.2   Definition of a Sharing Economy

At present, there is no uniform definition for a sharing economy in the academic world, the industrial world, and the world of policies. In addition, given the complicated appearance, diversity, and rapid change of a sharing economy, it is hard for us to define it for our research. Based on our review of related documents, and the on-site surveys of the platform enterprises of the sharing economy, in this report we take the position that the sharing economy is a new kind of economy using modern information technologies to integrate and share a huge number of dispersive resources and to realize the exchange of needed products, mass participation, and collaborative consumption, through the rapid flow and high-efficiency distribution of knowledge assets and resources. In practice, dependence on the online platform and the sharing of the user's rights are the two most outstanding features of the sharing economy. Based on this definition, in the survey, we define the sharing economy as sharing realized through network platforms. This is a broad definition of the sharing economy, covering both the B2C and C2C modes that exist in the sharing economy at present,[8] and we have distinguished between the two modes in fields with high vitality and an obvious pattern of coexistence between the two modes, such as traveling, accommodation, and catering. Finally, we need to point out that, considering the length of the questionnaire and the current conditions of the development of the sharing economy in different fields, we have focused on such fields as traveling, accommodation, catering, life services, and knowledge services that have developed early, without considering the development of the sharing economy in other fields.

1.3 *Data*

The data used herein are mainly from the Survey on the Public's Participation in the Sharing Economy conducted by the Chinese Academy of Science and Technology for Development from September to October in 2017. The survey was conducted in seven cities, namely, Beijing, Shenzhen, Zhengzhou, Chengdu, Lanzhou, Quanzhou, and Jingzhou, using the technique of random sampling at different stages. A total of 4,300 interviewees were selected from the districts and counties within these cities (the interviewees chosen had reached the age of 18 and lived in the area for more than three consecutive months), and some people who had used the Internet in the past year (from October 2016 to September 2017) were also interviewed. The survey was conducted by means of a door-to-door interview, and 2,061 questionnaires were recovered, with a recovery rate of 47.9%. In the calculations, the data were weighted based on the populations of the cities. We need to point out that the results of the survey were not used to deduce the situation of the whole population of China, since the subjects of the survey were limited to Internet users among the residents in the districts and counties within the seven cities, and not the whole population of China.

2 Major Findings

Given the concise nature of this report, we do not fully describe the social foundation of the development of the sharing economy and its influences but limit ourselves to reporting several major findings.

---

8 B2C means that the products or services are provided by businesses to consumers, which is similar to the traditional leasing mode, but the related services have been moved onto the Internet. A bike-sharing service is typical of this mode. C2C means that the platform enterprises only provide a supply-demand information matching service, without directly owning specific assets or employing service providers; this mode is well represented by Uber and Airbnb. Typically, we consider the C2C mode as the sharing economy in a narrow sense.

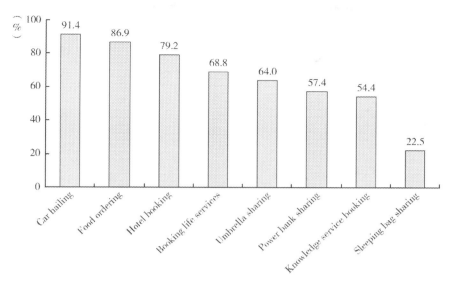

FIGURE 9.1 Public Awareness of the Services of a Sharing Economy in Different Fields

2.1   *The Public Awareness of the Sharing Economy Was High in General*

Since 2008, the sharing economy has witnessed rapid development throughout the world and is fully penetrating all aspects of life, becoming an integral part of our lives. The reports, analysis, and discussions in the media about it are countless. According to the survey results, the sharing economy is no stranger to the public of our country. The awareness rates of the interviewees regarding the services of the sharing economy in most fields were higher than 50%, and the awareness rates of online car hailing, food ordering, and hotel booking were as high as 91.4%, 86.9%, and 79.2%, respectively, ranking in the top three. In general, the awareness rates of those services in a sharing economy that appeared earlier to meet high-frequency demands, such as traveling and eating, are higher, while those for such sharing products/services as sharing power banks, booking knowledge services, and sharing sleeping bags were relatively low, due to their low-frequency nature or small scope of services or belated appearance (see Figure 9.1).

2.2   *The Sharing Economy Is Helpful in Addressing Aspects of People's Quality of Life that Are Difficult to Improve and in Promoting the Updating of Consumption*

The rapid development of the sharing economy was facilitated by rapid and highly efficient supply-demand information matching through online platforms. On the supply side, the global overcapacity and the policy of quantitative easing have reduced the prices of many products, and the financing difficulties and costs of the sharing economy industry are relatively low. After decades of high-speed economic growth, the idle assets held by ordinary households in our country have been increasing, such as cars and houses, and the storage of human capital such as knowledge and skills has become larger and larger. In other words, in an affluent society, if we have more resources that can be shared, the cost of sharing is lower. As for the demand side, on the one hand, many new aspects that help to determine the quality of people's lives but are difficult to improve have appeared during rapid urbanization in urban areas, such as difficulties in hiring a taxi and the problem of the last mile in shipping, as well as shopping difficulties due to the insufficient number of stores and reduced offerings of supermarkets in cities. All of these sore spots that are closely related to people's daily lives have gone unresolved for a long time. On the other hand, with the increase in disposable income and a change in consumption ideology, more and more people have begun to focus on better experiences related to consumption and quality of services. In recent years, with support from the rapid development and wide application of information technologies, the pushing force on the supply side and the pulling force on the demand side finally became a united force that is pushing forward the rapid development of the sharing economy.

According to the results of the survey, in the past one year, 88.9% of the public in the seven cities enjoyed at least one sharing economy service in a broad sense (including both B2C and C2C), and 71.5% of them enjoyed at least one sharing economy service in a narrow sense (only including C2C). For example, 68.9% of the people experienced a car-hailing service through online platforms; 63.8% of them used bike-sharing services; and 59.8% of them ordered food through online platforms. From the above information we can see that the rate of usage of sharing economy services in fields that address difficulties related to livelihood are high, such as traveling and catering. At the same time, the data also showed that in fields related to the updating of consumption, such as accommodation, life services, and knowledge services, a lot of people have begun to use sharing economy services (see Figure 9.2).

As mentioned above, in the fields of traveling, accommodation, and catering, the coexistence of B2C and C2C is quite obvious, and the services provided under these two modes are quite different. According to data from the survey, in the past year, 55.4% of participants used personalized taxi services, ride-sharing services, or fast vehicle services; 11.0% of them ordered food or snacks made by other people; and 12.8% of them booked accommodations with local residents through online platforms (see Table 9.1). We can see that new consumption needs that emphasize the understanding of local life and culture and improve consumption have driven forward the rapid development of the sharing economy in accommodation and catering.

SURVEY REPORT ON THE DEVELOPMENT OF THE SHARING ECONOMY 185

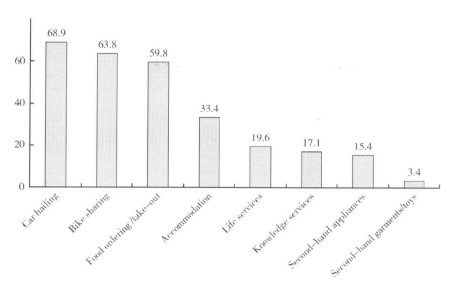

FIGURE 9.2 Proportions of the Sharing Economy Services Obtained by the Public
Note: The sharing economy services in such fields as traveling, accommodation, and catering combine both the B2C and C2C modes, but the modes are not separated in the figure. See the description in the report for the ratios of the two modes.

TABLE 9.1 Proportions of Sharing Economy Services in the Broad and Narrow Sense within Public Services

Unit: %

Type	Service field		
	Car hailing	Food ordering/take-out	Accommodation
Sharing economy in a broad sense	68.9	59.8	33.4
Sharing economy in a narrow sense	55.4	11.0	12.8

2.3   The Public's High Enthusiasm for Participating in the Sharing Economy

In the survey, we asked those who have used sharing economy services if they would like to continue to use those services; when speaking to interviewees who had never heard about the sharing economy services in certain fields, the

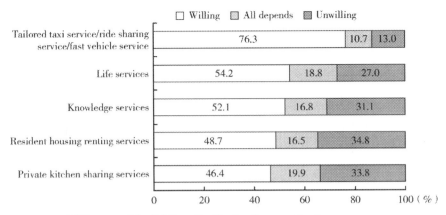

FIGURE 9.3 Willingness of the Public to Use Sharing Economy Services

researchers introduced the definition of the sharing economy in a standard way and then asked them if they would like to use the corresponding sharing economy services. According to statistics, the public was enthusiastic about participating in the sharing economy in the future, and the proportion of those who said that they would like to participate in the sharing economy and access tailored taxi service/ride sharing service/fast vehicle service, life services, knowledge services, resident housing renting services, and private kitchen sharing services was 76.3%, 54.2%, 52.1%, 48.7%, and 46.4%, respectively (see Figure 9.3). In addition, about 10% to 20% of the interviewees said that they would like to make a decision about participating in the sharing economy depending on the actual conditions. We can see that, in order to fulfill certain rigid demands in work and life, such as traveling and life services, people would like to use or try sharing economy services, but in the case of non-rigid services that require a higher requirement of social trust, such as private housing and kitchen sharing, the proportion of people who would like to use or try sharing economy service modes was lower.

2.4 Trust Is the Social Foundation for the Development of the Sharing Economy

Cultural factors are closely related to economic life. Some researchers believe that social trust has played an important role in the economic life of every country.[9] Trust can be discussed from two different perspectives. The first is the explanation of rational choices and the moral explanation of non-rational

---

9 Francis Fukuyama, *Trust*, translated by Peng Zhihua, Hainan Press, 2006.

choices;[10] the second is the distinction between ordinary trust and special trust.[11] Unlike trust in relatives, friends, and acquaintances, ordinary trust is about trusting strangers or other ordinary people in society. The shift from special trust to ordinary trust is a process of expanding the radius of one's trust and enhancing the inclusion of a moral community, a process that represents the degree of openness, advancement, and civilization of a society. There are two answers to the question regarding whom one should trust. One depends on a rational judgment of the results, while the other one depends on the inherent morality. However, most of the research is focused on discussing rational trust, and only some is devoted to morality and moral trust.[12]

The relationship between the sharing economy and social trust is an important issue to be considered when discussing the development of the sharing economy. In this aspect, there are two research directions: the first is whether social trust could influence the development of the sharing economy and to what extent; and the other is whether the influence of the sharing economy on social trust would enhance social trust. Given the fact that change in the degree of social trust is a slow process, in this report we have mainly focused on the first question, or the influence of social trust on people's acts of participating and willingness to participate in the sharing economy.

Following the classification method suggested by Uslaner,[13] in this report we have discussed the relationships between calculated trust and the sharing economy and between moral trust and the sharing economy. We have used the trust that people have in the Users' Comments on online platforms as the proxy variable of calculated trust, and the trust that people have in strangers as the proxy variable of moral trust. Typically, by extracting date from the Users' Comments, the sharing economy platforms could effectively disclose and gather information about the qualities, prices, and post-sales services of products and services, so as to reduce the degree of information asymmetry between buyers and sellers and promote the establishment of a relationship of trust. In the survey, we asked interviewees who have shopped or conducted other consumption activities online the following question: "When you were shopping or consuming online, did you check the comments related to the products or services (including opinions and photos)?" We provided four options, namely, "I checked every time," "I checked most times," "I sometimes

---

10   Eric M. Uslaner, *The Moral Foundations of Trust*, translated by Zhang Dunmin, Social Sciences Academic Press (China), 2006.
11   Zhou Yi, *Who Can We Trust? Scientific Exploration about the Trust Mode and Mechanism*, Social Sciences Academic Press (China), 2014.
12   Zhou Yi, *Who Can We Trust?*
13   Uslaner, *Moral Foundations of Trust*.

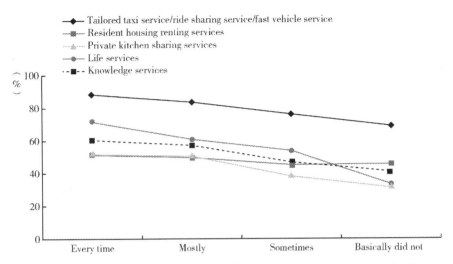

FIGURE 9.4 Review of Users' Comments and Willingness to Use Sharing Economy Services

checked," and "I basically did not check." According to our analysis, the more that people trust the system of comment-giving, the more they will use the sharing economy services, and this relationship is basically identical in all fields (see Figure 9.4). From this point of view, we thought that those who trust the information disclosure and credit evaluation systems provided by online platforms would have fewer concerns about the safety and security of the information regarding products and services when using the sharing economy, and so they would be more willing to use or try sharing economy services.

As mentioned above, in the B2C mode, since the service providers are enterprises, their brands, reputations, and strict supervision could enable consumers to calculate the degree of their trust in service providers. However, in the sharing economy in a narrow sense (or the C2C mode), the platforms only provide the service of information matching; services such as private housing and kitchen sharing and housekeeping are provided in relatively closed and private spaces, and the prices and safety of such services are highly uncertain, and thus the users of such services depend more on social trust. According to the analysis, those who used sharing economy services in a narrow sense in the past year had a much higher degree of trust in outsiders and merchants/businessmen than those who had never used such services (see Figure 9.5). In other words, those who have a high degree of ordinary trust would like to use or try sharing economy services.

According to the above results, the proportion of the public with a high degree of social trust would be more active in participating in the sharing

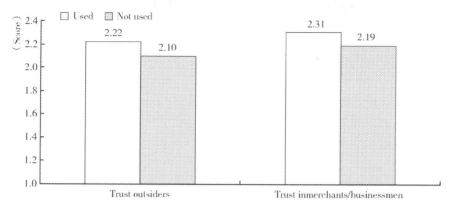

FIGURE 9.5 Relationship between Degree of Social Trust and Experiences with Sharing Economy Services
Note: We scored the degree of trust that the interviewees granted to people thus: 4 for total trust, 3 for trust, 2 for no trust, and 1 for never trust. The figure represents the average of the scores. The difference reached a significance of 0.001 after T-testing.

economy, and social trust has become the important social foundation for the development of the sharing economy.

2.4 *The Development of the Sharing Economy Is Inclusive but Manifests Differences with Respect to Social Class*

Mass participation and mass benefit are the developmental ideologies promoted by the sharing economy. Some scholars even believe that the development of the sharing economy can reduce unfairness in society. According to the survey data, the degree of public participation in the sharing economy in many fields was relatively high, which means that the benefits of the sharing economy could be shared by the public in general.

However, we also found that consumers of sharing economy services in different fields were obviously from different social classes. In terms of the use of sharing economy services in a broad sense, the data showed that among professional technicians, employees, and workers, the proportion of those who used bike-sharing services in the past year was relatively high, while the proportion of managers/leaders/employers/bosses who used them was low. In terms of users of online car-hailing services, the proportion of managers/leaders/employers/bosses was high, while that of employees and workers was low. Among those who have used sharing economy services in the accommodation field, the proportion of professional technicians was the highest and that of workers the lowest. Among those who used sharing economy services

TABLE 9.2   Usage of Sharing Economy Services by Different Groups
Unit: %

Occupational Group	Automobiles		Accommodations		Catering		Bike-sharing	Life Services	Knowledge Services
	Broad Sense	Narrow Sense	Broad Sense	Narrow Sense	Broad Sense	Narrow Sense			
Employers/ bosses	78.6	56.3	36.9	17.4	61.6	4.7	52.3	23.5	19.8
Managers/ leaders	80.0	65.3	32.4	16.5	46.7	21.7	61.5	22.4	16.9
Professional technicians	70.0	57.2	45.1	16.2	42.7	14.1	65.6	32.0	30.9
Employees	59.1	51.7	42.1	19.7	79.1	13.3	72.1	21.5	22.0
Workers	69.6	58.5	16.9	0.7	53.1	9.6	67.4	11.7	7.2

in the catering industry, the proportion of employees was high and that of professional technicians and managers/leaders was low. Among those who used life services, the proportion of the professional technicians was the highest and that of workers was the lowest. Among those who used knowledge services, the proportion of workers was the lowest. In terms of the usage of sharing economy services in a narrow sense, managers/leaders were the users most likely to use tailored taxi services/ride-sharing services/fast vehicle services; employees were most likely to use accommodation services provided by individuals; and managers/leaders were most likely to use private kitchen-sharing services.

In addition, we should emphasize three points: (1) The online car-hailing market is a multi-level market with high-end tailored taxi services and inexpensive fast vehicle and ride-sharing services. All walks of life in society may select an affordable service that meets their needs. This is why the differences among different social levels are small in using online car-hailing services. (2) In the field of private kitchen-sharing and life services, the low proportions among employers/bosses may be due to the fact that they have more disposable income and higher requirements for the quality of services, so they may hire related service providers directly. (3) The participation rate in life services and knowledge services was the highest among professional technicians, indicating typical consumption features of the middle class.

3 Conclusion and Suggestions

In this report, we used data from the Survey on the Public's Participation in the Sharing Economy to describe the attitudes and participation of the public in the sharing economy, paying special attention to the social foundation and social influence of the sharing economy. Our research led us to the following conclusions: (1) The public's rate of participation and their willingness to use the sharing economy were high, and difficulties in finding services related to quality of life and consumption updating jointly promoted the rapid development of the sharing economy. (2) Social trust could improve the willingness of the public to participate in the sharing economy. (3) Despite the class differences in the use of sharing economy services, the sharing economy is an inclusive economy mode that can benefit all walks of life in a particular society.

Based on the above findings, we think that we should make great efforts to develop the sharing economy and further optimize its developmental mode. Thus, we offer the following four suggestions.

First of all, we should further optimize the policy environment to promote the rapid development of the sharing economy. Based on programs such as Internet+ and Made in China 2025, we should strive to promote mass innovation and business start-ups, construct sharing platforms, and expand the developmental fields of the sharing economy. Based on the features of Internet+ and the sharing economy, we should accelerate the transformation of the economic administration of the government, explore a new governance mechanism in which all social subjects can participate, and promote the healthy development of the new modes, new industries, and new business patterns of the sharing economy according to the requirements for delegating powers, streamlining administration, and optimizing services.

Second, we should make great efforts in terms of both the improvement of the quality of people's lives and consumption updating at the same time. This will enable us to further improve the availability of sharing economy services and guide the sharing economy to promote social fairness and more balanced and sufficient development. We should combine mass innovation and business-starting with the development of the sharing economy to expand the fields of the sharing economy and facilitate the constant growth of the quality of people's lives and their welfare. By developing the sharing economy, we can activate idle skills and resources to help people explore new sources of income and promote structural reform on the supply side in the fields of education, health care, and the environment, as they relate to quality-of-life issues that are difficult to satisfy, in order to expand the capacity to supply products and services, resolve the issues caused by imbalanced and insufficient development, and meet the desire of the people for a better life.

Third, we should take the development of the sharing economy as an opportunity to promote the transformation of the system of social credit. We must fully understand the opportunities and challenges brought by new technologies, such as information technologies, and new business patterns, such as the sharing economy, to the transformation of the social credit system, so as to promote this transformation through the joint efforts made by governments, enterprises, the scientific world, and the public. We should fully take advantage of new information technologies such as big data and cloud computing to systematically exploit mass data to the largest extent while reasonably limiting and managing data collection and usage, so as to explore the establishment of a new system of social credit that can meet the needs of the information age.

Fourth, we should make more efforts to carry out research on the developmental mechanism of the sharing economy and its social influence. An accurate calculation of the economic and social influence of the sharing economy will be good for forming social consensus and making and adjusting related policies—a challenge that has become a hotspot for policy-makers and researchers in many countries. For these reasons, the related departments should further increase their input into related research in order to support institutes and research teams in carrying out research on the developmental mechanisms of the sharing economy and its economic and social influence. To begin with, we could focus on the influence of the sharing economy on economic growth, employment, business-starting, consumer surplus, the people's sense of gain, and their sense of happiness.

CHAPTER 10

Survey Report on Chinese College Students' Philosophy of Life and Social Attitudes: An Analysis of Data from a Longitudinal Survey of Students from Twelve Colleges and Universities

Liu Baozhong[1]

Abstract

With rapid economic growth and drastic social changes, the people's attitudes toward actions and values are experiencing a profound evolution. The changes in the social environment have significantly influenced the core values of college students, including their concepts of life and social attitudes. Most modern college students were born after 1990 and 1995, and they have active thoughts, outstanding individuality, and a strong thirst for knowledge, and they are in a critical period for the formation of their values. The "Longitudinal Survey on China's Employment, Lives, and Values of College Students and Graduates" started with a baseline survey in 2013 and has focused on the major features of and changes in the employment, lives, and values of modern college students in China. In this report, with the data from the aforementioned survey, we have analyzed the features and changing tendencies of the philosophy of life and social attitudes of college students in four dimensions, namely, outlook on employment, outlook on consumption, network participation, and social attitudes, and the results of the analysis could be used to further guide college students in determining the correct orientation of their values and in promoting their healthy development.

Keywords

college students – philosophy of life – social attitudes

In April 2017, the Central Committee of the Communist Party of China and the State Council issued the *Long- and Mid-Term Developmental Plan for Youth*

---

1 Liu Baozhong, assistant research fellow of the Institute of Sociology, Chinese Academy of Social Sciences.

© KONINKLIJKE BRILL NV, LEIDEN, 2022 | DOI:10.1163/9789004500723_011

(*2016–2025*), emphasizing that it is a fundamental and strategic project for the country to promote the development of youth in a better and faster way. As the youth group with the highest level of knowledge, college students are the backbone force pushing social development forward. The values of college students contain special content. Their value judgments on their lives and social environment do not only influence their development in the future, but they also represent to a large extent the changing tendency of values in the society of China. With rapid economic growth and drastic social changes, the people's attitudes toward action and their values are experiencing a profound evolution. Most modern college students were born after 1990 and 1995, and they have active thoughts, outstanding individuality, and a strong thirst for knowledge, and they can be easily influenced by the social environment. College students are in a critical period for the formation of their outlook on the world, life, and values. To accurately judge and analyze the new features and changes in terms of the philosophy of life and social attitudes of college students during the social transformation will be of important practical significance in guiding them to establish a correct orientation of their values and in promoting their healthy development.

The data used in this report are from the "Longitudinal Survey on China's Employment, Lives, and Values of College Students and Graduates" (hereinafter the College Student Survey). This survey was organized by the Institute of Sociology of the Chinese Academy of Social Sciences as a project for longitudinal research on modern college students in China, aiming at analyzing the developmental changes of college students against the background of social transformation in order to understand the conditions, attitudes, and activities of college students and graduates in a systematic and in-depth manner. The survey covered 12 colleges and universities in different regions at different levels, and about 10,000 effective survey samples were collected every year. This survey was started in 2013 and a new round was conducted in each of the following years. Unless otherwise specified, the data used herein are all from the fourth round of the College Student Survey in 2016. The number of valid samples was 10,765 and showed the following distribution: male, 47.4%; female, 52.6%; students born in the 1980s, 0.6% (almost all of them were postgraduates); students who were born after 1990, 23.2%; and students who were born after 1995, 76.3%. Students from urban areas (determined by their place of residence in the year they took the college entrance examination, and including counties and overseas locations) made up 49.9% of the sample; and students from rural areas (including townships) 50.1%. In addition to the data from the College Student Survey in 2016, data from the College Student Surveys in 2013, 2014, and 2015 have been used in the present study. Based on this data, we try to show the major features and changing tendencies of modern college students regarding their philosophy of life and their social attitudes in four dimensions,

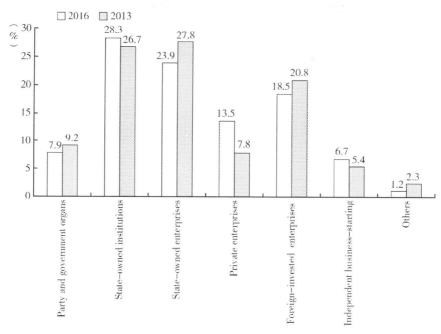

FIGURE 10.1   Employers Chosen as Ideal by College Students

namely their outlook on employment, outlook on consumption, their network participation, and their social attitudes.

1   Outlook on Employment

1.1   *Most College Students Would Like to Find Stable Jobs. College Students Are Very Much Attracted to Institutional Jobs and Those in Major Cities. However, the Choices Made by College Students Were Diversified and Tended to Be "Reasonable" or "Practicals"*

Figure 10.1 presents the types of employers selected by college students as ideal in 2016, compared with the baseline College Student Survey in 2013. According to the data, in 2016, among the ideal employers selected by college students, the top two were state-owned institutions and enterprises. Nearly one-third of students would like to work in state-owned institutions (28.3%) and about one-fourth of them chose state-owned enterprises (23.9%). From this we can see that the stable institutional jobs were the top choice for college students. It is worth mentioning that the proportion of college students who wanted to work in party and government organs was lower than one-tenth. The cooling of students' enthusiasm for working as public servants indicated that the job-finding

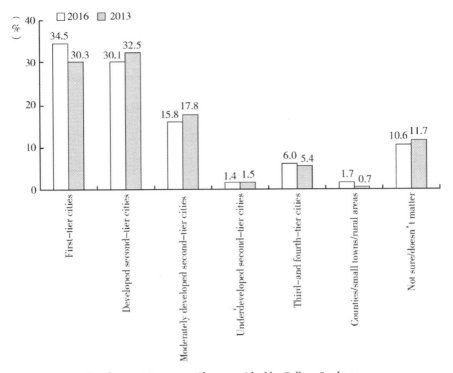

FIGURE 10.2   Employment Locations Chosen as Ideal by College Students

activities of college students have returned to a rational approach. In addition, nearly one-fifth (18.5%) of college students wanted to work in foreign-financed enterprises and 13.5% of them selected private enterprises. Compared to 2013, the types of employers desired by college students did not change too much. An obvious change was that the proportion of the students who wanted to work in private enterprise after graduation increased from 7.8% in 2013 to 13.5% in 2016.

Given the difficulties in finding jobs, the high liquidity of jobs, and the fierce competition in employment, most college students would like to find stable jobs in state-owned institutions and enterprises. However, with the growth of private enterprise in China, the number of college students who want to work in private companies increased significantly, indicating that college students' outlook on employment is changing.

In terms of job locations, according to the 2016 survey data, major cities such as Beijing, Shanghai, and Guangzhou were still the most popular among college students (preferred by 34.5%), followed by developed second-tier cities (preferred by 30.1%). The above two figures account for about two-thirds of the college students surveyed. On the other hand, in 2016, 15.8% of college students preferred to find jobs in moderately developed second-tier cities. Other options included in the survey attracted a relatively low proportion of students (see

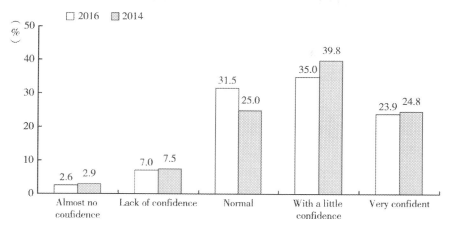

FIGURE 10.3   College Students' Confidence in Finding Employment

Figure 10.2). By comparing the data in 2013 and 2016, we can see that the choices of college students regarding employment locations did not change in general. Most students wanted to work in the developed first- and second-tier cities but not in the underdeveloped second-, third-, and fourth-tier cities, counties, townships, and rural areas.

The competitive pressures and cost of living in major cities did not deter college students. According to the data from the surveys in 2013 and 2016, there were still a lot of students who were enthusiastic about working in Beijing, Shanghai, Guangzhou, and Shenzhen. However, that data also indicated that the proportions of college students who wanted to work in developed second-tier cities were 32.5% and 30.1% respectively, which were basically the same as that of students who wanted to work in major cities. Strikingly, the proportion of college students who wanted to work in moderately developed second-tier cities was much higher than those wanting to work in first-tier cities. This indicated that major cities such as Beijing, Shanghai, Guangzhou, and Shenzhen were no longer the options preferred by college students seeking jobs, and second-tier cities have become the choice for many of them.

Since the expansion of college and university enrollment in 1999, the number of college graduates has increased rapidly year by year, and the employment situation for college students has become more competitive, leading to a huge amount of pressure on college students seeking employment. From the results of the analysis of the data, summarized in Figure 10.3, we can see that, with respect to finding satisfying jobs, compared to the survey in 2014,[2] the proportions of college students selecting "with a little confidence" and "very confident" decreased slightly, and the proportion of students selecting

---

2   In the 2013 survey, this indicator was not selected, so the data for 2014 were used.

"normal" increased to some extent. This means that the difficulties of college students in finding jobs did have some impact on their confidence in finding employment. However, college graduates were still confident about their ability to find satisfying jobs after graduation. In the 2016 survey, about one-fourth of the students were confident, and the proportion of those who selected "with a little confidence" and "very confident" was nearly 60%, while the proportion of those who selected "lack of confidence" and "almost no confidence" was lower than 10%. From this, we can see that most college students were confident and optimistic about finding satisfying jobs.

1.2 College Students' Dreams of Starting a Business Can Hardly Come True in Reality. Their Willingness to Start Up a Business Was Not High, Their Motivation to Do So Came from Successful Examples, and the System of Education in Colleges and Universities

In May 2014, the Ministry of Human Resources and Social Security and various other ministries and commissions jointly issued the *Notice on Implementing the Guiding Plan for the Starting up of Businesses by College Students* to provide policy support for those students at the national level. Against the background of Mass Entrepreneurship and Innovation, college students are considered the fresh force that will implement the strategy of using innovation to drive development and promoting the Mass Entrepreneurship and Innovation program. Indeed, various training classes and competitions aimed at preparing students for starting up a business have emerged in universities and colleges. However, according to the survey, college students' willingness to start up a business was still not high. Among the students covered by the survey, 72.3% of them said that they may start their own businesses, but those who were determined to start businesses only accounted for 7% (6.7%), and 21.0% of them said that they would never start their own business.

In terms of motivation for starting up a business, the number one motivation was stimulation by successful examples (34.0%), followed by the desire to obtain more wealth (26.0%). Influence from relatives or friends was higher than one-fourth, and only a few students (2.0%) said that they had to start businesses due to difficulty in finding jobs (see Figure 10.4). From this, we can see that college students who start businesses are making active choices motivated by personal needs or by environmental factors, such as relatives and friends.

What difficulties would be met by college students starting businesses? Among the students covered by the survey, 84.2% of those with the intention of starting up a business thought that the top difficulty in doing so would be a lack of work experience, resources, and social networks in the relevant fields. The number two difficulty would be a shortage of starting funds, but the proportion who cited this obstacle was relatively low, at about 12.4%. Given the above difficulties, when selecting the best time for starting up a business, more

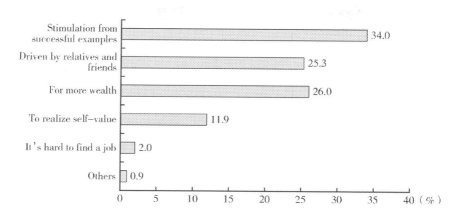

FIGURE 10.4   Major Business-Starting Motivations for College Students

than 70% of college students believed that they needed preparation before starting a business. For example, 33.7% elected to start a business within one to three years after graduation. More than 20% of them believed that it was better to start a business three years after graduation, and 23.1% of them thought that a business could be started at any time, provided one has been well prepared (see Figure 10.5). The proportion of students supporting the idea of starting up a business while studying was relatively low, but more than 20% of students would like to start a business during their undergraduate studies (10.1%) or postgraduate studies (11.8%). Starting a business is never an easy thing. College students need to prepare in many aspects before doing so—for example, by acquiring experience, a social network, and starting funds—in order to improve the possibility of success in their endeavor.

To cultivate innovation and talents that will enable college students to start their own businesses, we need to begin by improving the system of innovation and education toward starting a business. It is especially important for college students who are inexperienced in starting businesses to accept practical and specific training. The national government has attached great importance to innovation and education for starting businesses in colleges and universities, and to this end it has launched the Business-Starting Guiding Plan for College Students in 2014, aimed at promoting education for starting up a business among universities and colleges. However, according to current conditions, the educational system for starting businesses in colleges and universities needs to be improved as soon as possible. According to the survey, 75.2% of college students believed that consultation and training in starting a business are the most wanted educational services in colleges and universities, and 12.4% of them hoped that innovation and courses in starting a business will be provided, which means that college students need a great deal of guidance in starting up a business.

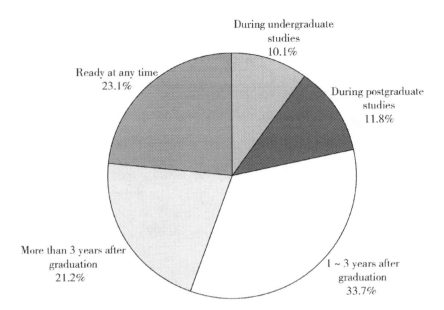

FIGURE 10.5   The Best Time to Start a Business according to College Students

2   Outlook on Consumption

2.1   *The Feature of Rational Consumption Was Prominent: College Students Were Consuming within Their Means and Bill Splitting Prevailed in Colleges and Universities*

In the opinion of the public, those who were born after 1990 and 1995 are considered a generation that has grown up in a greenhouse and they have been credited with negative qualities such as spending extravagantly, loving comparisons, and being sensitive about their reputations. However, according to data from the College Student Survey, these negative comments are exaggerated. Despite the better living conditions of college students who were born after 1990 and 1995, they were not blind consumers. For example, according to analysis of the motivations of college students who buy mobile phones, the three major motivations were qualities and functions (45.4%), the tastes and preferences of youth (15.4%), and high cost efficiency (14.8%). Only 3.2% of college students thought that good mobile phones would make them look great, and fewer than 2% of them had bought mobile phones on impulse (see Figure 10.6). The importance attached by college students to the practical value and cost efficiency of mobile phones shows that they practice a rational kind of consumption, while the attention they pay to the design of phones embodies their pursuit of taste.

SURVEY REPORT ON CHINESE COLLEGE STUDENTS' PHILOSOPHY OF LIFE

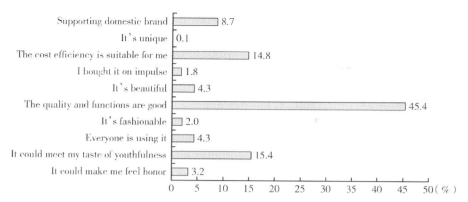

FIGURE 10.6 College Students' Motivations in Buying Mobile Phones

Next, we looked at students' attitudes toward dinner parties. When selecting places for dinner parties, 81.8% of college students chose restaurants with a good environment for chatting; 81.5% of them chose restaurants with special features, since having fun is very important; 83.2% of them chose restaurants with delicious dishes, since delicious food is very important; and 92.6% of them chose affordable restaurants, since nobody should incur an economic burden. The selections made by college students for dinner parties also display their pursuit of rational consumption and quality of consumption. When paying for dinner parties, most college students, including those who were born in the 1980s and after 1990 and 1995, would like to go dutch. Younger college students were more likely to prefer to go dutch. Among college students who were born after 1995, more than 30% would share dining costs equally with their lovers and more than 40% of them would do so with their good friends (see Table 10.1).

TABLE 10.1 Proportions of College Students Born after 1980, 1990, and 1995 Who Choose to Go Dutch for Restaurant Meals

Unit: %

Type	Roommates/ classmates	Good friends	Boy- or girlfriend	Ordinary friends	Friends of friends	Net friends/ strangers
After 1980	66.0	25.9	15.1	48.2	61.8	69.2
After 1990	78.2	35.0	25.8	67.5	78.4	84.7
After 1995	83.6	43.2	32.2	74.6	83.7	87.7

2.2 *The Traditional Concept of Housing Is Vanishing, and Younger College Students Would Not Like to Become Mortgage Slaves*

To the Chinese people, who have a great sense of family, housing has a special meaning and could even be seen as the symbol of family, to some extent. According to the survey, in terms of traditional housing concepts, such as "I can only feel the sense of being at home within my own house," "Owning a house is the necessary condition for marriage," "Owning a house is the necessary condition for having kids," and "I can only feel that I am one of the members of the city if I have my own house," most college students born after 1980, 1990, and 1995 still agreed that owning a house is the foundation for their lives and careers. However, compared to college students born after 1980, the proportion of students born after 1990 and 1995 who agreed with the above concepts has been decreasing. As for the concept that "I can only feel the sense of being at home within my own house," the proportion of college students born after 1980 who agreed with it was as high as 96.8%, while those of the college students born after 1990 and 1995 were 88.2% and 85.4%, respectively.

The change in the concept of housing is closely related to the high housing prices at present. In recent years, housing prices in China have witnessed a constant increase, which has become a nightmare for many people, especially young people. A lot of people have become slaves to heavy mortgages in order to buy a house. However, this condition was endorsed by more than 60% of the college students born after 1980 and rejected by half of the college students born after 1990 and 60% of the college students born after 1995. According to the survey, instead of becoming mortgage slaves like college students born after 1980, 44.7% of the students born after 1990 and 45.9% of the students born after 1995 would like to spend their money on enjoying their lives, but the proportion of college students born after 1980 who agreed with this choice of lifestyle was only 30% (see Table 10.2).

3 Social Network Participation

Chinese society today is a network-based society. According to statistics collected by the China Internet Network Information Center, as of December 2016, the number of Internet users in China had reached 731 million, and network coverage reached 53.2%, which was higher than the average level globally by 3.1 percentage points. College students are an important portion of Internet users. According to the College Student Survey, college students would spend more than 4.5 hours on surfing the Internet every day. Internet participation has gradually become an important part of college students' daily life. At the same time, the Internet is also affecting college students' behavior patterns

SURVEY REPORT ON CHINESE COLLEGE STUDENTS' PHILOSOPHY OF LIFE 203

TABLE 10.2 Differences among College Students Born after 1980, 1990, and 1995 in Concepts of Housing and Housing Purchases

Unit: %

Concept	After 1980	After 1990	After 1995
I can only feel the sense of being at home within my own house	96.6	88.2	85.4
Owning my house is a necessary condition for marriage	80.0	68.1	63.4
Owning my house is a necessary condition for having kids	83.6	83.3	81.2
I can only feel that I am one of the members of the city if I own my own house	72.6	69.4	59.5
Buying a house is the best way to maintain and increase the value of my assets	65.6	59.9	55.9
I would not buy a house if I had to use my parents' money	60.7	62.7	65.9
I prefer a free life, so I don't want to buy a house	22.6	28.8	26.3
To buy a house, I would reduce my living standard	41.9	37.5	35.1
I would not buy a house if I had to bear a heavy burden to do so	37.1	56.7	59.1
I would like to spend my money on enjoying my life rather than on buying a house	30.7	44.7	45.9
I would like to spend my money on starting a business or more meaningful things than buying a house	52.5	61.9	65.7

and values. In this part, we have reviewed the network participation of college students using the concepts and tools of network participation.

3.1 Social Network Activities, News and Information, and Entertainment Are the Three Major Types of Content in Network Activities of College Students

According to statistics about the frequency of various network activities of college students, the major types of content in the network activities of college students are "keeping in touch with friends and making new friends through the Internet (such as WeChat/QQ/Momo/Renren)," "browsing the news, understanding social conditions, and obtaining information on the Internet," and "having fun on the Internet (such as online videos, music and games)," and the proportions of college students who conduct the above three activities on the Internet reached 55.3%, 44.9%, and 40.6%, respectively.

College students are the audience and transmitters of public opinion on the Internet. However, according to the survey, most college students did not like expressing their opinions about social or public events on the Internet. Only 14.6% of them said they would express their opinions on the Internet, and more than 20% of the college students said they would never do so. From this we can see that only a few college students were part of the "Internet water army" or "keyboard men." In addition, only 30% of college students considered the Internet as a tool for study (see Table 10.3).

TABLE 10.3   Frequency of Social Network Activities of College Students
Unit: %

Activity type	Never	Occasionally	Sometimes	Often
Browsing the news, understanding social conditions, and obtaining information	4.7	26.5	23.9	44.9
Keeping in touch with friends or making new friends on the Internet (such as WeChat/QQ/Momo/Renren)	4.7	18.8	21.3	55.3
Expressing comments and opinions on current or social events on the Internet (such as forums, BBS, and microblogs)	21.7	39.9	23.8	14.6
Using the Internet as a diary to record moods	31.3	39.3	19.2	10.3
Having fun on the Internet (such as online videos, music, and games)	4.4	23.2	31.8	40.6
Learning professional or business knowledge on the Internet (such as encyclopedia and professional knowledge websites)	4.1	25.7	40.4	29.8

SURVEY REPORT ON CHINESE COLLEGE STUDENTS' PHILOSOPHY OF LIFE   205

TABLE 10.3   Frequency of Social Network Activities of College Students (*cont.*)
Unit: %

Activity type	Never	Occasionally	Sometimes	Often
Making life more convenient by using the Internet for tasks such as online shopping, ticket booking, looking for jobs, and investing in stocks	7.8	24.7	32.9	34.6

3.2   *WeChat Has Replaced the Microblog and Has Become the Most Popular Social App among College Students*

Microblog and WeChat are the most popular social apps in the age of We Media. WeChat in particular has experienced rapid growth. According to the survey data, 27.8% of the interviewees often use microblogs, about one-fifth of them have never used them, and the rest of them use them occasionally (see Figure 10.7).

College students' use of microblogs was far lower than their use of WeChat. According to the survey, 56.2% of the interviewees said they often use WeChat, less than 4% of them have never used it, 21.9% of them use it occasionally, and 18.3% of them use it sometimes (see Figure 10.8). According to data on the frequency of using microblogs and WeChat, although microblogs were invented and became popular among college students much earlier than WeChat, their popularity and rate of use is much lower than that of WeChat. WeChat and microblogs are different social apps. In terms of strong ties and weak ties, most college students would like to use WeChat, which can convey strong ties, and so microblogs, which represent weak ties, declined in popularity.

WeChat is not only a social app but also an important tool for college students seeking social information. The functions of WeChat, such as groups, friend circles, and official accounts, have made WeChat an important public platform for generating and spreading opinions on the Internet, and its influence on the thoughts and activities of college students should not be neglected. According to the survey, most college students have affirmed the huge influence of WeChat on network opinions (see Table 10.4). About 70% of college students agreed that WeChat has become the most influential communication media at present, and more than 60% of them believed that WeChat could help supervise the government and officials through public opinion. Most college students disagreed with negative opinions that affirmed that WeChat has become the source of opinions on social events, and that WeChat has aggravated the antagonism between different Internet users and between

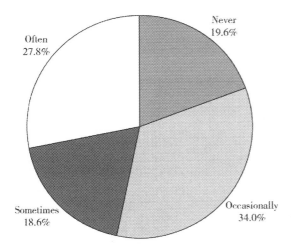

FIGURE 10.7   Usage of Microblogs among College Students

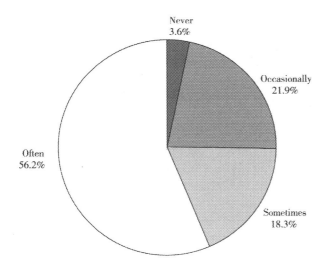

FIGURE 10.8   Usage of WeChat among College Students

Internet users and governments. However, more than half of college students agreed that the rumors generated through WeChat have significantly reduced the authenticity of Internet information. The acquaintance-society nature of the friend circle of WeChat and WeChat's system of information transmission could enable rumors to spread more easily. However, according to the results of the survey, college students had a rational and careful attitude toward WeChat and clearly recognized its negative effects. Of course, in order to guide network

SURVEY REPORT ON CHINESE COLLEGE STUDENTS' PHILOSOPHY OF LIFE 207

opinions, the related government departments should make more efforts to supervise Internet information in order to create good network entertainment.

3.3 While Making the Daily Life of College Students More Convenient, Smartphones Have Made College Students More and More Dependent on Them

The popularization of smartphones has greatly promoted the development of the mobile Internet. For college students, in addition to important communication tools, smartphones have become the major Internet surfing terminals. Smartphone Internet surfing has penetrated into all aspects of the daily lives of college students. The fast and convenient Internet surfing functions of smartphones have made the lives of college students more interesting. According to the survey, more than half of college students agreed that the use of smartphones could help them strengthen or expand their social networks. However, smartphone Internet surfing is a double-edged sword. The overuse of smartphones could generate

TABLE 10.4   College Students' Opinions of WeChat

Unit: %

Opinion	Completely agree	Agree	Disagree	Completely disagree	It's hard to say
WeChat has become the most influential communication media at present	24.1	45.4	24.2	2.7	3.6
WeChat has become the source of opinions on social events	9.3	32.8	46.3	6.4	5.2
WeChat could enable anyone to become a leader guiding social opinions	7.8	23.4	48.9	14.1	5.8
Rumors generated through WeChat have significantly reduced the authenticity of Internet information	16.2	41.8	30.6	5.0	6.4

TABLE 10.4 College Students' Opinions of WeChat (*cont.*)

Unit: %

Opinion	Completely agree	Agree	Disagree	Completely disagree	It's hard to say
WeChat has aggravated the antagonism among different Internet users and between Internet users and the governments	8.5	24.1	46.9	12.2	8.4
WeChat could help to supervise the government and officials through public opinion	14.6	51.5	21.4	3.5	9.0

negative consequences, and smartphone addiction is just one of them. In terms of the usage of smartphones, most college students have a serious smartphone addiction. More than 80% of college students said that they would feel uncomfortable if they forgot their smartphones; 70% of them would feel anxious if their smartphone could not access the Internet; and nearly 80% of them depend on smartphones to arrange their daily lives, studies, and entertainment. Compared to 2013, the dependence of college students on smartphones further deepened. Among the samples, the proportion of those who would feel uncomfortable if they forgot their smartphones increased from 80.7% in 2013 to 86.8% in 2016; and the proportions of those who would feel anxious if their smartphone could not access the Internet and those who depend on smartphones to arrange their daily lives, studies, and entertainment increased from 58.8% and 59.3% in 2013 to 75.8% and 78.3% in 2016, respectively (see Table 10.5).

TABLE 10.5 College Students' Addiction to Smartphones

Unit: %

Level of Addiction	2016	2013
I would feel uncomfortable if I forgot my smartphone	86.8	80.7
I would feel anxious if my smartphone could not get access to the Internet	75.8	80.7
I check my smart phone every 15 minutes at least	55.6	—

SURVEY REPORT ON CHINESE COLLEGE STUDENTS' PHILOSOPHY OF LIFE 209

TABLE 10.5   College Students' Addiction to Smartphones (*cont.*)
Unit: %

Level of Addiction	2016	2013
I often check my smartphone in class and at meetings	69.3	69.0
I watch my smartphone even when I am in bed	87.1	—
I depend on my smartphone for my schedule, studies, and entertainment	78.3	59.3
I cannot adapt to changing from a smartphone back to an ordinary mobile phone	70.6	56.1
I always check my smartphone, even when I am at parties	64.2	45.0
I try not to check my smartphone when I have nothing to do, but it is really hard	57.7	56.9

4   Social Attitudes

4.1   *College Students Have a High Level of Social Trust, but It Is Lower than the Average Level among the Public; They Also Have a High Level of Political Trust, but a Low Degree of Trust in Local Governments*

Trust is the reflection of social mentality. With the rapid economic transformation of China, the traditional trust modes have been constantly impacted, and the degree of trust among people has been decreasing. Many people believe that a crisis of trust has emerged in China. However, according to the 2014 World Values Survey (wvs), 64.4% of Chinese people thought that most people in society could be trusted, which was much higher than the world average (25.4%). According to the data of the 2015 "Longitudinal Survey on China's Employment, Lives, and Values of College Students and Graduates," 47.5% of college students thought that most people in society could be trusted. This proportion was lower than the Chinese public's average level of trust, but still much higher than the global average.

Political trust can be used to measure the public's recognition of the government's governance and to detect the image of the government among the public. According to transnational comparison research in the past, the level of the Chinese public's trust in politics was relatively high. According to the data of the 2015 "Longitudinal Survey on China's Employment, Lives, and Values of College Students and Graduates," the degree of college students' trust in government organs was generally high, and may increase with the level of government.

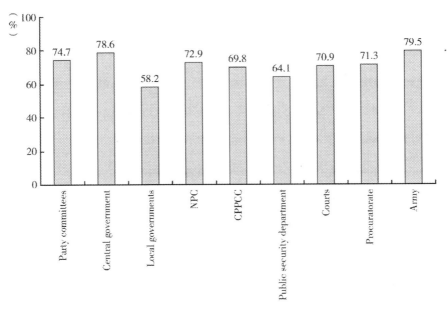

FIGURE 10.9   Degree of College Students' Trust in Different Government Organs (2015)

The degree of college students' trust in the party committees, the central government and the army was as high as 74.7%, 78.6%, and 79.5%, respectively (see Figure 10.9). The degree of college students' trust in local governments was the lowest—much lower than their trust in the superior organizations.

4.2   College Students Were Sensitive to Social Conflicts and Had a Clear Consciousness of Social Conflict

China is undergoing a rapid economic and social transformation with an aggravated differentiation of benefits, and the social contradictions and conflicts among various groups due to that differentiation are also being aggravated. How did college students sense such social conflicts and disputes? In the 2015 "Longitudinal Survey on China's Employment, Lives, and Values of College Students and Graduates," the researchers described social conflicts among six pairs of groups and asked the interviewees to judge the severities of those social conflicts. There were five options, including "No conflict," "Not so severe," "It's hard to say," "Relatively severe," and "Very severe." According to the results of the survey, college students had different opinions regarding the conflicts of interest among the various groups. In general, college students thought that the conflicts between the poor and the rich, the government officials and the people, and the bosses and employees were severe, but they regarded conflicts among different races/ethnic groups, different religious groups, and natives and outsiders as not so severe.

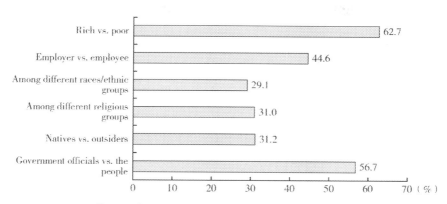

FIGURE 10.10   College Students' Feelings about Social Conflicts

College students thought that the gap between the rich and the poor is the most outstanding social conflict, and 62.7% of them believed that this conflict is relatively severe or very severe, which may reflect the relatively severe gap between the rich and the poor to some extent. In addition, about 56.7% of college students thought that the conflict between government officials and the people was relatively severe or very severe, indicating that the image of government officials in the eyes of college students was not good and that the credibility of the government should be improved as soon as possible (see Figure 10.10).

5   Conclusion

With the constant reformation and development of society, the values of college students have been changing, showing different features in different periods. In a China undergoing social transformation, all aspects of social entertainment change rapidly, and these changes have significantly influenced the important values of college students, including their philosophy of life and their social attitudes. Understanding the features of the changes in the values of college students is of great importance to guiding their development in a better way. We have analyzed the major features and changing tendencies of modern college students regarding their philosophy of life and social attitudes in four dimensions, which are their outlook on employment, their outlook on consumption, their network participation, and their social attitudes.

In terms of their concept of employment, modern college students have similar features to those in the past. For example, most of them would like to work in stated-owned institutions, enterprises, and governments as well as in major cities, but their job options are diversified. In terms of consumption, college students showed features of economical and rational consumption coupled with a pursuit of quality and fashion, and the quality of their lives has become the new consumption proposition for a new generation of college students. The rapid development of the Internet and the popularization of smartphones have significantly influenced college students. Cyberspace has gradually become an important place for social interaction, communication, and entertainment among college students, and smartphones enable them to get access to the Internet in any place and at any time. However, we should not neglect the negative consequences of the excessive usage of new media. For example, frequent online activities have been reducing the time and effort devoted by college students to studying, and the overuse of smartphones has aggravated their addiction to smartphones. In terms of social attitudes, college students have relatively high levels of social and political trust and are sensitive to social conflicts, indicating their obvious consciousness of social conflicts. We can say that college students have a high recognition of the nation and of society and a clear awareness of the social conflicts at present.

The new features and changes of college students in terms of philosophy of life and social attitudes are a result of various factors during the social transformation. We can see the values of the sharing of a social community, the sub-cultural elements on campus, the traditional historical heritage, the new thoughts within the new situation, and the unique values and activities of their age among college students.

Each generation of youth has its own challenges and opportunities. President Xi Jinping has spoken highly of modern college students: "Modern college students are full of youthful spirit and they are studious, with a wide sphere of points of view; they are open, confident, and trustful and are bound to make great achievements in the future." This comment shows trust and expectations. The analysis of the new features and changes in terms of the philosophy of life and social attitudes of college students during the social transformation will be of great importance in guiding them to establish a correct value orientation and promoting their healthy development.

References

China Internet Network Information Center. The 39th Statistical Report on the Development of the Internet Network of China, 2017.

Ma Deyong. "Political Trust and Its Origin—Comparison Research on Eight Countries in Asia." *Comparative Economic & Social Systems*, 2007(5).

Yang Qianqian. "Research on the Anomie of the Spread of WeChat." *Journal of News Research*, 2016(18).

CHAPTER 11

Survey Report on the Living Conditions of the New White-Collar Urban Workers: A Study of Shanghai in 2017

Sun Xiulin[1] and Shi Runhua[2]

Abstract

The new white-collar workers have become a very important social group in in China's cities. Attention to this group is of great importance to the future development of Chinese society. In this report, we have used sampling data from the Shanghai Urban Neighborhood Survey (SUNS) to analyze the social conditions of new white-collar urban workers in Shanghai, including their jobs, social lives, and social attitudes.

Keywords

Shanghai – new white-collar urban workers – social conditions – urban survey

With the rapid economic and social development of China, the middle-income group is expanding gradually, and the social structure is changing to an olive shape, where the bulk of the people belong to the middle-income group.[3] The new white-collar urban workers are an important part of the middle-income group and will play a more and more important role in the new stage of development. Therefore, understanding the living conditions of these new workers in cities is of great practical and theoretical importance to understanding the current conditions and future tendencies of the social development of China. Shanghai is one of the megacities of China, and it is in the final stage of becoming a modern cosmopolis. In addition, Shanghai is a typical immigrant city, and a lot of white collar workers have moved to this city, becoming the so-called

---

1 Sun Xiulin, Ph.D., professor of the School of Sociology and Political Science, Shanghai University, research orientation: city space.
2 Shi Runhua, master's degree, Shanghai Academy of Educational Sciences, research orientation: social development evaluation.
3 Li Peilin, "Growth of the Middle Class and a Middle Class–Dominated Society," *International Economic Review*, 2015(1).

© KONINKLIJKE BRILL NV, LEIDEN, 2022 | DOI:10.1163/9789004500723_012

new white-collar urban workers. These new workers are not only a special group in Shanghai, but they are also representative of the typical groups in China's megacities. Therefore, it is highly innovative and necessary to carry out research on the structure of this group of new white-collar workers and to analyze their social conditions from all angles, including jobs, lifestyles, and social attitudes, so as to explore the innovations in the system of social management for high-end immigrants, provide references for the policies made by governments, and promote the harmonious development of society.

1   A Definition of the New White-Collar Urban Workers and an Introduction to the Survey Data

"White collar" is defined differently in different countries. The term originated in the United States in the twentieth century. According to the *Collins Essential English Dictionary*, "white collar" refers to those employees working in offices and not engaged in manual labor. As it was first used in Western countries, the concept of "white collar" was supposed to contrast with "blue collar," or workers whose jobs involve manual labor. The group of white-collar urban workers has become the main body of the middle class today. To distinguish them from the traditional middle class, they are sometimes called the new middle class. Although scholars in Western countries have different explanations of who white-collar urban workers are, most would consider them as the middle class or the new middle class.[4]

At present, there is no definitive definition of white-collar urban workers in China.[5] The system of classification of professions in China is more complicated than that in Western society.[6] For example, according to Li Qiang, internationally, people think of the responsible people in government organs, party organizations, institutions, and enterprises, including professional technicians, clerks and employees, and business servants, as white-collar urban workers, and classify the operators of production and transportation facilities and workers in agriculture, forestry, animal husbandry, and the fishing industry as blue-collar workers. In China, however, given the backward development of the service industry, many people in this industry have a low social

---

4   Charles Wright Mills: *White Collar: The American Middle Classes*, translated by Zhou Xiaohong, Nanjing University Press, 2016.

5   Li Chunling, "Definitions of Concepts of the Middle-Income Group and Middle Class—Comparison between the Sociological and Economic Orientations," *Journal of Chinese Academy of Governance*, 2016(6).

6   Zhang Yi, "Research on the Tendency of Structural Change of the Social Classes of China—Analysis Based on the National CGSS Survey Data," *Studies on Socialism with Chinese Characteristics*, 2011(3).

status and they can hardly be classified as white-collar urban workers, as in Western countries.[7] According to the existing research, there are two definitions of new white-collar urban workers: The first one is a broad definition, in which white-collar urban workers are those who do brainwork; and the other one is a narrow definition that specifies white-collar urban workers as those with higher educational backgrounds, higher incomes, and higher positions. For example, Yang Xiong defined white-collar urban workers in Shanghai as personnel in management or technical posts who have higher educational backgrounds and higher incomes.[8]

Based on the opinions of scholars both at home and abroad, in the following analysis we have defined new white-collar urban workers as those who were not born in Shanghai, have an educational background higher than junior college, and are carrying out non-physical work in Shanghai.

The data used herein are from the Shanghai Urban Neighborhood Survey (SUNS), completed by the Center for Data and Urban Sciences (CENDUS) of Shanghai University in 2017. The SUNS is a longitudinal survey covering communities, households, and individuals at multiple levels. The survey at the community level covered community spaces and facilities, the community population structure, community organization, community resources, and community governance. The survey at the household level covered family structures, the social and economic status of households, family relationships, and family life. The survey at the individual level covered the basic features of individuals, including work, life, health, social attitudes and opinions, and community participation. The surveys were conducted with the Computer-Assisted Personal Interviewing (CAPI) system to ensure the effects of the complicated design of the survey at the community, household, and individual levels.

The SUNS has two sub-items, namely, a village (neighborhood) committee survey and a resident survey. (1) Village (neighborhood) committee survey: Among more than 5,700 village (neighborhood) committees, samples were taken at the proportion of 10% to survey various governance subjects within the communities, including village (neighborhood) committees, owner committees, property management companies, social organizations, and social workers. In 2015, survey questionnaires for 538 villages and communities were completed, in addition to 695 questionnaires for property management companies, 586 questionnaires for owner committees, 362 questionnaires for social organizations, and 531 questionnaires for social workers. (2) Resident

---

7 Li Qiang, "How Far Is China from the Middle Class–Dominated Society?—The Sociological Analysis of the Development of the Middle Class," *Exploration and Free Views*, 2016(8); Li Qiang and Wang Hao, "Issues of Scale and Structure of the Middle Class of China and Developmental Measures," *Society*, 2017(3).

8 Yang Xiong, "Survey of Occupational Lives of the White-Collar Urban Youth in Shanghai," *Youth Studies*, 1999(6).

survey: 180 representative villages and communities in the city were sampled from the above 538 villages and communities, and 30 households were chosen from each village and community for a survey of all the family members within each household. By working closely with the Population Office of Shanghai and the Shanghai Civil Affairs Bureau, more than 900 investigators worked for nearly 80,000 hours to complete the resident survey, including 5,100 household questionnaires, 8,600 adult questionnaires (over 15 years old), and 1,900 child questionnaires, after overcoming various difficulties in surveying the households in urban areas in July 2017 (see Figure 11.1). This survey has a complicated design as well as the largest samples among the various surveys and research projects on individual cities both at home and abroad, providing sufficient fundamental data for innovative research on the unique city communities in China and the development of the discourse system of the social sciences with Chinese characteristics.[9]

In this report, we have defined new white-collar urban workers as those who were not born in Shanghai, have an educational background that is higher than junior college, and carry out non-physical work in Shanghai. According to this definition, in our database there are 794 new white-collar urban workers. The following analysis exclusively treats this group in Shanghai.

2 Working Conditions of the New White-Collar Urban Workers in Shanghai

2.1 *The Yangtze River Delta Is the Major Source of the New White-Collar Urban Workers in Shanghai*

Among the interviewees, new white-collar urban workers from Jiangsu accounted for 27.89%, those from Anhui accounted for 13.61%, those from Jiangxi 10.88%, and those from Zhejiang 8.84%. From the above information we can see that new white-collar urban workers in Shanghai are mainly from the Yangtze River Delta (see Figure 11.2).

2.2 *The Jobs of the New White-Collar Urban Workers Are Concentrated in Secondary and Tertiary Industries*

According to the industry distribution of new white-collar urban workers, the proportion of workers in information transmission, software, and the IT service industry was the highest at 17.83%, followed by the manufacturing industry at 16.14%. The proportions in the financial industry and the wholesale

---

9 Wu Xiaogang and Sun Xiulin, "Basic Database for Urban Survey Facilitates Social Governance," *Chinese Social Sciences Today*, November 8, 2017, Ed. 006.

LIVING CONDITIONS OF THE NEW WHITE-COLLAR URBAN WORKERS 217

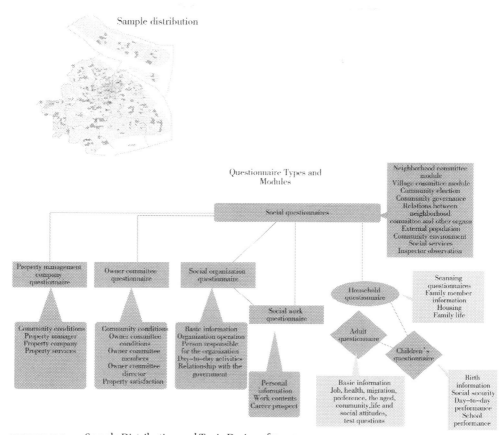

FIGURE 11.1   Sample Distribution and Topic Design of SUNS

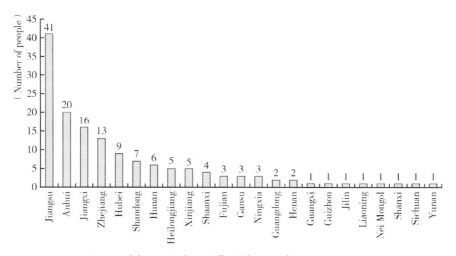

FIGURE 11.2   Origins of the New White-Collar Urban Workers

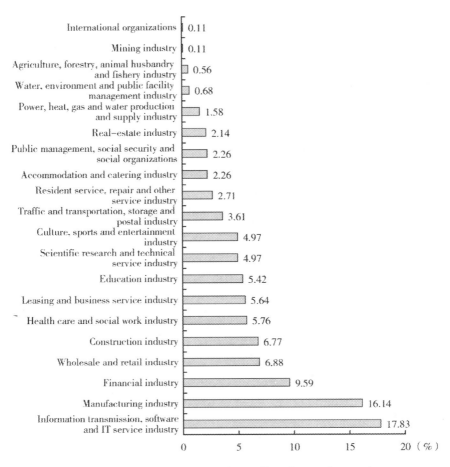

FIGURE 11.3   Industries in Which the New White-Collar Urban Workers Work

and retail industry were 9.59% and 6.88%, respectively. The proportions in the construction industry, health care industry, and social work industry were about 6%. The proportions in the power, heat, gas, and water production and supply industry (1.58%); water, environment, and public facility management industry (0.68%); agriculture, forestry, animal husbandry, and fishery industry (0.56%); mining industry (0.11%); and international organizations (0.11%) were relatively low, all below 2% (see Figure 11.3).

2.3   *The Jobs of the New White-Collar Urban Workers Are Concentrated in the Non-Public Sector*

In terms of employers, among the interviewees, 42.44% of the new white-collar urban workers were working for private enterprises, 20.49% were working for foreign-financed enterprises, 8.73% were running individual

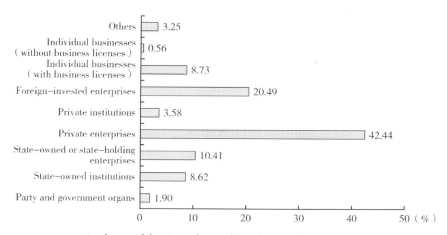

FIGURE 11.4   Employers of the New White-Collar Urban Workers

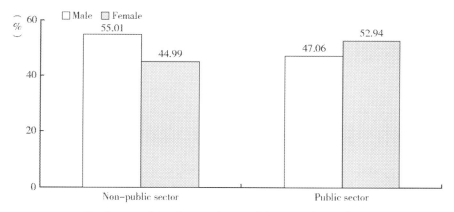

FIGURE 11.5   Employers and Gender Distribution of the New White-Collar Urban Workers

businesses, and 10.41% were working for state-owned or state-holding enterprises. A total of 8.62% were working for state-owned institutions, and 1.9% for party and government organs. If the party and government organs, state-owned institutions, and state-owned or state-holding enterprises are covered by the public-ownership sector, then the private enterprises, private institutions, foreign-financed enterprises, and individual businesses belong to the non-public sector. According to the distribution, most of the new white-collar urban workers in Shanghai were working in the non-public sector, and more than 70% of the employers of new white-collar urban workers were in the non-public sector (see Figure 11.4).

The public sector attracts more females. In terms of gender, more male new white-collar urban workers were working in the non-public sector, accounting

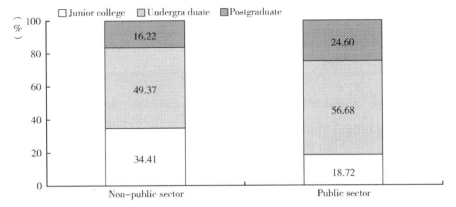

FIGURE 11.6   Employers and Educational Background of the New White-Collar Urban Workers

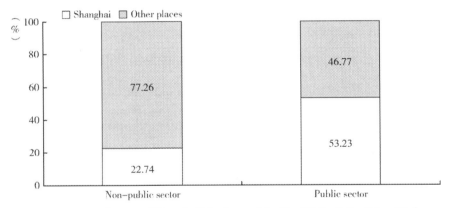

FIGURE 11.7   Employers and Household Registers of the New White-Collar Urban Workers

for 55.01%, while females accounted for 44.99%. More women were working in the public sector, accounting for 52.94%, while males accounted for 47.06% (see Figure 11.5).

The public sector attracts more talents with high educational backgrounds. The new white-collar urban workers working in the public sector had higher educational backgrounds than those working in the non-public sector (postgraduates accounted for 24.60%, undergraduates 56.68%, and junior college graduates 18.72%). In the non-public sector, postgraduates accounted for 16.22%, undergraduates 49.37%, and junior college graduates 34.41% (see Figure 11.6). In general, most of the new white-collar urban workers have an undergraduate background.

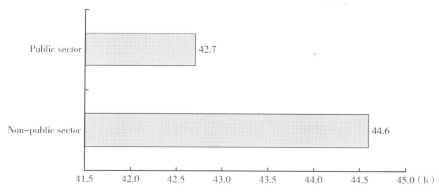

FIGURE 11.8 Working Hours of the New White-Collar Urban Workers in Units of a Different Nature

The non-public sector is more tolerant and inclusive of white-collar urban workers from other cities. According to the survey data, in the non-public sector, only 22.74% of the new white-collar urban workers have Shanghai household registers, and 77.26% of them have household registers from other places. In the public sector, however, the new white-collar urban workers with Shanghai household registers accounted for 53.23%, and those with household registers in other places accounted for 46.77% (see Figure 11.7).

2.4 A Great Difference Exists among the Different Types of New White-Collar Urban Workers in Terms of Working Hours and Income

According to the survey, the actual working hours for the new white-collar urban workers in Shanghai for each week were 44.2, and the average monthly salary was 12,573.8 yuan. When asked if their employers could provide or fund occupational skills training, 32.9% of the new white-collar urban workers said that they had never received any training. Among those who had received training, nearly half of them (47%) had not received any occupational qualification certificates acceptable to the national government or their industries. In terms of gender, type of employer, and household register, the new white-collar urban workers are different in terms of working hours and income.

In terms of actual working hours, the new white-collar urban workers in the non-public sector worked 44.6 hours per week, while the number of those working in the public sector was 42.7 (see Figure 11.8). The average monthly income of the new white-collar urban workers in the non-public sector (13,432 yuan) was also higher than that of those in the public sector (9,273 yuan) (see Figure 11.9).

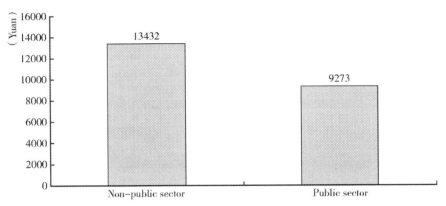

FIGURE 11.9   Monthly Salaries of the New White-Collar Urban Workers in Units of a Different Nature

The new white-collar urban workers with household registers in other places would work 44.9 hours per week, which was higher than the 42.5 hours of those with Shanghai household registers (see Figure 11.10). However, the average monthly income of the new white-collar urban workers with household registers in other places was 11,628 yuan, which was lower than the 14,961 yuan of those with Shanghai household registers (see Figure 11.11). From this we can see that, for the new white-collar urban workers with household registers in other places, their income was not commensurate with their hard work.

At the same time, the income of male new white-collar urban workers was much higher than that of the females. The monthly income of male new white-collar urban workers was 15,657.8 yuan, while that of the females was only 8,938.6 yuan (see Figure 11.12).

2.5   A Great Difference Exists among the Different Types of New White-Collar Urban Workers in Terms of Social Security

According to the data, the rate of participation of the new white-collar urban workers in basic health care insurance was 93.95%; in basic pension insurance, 92%; in unemployment insurance, 84.77%; and their rate of contribution to the housing provident fund was 83.37%. From the data, we can see that the rates of participation in the various social insurances among the new white-collar urban workers in the public sector were higher than those for the new white-collar urban workers in the non-public sector (see Figure 11.13).

In general, social security for female new white-collar urban workers was better than that for males, but the social security of the males was more inclusive. The females had higher rates of participation than the males in basic

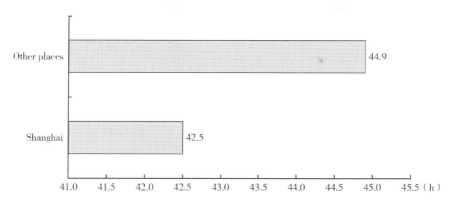

FIGURE 11.10   Working Hours of the New White-Collar Urban Workers with Different Household Registers

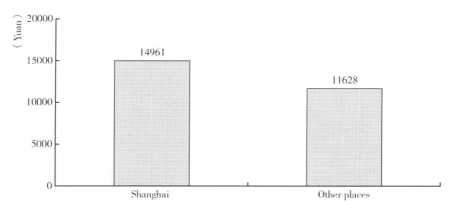

FIGURE 11.11   Monthly Salaries of the New White-Collar Urban Workers with Different Household Registers

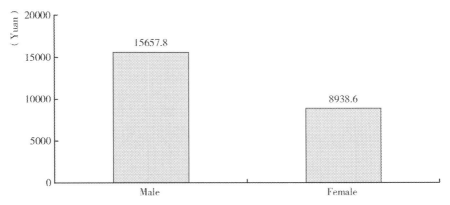

FIGURE 11.12   Gender Comparison of Monthly Salaries of the New White-Collar Urban Workers

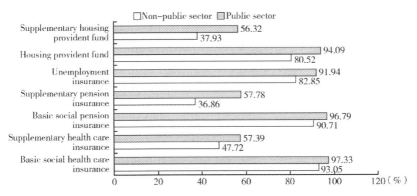

FIGURE 11.13   Rates of Participation in Social Insurance of the New White-Collar Urban Workers in Units of a Different Nature

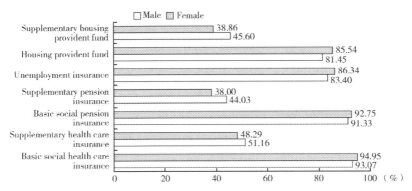

FIGURE 11.14   Gender Comparison of the Social Security of the New White-Collar Urban Workers

health care insurance, basic pension insurance, unemployment insurance, and the housing provident fund. In terms of supplementary health care insurance, supplementary pension insurance, and the supplementary housing provident fund, male new white-collar urban workers had more advantages than females (see Figure 11.14).

The social security of those with local household registers was better than that of those with household registers in other places. According to the data, the rate of participation of the new white-collar urban workers with Shanghai household registers in basic health care insurance was 96.90%, which was higher than the 92.72% among those with household registers in other places; the rate of participation of the new white-collar urban workers with Shanghai household registers in basic pension insurance was 96.89%, which was higher

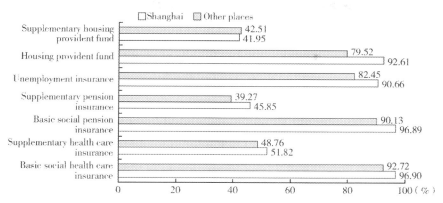

FIGURE 11.15   Social Security among New White-Collar Urban Workers with Different Household Registers

than the 90.13% for those with household registers in other places; the rate of participation of the new white-collar urban workers with Shanghai household registers in unemployment insurance was 90.66%, which was higher than the 82.45% for those with household registers in other places; and the rate of contribution of the new white-collar urban workers with Shanghai household registers in the housing provident fund was 92.61%, which was higher than the 79.52% for those with household registers in other places. The new white-collar urban workers with household registers in other places only had a higher rate of participation in the supplementary housing provident fund (42.51%), where they exceeded the participation rate of the new white-collar urban workers with Shanghai household registers (41.95%; see Figure 11.15).

3   Social Lives of the New White-Collar Urban Workers in Shanghai

3.1   *Residences of the New White-Collar Urban Workers*
The new white-collar urban workers had a high rate of movement, with a low rate of housing ownership and fixed types of residence. On average, each new white-collar urban worker in Shanghai changed his or her residence 2.6 times, and 71.2% of them did not own a house in Shanghai. In terms of types of residence, most of the new white-collar urban workers in Shanghai were living in ordinary commercial housing units (45.30%), old industrial / public housing units (24.44%), or flats/dorms provided by employers (7.33%; see Figure 11.16).

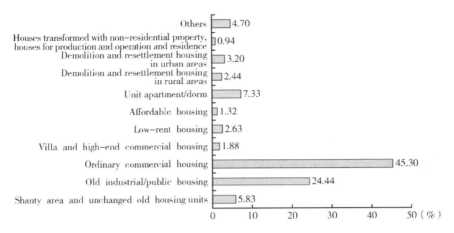

FIGURE 11.16   Types of Residence among the New White-Collar Urban Workers

3.2   *Commuting among the New White-Collar Urban Workers*

The new white-collar urban workers living in downtown areas accounted for 40.74%; those living in the near suburbs accounted for 42.08%, and those living in outer suburbs accounted for only 17.19% (see Figure 11.17).

In terms of commuting time, the new white-collar urban workers living in downtown areas had the shortest commuting time of 41.6 minutes every day; the time for those living in outer suburbs was 45 minutes; and the time for those living in the near suburbs was 49.5 minutes (see Figure 11.18).

3.3   *Physical Condition of the New White-Collar Urban Workers*

The new white-collar urban workers had healthier lifestyles and paid more attention to the management of their health. More than 80% of them did not drink or smoke, and more than 70% of them did not have any common diseases. Only 18.3% of the new white-collar urban workers included in the survey smoked, and 17.1% of them drank alcoholic beverages. According to the results of the survey, in the past 12 months, 70.4% of the new white-collar urban workers have received physical examinations. At the same time, 31% of them have purchased commercial medical insurance policies. This indicates that the new white-collar urban workers attach great importance to their health.

More than 60% of them would perform physical exercises and more than 70% of them had received a physical examination in the past year. According to the results of the survey, 14.52% of the new white-collar urban workers worked out almost every day in the past three months, 16.67% of them worked out two or three times per week, 17.55% of them once a week, and only 36.49% of them never worked out (see Figure 11.19).

LIVING CONDITIONS OF THE NEW WHITE-COLLAR URBAN WORKERS

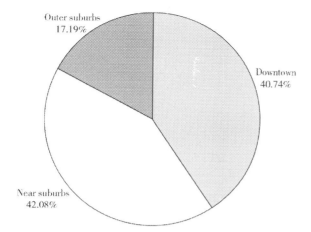

FIGURE 11.17   Living Areas of the New White-Collar Urban Workers

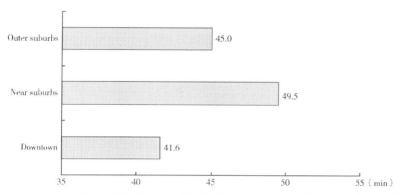

FIGURE 11.18   Place of Residence and Daily Commuting Time of the New White-Collar Urban Workers

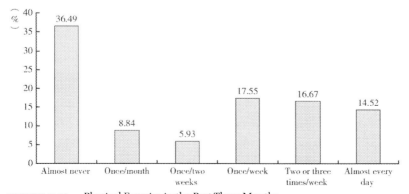

FIGURE 11.19   Physical Exercise in the Past Three Months

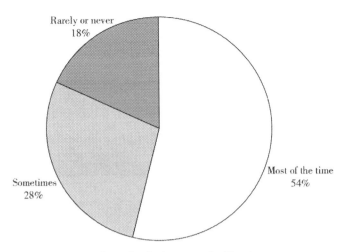

FIGURE 11.20　Feeling of Refreshment in the Morning

Most of the new white-collar urban workers had good sleep and rest conditions. In the past month, the average sleeping time of the new white-collar urban workers each night was 6.9 hours. More than half of the interviewees (54%) said that they felt refreshed in the morning, and only 18% of them said that they rarely or never rested sufficiently (see Figure 11.20).

Most (72.29%) of the new white-collar urban workers have not had any common diseases. Among the new white-collar urban workers diagnosed with diseases, those suffering from intestinal and stomach diseases accounted for 13.60%, those suffering from hyperlipidemia / high cholesterol accounted for 6.17%; and those suffering from lung diseases and high blood pressure accounted for 3.90% and 3.78%, respectively (see Figure 11.21).

3.4　Social Interactions of the New White-Collar Urban Workers

The new white-collar urban workers have widespread and diversified social interactions. Most of them did not have the experience of living in Shanghai when they were young, but their social interaction is sufficiently varied. According to the data, 86.2% of the interviewees did not live in Shanghai for more than 6 months before the age of 14. About 31% of the interviewees studied in Shanghai for an average period of 5.6 years. In terms of social interactions, nearly 40% (38.46%) of the interviewees said that most of their friends were from other places, and 3.53% of them said that all of their friends were from other places. About 20% of the interviewees said that most of their friends were Shanghai natives (see Figure 11.22).

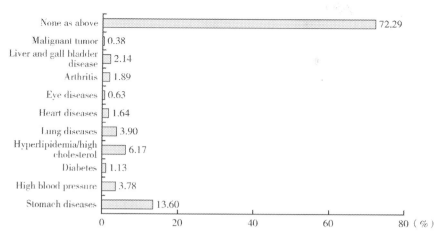

FIGURE 11.21   Common Diseases among the New White-Collar Urban Workers

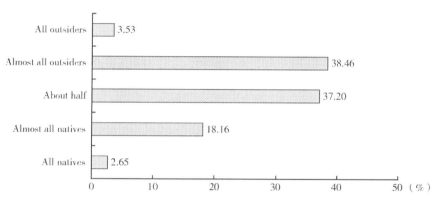

FIGURE 11.22   Composition of the Circles of Friends of the New White-Collar Urban Workers

More than half of the new white-collar urban workers (52.03%) said that most of their friends from other places were not fellow townsmen, while 20.25% of them said that nearly half of their friends from other places were fellow townsmen (see Figure 11.23). The social network and interactions of the new white-collar urban workers in Shanghai were relatively widespread and sufficiently varied.

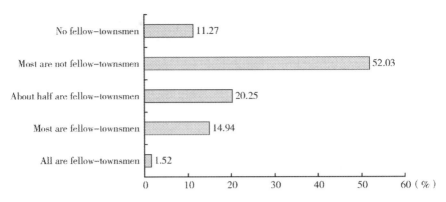

FIGURE 11.23   Proportion of Fellow Townsmen among the Friends of New White-Collar Urban Worker from Other Places

4   Social Attitudes of the New White-Collar Urban Workers in Shanghai

4.1   *The Degree of Satisfaction of the New White-Collar Urban Workers with Their Jobs Was Relatively High, but about 30% of Them Wanted to Change Jobs*

In general, about 60% of the new white-collar urban workers were satisfied with their jobs (satisfied: 47.93%; very satisfied: 12.74%). The new white-collar urban workers who were very unsatisfied with their jobs accounted for 0.45%; those who were dissatisfied with their jobs accounted for 1.90%; and those who were satisfied with their jobs accounted for 36.98% (see Figure 11.24). From this we can see that the new white-collar urban workers in Shanghai were relatively satisfied with their jobs.

Among the interviewees, 30% of them said that they wanted to change jobs and 70% of them did not want to do so. The more dissatisfied they were with their jobs, the more they wanted to change them. Among the new white-collar urban workers who were very dissatisfied and dissatisfied with their jobs, the proportions of those who wanted to change jobs were 75% and 88.24%, respectively (see Figure 11.25).

4.2   *The New White-Collar Urban Workers Had Good Living Conditions and Were Satisfied with Their Residences*

According to the data, the per capita living area of residences of the new white-collar urban workers in Shanghai was 24.4 square meters, which was basically the same as the per capita living area of 24.16 square meters that was obtained through the survey on the residences and properties of Shanghai

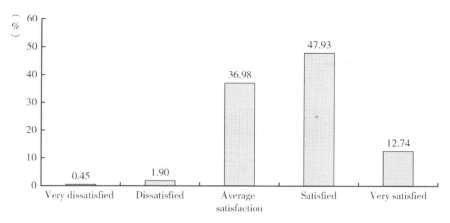

FIGURE 11.24　Feelings of Job Satisfaction among the New White-Collar Urban Workers in Shanghai

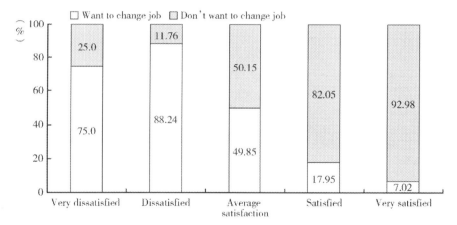

FIGURE 11.25　Job Satisfaction and Intention to Change Jobs among the New White-Collar Urban Workers in Shanghai

residents conducted by the Social Survey Center and the Institute of Sociology of the Shanghai Academy of Social Sciences.[10] When asked about their level of satisfaction with their residences, only about 10% of the interviewees said that they were dissatisfied (very dissatisfied: 1.56%; dissatisfied: 8.37%). More than half of the new white-collar urban workers were satisfied with their residences (very satisfied: 7.48%; satisfied: 42.63%; see Figure 11.26).

10　http://news.163.com/15/0414/10/AN5G8I8700014AED.html.

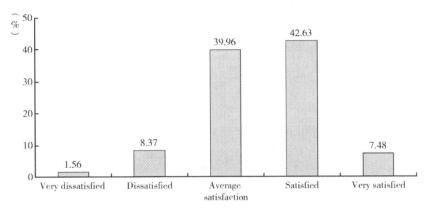

FIGURE 11.26   Satisfaction of the New White-Collar Urban Workers with Their Residences

4.3 Most New White-Collar Urban Workers Did Not Think That They Were a Vulnerable Group, and Only a Few of Them Thought Their Income Was Unfair

Nearly 60% (58.70%) of the new white-collar urban workers did not think they were a vulnerable group (totally not: 16.50%; not: 42.20%); and only 12.79% of the interviewees thought that they were or totally were a vulnerable group (see Figure 11.27).

Among the new white-collar urban workers, 33.63% of them thought that their incomes matched their educational backgrounds and capacities, and they obtained the returns they deserved. Those who thought their incomes were fair accounted for 30.32%, and 3.31% of them thought their incomes were very fair. Only 17.83% of the interviewees thought their incomes were unfair (see Figure 11.28). More than 70% (71.8%) of the new white-collar urban workers didn't want to leave Shanghai for other places to live or work.

4.4 The Values and Social Attitudes of the New White-Collar Urban Workers Are Diversified

More than half of the new white-collar urban workers agreed with marriages between two people who can match each other in all aspects; 10.1% of them totally supported such marriages and 46.1% of them relatively supported them. And 24.71% of the new white-collar urban workers did not care about this. Nearly 20% of the new white-collar urban workers did not agree that the precondition of a happy marriage should be that the two people match each other in all aspects.

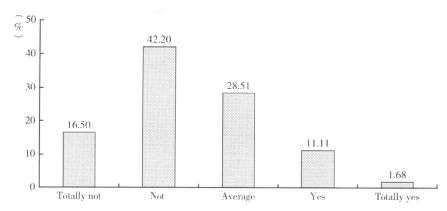

FIGURE 11.27   Vulnerable Group or Not

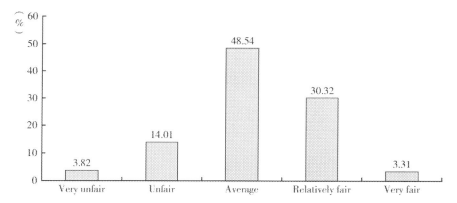

FIGURE 11.28   Opinions on Fairness of Current Income

More than 60% of the new white-collar urban workers agreed to pass legislation for euthanasia; 16.3% of them completely agreed and 44% of them agreed to a relative degree. And 24.7% of them thought it was fine. Those who did not agree with euthanasia accounted for nearly 15%.

In terms of passing laws to forbid eating dogs, the proportions of the new white-collar urban workers who agreed (33.5%), disagreed (32.1%), and were fine with it (34.4%) were about the same.

At the same time, in the past year, 53.2% of the new white-collar urban workers donated to institutions or individuals and 15.2% of them served as volunteers.

4.5 The New White-Collar Urban Workers in Shanghai Had a Good Level of Social Inclusion with a Low Degree of Self-Identity

In terms of attitudes to Shanghai natives, fewer than 8% of the new white-collar urban workers reported negative feelings about them (very much dislike: 2.53%; dislike: 5.32%), and those who liked Shanghai natives accounted for more than 30% (like very much: 9.25%; like to a relative degree: 25.60%; see Figure 11.29).

According to the scale of social distance, we found that more than 90% of the interviewees would like to work with natives (93.63%), live with them in the same community (96.44%), and be neighbors with them (92.98%). When asked if they welcome natives to their homes, 87.10% of the interviewees selected "Yes." And 89.45% of the new white-collar urban workers would agree to let their children or relatives date natives (see Figure 11.30). In general, the degree of social inclusion of the new white-collar urban workers in Shanghai was relatively good, with excellent social relationships.

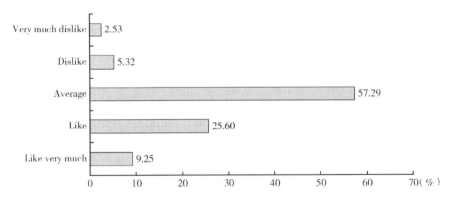

FIGURE 11.29   Attitudes of the New White-Collar Urban Workers toward Shanghai Natives

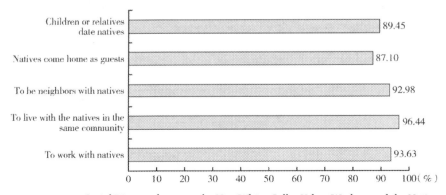

FIGURE 11.30   Social Distance between the New White-Collar Urban Workers and the Natives

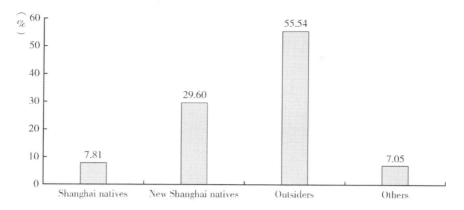

FIGURE 11.31 Self-Identity of the New White-Collar Urban Workers

In terms of self-identity, more than half (55.54%) of the new white-collar urban workers thought they were outsiders, nearly 30% (29.60%) of them thought they were new Shanghai natives, and only 7.81% of them thought they were Shanghai natives (see Figure 11.31). From the above information we can see that most new white-collar urban workers in Shanghai did not think they were Shanghai natives.

4.6 The New White-Collar Urban Workers Were Confident about the Safety of Their Community with a High Level of Neighborly Interaction

According to the survey, the rate of awareness among new white-collar urban workers of burglaries that occurred in their communities was only 6.9%. When asked if they dared to walk alone in their communities after 10 p.m., 85.8% of the interviewees said that they would not be concerned about their safety. This means that the new white-collar urban workers were confident about the safety of their communities.

At the same time, according to the survey, 62.5% of the interviewees had talked with or visited neighbors. About half of the interviewees (49.5%) knew their neighbors' jobs. When asked if they could ask their neighbors to receive express packages on behalf of them, more than half of the interviewees (54.23%) said that there would be no problem in doing so, including 30.97% for totally no problem and 23.26% for no problem on most occasions (see Figure 11.32).

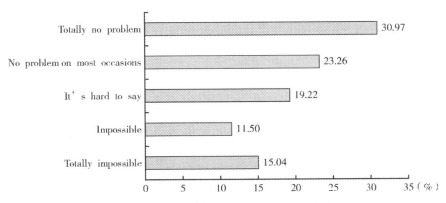

FIGURE 11.32   Willingness to Trust Neighbors to Receive Express Packages

4.7   New White-Collar Urban Workers' Rate of Participation in Community Activities Was Low, with an Ordinary Community Identity

According to the data, the new white-collar urban workers who voted during the owner committee meetings of their communities accounted for only 18.5%; those who participated in discussions about the public affairs of their communities only accounted for 7.9%, and those who provided suggestions or advice to their neighborhood committees, owner committees, or property management companies accounted for 17.7% (see Figure 11.33). In general, the rate of participation in community activities among the new white-collar urban workers was not high. At the same time, 91.3% of the new white-collar urban workers did not know the directors of their neighborhood committees, and 35.8% of them did not know the addresses of the offices of the neighborhood committees.

With the scale design, we obtained the sense of identity of the new white-collar urban workers with respect to their communities, and we scored each opinion from "completely disagree" to "completely agree" (1–5). The higher the score, the higher the sense of identity. According to the results, the community identity of the new white-collar urban workers in Shanghai was at an average level. The sense of identity for "I can trust the people in this community" was scored as 3.3; that for "The people living here would like to help each other" was 3.5; that for "I am qualified and able to participate in decisions related to the matters of the community" was 2.7; and that for "I can identify the major problems in the community in a good way" was 3.0 (see Figure 11.34).

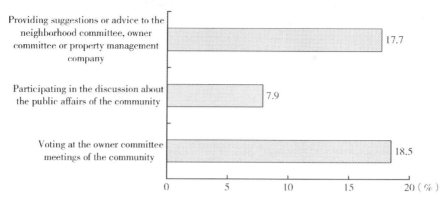

FIGURE 11.33 Participation of the New White-Collar Urban Workers in Community Activities

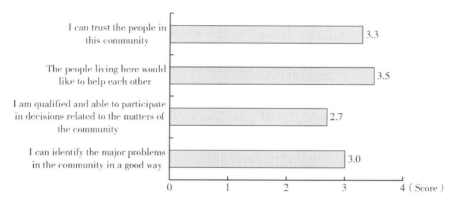

FIGURE 11.34 Community Identity of the New White-Collar Urban Workers

5   Conclusion

With the deepening of the reform and opening-up, population movement within Chinese society is becoming more and more frequent. At the same time, with the expansion of higher education, more and more well-educated youth would like to stay in cities to make their dreams come true. In Shanghai, the new white-collar urban workers have become an integral part of the metropolis. In recent years, with the implementation of a series of measures to deepen the reform in Shanghai, the city has become a pilot area for the new round of China's reform and opening-up policies, and it would take part in global competition more frequently, becoming an important link in the urban pattern of the world. The global flow and allocation of elements have left Shanghai needing more talents than ever before, especially high-quality talents. Only by understanding the actual conditions of the new white-collar urban workers can we effectively and accurately provide them with excellent working and living environments and better stimulate their innovative and creative abilities to make contributions to developing Shanghai into an excellent city with world-class influence.

From the empirical study we can see that against the macro background of the optimization of economic structure and structural reform on the supply side, the new white-collar urban workers in Shanghai are working in various industries in the non-public sector and tend to have a high degree of satisfaction with the city, frequent social interactions in Shanghai, a high degree of social inclusion, and great confidence in the city. However, we should also note that the degree of internationalization in Shanghai is still low, the integration of talents with its economic and social development has not been sufficient, and the capacity for aggregation of talents is still limited.

First of all, the new white-collar urban workers in Shanghai are chiefly from the Yangtze River Delta. In the industries that will be mainly developed in the future, such as financial services, information services, technological services, high-end manufacturing, and AI, the number, quality and the structure of distribution of the new white-collar urban workers were far from enough. In the non-public sector, the number of new white-collar urban workers with higher educational backgrounds was still low. The spatial distribution of the new white-collar urban workers in Shanghai was not uniform, with a limited degree of aggregation.

Second, the working conditions and life guarantees of the new white-collar urban workers in Shanghai were relatively good, with a generally high degree of satisfaction, but there were still some differences in terms of gender, household registration, and type of employer. For example, the male new white-collar urban workers had more advantages than females. Without Shanghai household registers, the new white-collar urban workers would face unfair treatment in terms of systems, economy, and society. Differences in the market and institutional environments would also force the new white-collar urban workers to separate themselves. Various factors have directly or indirectly led to the loss of the sense of identity and sense of gain among the new white-collar urban workers.

Third, regarding the new white-collar urban workers in Shanghai, we recognize the typical lifestyles of the middle class and features of social life in cities. In a metropolitan society with high risks, high liquidity, and a high-speed lifestyle, the new white-collar urban workers must deal with the dominant pressures, including the pressure of housing as well as the invisible pressure from themselves and the external environment, leading to the diversification of the values and social attitudes of this group.

Finally, we also found that the social interactions of the new white-collar urban workers were relatively sufficient, and their social inclusion was relatively high but their rate of participation in community activities and their sense of identity were relatively low. The new white-collar urban workers must be the group with the highest capacity for participation and potential public spirit in communities, and their social inclusion should be reflected through community inclusion. We should stimulate the activeness of the new white-collar urban workers in terms of their participation in the life of the community in order to improve their sense of belonging to their communities.

References

Li Chunling. "Definitions of Concepts of the Middle-Income Group and Middle Class—Comparison between the Sociological and Economic Orientations." *Journal of Chinese Academy of Governance*, 2016(6).

Li Peilin. "Growth of the Middle Class and a Middle Class–Dominated Society." *International Economic Review*, 2015(1).

Li Qiang. "How Far Is China from the Middle Class–Dominated Society?—The Sociological Analysis on the Development of the Middle Class." *Exploration and Free Views*, 2016(8).

Li Qiang and Wang Hao. "Issues of Scale and Structure of the Middle Class of China and Developmental Measures." *Society*, 2017(3).

Mills, Charles Wright. *White Collar: The American Middle Classes*. Translated by Zhou Xiaohong. Nanjing University Press, 2016.

Wu Xiaogang and Sun Xiulin. "Basic Database for Urban Survey Facilitates Social Governance." *Chinese Social Sciences Today*, November 8, 2017.

Yang Xiong. "Survey on Occupational Lives of the White Collar Youth in Shanghai." *Youth Studies*, 1999(6).

Zhang Yi. "Research on the Tendency of Structural Change of the Social Classes of China—Analysis Based on the National CGSS Survey Data." *Studies on Socialism with Chinese Characteristics*, 2011(3).

CHAPTER 12

Survey Report on Internet Use among Senior Citizens in China

Zhu Di,[1] Gao Wenjun,[2] and Zhu Yanqiao[3]

Abstract

More and more senior citizens have gained access to the Internet and created their own unique Internet culture. In this report, we describe the Internet life of senior citizens through typical phenomena, including the use of related hardware and functions of the Internet, Internet payment, the Internet and the participation of senior citizens in social networks, the preference for "chicken soup for the soul" and health maintenance articles, and Internet fraud. The data used herein include the survey data from eight cities and big data from several online platforms. According to our research, the capacity for Internet usage and the degree of participation of senior citizens were influenced by their social and economic status. However, their attitudes toward, perception of, and understanding of the Internet have also played an important role in their Internet lives. Their acknowledgment of the Internet and open, confident, and constant learning attitude could help them improve their capacities for using the Internet and protect them from risks on the Internet. The government, communities, and families should strengthen their intervention and cooperation to improve the Internet literacy of senior citizens and use the Internet and new technologies to improve the quality of life of senior citizens in real terms.

Keywords

the internet – senior citizens – capacity for action – image of the internet – internet safety literacy

---

1 Zhu Di, associate research fellow of the Institute of Sociology, Chinese Academy of Social Sciences.
2 Gao Wenjun, assistant research fellow at the Institute of Sociology, the Chinese Academy of Social Sciences.
3 Zhu Yanqiao, research fellow at the Tencent Center for the Internet & Society.

© KONINKLIJKE BRILL NV, LEIDEN, 2022 | DOI:10.1163/9789004500723_013

In the world, more and more senior citizens have gained access to the Internet. As early as 2012, a survey by the Pew Research Center in the United States found that the proportion of Internet users who were more than 65 years old surpassed 53%.[4] Despite the fact that the gap between senior citizens and youth in terms of Internet access (including devices, basic facilities, and skills) is narrowing, they are still relatively unskilled in using the Internet. In addition, we cannot deny that, with their life experiences and understanding, senior citizens have created a unique method of using the Internet, such as emojis for senior citizens and "chicken soup for the soul" and health maintenance articles, forming an Internet culture that is quite different from that of youth.

In this report, we have studied the group of over-50-year-olds in order to describe the Internet lives of senior citizens by analyzing typical phenomena. We have not only focused on differences in the way that senior citizens use the Internet due to population characteristics and social and economic status, but we have also tried to understand the actions and options of senior citizens through their action vision (their attitudes toward, perception of, and understanding of the Internet) and the mental mechanisms involved.

The data include survey data and big data. The survey data are from a questionnaire survey jointly conducted by the Survey and Data Center of CASS and the Tencent Center for Internet & Society in eight cities. There are two sources for the big data: (1) the Tencent Browsing Index (TBI), based on the Tencent Browsing Service (TBS); using access devices such as smartphones, the number of samples complying with the age requirement was 35,759,363 (data collection duration: July 27 to October 27, 2017); and (2) the data on the users of Himalaya FM Internet audio, which was provided by the Himalaya Research Institute; using access devices such as smartphones and smart pads, the number of samples complying with the age requirement was 20,970 (data collection duration: September 26 to October 26, 2017). In this report, typical phenomena of senior citizens in their Internet lives have been selected for analysis, including the use of related hardware and functions of the Internet, Internet payment, the Internet and participation in social networks on the part of senior citizens, their preference for articles regarding "chicken soup for the soul" and health maintenance, and Internet fraud. In addition, as important explanatory mechanisms, Internet action vision and mental mechanisms have also been discussed in the report.

---

4 http://www.pewinternet.org/2012/06/06/older-adults-and-internet-use.

1 Usage of Related Hardware and Functions of the Internet

1.1 The Requirements That Senior Citizens Have regarding the Operational Speed and Storage Space of Smartphones

The survey data of this report are from the sampling survey conducted in eight cities in 2017 with WeChat users who are over 50 years old as subjects. A total of 800 valid samples were obtained, and the basic information is listed in Table 12.1.

TABLE 12.1   Basic Population Characteristics of the Survey Subjects
Unit: %

Population characteristics	Type	Percentage
Gender	Male	46.8
	Female	53.3
Age	50–60	62.3
	61–70	29.9
	71–80	7.9
Educational background	No schooling (including literacy class)	0.6
	Primary school (including old-style private school)	12.6
	Junior high school	38.1
	Senior high school / technical secondary school / secondary vocational school	38.9
	Junior college	6.5
	Undergraduate and above	3.3
Marital status	Married	92.0
	Widowed	5.3
	Divorced	2.5
	Never married	0.3

Smartphones are an important piece of hardware for senior citizens in accessing the Internet. Among the interviewees, most senior citizens thought large screens were an important feature of smartphones, as shown in Table 12.2. This could be considered to be a performance demand corresponding to their conditions of eyesight. In addition, large storage capacity, high cost efficiency, and high operational speed were aspects emphasized by more than one-third of senior citizens; the stress on high cost efficiency reflected the characteristically careful and strict budget-keeping of senior citizens. Meanwhile, the

SURVEY REPORT ON INTERNET USE AMONG SENIOR CITIZENS IN CHINA   243

TABLE 12.2   Performance Requirements of Senior Citizens Regarding Smartphones
Unit: Number, %

Important smartphone functions	Percentage of people selecting this item	Reason for dissatisfaction	Percentage of people selecting this item
Large screen	65.80	Small screen	46.70
Large storage space	37.40	Low operational speed	42.70
High cost efficiency	37.00	Insufficient storage space	36.00
High operational speed	33.50	Poor appearance	18.70
Good sound effects	25.60	Unstable operations	18.70
Good photography function	24.30	Poor photography function	17.30
Fashionable appearance	14.30	Poor sound effects	16.00
Small and smart	7.30	Old type	14.70
Others	0.90	Too large	8.00
Sample quantity	800	Sample quantity	75

requirements of the senior citizens regarding smartphones have not been limited to communication; they have proposed higher requirements for operational speed and storage space, which are related in the fact that they have started to use more Internet functions and smartphone functions, such as browsing and storing photos and videos online. In addition, about one-fourth of the senior citizens said that they would emphasize the functions of sound effect and photography of the smartphones.

Most (90.6%) senior citizens were satisfied with their smartphones, and only 9.4% of them were unsatisfied with them, with the top three complaints being small screens, low operational speed, and insufficient storage space, which again reflects the high degree to which senior citizens are active on their smartphones.

1.1   *The Internet Experiences of Senior Citizens Have Become More Comprehensive*

In the survey, we asked senior citizens about the functions they use on the Internet, including obtaining information, communicating, and seeking

TABLE 12.3   Use of Internet Functions by Senior Citizens

Unit: %

Type	Internet functions	Proportion of senior citizens who can use them
Obtaining knowledge	Read news and information through WeChat or the Internet	75.8
	Read articles from the Official Accounts in WeChat	45.9
	Search for information and news on the Internet	56.6
WeChat communication	Chat via WeChat	98.5
	Send emojis and pictures in WeChat	81.8
	Make and forward small videos in WeChat	68.9
	Click likes and make comments in the Moments of WeChat	81.6
	Receive or send red packets in WeChat	83.0
Life applications	Pay mobile phone charges online	40.6
	Pay utility bills	22.1
	Shop online	32.6
	Register for medical appointments online	12.1
	Book tickets online	15.4
	Book hotels online	11.6
	Use apps such as DiDi and Kuaiche to hail taxis	25.8
	Smartphone navigation	33.1
	Smartphone payment	51.5
	WeChat applets	22.0
Entertainment	Use entertainment apps, such as WeSing and Sing Bar	16.4
	Use smartphones to listen to programs, such as Himalaya FM and LanRenDuShu	19.0
	Use smartphones to watch videos, such as those from Tencent Video	59.3
	Make photo albums with smartphones	25.0
	Make WeChat emojis	20.0

entertainment. In general, most senior citizens were using the Internet for communication and for obtaining information. However, according to the data, some functions previously unique to youth have gradually been integrated into the lives of senior citizens, such as watching videos, smartphone payments, smartphone navigation, car-hailing apps, and WeChat applets.

As can be seen in Table 12.3, with regard to obtaining knowledge, 75.8% of senior citizens browsed news on the Internet, more than half (56.6%) of them were able to search for news and information by themselves, and some senior citizens (45.9%) read the articles of the Official Accounts in WeChat. In terms of communication via WeChat, most senior citizens (98.5%) chat by using WeChat; more than 80% of them could send emojis, click likes in Moments, and receive or send red packets; and nearly 70% of them could make and forward small videos.

In terms of life applications, the proportion of senior citizens using the Internet was relatively low. About 40% of them could pay mobile phone charges online, about 30% of them could carry out online shopping and navigation, and about one-fourth of them could use car-hailing apps or pay utility bills online. The proportion of senior citizens who could register for medical appointments, book tickets and hotels, and use other convenient services was even lower. However, more than half of senior citizens said that they could use the smartphone payment function, indicating that mobile payment is currently popular among senior citizens.

In terms of entertainment, most senior citizens (59.3%) used smartphones to watch videos, but less than 20% of them could use smartphones to listen to audio. Some senior citizens could use smartphones to make photo albums (25.0%) and emojis (20.0%). We believe that more and more senior citizens can enjoy the convenient and interesting life provided by the Internet in an all-around way.

1.3 Most Popular Information among Senior Citizens: "Chicken Soup for the Soul" Articles, Humorous Stories, and Current News

According to the TBI index, the top 20 topics for senior citizens to browse are listed in Table 12.4. The top two topics were "chicken soup for the soul" articles and humorous stories, and 76.5% and 72.0% of senior citizens would browse them; next came current news, browsed by 67.0% of senior citizens; and then topics about health and sex, browsed by 66.9% and 60.7% of the senior citizens, respectively.

TABLE 12.4 Analysis of the Top 20 Topics Browsed by Senior Citizens (N = 35.76 Million)
Unit: %

No.	Topic	Percentage	No.	Topic	Percentage
1	"Chicken soup for the soul" articles	76.5	11	Culture	45.7
2	Humorous stories	72.0	12	Food	43.6
3	Current news	67.0	13	Education	41.2
4	Health	66.9	14	Astrology	39.8
5	Sex	60.7	15	Story-type articles	36.8
6	Society	56.5	16	Real estate	34.7
7	Tourism	55.1	17	History	34.2
8	Entertainment	49.9	18	Commerce	32.9
9	Military	49.8	19	Finance	32.0
10	Science and Technology	46.4	20	Curiosity	30.7

It is safe to say that the above topics could meet the common needs of senior citizens, including emotional needs (comforting and delighting), cognitive needs (obtaining information), and physiological needs (health and sex). In addition, the top topics also reflected the diversified interests of senior citizens, such as tourism, military affairs, science and technology, and culture and food, as well as the attention paid by senior citizens to investment, finance, and real estate.

1.4 *Audio Files Related to Psychological Counseling Were Most Popular among Senior Citizens*

With the popularization of audio apps, people could use smartphones to listen to radio, music, novels, lectures, and many other things regarding health, feelings, and finance, and even Party classes. According to the big data provided by Himalaya FM, the number of users over 50 was 20,790, accounting for 0.38% of the total number of users, including 56.4% males and 41.2% females (users who did not report their gender accounted for 2.4%). Therefore, the level of popularity of mobile audio among senior citizens was relatively low.

What did those senior citizens who used audio platforms earlier prefer to listen to? What did they search for? The top 20 results are listed in Table 12.5. Among the most popular contents among senior citizens, audio books ranked at the top, indicating that senior citizens often use audio apps to listen to books. Musical hits and cultural albums also ranked high, reflecting the

TABLE 12.5 Types of Audio Files Listened to and Ranking of Topics Searched for by Senior Citizens (N = 20970)

Unit: Times, %

No.	Audio type	Percentage (%)	Search content	Search quantity
1	Audio books	32.3194	Attachment	1708
2	Educational training	9.0966	Ai Baoliang	605
3	Music	8.8037	Groundless talk of A Dream of Red Mansions	373
4	Culture	8.7509	The Historical Records	336
5	Others	6.1868	The Ming Dynasty _ 97	327
6	Children	5.1521	A Dream of Red Mansions	280
7	Emotional life	4.4030	Ai Mo systematic capital investment training	278
8	Health	3.7908	Time Raiders	257
9	History	3.6588	Shaanxi Opera	222
10	Cross talks and storytelling	3.3347	Romance of the Three Kingdoms	210
11	Foreign languages	3.0730	Plants vs. Zombies	201
12	Business and finance	2.6889	Rocky Liang	193
13	Traditional operas	1.7550	Henan Zhuizi (a Chinese folk art form in Henan Province)	186
14	Entertainment	1.5293	New Concept English	175
15	Tourism	1.0563	Horoscope	173
16	Fashionable life	0.8883	Xu Shufen, the psychological counselor	168
17	Radio plays	0.8259	Zhou Jianlong	166
18	Headlines	0.8067	Jin Yong	160
19	Radios	0.4706	Diamond Sutra	159
20	IT	0.4129	Lecture Room	157

major interests of the senior citizens. Educational training and children also received a certain percentage of hits because senior citizens would like to meet their learning needs and fulfill their duty to take care of their grandchildren. Therefore, educational content was sought on behalf of their grandchildren.

The No. 1 topic searched for by senior citizens was Attachment, an audio program related to psychological counseling, reflecting that the senior citizens need understanding and caring. Content with a lower search ranking included names of novels or writers, as well as traditional operas, which could match with the interests of senior citizens.

2 Internet Payment

For both online and offline consumption, Internet payment and mobile payment have become more and more popular. From shopping malls and supermarkets to small stalls, all products or services can be bought via smartphone payment. Under such macro conditions, what are the attitudes of senior citizens toward Internet payment?

2.1 *More than Half of Senior Citizens Would Use Smartphone Payment*
According to the survey, 46.3% of senior citizens had never used smartphone payment, 36.4% of them had used it occasionally, and 17.4% of them had used it often. The use of smartphone payment by senior citizens is closely related to the connection of bank cards, as shown in Figure 12.1. Among the senior citizens who have connected their smartphones to their bank cards, 92.4% of them use smartphone payment, including 41.5% who use them frequently and 50.9% who use them occasionally. Among the senior citizens who have not connected their smartphones to their bank cards, 28.5% of them use smartphone payment, including 1.7% who use them frequently and 26.8% who use them occasionally. According to research, connection to their bank cards promotes the usage of smartphone payment by senior citizens. Of course, we can say that most senior citizens who would like to use smartphone payment have connected their bank cards to their smartphones.

With regard to the common payment platforms, such as WeChat and Alipay, 39.5% of senior citizens have connected their bank cards to their WeChat or Alipay accounts (credit or debit cards). For example, 32.1% of them connected their debit cards, 4.6% connected their credit cards, and 2.8% connected both. Among these senior citizens who have connected their bank accounts, 91.8% of them connected their own cards, 6.6% connected the bank cards of their children, and 1.6% connected the bank cards of their spouses.

According to Table 12.6, the balances of the connected bank cards of more than half of the senior citizens (55.7%) were lower than 5,000 yuan, mostly between 501–1,000 yuan and 1,001–5,000 yuan. Only a few senior citizens (7.9%) have connected the bank cards of more than 10,000 yuan.

The senior citizens who have connected their bank cards were relatively independent, and 58.2% of them connected their bank cards by themselves, while nearly 40% of them did so with assistance from their children (36.7%).

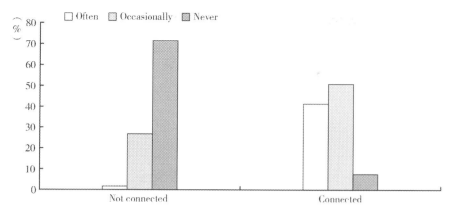

FIGURE 12.1   Relationship between Smartphone Payment and Bank Card Connection among Senior Citizens

TABLE 12.6   Balances on Bank Cards Connected by Senior Citizens (N = 316)
Unit: %

Balance	Percentage of the people selecting this item
< 100yuan	2.2
100–500yuan	9.8
501–1000yuan	20.6
1001–5000yuan	23.1
5001–10000 yuan	12.3
> 10000 yuan	7.9
I don't know	7.3
Refuse to reply	16.8

In addition, given issues related to safety and privacy, it was unusual for them to seek help from friends or relatives. However, strangers, such as the employees of mobile phone business offices or banks, were trusted by some senior citizens due to their professional identities, and some senior citizens would seek help from them (8.9%).

2.2   *Safety Perception and Easy Operation Were the Key Factors Promoting the Usage of Smartphone Payment among Senior Citizens*
According to our analysis, the perception that smartphone payment is safe was closely related to the use of smartphone payment, as can be seen in Figure 12.2. Among the senior citizens who believed that smartphone payment was safe, 97.6% used smartphone payment in their daily lives, including 70%

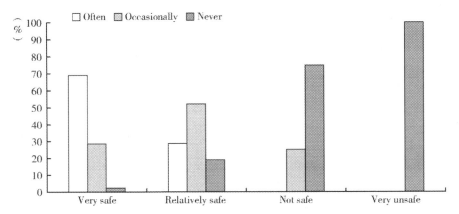

FIGURE 12.2   Relationship between Perception of Safety and the Use of Smartphone Payment by Senior Citizens

for frequent use and 30% for occasional use. Among the senior citizens who believed that smartphone payment was relatively safe, 80.9% used it in their daily lives, including 30% for frequent use and more than half for occasional use. Among the senior citizens who thought that smartphone payment was not very safe, 74.8% had never used that kind of payment, and 25.2% have used it occasionally. None of the senior citizens who thought smartphone payment was very unsafe used it. Therefore, perception of safety is one of the key factors determining the use of smartphone payment by senior citizens.

To understand the physical and mental experiences of senior citizens in using smartphone payment, we have analyzed their opinions on the operation and safety of information on smart-phone payment and experiences of being cheated among senior citizens who have used smartphone payment (430 persons). See Table 12.7 for the results. Most senior citizens said that using smartphone payment was easy and they did not experience any online fraud, but half of them were concerned that using smartphone payment would disclose their private information. In general, senior citizens were relatively active in using smartphone payment. However, the data also reflected that senior citizens were not careful enough in protecting their personal information, leading to some safety risks.

3   The Internet and Senior Citizens' Participation in Social Networks

According to the survey, the most popular group activities in which senior citizens participated were physical exercise and traveling, with rates of participation of 70.1% and 67.4%, respectively. In addition, more than half of female senior citizens participate in dancing and singing activities, in the proportions of 58.9%

TABLE 12.7   Experiences of Senior Citizens in Using Smartphone Payment
Unit: %

Item	Option	Percentage of the people selecting this item
Easy operation of smartphone payment	Easy	87.0
	Not easy	13.0
Experienced Internet fraud in using	Yes	13.5
smartphone payment	No	86.5
Concern about the leakage of personal	Yes	50.0
information during payment	No	50.0

and 53.5%, respectively; fewer male senior citizens participate in such activities. Similarly, the proportions of female senior citizens participating in community activities and volunteer services were higher than those of male senior citizens. About 45.3% of female senior citizens had participated in community activities, and 27.9% of them had participated in volunteer services, while the proportions of male senior citizens were 32.1% and 19.8%, respectively. However, the proportion of male senior citizens participating in calligraphy and painting activities (23.3%) was higher than that among female senior citizens (24.9%). The proportion of male senior citizens interested in reading and writing was also higher than that of the female senior citizens (16.4%; see Figure 12.3).

Telephones and WeChat were the major communication methods for senior citizens in participating in and organizing group activities. For square dancing, singing, and doing exercises with a high degree of organization, fixed members, and concentrated places, the most common communication method was WeChat, and 69.4%, 61.9%, and 59.5% of the senior citizens selected WeChat for communication. Some of the senior citizens use telephones and face-to-face communication. For group activities in communities and exchange activities such as calligraphy, painting, reading, and writing, the proportion of telephone communication was a little higher than WeChat, followed by face-to-face communication. Traveling activities were mainly communicated and organized through WeChat, and 67.2% of senior citizens use WeChat for this task, followed by telephones.

In terms of frequency of participation and means of communication, as shown in Figure 12.4, the senior citizens who often took part in various group activities used WeChat for communication with the highest frequency, although they used face-to-face communication or telephones when they took part in some activities (such as traveling and community activities). According

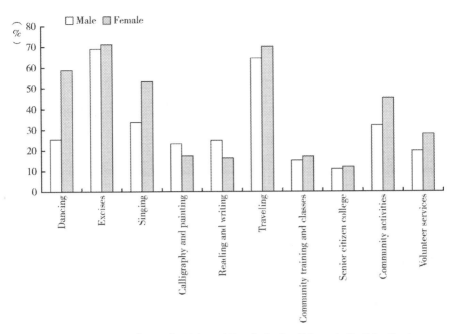

FIGURE 12.3　Basic Conditions for Male and Female Senior Citizens in Participating in Group Activities

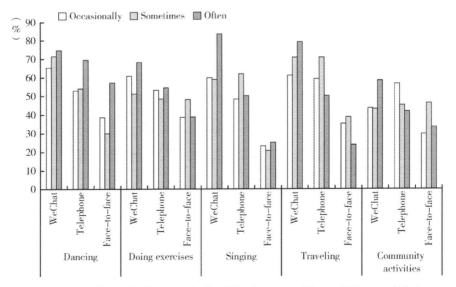

FIGURE 12.4　Relationship between the Social Participation of Senior Citizens and Their Means of Communication

SURVEY REPORT ON INTERNET USE AMONG SENIOR CITIZENS IN CHINA 253

to our findings, we can also say that those senior citizens who used WeChat more frequently participated in more group or cultural activities, and that usage of WeChat has improved the social participation of senior citizens.

4 Preference for Articles Regarding "Chicken Soup for the Soul" and Health Maintenance

With the deepening participation of senior citizens in the Internet, their life experiences, preferences, and cultural tastes have been reflected in the world of the Internet, creating a unique Internet using method and culture. The most representative Internet culture of senior citizens is the preference for articles regarding "chicken soup for the soul" and health information.

4.1 Articles about Health Were the Articles Most Favored by Senior Citizens

When using WeChat, most senior citizens like to search for information about health and the common sense of life, and 74.9% and 72.8% of senior citizens like to read articles about these two topics on WeChat, respectively. In addition, a lot of senior citizens like to read articles about news, government policies, tourism, and emotions (see Table 12.8).

As mentioned above, according to the TBI index, information on health browsed by senior citizens accounted for a high proportion, and most of that information was used mainly for maintaining their health, but not for losing

TABLE 12.8   Types of Articles Favored by Senior Citizens on WeChat

Unit: %

Article type	Proportion	Article type	Proportion
Emotions	42.5	Common sense of life	72.8
Current news	68.3	Health	74.9
Government policies	59.5	Investment and finance	31.0
Patriotism/military	46.1	Tourism	52.0
History and culture	39.1	Dancing / square dancing	36.0
Social sciences and ideologies	27.1	Photography	19.8
High-techs	30.1	Encouragement / attitudes toward life	33.1

weight and keeping fit. According to further analysis, 55.28% of senior citizens like to browse daily health information, 41.18% of them like to browse TCM health information, and only 13.13% and 9.6% of them like to browse information about losing weight or keeping fit.

The senior citizens who liked reading articles regarding the maintenance of their health attach a great deal of importance to their health. For example, 74.8% of senior citizens thought that health is vital to the happiness of their twilight years, and 21.1% thought that health is relatively important. Similarly, 79% of them thought that their health should be improved. The senior citizens who forward such articles to their Moments made up 33.4% of the sample, and those who forward such articles to their children and family members accounted for 24.5%.

Only one-third of senior citizens said that they like articles about encouragement / life attitudes, which was quite different from the common perception of senior citizens—the WeChat Moments of senior citizens are full of "chicken soup for the soul articles." For example, female senior citizens like to read chicken soup for the soul articles, accounting for 58.9%; within this group, those with an educational background of senior high school, technical secondary school, or secondary vocational school account for 42.3%.

According to the data, those senior citizens who liked articles regarding the maintenance of health like to read articles about the common sense of life, current news, government policies, tourism, and emotions. As shown in Table 12.9, 84.3% of senior citizens who liked articles regarding health maintenance like to read articles about the common sense of life, 69.4% of them like articles about current news, 60.1% like articles about government policies, 58.6% like articles about tourism, and 47.2% like articles about emotions. According to the interview with the focus group, we found that senior citizens are concerned about current political events both at home and abroad and about policies closely related to their benefits, including the increase in their pensions and reform of the pension system. However, there are a lot of rumors regarding such information, which may bother senior citizens.

4.2 The Senior Citizens Concerned about Their Lives and Health Depend More on "Chicken Soup for the Soul" Articles

In this report, we have analyzed the influence of mental mechanisms on the preference of the senior citizens for "chicken soup for the soul" and health maintenance articles. The scale used to measure anxiety over death included: "I am very afraid of death"; "I feel anxious when I think that I will die"; and "I will try my best not to think about death." The scale used to measure the acceptance of death included: "Death is a natural part of life"; and "It's hard to say that death is good or bad." There were four options: completely disagree, disagree, agree, and completely agree, which were assigned 1 to 4 points.

SURVEY REPORT ON INTERNET USE AMONG SENIOR CITIZENS IN CHINA 255

TABLE 12.9 Types of Articles Liked by Senior Citizens Who Also Like Articles Regarding the Maintenance of Health

Unit: %

Article type	Proportion	Article type	Proportion
Common sense of life	84.3	History and culture	40.6
Current news	69.4	Encouragement / attitudes toward life	36.1
Government policies	60.1	Investment and finance	35.1
Tourism	58.6	High-tech	28.2
Emotions	47.2	Social sciences and ideologies	27.0
Patriotism/military	44.6	Photography	22.5
Dancing / square dancing	43.4		

TABLE 12.10 Anxiety of Senior Citizens over Birth, Aging, Disease, and Death

Unit: %

Degree	Anxiety over death	Acceptance of death
Low	34.9	11.5
Moderate	51.3	53.0
High	13.9	35.5

TABLE 12.11   Relationship between Mental Mechanisms and the Reading Preferences of Senior Citizens

Unit: %

Type	Encouragement/attitudes toward life	Health
Anxiety over death		
Low	31.5	78.3
Moderate	31.7	75.1
High	42.3	65.8
Acceptance of death		
Low	78.3	28.3
Moderate	75.0	32.5
High	73.6	35.6

One possible reason for the popularity of "chicken soup for the soul" articles could be that senior citizens who are too concerned about their health and death are afraid of understanding their physical condition or seeing doctors, so they need to read "chicken soup for the soul articles" to guide their attitudes toward life or to find spiritual ballast. However, dependence on "chicken soup for the soul" articles might not be good for senior citizens if it prevents them from dealing with their health problems correctly, which might in turn lead to a delay in seeking timely and efficient medical measures.

5   Internet Frauds

Senior citizens have made significant progress in using various Internet functions, but they are still weak in terms of cybersecurity. In this section, we have analyzed the causes of incidents of fraud experienced by senior citizens by discussing the perceptions of senior citizens regarding false information on the Internet and their experiences of fraud, and we have established an indicator to measure the literacy of internet safety.

5.1   *Senior Citizens Trust the Information Published by Official Media and Government Departments*

According to the survey data, senior citizens have doubts about information on the Internet. About 23.5% of them think that 50% to 60% of the information on the Internet is fake. This finding corresponds to the results of our

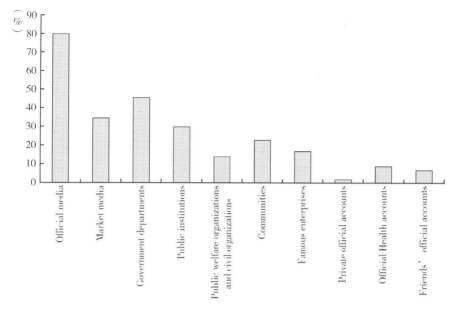

FIGURE 12.5   Sources of Online Information Trusted by Senior Citizens

research on the focus group in northern China and eastern China. Especially in developed areas and major cities, more senior citizens think that more than 50% of the information on the Internet is fake.

In the eyes of senior citizens, sources of reliable information include the official media and government departments, and 80.4% and 45.6% of them think that the information published by official media and government departments, respectively, is reliable. By contrast, in the eyes of senior citizens, the reliability of the information issued by private official accounts and health official accounts is relatively low (see Figure 12.5). This indicated that the senior citizens had a certain capacity for identifying false information and tended to trust information issued by the government and authoritative organizations.

5.2   Senior Citizens with a Mid-Level Income and Economic Independence Are More Likely to Be Cheated

If cheating is understood to cover matters of money, emotions, rumors, and false advertisements, the proportion of senior citizens who have been cheated (or who suspect that they have been cheated) would be 67.3%. As shown in Figure 12.6, most senior citizens were cheated through the Moments of WeChat (69.1%), WeChat groups (58.5%), and WeChat friends (45.6%). As shown in Figure 12.7, the top three types of fraudulent messages that are easily accepted by senior citizens include offers of free red packets (60.3%), free smartphone data (52.3%), and discounted products (48.6%).

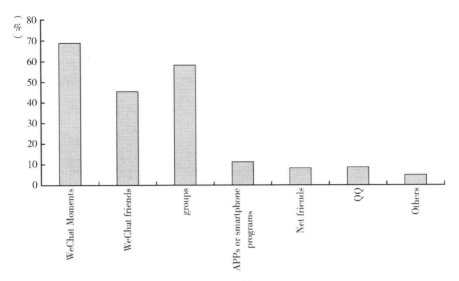

FIGURE 12.6   Channels of Cheating Experienced by Senior Citizens

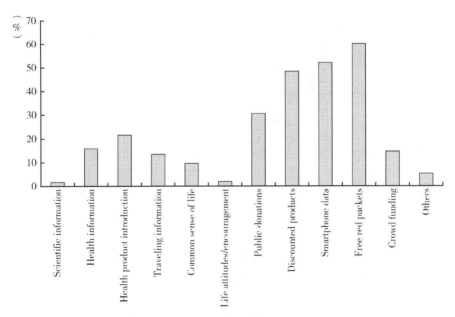

FIGURE 12.7   Types of Cheating Messages Received by Senior Citizens

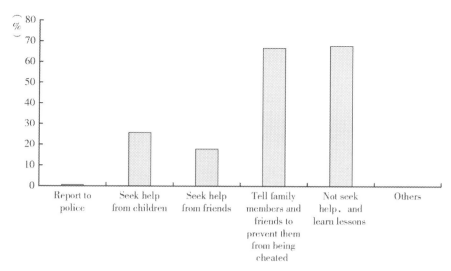

FIGURE 12.8   Sources of Help Sought by Senior Citizens after Incidents of Internet Fraud

After finding out that they have been cheated, only a few senior citizens seek help. About 68.3% of them said that they would not seek help and just viewed the experience as a lesson; 67.2% of them chose to tell their family members and friends to prevent them from being cheated; only 25.9% and 17.9% of them sought help from their children and friends, respectively; and only 0.6% of them summoned police for help (see Figure 12.8). From this we can see that senior citizens' ability to protect their own interests needs to be improved.

According to the analysis, most of the senior citizens who were defrauded had a relatively high social and economic status and level of economic independence. The defrauded senior citizens who had educational backgrounds of junior high school and senior high school / technical secondary school / secondary vocational school accounted for 39.4% and 37.7%, respectively, while those with a primary school educational background only accounted for 12.3%. Most of the defrauded senior citizens had middle or high incomes, accounting for 67.1% and 24.3%, respectively, and low-income senior citizens only accounted for 8.6%. Those who had health care insurance accounted for 99.4%. In terms of economic independence, 41.1% of senior citizens who were cheated said that the major expenditures of their families were determined by themselves; 37.5% said such expenditures were determined jointly with their family members; and only 16% and 5.4% of them, respectively, said their expenditures were determined by their spouses or children.

Therefore, fraud encountered by senior citizens in the age of the Internet has displayed new features, and the victims of fraud were not limited to senior citizens with low educational backgrounds and living guarantees. Many educated and high-income senior citizens with economic independence also experienced fraud. Such senior citizens feel more confident about their judgments and thus might be more likely to suffer heavier economic losses.

The data showed that 66.6% of senior citizens who liked articles regarding health maintenance had been cheated online, and most of them were cheated due to offers of free red packets, free smartphone data, or discounted products. More than 50% of senior citizens said that they were cheated through such messages. Therefore, we need to strengthen the supervision and control over health information for senior citizens, especially the related marketing information.

5.3 It Is Especially Important for Senior Citizens to Improve Their Ability to Identify False Information on the Internet

In this report, we have created a scale of literacy of internet safety for senior citizens with four dimensions, namely, capacity for obtaining information, capacity for the identification of information, consciousness of internet safety, and capacity for the protection of one's personal information. Each question on the scale was scored from 1 to 4 (see Table 12.12). Among the samples, the average degree of literacy regarding the internet safety of senior citizens was 22.494, indicating that the general degree of literacy regarding internet safety following self-evaluation was at the mid to high level. In terms of the four dimensions, senior citizens' capacity for the identification of information was the weakest, indicating that supervision regarding false information and rumors and development of the capacity of senior citizens to identify information were of great importance to the improvement of the degree of senior citizens' literacy regarding internet safety.

According to the data, senior citizens' degree of literacy regarding internet safety is obviously related to their social and economic status. As shown in Figure 12.9, the average score of the degree of literacy regarding internet safety among senior citizens with an educational background of junior college and undergraduate and above was higher than 23, while the score for senior citizens with no schooling or a primary school educational background was about 20. Scores for degree of literacy regarding internet safety among senior citizens working as enterprise managers, ordinary clerks, and professionals at present or before retirement were relatively high, while the scores of those working as freelancers or in the agriculture, forestry, animal husbandry, or fishery industries were relatively low (see Figure 12.10). In addition, the higher the income of the senior citizens, the higher their degree of literacy regarding internet safety.

SURVEY REPORT ON INTERNET USE AMONG SENIOR CITIZENS IN CHINA 261

TABLE 12.12 Senior Citizens' Degree of Literacy Regarding Internet Safety
Unit: Point(s)

Measurement dimension	Scale	Score
Capacity for obtaining information	I know where I can find the latest news I can find the information I need	5.875
Capability of identifying information	I can identify false information I can verify the information through websites and apps	4.918
Consciousness of internet safety	I never browse unsafe websites I would not easily open the links in WeChat articles or messages	5.918
Capacity for protecting personal information	I have no secrets and I do not need to protect my personal information I never leave my telephone number or address at any untrusted sites	5.783
Degree of literacy regarding internet safety		22.494

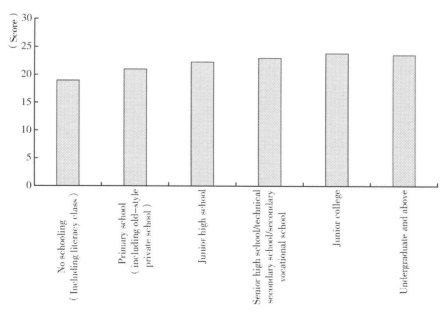

FIGURE 12.9 Degree of Literacy Regarding Internet Safety of Senior Citizens with Different Educational Backgrounds

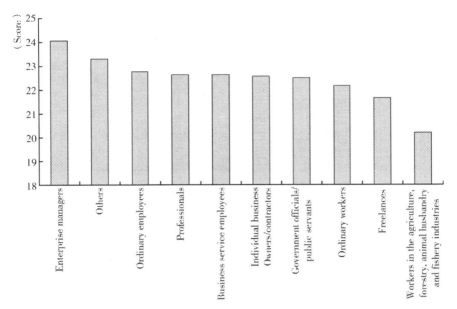

FIGURE 12.10 Degree of Literacy Regarding Internet Safety of Senior Citizens with Different Jobs at Present or before Retirement

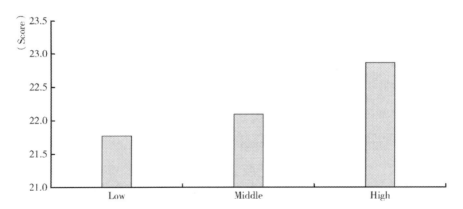

FIGURE 12.11 Degree of Literacy Regarding Internet Safety of Senior Citizens with Different Incomes

6 Capacity for Activity on the Internet and Vision

6.1 *Technology Phobia Influenced the Capacity for Internet Activities among Senior Citizens*

In this report, we measured senior citizens' capacity for activity on the Internet based on three indicators, including: "If I try, I will be able to learn various Internet operations"; "if I have any trouble, I can find solutions on the Internet"; and "I can deal with any problem on the Internet based on my talent." Each question is assigned 1 to 4 points, and the range of scores on the scale is from 3 to 12. The data showed that the average score of the senior citizens' capacity for action was 7.78, at the middle level.

Under the influence of their physiological features, life cycle features, and social changes, the representation and mechanisms of the Internet lives of senior citizens were more complicated; this was due not only to their social and economic status but also to their attitudes toward, perception of, and understanding of the Internet. We deemed the attitudes toward, perception of, and understanding of senior citizens as the vision of action. An individual's image of the Internet is an important factor in explaining the capacity for action.

According to the survey, 44.3% of senior citizens thought that they need to learn more functions of the Internet and smartphones, and had a higher score on their capacity for Internet action, at 7.80 (the score of those who did not think it was necessary to learn more was 7.63).

Senior citizens' understanding and evaluation of the Internet were positive. About 82.3% of senior citizens thought that the Internet could make communication among people easier; 78.8% and 74.3% of them, respectively, thought the Internet had made their lives more convenient and more replenished; 75.5% of them said that they could keep up with the times due to the Internet; and 65.4% of them agreed that the Internet was an important channel for obtaining related information. By contrast, only a few senior citizens thought that the Internet was something for youth and that senior citizens could not use it fluently, and that only those with a higher educational background could use smartphones well. The results of the research showed that senior citizens have accepted the involvement of the Internet in their lives.

Typically, senior citizens reject new things, because, on the one hand, they are afraid that they are unable to control those things, and, on the other hand, they are reluctant to accept new things due to self-esteem. According to the survey, senior citizens did express their technology phobia regarding smartphones. As shown in Figure 12.12, more than half of senior citizens are concerned about fraud, the safety of private information, and the costs and

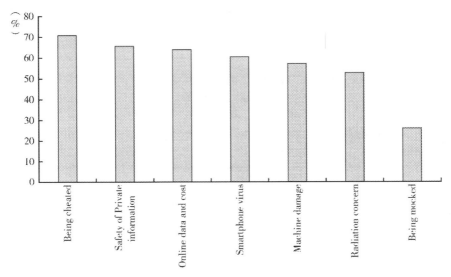

FIGURE 12.12   Concerns of Senior Citizens about Smartphone Use

risk of viruses that smartphones carry. We have established a scale for technology phobia based on these indicators ranging from 0 to 7. The average score of technology phobia among the senior citizens was 3.99, and 48.5% of the senior citizens scored 5 or above. The higher the degree of phobia,[6] the lower the senior citizens' capacity for Internet activity. The analysis showed that senior citizens with a low degree of technology phobia had a much higher degree of capacity for activity on the Internet, with an average score of 8.20, while the score for senior citizens with a high degree of technology phobia was 7.75.

Therefore, although more and more senior citizens have started to use smartphones and the Internet, they still have some concerns which have stopped them from further improving their capacity for carrying out activities on the Internet. Therefore, to improve the Internet lives of the senior citizens, intervention from the government and social workers and the support of families are needed.

6.2   *Senior Citizens' Acceptance of and Confidence in the Internet Could Improve Their Capacity for Carrying Out Internet Activities and Their Capacity to Resist Risks*

In this report, we considered two statements—"The Internet is something for youth and senior citizens cannot use it fluently" and "Only those with higher

---

6   2 and below for a low degree of fear; 3–5 for a medium degree of fear; and 6–7 for a high degree of fear.

educational backgrounds can use smartphones well"—and "technology phobia" as the three major indicators for measuring senior citizens' perception of and understanding of the Internet. Then we discussed the influences of senior citizens' image of the Internet on their use of smartphone functions, their capacity for carrying out activities on the Internet, their attitude toward Internet fraud, and their degree of literacy regarding internet safety.

As mentioned before, we divided the functions of smartphones into four categories: knowledge obtaining, WeChat communication, life application, and entertainment, with 23 functions. We have divided the degrees of smartphone use among senior citizens into three levels, with a low level for using 8 functions, a middle level for using 9–16 functions, and a high level for using 17 functions or more. In term of the degree of smartphone use, among the interviewed senior citizens, low-level users accounted for 44.9%, mid-level users accounted for 40.1%, and high-level users accounted for 15%.

From Table 12.13 we can see that senior citizens who disagreed with the idea that "The Internet is something for youth and senior citizens cannot use it fluently" had a higher degree of smartphone use, and that those who agreed with the idea were far outnumbered by mid-level and high-level users. The related analysis of the idea that "Only those with higher educational backgrounds can use smartphones well" showed a similar tendency. The results revealed that the more that senior citizens accepted the Internet and smartphones, the lower their feeling of dread and the higher their degree of smartphone use.

One's image of the Internet has a significant influence on the capacity for action. Compared to the senior citizens who agreed with the idea that "Only those with higher educational backgrounds can use smartphones well," those who disagreed had a higher score in their capacity for action, a score of 7.83.

TABLE 12.13   Influence of Senior Citizen's Image of the Internet on Smartphone Use
Unit: %

Image of the Internet	Attitude	Degree of using smartphones		
		Low	Middle	High
The Internet is something for youth and senior citizens cannot use it fluently	Disagree	37.7	43.4	18.9
	Agree	53.6	36.2	10.2
Only those with higher educational backgrounds can use smartphones well	Disagree	41.3	42.3	16.4
	Agree	52.6	35.5	12.0

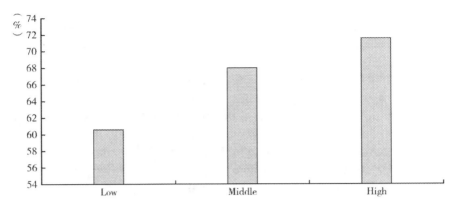

FIGURE 12.13   Relationship between Concern about Smartphones and Experiences of Internet Fraud

According to the data, a higher degree of technology phobia led to a higher possibility of being defrauded on the Internet. Among senior citizens with a high degree of technology phobia, 71.6% of them have been cheated (see Figure 12.13). The reason for this situation may be that the more that senior citizens are afraid of new things and high technologies, the lower their confidence in their own capacities and the higher the possibility that they will become targets of fraud. Of course, senior citizens may become more afraid of high technologies such as smartphones if they have been cheated before.

Senior citizens' image of the Internet also has a significant influence on the degree of literacy regarding internet safety. The senior citizens who disagreed with the idea that "The Internet is something for youth and senior citizens cannot use it fluently" had a higher score in their degree of literacy regarding internet safety (23.09) than those who agreed with it (21.77). According to Table 12.14, 34.9% of senior citizens who disagreed with the idea that "The Internet is something for youth and senior citizens cannot use it fluently" had a high degree of literacy regarding internet safety,[7] and only 16.0% of those who agreed with that idea had a high degree of literacy regarding internet safety.

---

7   The total score range for the degree of literacy regarding internet safety is from 8 to 32; 18 and below for a low degree of literacy; 19 to 24 for a medium degree; and 25 and above for a high degree.

SURVEY REPORT ON INTERNET USE AMONG SENIOR CITIZENS IN CHINA 267

TABLE 12.14 Relationship between the View That "The Internet Is Something for Youth and Senior Citizens Cannot Use It Fluently" and Degree of Literacy Regarding Internet Safety

Unit: %

Attitude	Degree of Literacy Regarding Internet Safety		
	Low	Middle	High
Agree	13.0	71.0	16.0
Disagree	7.8	57.3	34.9

Senior citizens who disagreed with the idea that "Only those with higher educational backgrounds can use smartphones well" had a higher score in their degree of literacy regarding internet safety (22.88) than those who agreed with it (21.64). According to Table 12.15, 31.1% of senior citizens who disagreed with the idea that "Only those with higher educational backgrounds can use smartphones well" had a high degree of literacy regarding internet safety, and only 15.9% of those who agreed with the idea had a high degree of literacy regarding internet safety.

TABLE 12.15 Relationship between the View That "Only Those with Higher Educational Backgrounds Can Use Smartphones Well" and Degree of Literacy Regarding Internet Safety

Unit: %

Attitude5	Degree of Literacy Regarding Internet Safety		
	Low	Middle	High
Agree	11.6	72.5	15.9
Disagree	9.5	59.4	31.1

In general, according to the above analysis, the more that senior citizens accept the Internet and smartphones, the higher their confidence in their own capacities; the more functions of smartphones they can handle, the higher their capacity for carrying out activities, the lower the possibility of being cheated, and the higher their degree of literacy regarding internet safety.

7 Conclusion

According to our research, senior citizens' capacity for using the Internet and the depth of their participation were influenced by their social and economic status. However, the data showed that their attitudes toward, perception of, and understanding of the Internet have also played an important role in their Internet lives. Their acknowledgment of the Internet and open, confident, and constant attitude could help them improve their action and their capacity to avoid risks. If their objective economic status, social status, and physiological features have created a 3D life world for senior citizens, then the Internet has become the fourth dimension in their life, to some extent. Although it is not a time-traveling machine, the Internet may create a new life world and new life visions for senior citizens.

Government, communities, and families should strengthen their intervention and cooperation to improve senior citizens' capacity for carrying out activities on the Internet. On the one hand, we should provide diversified training and technical support to break down fears or wrong perceptions of technology among senior citizens so as to integrate the Internet and AI technologies into the pension guarantee and twilight years of senior citizens; on the other hand, we need to establish a system of Internet protection for senior citizens in order to increase publicity about the prevention of fraudulent activities and to improve the degree of senior citizens' literacy regarding internet safety.

References

Fang, Yang, Chau, Anson, Wong, Anna, Fung, Helene, and Woo, Jean. "Information and Communicative Technology Use Enhances Psychological Well-Being of Older Adults: The Roles of Age, Social Connectedness, and Status of Frailty." *Aging & Mental Health*, 2017.

Guo Zhigang and Liu Peng. "Analysis of the Factors of the Life Satisfaction and Need Fulfillment Methods of Senior Citizens in China—Influence from Core Family Members." *Journal of China Agricultural University* (Social Sciences Edition), 2007(3).

Hargittai, E., and Dobransky, K. "Old Dogs, New Clicks: Digital Inequality in Skills and Uses among Older Adults." Canadian Journal of *Communication*, 42(2), 2017.

He Tiantian. "Overview of the Research on Internet Usage by Senior Citizens." *Press Outpost*, 2015(9).

Le Xin and Peng Xizhe. "New Cognition on the Consumptions of Senior Citizens and Thoughts Regarding Public Policies." *Fudan Journal* (Social Sciences Edition), 2016(2).

CHAPTER 13

Survey Report on the Conditions of Urban and Rural Residents Living under Economic and Material Hardship

Jiang Zhiqiang,[1] Wang Jing,[2] and Tian Feng[3]

Abstract

Since the 18th National Congress of the CPC, governments at all levels have devoted a great number of resources to social security for urban and rural residents living under economic and material hardship, reducing the number of poor households and improving their living standards. With the acceleration of urbanization, poor urban and rural groups still face some pressures in terms of health care, education, and housing. In particular, poor households in motion can only obtain low levels of social security and assistance in cities, so social policies in the future should focus on the demands of these groups.

Keywords

urban and rural residents living under economic and material hardship – economic poverty – social poverty – precision

Since the 18th National Congress of the CPC, the central government has devoted a lot of resources into eliminating the shortcomings in the improvement of people's quality of life and in promoting social fairness and justice, aiming at building a moderately prosperous society in all respects. In terms of social security for urban and rural residents living under economic and material hardship, the government has integrated and improved the system of

---

1 Jiang Zhiqiang, associate research fellow of the Policy Research Center of the Ministry of Civil Affairs.
2 Wang Jing, associate research fellow of the Institute of Sociology, the Chinese Academy of Social Sciences, research orientation: pension guarantee and housing guarantee.
3 Tian Feng, research fellow of the Institute of Sociology, the Chinese Academy of Social Sciences, research orientation: network society and social stratification.

© KONINKLIJKE BRILL NV, LEIDEN, 2022 | DOI:10.1163/9789004500723_014

social assistance and the system of subsistence allowance to greatly improve the living conditions of urban and rural residents. In the Report to the 19th CPC National Congress, Xi Jinping further required to ensure and improve the quality of people's lives during the process of development. The fundamental purpose of development is to improve the quality of people's lives and their welfare. New progress should be made in educating all children, teaching all students, benefiting all workers, treating all patients, supporting all senior citizens, providing housing to all those in need, and helping the vulnerable groups; likewise, poverty reduction programs should be further implemented to make sure that all the people of our country have a greater sense of gain in building and sharing in development, so as to constantly promote the comprehensive development of the people and the common wealth of the whole population. Over the next five years, it will remain an important task for governments at all levels to gradually improve the living conditions of urban and rural residents living under economic and material hardship. In this report, we have mainly discussed the changing tendencies and some core issues of urban and rural residents living under economic and material hardship since the 18th National Congress of the CPC, based on macro data and data from three rounds of a sampling survey of poor households in urban and rural areas from 2015 to 2017.

1 Basic Conditions of the Sampling Survey of Poor Households in Urban and Rural Areas

1.1 *Types of Poor Households in Urban and Rural Areas*
Within the program of Constructing a System of Social Policy Support for Poor Households in Urban and Rural Areas, longitudinal surveys have been conducted every year on poor households in urban and rural areas since 2015.[4] Survey subjects under the program were divided into three categories: (1) Poor households in cities, including households receiving subsistence allowances in communities in cities ("subsistence allowance households") and households that applied for subsistence allowances but failed ("margin subsistence allowance households"). (2) Poor households in rural areas, including subsistence allowance households and margin subsistence allowance households in rural communities. (3) Poor households that have relocated to cities, which should meet four conditions under survey: (a) The interviewees come from counties and cities outside their places of residence (excluding the districts of one city); (b) the interviewees were living in urban communities in households (the

---

4   Unless specified otherwise in the tables and figures herein, all statistical results are based on the survey data of the program.

SURVEY REPORT ON THE CONDITIONS OF URBAN AND RURAL RESIDENTS 271

interviewees should live with their immediate family members); (c) the interviewees have been in their place of residence for more than six months; and (d) the economic conditions of the households of the interviewees should be at the mid to low range of households in their place of residence.

In 2017, 9,269 poor households were interviewed successfully, including 4,124 poor urban households, 3,095 poor rural households, and 2,050 poor households transferred into cities. Among the poor urban households, subsistence allowance households accounted for 56%; among the poor rural households, subsistence allowance households accounted for 47%; and subsistence allowance households among the poor households transferred into cities accounted for 9% (see Table 13.1). Among the poor urban and rural households, the subsistence allowance households were determined according to self-reporting, and among the poor households transferred into cities, the subsistence allowance households were determined according to the amount of subsistence assistance they received in their current native places and places of residence.

TABLE 13.1 Types and Proportions of Poor Urban and Rural Households in the 2017 Survey
Unit: Number, %

Type of poor households	Urban	Rural	Floating population in urban areas
Subsistence allowance households	56	47	9
Margin subsistence allowance households	44	53	91
Total	100	100	100
Sample size	4124	3095	2050

1.2   *Population Structure of Poor Urban and Rural Households*

Among the samples in the 2017 survey, the average size of poor urban households was 3.1 people, and the average number of people able to work was 1.3, accounting for 39% of the average number of family members; the average number of people with an income from working was 0.7, accounting for 24%; and the average number of people without self-help ability was 0.5, accounting for 16%. The average size of poor rural households was 3.2 people, which was a little higher than that in urban areas; the average number of people able to work was 1.2, accounting for 33% of the average number of family members, which was a little lower than that in urban areas; and the average number of people without self-help ability was 0.5, accounting for 16%, the same as in urban areas. The average size of poor households who had transferred

TABLE 13.2 Population Structure of Poor Urban and Rural Households

Type	Average number of family members (person)	Average number of people who are able to work, and the average proportion (person, %)		Average number of people with an income from working, and the average proportion (person, %)		Average number of people without self-help ability, and the average proportion (person, %)		Sample size
Urban	3.1	1.3	39	0.7	24	0.5	16	4124
Rural	3.2	1.2	33	—	—	0.5	16	3095
Floating population in urban areas	3.5	2.1	63	1.6	49	0.2	6	2050

into cities was 3.5 people, which was the highest among the three categories, whereas the average number of people able to work was 2.1, accounting for 63% of the average number of family members; the average number of people with an income from working was 1.6, accounting for 49%; and the average number of people without self-help ability was 0.2, accounting for 6% (see Table 13.2). In general, poor households that transferred to cities were mainly made up of persons of working age, who were the main income generators of their families. The population transferred to cities was moving between urban and rural areas, and the major supporters of the poor rural households.

1.3 *Human Capital of Poor Urban and Rural Households*

A shortage of human capital is usually the major cause of household poverty. In this report, we first analyze the health conditions of members of poor urban, rural, and urban transferee households. Among the poor urban households, 26% of family members had relatively poor health conditions and 20% had very poor health conditions according to their self-evaluation, totaling 46%. Among the poor rural households, 27% of family members had relatively poor health conditions and 23% had very poor health conditions according to their self-evaluation, totaling 50% of the poor rural households. Among the poor households who had transferred to cities, 7% of family members had relatively poor health conditions and 5% had very poor health conditions according to their self-evaluation, totaling 12%. In the three categories of households, the number of family members of poor urban and rural households with poor

TABLE 13.3 Health Conditions of the Members of Poor Urban and Rural Households Based on Self-Evaluation

Unit: Number, %

Health conditions	Urban	Rural	Floating population in urban areas
Very good	8	8	31
Good	8	6	20
Normal	38	36	37
Bad	26	27	7
Very bad	20	23	5
Total	100	100	100
Sample quantity	4124	3095	2050

health conditions according to their self-evaluation was close to or equal to half of the total survey samples. The health conditions of the members of poor households who had transferred to cities were better, and the proportion of members with good health conditions was 88% (see Table 13.3).

In terms of educational background, most of the members of poor urban households had a junior high school education, accounting for 36% of the total number of samples of poor urban households, followed by a primary school education, accounting for 26%; those who had received no education accounted for 14%. This means that people with a junior high school education and below among the poor urban households accounted for 76% of the total samples. Most members of poor rural households had a primary school education, accounting for 42% of the total samples, followed by those with a junior high school education, accounting for 26%, and then those with no schooling, accounting for 25%. Across the three categories, the illiteracy rate among poor rural households was the highest. People with a junior high school education or below accounted for 93% of the total samples of poor rural households. Most members of poor households who had transferred to cities had a junior high school education, accounting for 37% of the total samples of poor households who had transferred to cities, followed by those with a senior high school / technical secondary school education, accounting for 23%, and then those with a primary school education, accounting for 18% (see Table 13.4). Among the three categories, the overall human capital of the poor households who had transferred to cities was the highest.

TABLE 13.4 Educational Backgrounds of the Members of Poor Urban and Rural Households
Unit: Number, %

Educational background	Urban	Rural	Floating population in urban areas
No schooling	14	25	5
Primary school	26	42	18
Junior high school	36	26	37
Senior high school / technical secondary school	18	6	23
Junior college	3	1	11
Undergraduate and above	3	—	6
Total	100	100	100
Sample quantity	4124	3095	2050

1.4   *Employment Structure of Poor Urban and Rural Households*
The employment structure of poor urban and rural households was relatively complicated. At first, in terms of the employment structure of poor urban households, those with stable jobs only accounted for 1%, and those who were self-employed accounted for 14%. People who are not able to work but are of working age, the unemployed, and people taking care of family affairs for a long time accounted for 29%, which means that dependent family members in cities accounted for about 29%. Second, in terms of the employment structure of poor rural households, members who were farmers accounted for 35%, while those who were doing temporary jobs accounted for 10%. The proportion of dependent family members (the people who are not able to work, but are of working age, the unemployed, and those taking care of family affairs for a long time) was 22%. Finally, among the poor households who had transferred to cities, family members with stable jobs accounted for 21%, those doing temporary jobs accounted for 17%, and those who were self-employed accounted for 25%. The total proportion of people who are not able to work but are of working age, the unemployed, and those taking care of family affairs for a long time was only 15% (see Table 13.5).

SURVEY REPORT ON THE CONDITIONS OF URBAN AND RURAL RESIDENTS 275

TABLE 13.5 Employment and Schooling of the Members of Poor Urban and Rural Households
Unit: Number, %

Employment and schooling	Urban	Rural	Floating population in urban areas
Students at school	1	1	1
Stable jobs	1	1	21
Temporary jobs	5	10	17
Self-employed	14	2	25
Retired (elderly and unemployed)	14	25	12
Farmer	3	35	3
Taking care of family affairs for a long time	7	7	7
The unemployed	10	3	6
People without the capacity to work, but of working age	12	12	2
Others	33	4	6
Total	100	100	100
Sample quantity	4124	3095	2050

In terms of employment industries, in poor urban households, the employed people who could not be classified accounted for 32%; those in the commercial and service industry accounted for 13%; those in the agriculture, forestry, animal husbandry, or fishery industry accounted for 6%; and those working as professional technicians and clerks accounted for 4%, respectively. The employed members of poor rural households were mainly working in agriculture, forestry, animal husbandry, the fishery industry, or the hydraulic engineering industry, accounting for 34% of the total samples, and other employed people who could not be classified accounted for 26%. Among the employed members of poor households who had transferred to cities, other employed people who could not be classified accounted for 31%, and those working in the commercial and service industry accounted for 31% of the total sample (see Table 13.6). In general, members of poor urban and rural households were mainly working in mid- to low-end industries.

TABLE 13.6 Employers of the Members of Poor Urban and Rural Households
Unit: Number, %

Jobs of the main family supporters	Urban	Rural	Floating population in urban areas
Person with responsibilities in government organs, party and mass organizations, institutions, and enterprises	3	1	5
Professional technicians	4	2	10
Clerks and related personnel	4	1	6
Employees in the commercial and service industry	13	5	31
Workers in the agriculture, forestry, animal husbandry, fishery, or hydraulic engineering industries	6	34	3
Operators of production and transportation facilities and related personnel	8	5	7
Soldiers	0.4	0.2	0.6
Other employed people who could not be classified	32	26	31
No job	30	26	31
Total	100	100	100
Sample quantity	4124	3095	2050

2 Economic Poverty in Poor Urban and Rural Households and Its Changing Tendency

2.1 *The Changing Tendency of Economic Poverty in Poor Urban and Rural Households, 2014–2016*

The sampling survey of urban and rural residents living under economic and material hardship started in 2015, and three rounds of surveys have been completed to date. In terms of the changing tendency of the income of poor urban and rural households, in general, the per capita income of such households witnessed a significant increase. The per capita income of poor urban households increased from 9,170 yuan to 13,393 yuan, an increase of 46%; that of

SURVEY REPORT ON THE CONDITIONS OF URBAN AND RURAL RESIDENTS   277

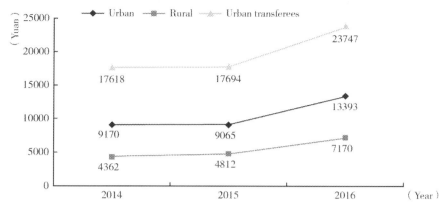

FIGURE 13.1   Changing Tendency of the Per Capita Income of Poor Urban and Rural Households, 2014–2016

poor rural households increased from 4,362 yuan to 7,170 yuan, an increase of 64%; and that of poor households who had transferred to cities increased from 17,618 yuan to 23,747 yuan, an increase of 35% (see Figure 13.1). In terms of relative growth, the growth of the per capita income of poor rural households was the highest.

In terms of the changing tendency of per capita expenditures of poor urban and rural households, the per capita expenditure of poor urban households did not change too much, increasing from 15,758 yuan to 16,693 yuan, an increase of 6%; that of poor rural households increased from 11,963 yuan to 13,416 yuan, an increase of 12%; and that of poor households who had transferred to cities increased from 20,071 yuan to 28,983 yuan, an increase of 44% (see Figure 13.2). Among the three categories, the per capita expenditure of the poor households who had transferred to cities witnessed the largest change, indicating that they would face higher subsistence pressure with the expansion of urbanization.

The Engel coefficient (ratio of food expenditure to total household expenditure) is an internationally recognized index of poverty. According to the results of the analysis of the sampling survey, the Engel coefficient of poor urban households was stable at 0.34 from 2014 to 2016; that of poor rural households decreased slightly from 0.31 in 2014 to 0.28 in 2016; and that of poor households who had transferred to cities witnessed a large fluctuation, increasing from 0.30 in 2014 to 0.55 in 2015 and then decreasing to 0.27 in 2016 (see Figure 13.3). In general, the ratio of food expenditures of poor urban and rural households decreased to different extents, and expenditures on other items of spending increased year on year, indicating a more diversified type of consumption.

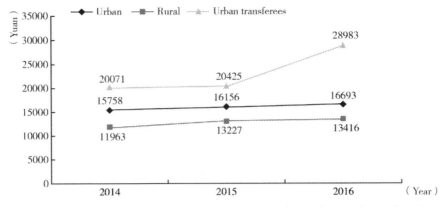

FIGURE 13.2   Changing Tendency of the Per Capita Expenditure of Poor Urban and Rural Households, 2014–2016

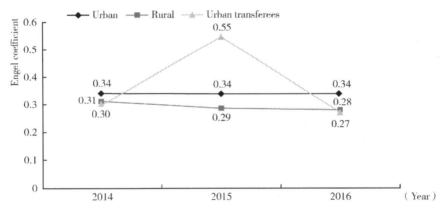

FIGURE 13.3   Changing Tendency of the Engel Coefficients of Poor Urban and Rural Households, 2014–2016

2.2   *The Structure of Income and Expenditures of Poor Urban and Rural Households in 2016*

The structure of household income is an indicator of household economic sustainability. According to the latest survey statistics in 2017, in the structure of the income of poor urban households in 2016, the income from labor accounted for 40% of the total household income, the transfer income accounted for 38%, and the income from government assistance accounted for 16%. The latter two incomes accounted for 54% of total income, indicating that poor urban households needed a high rate of transfer payment to maintain their income-expenditure balance.

SURVEY REPORT ON THE CONDITIONS OF URBAN AND RURAL RESIDENTS 279

TABLE 13.7 The Structure of Income of Poor Urban and Rural Households in 2016
Unit: Number, %

Type	Total income	Ratios of various incomes					
		Income from labor	Operating income	Property income	Transfer income	Income from government assistance	Other incomes
Urban	38409	40	3	2	38	16	2
Rural	22903	34	15	2	31	16	1
Floating population in urban areas	74971	71	14	2	11	2	0.7

In the structure of income of poor rural households, income from labor accounted for 34% of total household income, transfer income accounted for 31%, and income from government assistance accounted for 16%. The latter two sources accounted for 47% of total income, indicating that nearly half of the structure of income of poor rural households was made up of income from various transfer payments.

In the structure of income of poor households who had transferred to cities, income from labor accounted for 71% of total household income, transfer income accounted for 11%, and income from government assistance accounted for 2% (see Table 13.7). Compared to poor urban households and poor rural households, the economic sustainability and independence of the poor households who had transferred to cities were the highest.

In terms of the structure of the expenditures of poor urban and rural households in 2016, the expenditures of poor urban households were mainly directed toward food and health care, with food expenditures accounting for 34% and health care expenditures accounting for 23%. The expenditures of poor rural households were also mainly spent on food and health care, with food expenditures accounting for 28% and health care expenditures accounting for 28%. The expenditures of poor households who had transferred to cities were diversified, with food accounting for 27%, education for 9%, health care for 10%, housing for 9% and other sources accounting for 44% (see Table 13.8).

TABLE 13.8 Structure of the Expenditures of Poor Urban and Rural Households in 2016

Type	Total expenditures	Ratios of various incomes				
		Food	Education	Health care	Housing	Others
Urban	47058	34	8	23	3	32
Rural	40800	28	7	28	2	36
Floating population in urban areas	90901	27	9	10	9	44

3 Social Poverty of Poor Urban and Rural Households and Its Changing Tendency

3.1 Analysis of the Factors of Social Poverty for Poor Urban and Rural Households

From 2014 to 2016, the ratio of poor urban and rural households with a heavy economic burden due to diseases of family members decreased from 59% to 51%. Despite the reduction, economic burdens caused by diseases were still the major cause of poverty in poor urban and rural households. The ratio of households in which the main members had no capacity to work decreased from 48% to 44%. The ratio of households in which the main labor force had no job decreased from 46% to 42%. The ratio of households with poor living conditions decreased from 45% to 43%. The ratio of households that could not bear the cost of their children's education decreased from 30% to 28% (see Figure 13.4). In general, the difficulties faced by poor urban and rural households decreased to some extent, but the general pattern did not change much. Burdens due to costs in health care, housing, and education were still the main problems faced by poor urban and rural households.

Different households faced different resource restrictions and problems. In terms of the problems faced by poor urban households, the number one problem was that "the burden due to diseases of family members was too heavy," accounting for 58%; the number two problem was that "the main family members were not able to work," accounting for 51%; and the number

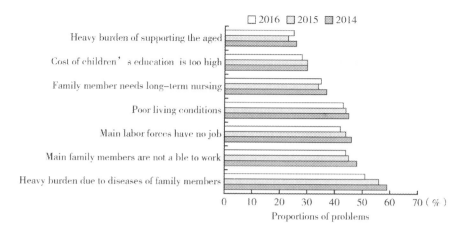

FIGURE 13.4   Changing Tendency of the Causes of Poverty in Poor Urban and Rural Households, 2014–2016

three problem was that "the main labor forces of the households had no job," accounting for 48%. In terms of the problems faced by poor rural households, the number one problem was still that "the burden due to diseases of family members was too heavy," accounting for 62%, higher than that of the poor urban households by 4 percentage points; the number two problem was that "the main family members were not able to work," accounting for 57%, higher than that of poor urban households by 6 percentage points; and the number three problem was that "the main labor forces of the households had no job," accounting for 46%. For the poor households who had transferred to cities, the number one problem was "poor living conditions," accounting for 45%; the number two problem was that "the cost of their children's education was too high," accounting for 26%; and the number three problem was that "the burden of supporting elderly members was too heavy," accounting for 25% (see Table 13.9). The problems faced by poor households who had transferred to cities were quite different from those faced by poor urban and rural households. The problems concerning living conditions, the burden of children's education, and the burden of supporting elderly family members were problems that derived gradually from urbanization. Most of the difficulties encountered by those households were a result of the accumulation of weaknesses during urbanization.

TABLE 13.9 Problems Faced by Poor Households in 2016

Unit: Number, %

Problem	Urban	Rural	Floating population in urban areas
Heavy economic burden due to diseases of family members	58	62	21
Main family members are not able to work	51	57	14
Main labor forces of the households have no job	48	46	24
Poor living conditions	41	44	45
A family member needs long-term nursing	40	42	16
Cost of children's education is too high	30	26	26
Burden of supporting elderly members is too heavy	25	24	25
Sample quantity	4124	3095	2050

3.2 Changing Tendency of Poverty Caused by Diseases in Poor Urban and Rural Households

As mentioned above, diseases were still the major cause of poverty for poor urban and rural households. Expenditures for disease included chronic disease expenditures and major disease expenditures. The per-time cost of chronic disease was not high but the duration was long, resulting in a heavy burden on poor households. From 2014 to 2016, the absolute amount of chronic disease expenditures of poor urban and rural households decreased from 13,612 yuan to 12,530 yuan with a reduction of 8%, and the proportion of those expenditures in the total household expenditures decreased from 39% to 31%.

The absolute amount of major disease expenditures of poor urban and rural households decreased from 42,801 yuan to 30,533 yuan, a reduction of 29%, and the proportion of those expenditures in the total household expenditures decreased from 102% to 63%. The amount of debt resulting from diseases decreased from 16,804 yuan to 12,802 yuan. The absolute amount decreased by 24% and the proportion of debt in the total household expenditures decreased by 11 percentage points (see Table 13.10).

In general, the burden due to disease expenditures decreased to some extent from 2014 to 2016, which might be related to the zero addition of grassroots drug prices and the increase in the reimbursement ratio for major diseases

TABLE 13.10 Expenditures on Disease in Poor Urban and Rural Households as a Proportion of Household Expenditures, 2014–2016

Unit: yuan, %

Year	The amount and proportion of chronic disease expenditures		The amount and proportion of major disease expenditures		The amount and proportion of debt taken on to pay medial bills	
2014	13612	39	42801	102	16804	38
2015	12193	39	46306	104	17851	40
2016	12530	31	30533	63	12802	27

in the medical reform. The health care insurance reimbursement will be analyzed specifically in a later article.

The burden caused by major disease expenditures was the number 1 cause of poverty for poor urban households, poor rural households, and poor households who had transferred to cities. The changing tendency of major disease expenditures by household types are as follows: In poor urban households, major disease expenditures increased from 45,597 yuan in 2014 to 52,142 yuan in 2015 and then decreased to 31,092 yuan in 2016. In poor rural households, major disease expenditures also increased from 38,183 yuan in 2014 to 40,864 yuan in 2015 and then decreased to 26,434 yuan in 2016. In poor households who had transferred to cities, major disease expenditures reduced from 44,056 yuan in 2014 to 31,363 yuan in 2015 and then increased to 44,015 yuan in 2016 (see Figure 13.5).

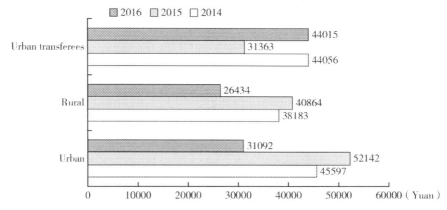

FIGURE 13.5 Changing Tendency of the Major Disease Expenditures of Poor Urban and Rural Households, 2014–2016

3.3 Changing Tendency of the Burden of Education in Poor Urban and Rural Households

In 2016, the proportion of poor urban and rural households with too heavy a burden from their children's education was 28%. In this section, we have analyzed preschool education, compulsory education, senior high school education, and college education. From 2014 to 2016, the average annual cost of preschool education for poor urban and rural households increased from 4,647 yuan to 5,981 yuan, an increase of 29%. At present, public preschool educational organizations are in serious demand in urban and rural areas, private preschool educational organizations are not standardized, and there is a great gap in terms of preschool educational resources, which are the key factors leading to the increase in the cost of preschool education year by year.

Compared to the other three educational stages, the cost of compulsory education was relatively low. In 2016, the average annual expenditure on compulsory education was 3,199 yuan, while the expenditures on preschool education, senior high school, and college education were 5,981 yuan, 8,137 yuan, and 12,097 yuan, respectively. From 2014 to 2016, the average annual expenditure on compulsory education increased from 2,864 yuan to 3,199 yuan, an increase of 12%. During the period of the 13th Five-Year Plan, the national government has gradually increased the financial input in the compulsory educational stage, which has played an important role in reducing the burden from the cost of compulsory education on urban and rural households.

In the senior high school educational stage, the average annual expenditure increased significantly. In 2016, the average annual expenditure on senior high school education was 2.5 times that on compulsory education, and the households with senior high school students had a much heavier burden. President Xi Jinping proposed that senior high school education should be integrated into the stage of compulsory education gradually, which is of great importance to reducing the educational burden on households.

In the college educational stage, the average annual expenditure of households was much higher than that of senior high school education. In 2016, the average annual expenditure on college education was 3.8 times that on compulsory education. From 2014 to 2016, the average annual expenditure on college education decreased from 14,555 yuan to 12,097 yuan, a reduction of 17% (see Table 13.11).

Among the four educational stages, college education imposes the heaviest burden. Do the college educational burdens for poor urban households, poor rural households, and poor households who have transferred to cities differ at different time points?

SURVEY REPORT ON THE CONDITIONS OF URBAN AND RURAL RESIDENTS 285

TABLE 13.11   Education Expenditures of Poor Urban and Rural Households in Different
Educational Stages, 2014–2016

Unit: yuan

Year	Preschool education	Compulsory education	Senior high school education	College education
2014	4647	2864	7369	14555
2015	4807	2755	7924	15292
2016	5981	3199	8137	12097

In terms of the absolute amount of college education expenditures of poor urban households, in 2014, the college education expenditures of poor urban households were 13,842 yuan, accounting for 33% of household expenditures. In 2016, expenditures increased to 14,475 yuan, accounting for 31% of household expenditures. Although the absolute amount increased by 5%, the ratio of household expenditures decreased by 2 percentage points.

In terms of the absolute amount of college education expenditures of poor rural households, in 2014, the college education expenditures of poor rural households were 16,840 yuan, accounting for 55% of the household expenditures, which means that half of the total expenditures of poor rural households with college students went toward college education. In 2016, the college education expenditures of poor rural households decreased to 16,243 yuan, accounting for 34% of total household expenditures. In 2016, the ratio of college education expenditures to total household expenditures decreased by 21 percentage points over that in 2014, mainly because of the increase in the income of rural households in the past three years.

In terms of the absolute amount of college education expenditures of poor households who had transferred to cities, in 2014, college education expenditures were 14,521 yuan, accounting for 29% of household expenditures. In 2015, college expenditures increased to 17,580 yuan, an increase of 21% of the absolute amount. In 2016, college education expenditures were kept at 17,705 yuan (see Table 13.12). As mentioned above, the number two problem faced by poor households who had transferred to cities was that "the cost of their children's education was too high" (26%). After integrating into the cities, poor households who had transferred gradually accepted the education model in cities and recognized the importance of cultural capital to the improvement of the social status of the households. Therefore, the expectation for children's education in those households was higher than that of the poor rural

TABLE 13.12   Expenditures on College Education in Poor Urban and Rural Households as a Proportion of Household Expenditures, 2014–2016

Unit: yuan, %

Year	Urban		Rural		Floating population in urban areas	
	Amount	Proportion	Amount	Proportion	Amount	Proportion
2014	13842	33	16840	55	14521	29
2015	13857	33	16092	37	17580	41
2016	14475	31	16243	34	17705	25

households. For example, in 2016, the expenditures on college education of poor households who had transferred to cities was higher than that of poor rural households by 1,462 yuan.

3.4   *The Changing Trends in Housing Burden in Poor Urban and Rural Households*

As mentioned above, "poor living conditions" were a common feature of poor urban and rural households. In 2016, poor urban households with poor living conditions accounted for 41% of the total number of poor urban households; the proportion was 44% for poor rural households and 45% for poor households who had transferred to cities. The feature of "poor living conditions" was closely related to the living structures of different households. Among poor urban households, 29% of them were living in self-built housing units, 17% in displacement and resettlement housing units, 10% in purchased commercial housing units and 9% in low-rent housing. Among poor rural households, 74% were living in self-built housing units and 7% of them were living in housing units built with government subsidies (see Table 13.13). Given the high proportion of self-built housing units, the cost of repairing and maintaining them has become a common problem for poor urban and rural households. Both poor urban and rural households were facing the problem of a high proportion of dilapidated buildings. From 2014 to 2016, the proportion of dilapidated buildings among poor urban households was 22% to 23%. In 2014, the proportion among poor rural households was 37%, which decreased to 32% in 2016, a reduction of 5 percentage points in three years (see Table 13.14).

SURVEY REPORT ON THE CONDITIONS OF URBAN AND RURAL RESIDENTS

TABLE 13.13   Dwelling Structures of Poor Urban and Rural Households in 2016

Unit: %

Housing type	Urban	Rural	Floating population in urban areas
Self-built housing	29	74	12
Displacement and resettlement housing	17	4	—
Self-purchased commercial housing	10	—	24
Low-rent housing	9	—	—
Government subsidy housing	—	7	—
Market-rent housing	—	—	30

Note: Statistics for other types of housing are not included.

TABLE 13.14   Proportion of Poor Urban and Rural Households in Dilapidated Buildings, 2014–2016

Unit: %

Year	Urban	Rural
2014	22	37
2015	23	36
2016	23	32

Among the three categories of households, only poor households who had transferred to cities considered the feature of "poor living conditions" as the number one problem, because the transferee population was mostly living in market-rent housing units, accounting for 30% of the total samples, followed by self-purchased commercial housing units and self-built housing units. Most of the transferee population was living on the edges of cities with a poor living environment. Zhou Daming used to say that there were binary communities in urban society. Migrant workers in the Pearl River Delta are living either in the houses of the local farmers or in the dorms offered by their employers, while the local people are living in communities with good facilities. Locally based policies and a parasitic economy are the fundamental factors leading to this binary mode.[5]

---

5 Zhou Daming, "Migrant Workers and Binary Communities—Investigation in the Pearl River Delta," *Journal of Sun Yat-Sen University* (Social Science Edition), 2000(2).

4 Functions of Social Security Policies in Poverty Reduction

4.1 *The Overall Effect of Social Policies since the 18th National Congress of The CPC*

At present, the number of subsistence allowance households in urban and rural areas has witnessed a stable reduction. According to data from the National Bureau of Statistics, at the end of 2016, 14.802 million people had received subsistence allowances for urban residents, 45.864 million people had received subsistence allowances for rural residents, and 4.969 million people had received assistance for extremely impoverished people in rural areas,[6] totaling 65.636 million people and accounting for 5% of the total population of the country. According to the changing tendency in recent years, both the population receiving subsistence allowances in urban and rural areas and the extremely impoverished population in rural areas have been decreasing. In 2012, the total number of that population was 80.336 million, accounting for 6% of the total population of the country, and it started to decrease continuously in 2012. At present, the number has declined to lower than 70 million, accounting for 5% of the total population (see Table 13.15).

The size of the urban subsistence allowance population witnessed the largest reduction, at an annual average rate of 8% beginning in 2012. The size of the rural subsistence allowance population decreased at a rate of 4% per year, and that of the rural extremely impoverished population decreased at a rate of 2% per year (see Figure 13.6).

According to the rural poverty reduction standard of 2,300 yuan per person per year (calculated at a constant price in 2010), the rural impoverished population in 2016 was 43.35 million, decreasing by 12.40 million over the previous year. From 2012 to 2016, more than 12 million rural impoverished people were able to rid themselves of poverty every year, at an annual poverty reduction rate of 19%. Poverty incidence among the rural population also decreased from 15% in 2012 to 7% in 2016 (see Table 13.16).

---

6 "Rural extremely impoverished people" refers to the elderly, the disabled, and those under 16 years old in rural areas who are not able to work, have no income or anyone to support them legally, or whose legal supporters are not able to perform their duties.

TABLE 13.15 Size and Proportion of the Subsistence Allowance and Extremely Impoverished Populations in China, 2012–2016

Unit: 10,000 persons, %

Year	Urban subsistence allowance population	Rural subsistence allowance population	Rural extremely impoverished population	Total number of the urban and rural subsistence allowance population and the rural extremely impoverished population	Proportion of the urban and rural subsistence allowance population and the rural extremely impoverished population
2012	2143.5	5344.5	545.6	8033.6	6
2013	2064.2	5388.0	537.2	7989.4	6
2014	1877.0	5207.2	529.1	7613.3	6
2015	1701.0	4903.6	516.7	7121.3	5
2016	1480.2	4586.5	496.9	6563.6	5

SOURCE: STATISTICAL BULLETIN OF THE DEVELOPMENT OF SOCIAL SERVICES, 2016

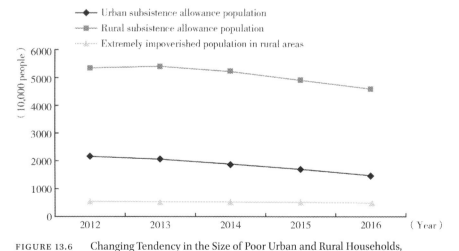

FIGURE 13.6 Changing Tendency in the Size of Poor Urban and Rural Households, 2012–2016
SOURCE: STATISTICAL BULLETIN OF THE DEVELOPMENT OF SOCIAL SERVICES IN 2016

TABLE 13.16   Size, Incidence, and Growth Rate of the Rural Impoverished Population, 2012–2016

Unit: 10,000 persons, %

Year	Rural impoverished Population	Amount of poverty reduction	Growth rate of the rural impoverished population	Incidence of rural poverty	Poverty standard
2012	9899	2339	-19	15	2,300 yuan/
2013	8249	1650	-17	13	person/year
2014	7017	1232	-15	11	(calculated at a
2015	5575	1442	-21	9	constant price in
2016	4335	1240	-22	7	2010)

SOURCE: STATISTICAL BULLETINS OF NATIONAL ECONOMIC AND SOCIAL DEVELOPMENT FOR PREVIOUS YEARS

4.2 Social Assistance Has Been Diversified and Has Become More Accurate

According to the survey results in Table 13.17, the assistance and preferential items that poor urban and rural households are eligible to receive have been diversified. In general, most assistance consisted of regular programs supplemented by irregular programs. Subsistence allowances, medical assistance, educational assistance, and housing assistance now cover both poor urban and rural households. The proportion of poor urban households enjoying subsistence allowances was 64%, which was higher than that for poor rural households (58%). The proportion of members of poor households who had transferred to cities who were eligible to receive subsistence allowances in their working places was relatively low, at 9%. In terms of medical assistance, the proportion of members of poor urban households who were eligible to receive medical assistance was the highest among the three groups, at 24%. The proportion for poor rural households witnessed a significant increase in the past three years, reaching 21%. The proportion of members of the poor households who had transferred to cities enjoying medical assistance was 11%. In addition to the above regular assistance programs, more poor urban households were able to benefit from preferential policies in terms of utility charge reductions or exemptions, commodity price subsidies, or holiday assistance than poor rural households and poor households who had transferred to cities.

SURVEY REPORT ON THE CONDITIONS OF URBAN AND RURAL RESIDENTS   291

TABLE 13.17   Ratios of Coverage under the Social Security Policies for Poor Urban and Rural Households in 2016

Unit: %

Assistance and preferential programs	Urban	Rural	Floating population in urban areas
Subsistence allowance	64	58.0	9
Medical assistance	24	21	11
Educational assistance	15	13	6
Housing assistance	8	4	3
Reduction or exemption of utility charges	22	13	3
Commodity price subsidy or holiday assistance	15	7	—
Temporary assistance	9	7	2
Charity assistance	6	5	
Other assistance or preferential programs	4	3	28
Natural disaster assistance	2	4	—
Reduction or exemption of other charges	3	2	—
Unemployment assistance	1	0.1	3
Legal assistance	1	0.2	1

4.3   *The Four Categories of Regular Assistance Programs Did Not Change Much, and the Overlap of Assistance Programs Was Common*

In terms of the tendency to vertical development, according to the statistics of the sampling survey, the coverage of the four categories of assistance systems has not changed much in the past three years. By the end of 2014, the coverage of subsistence allowances was 47%, which increased to 50% in 2016. The coverage of medical assistance decreased slightly from 22% in 2014 to 20% in 2016. The coverage of educational assistance increased slightly from 10% in 2014 to 13% in 2016. The coverage of housing assistance did not change too much, remaining at about 5% (see Table 13.18).

According to statistics, the overlaps among social assistance and preferential programs were high. Some poor urban and rural households enjoying subsistence allowances were also receiving medical assistance, educational assistance, and housing assistance. From 2014 to 2016, about 28% of the poor households enjoying subsistence allowances were still receiving medical

292   JIANG, WANG, AND TIAN

TABLE 13.18   The Changing Tendency in Different Assistance Policies for Poor Urban and Rural Households, 2014–2016

Unit: %

Year	Subsistence allowance	Medical assistance	Educational assistance	Housing assistance
2014	47	22	10	6
2015	51	21	11	5
2016	50	20	13	5

TABLE 13.19   Proportion of Households Receiving Subsistence Allowances and Other Preferential Policies, 2014–2016

Unit: %

Year	Medical assistance	Educational assistance	Housing assistance
2014	28	14	8
2015	27	15	7
2016	28	19	8

assistance. The number of people enjoying educational assistance increased year by year. In 2014, the proportion of households receiving both the subsistence allowance and educational assistance was 14%, which increased to 19% in 2016. The proportion of households receiving both the subsistence allowance and housing assistance was about 8% (see Table 13.19).

4.4   *The Role of Social Insurance in Poverty Reduction Has Become More Prominent*

As mentioned above, the ratio of health care expenditures to household expenditures has been decreasing, and the importance of social insurance has become prominent. According to the statistics of the sampling survey, in 2014, the average amount of health care insurance reimbursement for chronic diseases for poor urban and rural households was 3,937 yuan, accounting for 22% of the health care expenditures for chronic diseases. In 2016, the average amount of health care insurance reimbursement for chronic diseases increased to 4,247 yuan, with a reimbursement ratio of 23%, having increased slightly. In 2014, the average amount of health care insurance reimbursement for major diseases for poor urban and rural households was 14,248 yuan, and

SURVEY REPORT ON THE CONDITIONS OF URBAN AND RURAL RESIDENTS   293

TABLE 13.20   Health Care Insurance Reimbursements for Chronic and Major Diseases for Poor Urban and Rural Households, 2014–2016

Unit: yuan, %

Year	Health care insurance reimbursement amount for chronic diseases	Ratio of reimbursement	Amount of health care insurance reimbursement for major diseases	Ratio of reimbursement
2014	3937	22	14248	27
2015	3715	22	14383	30
2016	4247	23	11515	30

the absolute reimbursement amount decreased slightly in 2016 (11,515 yuan). However, the ratio of health care insurance reimbursement for major diseases increased from 27% in 2014 to 30% in 2016 (see Table 13.20).

Health care insurance in rural and urban areas has not been unified. In general, there are four types of insurance: urban worker health care insurance, urban resident health care insurance, new rural cooperative health care insurance, and the health care insurance systems established for the transferee population in some regions. Given the diversified financing systems, the social security systems participated in by urban residents, rural residents, and the transferee population in urban areas are different in terms of types and ratios of reimbursement. According to the results of the sampling survey in 2017, the amount of absolute health care insurance reimbursement for chronic diseases for poor urban households was 4,672 yuan, which was higher than that of the poor rural households and the poor households who had transferred to cities. However, in terms of relative ratios, the ratios of reimbursement of the three groups have been approaching equality. The ratio of reimbursement for chronic diseases for poor urban households was 24%, and that for poor rural households and poor households who had transferred to cities was 22%, indicating that, with the improvement of the social security system, the gap between poor urban and rural households in terms of reimbursement for chronic diseases was gradually narrowing.

In terms of the amount of reimbursement for major diseases, the average amount of health care insurance reimbursement for major diseases for poor urban households was 12,658 yuan, and that for poor rural households was 10,135 yuan, which was lower than that for poor urban households by 2,523 yuan. The average amount of health care insurance reimbursement for major

TABLE 13.21   Ratio of Health Care Insurance Reimbursement for Chronic and Major
Diseases among Poor Urban and Rural Households, 2014–2016

Unit: yuan, %

Type	Amount of health care insurance reimbursement for chronic diseases	Ratio of reimbursement	Amount of health care insurance reimbursement for major diseases	Ratio of reimbursement
Urban	4672	24	12658	32
Rural	3913	22	10135	30
Floating population in urban areas	3569	22	10385	25

diseases for the poor households who had transferred to cities was 10,385 yuan, which was lower than that for the poor urban households by 2,273 yuan. In terms of relative ratios, the ratio of health care insurance reimbursement for major diseases for poor urban households was 32%, the ratio for poor rural households was 30%, and that for poor households who had transferred to cities was 25% (see Table 13.21). The ratios of health care insurance reimbursement for major diseases for the three groups decreased one by one. In general, health care insurance benefits for poor urban households were still better than those for poor rural households and poor households who had transferred to cities.

5   Prospect for Future Policies

In the Report to the 19th CPC National Congress, President Xi Jinping pointed out, "We should comprehensively establish a sustainable social security system at all levels covering the whole population with urban and rural integration, clear credibilities, and moderate guarantees based on the requirements of ensuring bottom-line coverage, forming a network, and building a mechanism," and "integrate the rural and urban social assistance systems and improve the system of subsistence allowances." This has set the course for innovations in policies for civil work in the new age, and social security policies in the future should focus on the following aspects.

First of all, we should strive to establish a multi-level social security system. We should gradually establish a multi-level pension system based on social pension insurance + enterprise annuity + commercial insurance + personal savings, and a multi-level medical insurance system based on social medical insurance + supplementary enterprise medical insurance + commercial health care insurance, in order to diversify the sources of the funds of the pension and medical insurances. Based on the social security system, we should gradually improve the risk-withstanding capacity of poor urban and rural households and reduce the financial burden on governments at all levels.

Second, we should gradually narrow the gap between different social security systems. At present, the social security systems of our country are not unified and the levels of guarantee are imbalanced. In the future, we should gradually integrate the worker pension insurances in urban areas, the pension insurance for urban and rural residents, and the pension insurances of institutions and enterprises, in order to gradually narrow the differences between the social security systems for different groups.

Third, we should improve the accuracy of the social assistance system in preventing repeated overlaps. At present, overlaps of subsistence allowance and assistance funds in terms of health care, education, and housing are common. In the future, we should gradually define the boundaries of different types of assistance and meet the social needs of the impoverished people more accurately.

Fourth, we should gradually improve a mechanism of interlocking among the social assistance and guarantee standards and the price increase to make sure that the living standards of impoverished people do not decrease due to price increases. We should ensure the minimum living standard of the people in the new age, and pay close attention to the core economic data related to the quality of people's lives, such as CIP, average social income, minimum income, average income after retirement, basic living expenditures, utility charges, parking charges, property management fees, educational expenditures, and medical expenditures.

CHAPTER 14

Analytical Report on Online Public Opinion in China in 2017

Zhu Huaxin,[1] Liao Canliang,[2] and Pan Yufeng[3]

Abstract

Governance over the Internet has been improved by expanding its coverage from information on current politics to information about entertainment and gossip, and from a few opinion leaders to common Internet users. The development of We Media on the Internet has met an inflection point. At present, the middle-income group has become the major force of Internet public opinion. The public opinion caused by extreme individual cases has decreased, but the public uses small hotspots in daily life to express their collective concerns about deep social issues such as reduced inter-class mobility. To balance the governance of chaotic phenomena on the Internet and the guarantee of expression on the Internet is a key point on which the governance of the Internet should be focused in the future.

Keywords

internet public opinion – real-name system – collective anxiety – public opinion structure – public opinion differentiation

The Internet has made it convenient for more and more Chinese people to be informed and to express their opinions. As of June 2017, the number of Internet users in China had reached 751 million, with 96.3% of them using smartphones for Internet surfing. In addition, 92.1% of Internet users use QQ and WeChat as well as other real-time communication APPS, and 81.0% of them use search

---

1 Zhu Huaxin, public opinion analyst of the Public Opinion Monitoring Office of *People's Daily Online*.
2 Liao Canliang, public opinion analyst of the Public Opinion Monitoring Office of *People's Daily Online*.
3 Pan Yufeng, special expert of the new media think tank of *People's Daily Online*.

© KONINKLIJKE BRILL NV, LEIDEN, 2022 | DOI:10.1163/9789004500723_015

engines.[4] The smartphone reading contact rate of people in China witnessed an increase for eight consecutive years, reaching 66.1% in 2016. In 2016, 62.4% of adults read using WeChat, with an average reading time of about 26.00 minutes.[5] The number of active users of Sina Microblog every day was 159 million;[6] it was estimated that there were 20 million official WeChat accounts and about 10 million active apps (including information and service apps). The current hotspots of public opinion have been described as screen flooding. Based on its information sharing and opinion exchange functions, such as WeChat, microblogs, and news clients, the Internet has become both the source of and the platform for spreading social public opinion.

1   Quantitative Analysis of Public Opinion Pressure in 2017

In this report, we have established such indicators as popularity and public opinion pressure to analyze the 600 public opinion hotspots that were ranked in the top 50 during each month of the period covered by the report (from November 1, 2016, to October 31, 2017).

Among the top 20 topics, the 19th National Congress of the CPC has become the top topic of concern on various Internet public opinion platforms; it was followed by the movie *Wolf Warriors II* and the TV series *In the Name of the People*, and the border clash between China and India and the establishment of the Xiong'an New Area ranked in fourth and fifth place, respectively (see Table 14.1). The top five events of the year have a positive public opinion tendency, and among the top ten events, only the Luo Yixiao event and the Shandong Yu Huan case had positive public opinion pressure, leading to a certain amount of public opinion rebound and differentiation. The number of events with positive public opinion pressure in 2016 and 2015 was six.

In this report, we have divided the hot-button issues into eight categories, among which are public management, social contradictions, public safety, and enterprise public opinion. We can make the following observations: (1) Social contradictions are still subject to high public opinion pressure, and public opinion on public management has diminished greatly over the previous year. The issuance and implementation of various public policies, laws, and regulations have been highly recognized in public opinion. (2) Famous

---

4   China Internet Network Information Center, "The 40th Statistical Report on the Development of the Internet Network of China," August 4, 2017.

5   Chinese Academy of Press and Publication, "The 14th Survey on the Reading Habits of the Population," April 18, 2017.

6   2017 Q2 Financial Statements published on microblog.

TABLE 14.1   Top 20 Hot-Button Issues in 2017

Unit: 1,000 articles

Ranking	Event	News-paper	News	Forum	Blogs	Micro-blog	WeChat	App	Level of Media Coverage
1	19th National Congress of the CPC	76.5	550.7	42.3	3.9	66.3	314.6	161.0	97.03
2	*Wolf Warriors II*	6.3	247.1	97.5	14.0	356.6	174.0	59.3	91.24
3	*In the Name of the People*	14.3	303.9	126.8	15.1	147.6	191.6	15.7	91.09
4	China–India Dong Lang Stalemate	4.6	150.5	24.9	20.9	44.7	158.8	16.4	85.56
5	Establishment of the Xiong'an New Area in Hebei	6.5	194.1	41.2	17.7	13.8	63.7	8.2	83.57
6	The Shandong Yu Huan Case	3.9	100.3	33.3	5.5	69.4	114.7	5.2	82.73
7	The Luo Yixiao Event	2.1	143.8	30.5	9.4	9.7	161.9	11.9	81.65
8	Topics about school district housing and the policies issued in different regions for equal rights for home tenants and owners	4.1	137.3	8.6	4.8	8.9	50.7	14.0	80.63
9	The 2017 Belt and Road Forum for International Cooperation	7.2	118.9	11.9	9.1	6.3	64.4	3.4	80.29
10	Topics related to bike sharing	5.1	134.9	11.6	3.5	6.2	48.3	9.1	80.09

ANALYTICAL REPORT ON ONLINE PUBLIC OPINION IN CHINA IN 2017   299

TABLE 14.1   Top 20 Hot-Button Issues in 2017 (*cont.*)

Unit: 1,000 articles

Ranking	Event	News-paper	News	Forum	Blogs	Micro-blog	WeChat	App	Level of Media Coverage
11	Death of Li Wenxing due to pyramid selling	5.5	62.0	6.6	2.5	13.7	52.1	7.0	79.14
12	Protest against the THAAD in South Korea	1.4	65.5	46.4	6.9	49.0	70.7	4.4	78.93
13	Dispute regarding the speech of Deng Xiangchao	4.9	61.3	6.3	3.5	11.6	43.1	4.8	78.18
14	Collective withdrawal of the Chinese men's table tennis team	1.7	24.5	4.8	1.7	98.9	18.9	2.3	74.22
15	Debut of the first aircraft carrier made in China	0.7	40.1	43.7	4.2	19.3	20.6	6.5	74.12
16	Babysitter arson in Hangzhou	0.7	26.3	4.2	1.6	97.5	23.6	2.6	72.84
17	3rd comment on *Honor of Kings* by people.cn	0.6	55.0	7.6	2.4	3.2	30.8	8.6	72.42
18	Pregnant woman who died from a fall in Yulin	0.8	20.6	3.2	1.5	21.1	11.3	8.3	71.32
19	Issuance of the Regulations on Managing Group Information Services on the Internet	1.2	30.5	4.6	0.6	3.3	19.5	4.9	70.63
20	Overseas rumors spread by Guo Wengui	1.1	46.8	3.3	0.9	1.3	11.7	1.5	68.44

enterprises such as Letv, Hannan Airline, Wanda, and Baidu have encountered a greater public opinion crisis, and the quantities, popularities, and pressures of hot-button issues related to enterprise public opinion have increased over the previous year. (3) With the opening-up of China to the world, more and more public opinion hot-button issues have occurred in foreign countries, including many negative events, such as disappearances and kidnappings of Chinese people, leading to an increase in public opinion pressure related to foreign and military affairs. At the same time, the Great Power Mindset has taken shape among Internet users, further cohering patriotic enthusiasm. (4) The quantity and pressure of public opinion on sports, entertainment, and public figures has been increasing. In the age of total population entertainment, people's attention has been increasingly attracted by gossip regarding pop stars, challenging the moral bottom line of the people. (5) Public opinion pressure on official government management and anti-corruption has decreased, and the negative public opinion crisis caused by government officials has been reduced to a very low level, which is not able to stimulate public discourse (see Table 14.12). According to the geographical distribution of the pressure index, public opinion pressure in most regions has diminished over the previous year; pressure in Beijing, Jiangsu, Shanghai, Sichuan, and Gansu witnessed the largest reduction. By contrast, public opinion pressure increased in some regions, such as Zhejiang, Yunnan, Shaanxi, and Tianjin, under the influence of individual negative events, such as the babysitter arson case in Hangzhou, Zhejiang Province; the public opinion events related to tourism in Yunnan; the pregnant woman who died of a fall in Yulin, Shaanxi Province; and the death of Li Wenxing due to pyramid selling in Tianjin.

Among the 600 hot-button issues this year, there were 131 public opinion events related to social contradictions, decreasing by 22 over the previous year, but the total public opinion pressure has increased. Three points are worth noting: (1) Contradictions in social moral disputes, the protection of juveniles and vulnerable groups, social fraud, and ideology were the most prominent topics, witnessing the highest growth of public opinion pressure. (2) Public opinion pressure due to focus on contradictions in terms of labor disputes, land requisition and demolition, and the protection of group rights decreased noticeably, and no real hotspot occurred among events regarding the protection of rights (see Table 14.3).

ANALYTICAL REPORT ON ONLINE PUBLIC OPINION IN CHINA IN 2017 301

TABLE 14.2 Index of the Pressure in Different Public Opinion Areas, 2015–2017
Unit: Number, %

Classification	Event number	2017 event propor- tion	2016 event propor- tion	2015 event pro- portion	2017 average heat	2016 average heat	2015 average heat	2017 public opinion pressure	2016 public opinion pressure	2015 public opinion pressure
Social contradictions	131	21.8	25.5	20.6	47.04	41.3	56.86	110.87	102.41	105.09
Public management	211	35.2	38.0	31.2	51.58	50.14	65.67	67.86	103.69	91.71
Public safety	75	12.5	10.7	11.6	53.49	48.72	62.54	65.46	59.83	61.41
Enterprise public opinion	48	8.0	5.2	14.0	55.93	53.74	61.81	34.17	24.94	49.82
Sports, entertainment, and public figures	37	6.2	6.0	5.4	56.01	60.25	66.10	17.10	12.57	12.41
Foreign and military affairs	61	10.2	7.2	9.4	56.51	59.73	65.72	11.66	9.76	11.02
Official government management and anti-corruption	16	2.7	6.5	4.4	52.91	45.54	58.41	6.91	20.08	12.99
Other	21	3.5	1.3	3.4	50.20	48.97	66.76	2.11	5.27	8.00

TABLE 14.3 Index of the Pressure Due to the Focus on Social Contradictions, 2015–2017
Unit: Number, %

Contradic- tion focus	Event number	2017 event propor- tion	2016 event propor- tion	2015 event propor- tion	2017 average heat	2016 average heat	2015 average heat	2017 public opinion pressure	2016 public opinion pressure	2015 public opinion pressure
Social moral disputes	56	9.3	7.7	6.4	45.46	38.98	59.30	38.38	19.65	25.37

TABLE 14.3   Index of the Pressure Due to the Focus on Social Contradictions, 2015–2017 (*cont.*)
Unit: Number, %

Contradiction focus	Event number	2017 event proportion	2016 event proportion	2015 event proportion	2017 average heat	2016 average heat	2015 average heat	2017 public opinion pressure	2016 public opinion pressure	2015 public opinion pressure
Protection of juveniles and vulnerable groups	15	2.5	2.3	2.2	49.00	30.75	52.32	15.16	7.23	11.70
Social fraud	7	1.2	0.5	0.2	53.98	50.12	0.0	10.25	4.13	1.20
Ideology	6	1.0	1.0	1.2	54.29	53.79	56.87	8.49	5.04	10.35
Social violence	8	1.3	1.7	2.6	43.80	41.43	54.37	8.14	8.57	10.11
Relations between officials and the people	7	1.2	2.8	1.2	43.79	36.43	59.41	7.02	11.48	9.85
Relations between police and the people	3	0.5	1.3	1.2	62.99	44.03	57.96	5.70	8.69	9.16
Relations between doctors and patients	4	0.7	1.3	0.8	44.85	38.62	58.02	4.09	5.01	4.80
Gap between rich and poor and between urban and rural areas	11	1.8	2.7	0.4	50.97	47.56	66.08	2.23	12.37	1.78
Labor disputes	1	0.2	1.3	2.4	34.11	46.75	52.62	0.62	7.55	10.96

TABLE 14.3   Index of the Pressure Due to the Focus on Social Contradictions, 2015–2017 (*cont.*)
Unit: Number, %

Contradiction focus	Event number	2017 event proportion	2016 event proportion	2015 event proportion	2017 average heat	2016 average heat	2015 average heat	2017 public opinion pressure	2016 public opinion pressure	2015 public opinion pressure
Land requisition, demolition, and the protection of group rights	0	0.0	1.0	0.6	0.00	41.84	57.84	0.00	5.56	5.52

2   Internet Hot-Button Issues Reflecting Deep Social Issues

2.1   *A Profound Structural Change Occurred in the Field of Public Opinion*

The influence of news media and opinion leaders on the field of public opinion has decreased, the opportunities for ordinary people to express their opinions have increased, the right to speak in the field of public opinion has been equalizing, and the government has strengthened its agenda to play a main role in the field of public opinion in key nodes.

In 2017, public opinion on the Yu Huan case in Shandong in March was generated by a report in the newspaper *Southern Weekly*, in the classic vehicle for public opinion generation, and spread via portal websites and social media discussion. With the exception of the Yu Huan case, the capacity of the news media and opinion leaders to set agendas has been further reduced. On June 24, a landslide occurred in Xinmo Village, Diexi Town, Maoxian County, Sichuan Province, leading to several deaths. Some landslide videos were spread via microblogs and WeChat Moments, causing panic among Internet users. Afterward, the local police department refuted the rumor by saying that those videos were from Hangzhou, not Maoxian County. In case of emergencies, local governments should pay close attention to how to use news media to curtail rumors that spread on We Media.

WeChat has reduced the threshold for Internet expression and browsing. In the age of BBS and the early stage of microblogs, Internet public opinion was led by a few social media influencers, but now public opinion is led by people of all walks of life, including ordinary people. Everyone can express their opinions and make requests by moving a finger, and the right to voice one's opinion is being equalized. On the Internet, the unique opinions of opinion leaders have decreased, as they attract fewer supporters, and public topics have aroused sympathy more easily. An article entitled "How to Avoid Becoming a Fat Middle-Aged Man" was read more than 5 million times. During the 90th anniversary of the PLA in 2017, an H5 product published on the client page of the *People's Daily*, titled "Look! Our New Military Uniforms," was viewed more than 1.5 billion times. This phenomenon-level product had become popular due to the elements of youth and narcissism, which could reflect the sentiments of family and country among Internet users.

In 2017, a lot of great and good events occurred, from the Belt and Road Forum for International Cooperation and the meeting of the leaders of the BRICS countries in Xiamen to the 19th National Congress of the CPC; with regard to some important nodes and topics of political importance, the government showed a powerful capacity for agenda-setting and obtained overwhelming public opinion influence. In 2017, *Wolf Warriors II* was broadcast; it tells a story about a retired Chinese soldier saving compatriots in Africa. Within three months, the movie had been seen by more than 159 million people, and the sense of national pride among grassroots Internet users was overwhelming. The praise the movie received allayed the doubts expressed by Internet users in intellectual circles over whether the movie was encouraging arrogance within the nation.

2.2 The Number of Broad Topics Related to Social Systems Diminished

In 2017, public opinion had more to say on quality of life as it relates to the benefits of ordinary people. Internet users showed strong empathy, reflecting the collective anxiety of the public during the social transformation and demonstrating the feature of small hot-button issues that generate an enormous amount of public opinion. An image of the middle-aged drummer of the Black Panther Band holding a vacuum cup containing wolfberries led Internet users to cherish a memory from their youth. The article entitled "I'm Fan Yusu," contributed by a female housekeeper, became popular on the Internet overnight; the author used the sad and happy stories of small figures in society to express her sympathy for those who are struggling for their lives at the bottom of society and stimulated discussion about the living conditions of the grassroots people.

Since February 2017, the topic of school district housing has aroused heated discussions, and it has become a consensus among Internet users that we should not let the kids lose at the beginning. Internet articles about the high price of school district housing, including "The Confession of a Research Fellow at the Chinese Academy of Sciences: Why I Chose to Leave" and "I Have Felt a Little Sad for Beijing Recently," were widely disseminated via WeChat Moments and read more than 700,000 times.

During the college entrance examination in 2017, a contemptuous view of middle-class education spread widely on the Internet. The opinion expressed on the Internet that the capacity of education to reverse reduced inter-class mobility is weakening has been accepted by many people. Some Internet users think that the topic assigned for the composition on the 2017 college entrance examination may validate the sentiment that it is hard for poor households to educate talented youths. "In remote areas, things such as high-speed trains, bike sharing, and mobile payment that are common for urban kids are very abstract to kids in rural areas. You can image the difficulties they had when writing the composition." In October, a student at the Tsinghua University Primary School wrote a thesis entitled "Big Data Helps You Know about Su Shi in a Better Way," resulting in a discussion about reduced inter-class mobility.

2.3 Public Opinion Focused on the Environment of Business Operations and Expected the Stabilization of the Future Prospects of the Non-public Sector of the Economy

At the end of 2016, an auto glass plant financed by Cao Dewang, the president of Fuyao Glass, with 600 million US dollars went into operation in the United States, leading to the Internet rumor that Cao Dewang was trying to escape to the United States. Cao Dewang said: "In China, except for laborers, everything in the entity economy is more expensive than in the United States." Some scholars said that Chinese enterprises have encountered a death tax rate. The State Administration of Taxation published an article on its website pointing out that the macro taxation burden has been regularly decreasing in recent years. As a response, the Ministry of Finance proposed a theory of "fishing in good water" to research new tax reduction measures to further relieve the burdens on enterprises.

In 2017, during the NPC and CPPCC at the levels of the nation, provinces, autonomous regions, and municipalities, the optimization of the environment of business operations was a hot topic. At the current stage of the slowdown of the economic growth rate, we should strive to reduce the trading costs of the main market players, which would help business owners to regain and improve their confidence. At the central political and legal work conference in January, the government pointed out that the ownership system was the cornerstone of the market economy and that the strengthening of ownership protection could stabilize the expectations of various market players and improve social confidence. Before the 19th National Congress of the CPC, the Central Committee of the Communist Party of China and the State Council issued the *Opinions on Creating an Environment for the Healthy Development of Entrepreneurs to Promote Excellent Entrepreneurship and Give Play to the Role of Entrepreneurs in a Better Way*, emphasizing that we should protect the property rights of entrepreneurs; that governments at all levels and government agencies and officials should not intervene in the operations conducted by entrepreneurs according to law; that enterprise fees should be reduced; and that a service platform for the protection of uniform enterprise rights should be established in the country.

2.4 *A Public Call for Social Morality*

In 2017, bike-sharing services became popular in many cities, and Internet users criticized those who damaged the bikes on purpose. The improvement of social morality involves personal moral cultivation and a guarantee based on industry management and legislation. Internet users proposed that related enterprises should conduct credit management for users and hoped that the government could integrate the bike-sharing service into the social credit system to punish those who break public orders.

Many sexual assaults have been exposed through the Internet. The offenders in such assaults were always the more powerful party in teacher-student relationships or classmate relationships—a reminder of the defects in school management, especially the deficiencies of teachers' ethics. Some deputies to the national congress, members of the national committee of the CPPCC, and experts in the industry recommended integrating sexual assault prevention into the normal teaching programs oriented around the curricula of compulsory education, publicizing the personal information of the offenders, and forbidding them from holding any jobs related to children.

In Shandong, Yu Huan was condemned to life imprisonment during the first trial. The report of the *Southern Weekly* raised a huge emotional outcry among the public. A single piece of news reported by Netease attracted more than 2.7 million comments. It is valuable that overall, public opinion respected judicial procedure and looked forward to a just settlement in the second trial. Yu Huan was sentenced to five years of imprisonment in the second trial. Rational voices finally won over the public and overwhelmed the extreme words supporting revenge. As a result of the Yu Huan case, a new round of benign interaction between justice and public opinion was initiated to restore facts and resolve disputes through law, in order to avoid the rupture in public opinion after the Lei Yang case and to gain the highest recognition of the society.

2.5 *Increased Debates about Ideology*

In 2017, many events related to ideological topics occurred on the Internet, and some of those topics have stirred controversy that has led to actions in the offline world. At the beginning of the year, Deng Xiangchao, a former professor from Shandong Jianzhu University, Zuo Chunhe, the deputy director of the Culture, Radio, Television, and Press and Publication Bureau of Shijiazhuang, and Liu Yong, an employee of Luohe TV station of Henan Province, were suspended from their posts and became unemployed because they made speeches on the Internet containing false information and violated political disciplines. Some Internet users grew furious and thought that the purpose of the speeches made by the above three people was to destroy their employers, and so they gathered offline to protest, putting pressure on the employers of the three people. However, some Internet users also supported their freedom of expression. Opinions were polarized.

In March, the United States and South Korea jointly deployed the THAAD missile system in South Korea; a lot of people proposed boycotting products from the United States and South Korea, and they gave expression to extreme nationalist sentiments. This event shows that some arguments about ideological topics on the Internet have had an impact offline. Online arguments can easily develop into offline gatherings and protests, and aimless online protests can become offline assaults with malicious purposes.

At the same time, colleges and universities should strengthen their governance over cyberspace and schools based on the principle that they are responsible for ideological work. Some college teachers were fired due to improper speeches in class or on the Internet that crossed the red line imposed by ideological management, which caused shock in society. In July, a national teaching material commission was established for the first time in our country to handle the ideological content of teaching materials and ensure ideological safety in the country.

2.6 Topics Related to Ethnic Groups, Religion, and Hong Kong Have Become Prominent

Against the general background of rampant terrorist activity in the world, anti-terrorism, anti-splitting, and anti-extremism have become the consensus position of the public. Some Internet users from minority groups are sensitive to affairs related to ethnic groups and religion, and the names of some business service enterprises, such as Afanti and Flying Pig, have triggered protests. At the same time, public opinion did not wholly turn against extreme claims directed at national religions. In April 2017, the government of Tancheng County, Linyi City, Shandong Province disclosed through the government microblog account "@Tancheng Release" that resident Hou had been arrested by the public security organ because he had used improper expressions to defame religious beliefs in his WeChat Moments. In their comments, Internet users expressed their doubts about his arrest, arguing that local law enforcement had acted excessively.

In July, someone disclosed on the Internet that Meituan had established special channels for ordering halal food and made halal food boxes, causing arguments online. Mainstream public opinion opposed Meituan's actions on the grounds that halal food was spreading a symbol with specific religious significance throughout the entire society. On the Internet, some extreme posts connected Muslims with extremism, bringing shame on the Islamic public, which we should guard against.

In 2017, the issue of "Hong Kong independence" continued to be a focus of public opinion. At the beginning of the year, a member of the legislative council of Hong Kong made a vow insulting China's mainland, resulting in the interpretation of the basic law of the National People's Congress. After that, the central government and ordinary Internet users maintained high pressure against speeches and acts favoring independence for Hong Kong. At the beginning of the new semester in September, some banners and posters supporting Hong Kong independence were seen in some universities in Hong Kong, leading to conflicts between Hong Kong students and students from China's mainland. The majority public opinion on the Internet opposed acts supporting Hong Kong independence, indicating that such acts violated both the Constitution of China and the basic law of Hong Kong. The youth groups from China's mainland did very well in this aspect, taking an active role in making their voices heard online. Internet users of the Liyiba social platform on Baidu launched an initiative[7] to log into their Facebook accounts to lodge protests on the accounts of the student unions of the Chinese University of Hong Kong and the University of Hong Kong and the account of the Consulate General of the United States in Hong Kong and Macau.

In addition, some soccer fans from Hong Kong booed during the national anthem of China in some international games, and a Chinese overseas student, Yang, delivered a speech at his graduation ceremony in the University of Maryland in which he praised the fresh air and free expression in the United States, drawing a contrast with China. All of these acts have elicited condemnation via public opinion. For more and more Internet users, the Chinese state has become a concept that is too sacred to be violated. The opinions against Hong Kong independence have been firm and clear. At the same time, a discussion about speech boundaries was started on the Internet.

3 Management and Guarantee: Tension in the System

3.1 *Governance over the Internet Has Been Improved to an Unparalleled Level, and the Golden Age of We Media Has Ended*

On June 1, 2017, the *Cyber Security Law* was put into operation to establish legal norms for the use of the Internet by individuals and organizations. On the same day, the new version of the *Regulations on Managing Internet News*

---

7 Football player Li Yi's Post Bar. Li Yi was called the Great Li Yi by Internet users, and he has totally shaken off the tag of footballer. Post Bar is a social platform for large-scale Internet group activities. The Internet users of Li Yi's Post Bar have participated in protests against the Taiwan Independence acts of Tsai Ing-wen on Facebook many times.

Information Services was also put into practice to standardize and manage news information services, ranging from the PC websites of 12 years ago to microblogs, official accounts, real-time communication tools, network broadcasting, and other mobile platforms.

The management of the Internet should emphasize the entities responsible for network platforms, such as requiring news aggregators, which were considered information distribution centers in the past, to implement the system of holding the chief editor accountable for content. In addition, even those young Internet users who do not care about politics have felt pressure from Internet management in the past year.

In June, the Beijing Internet Information Office met with many website principals, requesting them to take effective measures to prevent online reporting of private information about pop stars and their lives, and a group of gossip accounts such as "All-Star Detective," "China No. 1 Paparazzo Zhuo Wei," and "Famous Detective Zhao Wuer" were shut down. This act was a severe condemnation of the wild development of We Media over the past several years, and it was theorized that the shutdown of these accounts would lead to the disappearance of hundreds of millions of yuan in assets. Some gossip accounts were mainly used to report on the affairs and luxurious wedding ceremonies, cars, and residences of pop stars. The measure taken by the government not only stipulated the restrictions in laws, but also promoted a set of values. For some Internet users, this means that they have lost some of the content of their online entertainment. In July, due to copyright protection, overseas movies and TV plays were removed from bilibili and AcFun, causing some youth to feel a great sense of loss. In October, the section of the Tianya BBS that serves homosexual users was shut down. Whereas the entertainment fields had been relatively free in the past, people could now feel an invisible hand there.

3.2 The Management of Dependent Territories and New Group Regulations Are a Reminder of the Standards for Collective Online Lives

Another management measure instituted by the Internet Information Office triggered shock within society. In October, the *Regulations on Managing Internet Group Information Services* declared that the creators and administers of Internet groups on WeChat or QQ should carry out their group management responsibilities. Thus, in 2017, some regions tried to conduct dependent territory management for We Media accounts. For example, in Xi'an, registration requirements were imposed on the following categories: personal microblog accounts with more than 30,000 subscribers; the creators of such accounts with their ID cards, residence, or business addresses in the areas under administration of Xi'an; and the registers, administrators, or users of official WeChat

TABLE 14.4 Gender, Region, and Age of Internet Users Concerned about Hot-Button Issues
Unit: %

Event	Male rate	First-tier city	Developed second-tier city	Moderately developed second tier city	Third-tier city	Born in 2000–2009	Born in 1990–1999	Born in 1980–1989	Born in 1970–1979	Born before 1970s
Pregnant woman who died of a fall in Yulin	32.90	21.14	12.09	35.29	16.25	3.63	68.15	22.64	4.28	1.31
The Shandong Yuhuan Case	47.20	21.62	12.87	33.70	16.71	5.48	72.89	15.20	4.94	1.49
The suicide of programmer Su Xiangmao	37.10	30.89	12.74	33.04	12.67	3.89	66.39	23.33	4.91	1.48
The Luo Yixiao Event	26.61	29.80	12.99	32.35	13.15	4.53	66.93	22.73	4.56	1.25
The speech of Deng Xiangchao containing false information	84.48	32.70	12.70	30.15	13.61	3.33	29.83	25.19	20.94	20.72
Old ladies occupying the basketball playground for dancing	68.62	27.01	12.28	32.39	17.24	2.90	66.95	23.12	5.49	1.55
Movies and TV plays removed from bilibili and AcFun	34.68	21.50	13.57	33.05	15.45	15.52	75.63	4.42	3.20	1.22
Shanghai police officer kicked down a woman holding a child	62.09	30.17	12.38	30.55	14.13	3.35	52.40	33.29	8.08	2.89
Comment on *Honor of Kings* by people.cn	58.55	24.61	12.03	34.50	14.11	10.82	71.95	12.19	4.15	0.88

ANALYTICAL REPORT ON ONLINE PUBLIC OPINION IN CHINA IN 2017 311

TABLE 14.4   Gender, Region, and Age of Internet Users Concerned about Hot-Button Issues (*cont.*)
Unit: %

Event	Male rate	First-tier city	Developed second-tier city	Moderately developed second tier city	Third-tier city	Born in 2000–2009	Born in 1990–1999	Born in 1980–1989	Born in 1970–1979	Born before 1970s
Speech of a Chinese overseas student at the University of Maryland	54.27	26.69	11.56	34.33	13.93	4.99	65.65	20.39	6.61	2.35
Wolf Warriors II	44.54	21.56	11.98	34.04	16.06	12.09	70.58	13.17	3.42	0.75
Dispute caused by the articles of Zhou Xiaoping	82.81	33.66	12.93	30.22	12.42	3.76	36.59	29.06	19.71	10.87

SOURCE: SYSTEM OF THE PUBLIC OPINION MONITORING OFFICE OF *THE PEOPLE'S DAILY ONLINE* AND SINA MICROBLOG. DATA CAPTURE DURATION: NOVEMBER 2016–NOVEMBER 2017

accounts who are in Xi'an. To enact the dependent territory management of We Media accounts, we need to carefully strike a balance between the standardization of Internet speech and the guarantee of the public's right of expression, so as to prevent grassroots government officials from suppressing the democratic rights of the public.

Government officials in some places have even required the police to take into custody some Internet users who complained about the compulsory donations required by government officials or the bad, overpriced food provided in the dining halls of hospitals, on the grounds that these users were making trouble and causing an uproar among the public. To govern the chaos on the Internet and properly carry out the supervision of public opinion, the related departments should respect the rights of governments as well as the boundaries of the rights of Internet users, accept the supervision of the public, and properly respond to the concerns of the public.

TABLE 14.5 Educational Background of Internet Users Concerned about Hot-Button Issues
Unit: %

Event	Primary school	Middle school	College and university	Overseas study returnees	Unknown
Pregnant woman who died of a fall in Yulin	0.73	11.15	46.98	1.86	39.28
The Shandong Yuhuan Case	0.64	11.84	47.74	1.96	37.81
The suicide of programmer Su Xiangmao	1.43	8.21	52.65	2.63	35.07
The Luo Yixiao Event	1.09	10.48	51.87	4.30	32.26
The speech of Deng Xiangchao containing false information	1.91	8.18	63.27	2.18	24.45
Old ladies occupying the basketball playground for dancing	1.36	10.34	52.21	2.78	33.31
Movies and TV plays removed from bilibili and AcFun	0.00	21.41	43.07	3.02	32.49
Shanghai police officer who kicked down a woman holding a child	1.27	11.94	45.62	1.90	39.27
Comment on *Honor of Kings* by people.cn	1.03	11.60	52.49	2.45	32.44
Speech of a Chinese overseas student at the University of Maryland	0.93	9.62	52.04	6.07	31.33
Wolf Warriors II	0.64	14.32	44.12	2.05	38.87
Dispute caused by the articles of Zhou Xiaoping	2.04	8.78	59.36	3.15	26.67

SOURCE: SYSTEM OF THE PUBLIC OPINION MONITORING OFFICE OF *THE PEOPLE'S DAILY ONLINE* AND SINA MICROBLOG. DATA CAPTURE DURATION: NOVEMBER 2016– NOVEMBER 2017

4 Research on Demographic Structure and the Splintering of Internet Public Opinion on Hot-Button Issues

4.1 *The Demographic Composition of Internet Users Concerned with Hot-Button Issues*

The Public Opinion Monitoring Office of the *People's Daily Online* conducted a statistical analysis on the gender and age of 820,000 Internet users who were concerned about 12 hot-button issues related to social conflict that generated significant public attention. The results are listed in Tables 14.4 and 14.5.

In terms of social stratum, the middle-income group has become the major contributor to Internet public opinion. According to statistics, the Internet users with an undergraduate education and above accounted for 50.9% of those sharing opinions, and those with occupations such as media workers or white-collar workers in enterprises accounted for 7.48% and 27.75%, respectively. The middle-income group commonly has an undergraduate education or above, and media workers and white-collar workers have knowledge-intensified middle-income occupations. Therefore, in terms of educational background and occupation structure, most Internet users expressing their opinions on hot-button issues could be included in the middle-income group.

The fact that the middle-income group is the main force of public opinion could explain why hot-button issues have mostly focused on safety, education, health care, income distribution, and housing for years. In terms of public opinion guidance and social governance, since the middle-income group is concerned mostly about health care, personal safety, and the fairness of education, which are topics related to quality of life and developmental prospects, and since they have a certain right to speech and would like to use the Internet to express their opinions, topics related to police, health care, education, and income distribution have become sensitive areas of public opinion. Beyond the public opinion events, some members of the middle-income group have started to express their anxiety and concerns about reduced inter-class mobility.

In addition, with the increase in the amount of public opinion expressed by the middle class year after year, the voices from other classes may be squeezed out. In particular, when the major social conflict has become the one between the people's desire for a better life and imbalanced and insufficient development, the government should make more efforts to capture the muffled voices to balance the interests of different parties.

In terms of gender, no obvious difference could be seen among Internet users concerned about hot-button issues, but there was an obvious difference in terms of the types of hot-button issues they were concerned about. According to the data, the ratio of male to female Internet users was 52.8:47.2. In terms of topics, female Internet users were more concerned about topics related to themselves or topics with female subjects. For example, the female Internet users who paid attention to the pregnant woman who had died of a fall in Yulin, Shaanxi Province, accounted for 68.1% of those interested in the topic, and women made up 73.4% of the users who were concerned about the Luo Yixiao event.

In terms of geographical distribution, in bigger cities, the rate of expression and participation in public opinion events tends to be higher. The 1980s generation of Internet users in cities has become the most stable group in the field of public opinion. First- and second-tier cities have become the major sources of Internet public opinion on hot-button issues, accounting for 71.6%. Internet users from first-tier cities accounted for 26.65%, and those from second-tier cities accounted for 45.1%. Internet users from first-tier cities were inclined to guide public opinion and participate in discussions on macro topics. Internet users from second-tier and third-tier cities paid more attention to public opinion as it related to social life. The attention paid by some groups (such as the 1980s generation from developed second-tier cities) to various events had a minimum degree of fluctuation, and so they could be considered the most stable groups in the field of public opinion.

In terms of age structure, the 1990s generation has become the main force behind public opinion on hot-button issues, and the voices of the 2000s generation have become more and more numerous in discussions of some hot-button issues. Internet users of the 1990s generation accounted for 61.9% of all Internet users, but they were less concerned about topics related to ideology on the Internet. The 1980s generation accounted for 20.4%, and their participation in various public opinion topics was balanced; the 2000s generation accounted for 6.1%, with a high degree of participation in entertainment topics.

4.2 *Differentiation of Internet Public Opinion on Hot-Button Issues*
Due to the differentiation of interests and the fragmentation of the social stratum, social classes and groups that differ in age, gender, and geographical distribution have differences and conflicts in values. On the Internet, these conditions are reflected by the splintering of Internet public opinion.

First of all, public opinion on the Internet was divided over issues related to Internet users' quality of life. In September 2017, media sources reported that in some compound communities in Beijing and Shenzhen, the owners of commercial housing units had built separation barriers between the commercial housing units and the indemnificatory housing units, resulting in a discussion among the public. The articles published on WeChat official accounts, such as "Owners vs. Low-Rent Housing Tenants—Another Class Combat in Communities" and "Low-Rent Housing—From Swimming Pools to Separation

Barriers," have been widely disseminated, keeping public opinion on the topic warm. Behind the event, we can see the conflict between the imbalanced and insufficient development of the housing demands of different social classes, which deserves profound consideration.

Second, the splintering of Internet public opinion on ideological topics was intense, and could even spill over into offline incidents, causing an intervention in the social order—as, for example, in the case of the opinions expressed by Deng Xiangchao, Zuo Chunhe, and Liu Yong mentioned above.

Third, the measures taken by some local governments were improper, lacking in effective communication or response, and caused situations in which each group in the field of public opinion was only concerned with its own voice. For example, some grassroots units have fallen into the "Tacitus Trap"—i.e., when a department loses its credibility, it will never be trusted by the public, no matter what it does or says. When a student in Luxian, Sichuan Province, died of a fall in April 2017, a lot of rumors were spread, claiming that the student had been beaten to death, that some children of government officials were involved, and that the event was covered up by the government. Although these rumors were proved false, other information published by the local government was consequently questioned by Internet users.

Fourth, Internet public opinion on hot-button issues tended to divide into groups of users. Members of the same group might support each other, leading to a perception gap between different groups. In addition, different groups have different areas of interest on the Internet, forming a community of shared values and interests. For example, young Internet users tend to gather at QQ spaces, bilibili, and online broadcasting communities, while the middle-income group in cities tends to join Zhihu and Guokr. Views on hot-button issues may serve as an identifying mark in such network communities, and these views could be further strengthened through Internet public opinion to become the consensus of an entire class or group.

The grouping of users who share a particular view could not help to cool down public opinion and reconcile opposing groups. In September, a video about the rude law enforcement practices of Shanghai police caused heated discussions among the public. Opinions among Internet users were divided. Many female Internet users took a critical stance, saying that a traffic police officer should not have enforced the law when a woman was holding a baby, since the baby would be endangered. Some police groups thought that the woman made the first wrong move by trying to attack the police officer, using her baby as a shield, and by challenging the authority of the police officer. Thus, these police groups believed that the police officer's compulsory enforcement of the law was justified.

We should note that division in Internet public opinion on hot-button issues is a normal social phenomenon accompanied by changes in basic social conflicts. It is safe to say that imbalanced and insufficient development has influenced public opinion, and that the splintering of Internet public opinion is a reflection of the basic social conflicts that are embedded within public opinion. However, diversified differentiation of opinions is not good for social solidarity or the achievement of social consensus. In such cases, the relevant departments should take action to eliminate the negative influences generated by the differentiation of opinions.

5 Prospects for Public Opinion in 2018

After the 19th National Congress of the CPC, strengthening and maintaining the centralized leadership of the Central Committee of the Party to guide the people of China into a new age of socialism with Chinese characteristics has become the theme of news publicity and ideological construction. Supporting main themes and spreading positive energy have become the characteristic features of Internet public opinion in 2018.

5.1 *Mainstream Media Could Further Promote Media Integration, and the Construction of New Media for Government Affairs Would Enter a New Stage*

In August 2017, the *People's Daily* launched an initiative to construct a Public Platform for National Party Media, and the first 38 party media clients joined the platform to realize integrated development in terms of contents, channels, operations, and profit-making models for joint construction, sharing, and win-win purposes. Take the *People's Daily*, for instance: its Sina Microblog account had 54.46 million subscribers, its WeChat official account had 14 million subscribers, and its clients were downloaded 210 million times. The media studios under the *People's Daily*, such as @Dajiangdong, @Malacaijing, and @Xiakedao, have played an outstanding role in explaining policies and news and guiding public opinion. In terms of the integrated transmission of information via clients, the leading advantage of the central media over the market media would continue to expand.

Overseas transmission of the central media would further expand to tell stories about China in a good way using small starting points and sensitive materials (see Table 14.6). Even the efforts at preventing and dealing with heresy have been exposed. Since its opening in May 2017, the Twitter account

ANALYTICAL REPORT ON ONLINE PUBLIC OPINION IN CHINA IN 2017

TABLE 14.6 Transmission Data of Overseas Social Platforms Linked to Mainstream Media in China

Type	Facebook		Twitter		YouTube	Instagram	
	Subscribers (people)	Likes (Times)	Subscribers (people)	Message amount (Times)	Subscribers (people)	Subscribers (people)	Comments (pieces)
People's Daily	39566865	39708893	4119821	55171	20435	699376	12367
CGTN*	52107586	52258526	4740270	38747	235677	1203778	3202
CCTV	43729264	43742682	370195	33127	233673	552051	2959
Xinhua News Agency	30113839	30106381	11079151	99312	121982	75233	2897
China Daily	26422353	26413600	1349205	53994	3215	5246	1016

China Facts has issued more than 1,000 messages to spread Chinese culture and refute the rumor of organ removal spread by Falungong to introduce information about anti-heresy.

5.2 *We Should Adhere to the Correct Guidance of Public Opinion by Using the Art of Transmission and Paying Attention to Spam*

News reporting should demonstrate greater political awareness, a keener sense of perspective, and continued commitment to the CPC leadership and its overall objectives for national development. Political motivation should be tested by examining political effects. We should understand public opinion without touching sensitive nerves among the public. Also, we should avoid the style of speech popular during the Cultural Revolution.

The workers responsible for news publicity should improve their knowledge so that they can share the same feelings with Internet users, so as to improve the transmission, guidance, influence, and credibility of the news. Some misguided articles meant to communicate positive energy, such as an article that described the movie *Dunkirk* as demonstrating the courage of the British army in fighting against the Japanese intruders in Asia, have overlooked or diminished the great efforts of the Chinese people in fighting the intrusion by the Japanese army.

5.3 The Super Online Platforms Should Be Jointly Governed by the Government, Industry, and Internet Users

In 2017, people.cn criticized three times the opinion that the mobile game *Honor of Kings* had affected the healthy development of the youth, causing a fluctuation in the share price of Tencent. The information push of Jinri Toutiao based on machine algorithms has often caused people to doubt the official media and experts. It seems that machine algorithms can understand the needs of users, but they are not good for balancing the psychology and ensuring the rationality of users, which may lead to an information cocoon that generates knowledge, views, and values with shallow interests. Some people believe that the network platforms are neutral suppliers that should not take on too many social responsibilities. For a socialized product with such a huge user group, the social responsibilities of network platforms should be higher than those of ordinary Internet enterprises. The rules for network platforms should be jointly set down by users and the diversified subjects. The Internet is the largest variable in the period of social transformation, and it has the potential to impact the orderly operation of the market and society, generating a disturbance of social mentality. To handle this largest variable, the network platforms, related parties, and the government should work together to create a new open and sharing Internet environment.

5.4 Fee-Based Access to Online Content Has Become a Trend, and the Knowledge-Sharing Economy Could Become the Next Hotspot of the Internet

At present, free and fee-based access to online content are two different operational strategies. However, since access to the World Wide Web was established in China more than 20 years ago, Internet users have been accustomed to free access to online content. Nevertheless, content creation is a costly undertaking. For example, it costs *Southern Weekly* 12 yuan to create each Chinese character in its news reports. If free sharing and reading on the Internet cannot be controlled, the writers will not be able to make any profit or even recover their costs, leading to a vicious circle: more talents will be lost, and the new websites will depend on searching and copying information to catch the attention of the audience, leading to a serious homogenization of content.

The Internet world has developed from offering paid videos and music in the early stage to paid original literature, scientific introductions, and ideological articles. Many Internet companies, such as Zhihu, Douban, Himalaya, Guokr, Fenda, and Logical Thinking have tried to cash in on their content. Caixin Media has charged readers for all news information since November 2017.

After a charge is imposed, the number of readers may diminish, but the quality of the information will be improved. In turn, the loyalty of the user base generated by paid reading will be improved.

5.5 Internet Use among Seniors Has Yet to Peak, and More Encouragement Is Needed

Li Kaifu predicted a rise in the third-wave population of the Internet, namely, elderly mobile Internet users in third- and fourth-tier cities and rural areas. However, senior citizens have a lower ability to identify fake information on the Internet, and they may easily be misled by rumors on WeChat Moments. Although senior citizens are experienced and can access simple information sources after retirement, they cannot understand new things thoroughly, so they will be easily cheated in the new media age. Some senior citizens have even lost their property after buying fake financial products.

In the field of Internet public opinion, senior citizens have a relatively weak voice. Senior citizens are habitually mocked by Internet users, for example, in reports that old ladies took over a basketball playground for dancing or that an elderly walking group occupied driveways and small roads in parks. On the Internet, we need to listen to the requests and feelings of senior citizens to make it easier for groups in other age brackets to understand and respect them.

CHAPTER 15

Analytical Report on China's Food and Drug Safety Situation in 2017

Luo Jie[1] and Tian Ming[2]

Abstract

Following the official implementation of the *Food Safety Law* and the proposal of the Four Strictest Standards, food and drug inspection work, focusing on supervision and sampling inspection, has been conducted effectively in order to urge enterprises to fulfill their responsibilities, guide the scientific consumption of the public, and make comprehensive shared governance the goal of society, so as to promote the supervision and governance of the safety of food and drugs in an orderly and comprehensive way. In the past year, the number of crimes related to food and drug safety witnessed a significant reduction and the passing rate of random checks increased steadily. Thus, the foundation of the food and drug safety of our country has been gradually stabilized, but there are still some safety risks. The people's sense of safety and satisfaction should be further improved, and we still have a long way to go to ensure the safety of food and drugs. In this report, we have summarized the general conditions of the food and drug industry in our country in the past year, discussed the existing issues in this industry based on typical food and drug incidents, analyzed the situation of food and drug work in the future, and proposed some creative suggestions.

Keywords

food and drugs – national strategy – food safety – drug safety

---

1   Luo Jie, deputy party secretary of the National Medical Products Administration Institute of Executive Development, professor, doctor of laws, and postdoctoral fellow of food safety and engineering, with research interests in constitutional and administrative law, and food and drug supervision.
2   Tian Ming, postdoctoral fellow at the National Medical Products Administration Institute of Executive Development, and food science doctor with research interests in food and drug supervision.

© KONINKLIJKE BRILL NV, LEIDEN, 2022 | DOI:10.1163/9789004500723_016

Food and drug safety is closely related to the health and lives of the public and is thus important for building a harmonious socialist society. In the past year, governments and food and drug administrations at all levels have performed their functions regarding market supervision, social administration, and public services to strictly implement the Four Strictest Standards, and they have strived to promote the reform of power delegation, thereby streamlining administration and optimizing services. The focus should be placed on controlling the illegal use of veterinary drugs and food additives as well as the manufacturing and sale of fake drugs and medical devices. At the same time, the systems and mechanisms of review and approval should be reformed and innovated to steadily implement consistent standards of evaluation for generic drugs, fully publicize law enforcement information, completely ensure the food safety of cities, and create an excellent environment for food and drug safety. However, there are still some issues regarding food and drug safety in China. In terms of food, pollution at the source is a prominent problem, the foundation of the food industry is weak, food safety standards lag behind those of developed countries, and the capacity for supervision and governance is not able to meet the needs. In terms of drugs, major issues include flaws in quality control and assurance, document management, and equipment. Plus, given the gap between supervisory work and the expectations of the people, the situation of food and drug safety remains complicated.

In this report, we have summarized the general conditions of the food and drug industry of our country in the past year, discussed the existing issues in this industry as they are reflected in typical food and drug incidents, analyzed the situation of food and drug work in the future, and proposed some creative suggestions.

1 The General Situation of Food and Drug Safety

1.1 *Permissions for the Production and Operation of Food and Drugs*
In 2016, food and drug administrations at the provincial (autonomous region and municipal) level issued 18,854 food production licenses, about 8,000 fewer than in 2015, and issued 462 food additive production licenses, 200 fewer than in 2015.

As of the end of November 2016, there were 4,176 API and preparation manufacturing enterprises in China, 800 fewer than in 2015. There were 465,618 enterprises with drug distribution certificates, 1,000 fewer than in 2015.

Among them, the number of corporate wholesale enterprises decreased by 200 and that of non-incorporated wholesale enterprises decreased by 400.[3] In 2016, the number of drug production enterprises as well as API and preparation enterprises witnessed a decrease because some enterprises did not pass the GMP certification during the certificate renewal period.

Production and operation certification of food and drugs has been making steady strides and developing in a more standardized direction under the guidance of the correct policies of the country.

1.2   Review and Approval of Food and Drug Registration

In 2016, 312 initial food and drug registration applications, 738 modification applications, 143 technical transfer applications, and 118 re-registration applications were approved.[4] Compared to 2015, the number of food and drug registrations and modifications decreased significantly. Since the new *Method of Managing Health Food Registration and Filing* was issued on July 1, 2016, a parallel management method integrating registration and filing was used for health food, making the review and approval system for health food stricter and more complete. Therefore, the number of registration applications for health food in the past year decreased slightly.

In 2016, 4,011 new drugs were approved for clinical use, seven times the number in 2015; five new drug certificates and approval documents were issued, an increase of three over 2015; and 13 approval numbers were issued, 24 fewer than in 2015. At the same time, approvals of clinical applications of generic drugs, imported drug applications, supplementary drug applications, and production applications of packaging materials and containers in contact with drugs witnessed a significant increase over 2015.

1.3   Food Safety Supervision and Random Checks[5]

In 2016, the China Food and Drug Administration (CFDA) randomly checked 257,000 batches of food samples nationwide, with a general passing rate of 96.8%; this was the same as the passing rate in 2015 and higher than that in 2014 by 2.1 percentage points. The samples checked were mainly from the following categories:

---

3   The data are from *The 2016 Food and Drug Supervision Statistical Yearbook*, http://www.sda .gov.cn/WS01/CL0108/172895.html.
4   The data are from *The 2016 Food and Drug Supervision Statistical Yearbook*.
5   The data in this section are from the "Press Conferences for Food Safety Random Check Information in 2016 and the Random Check Plan in 2017," official website of the China Food and Drug Administration, http://www.sda.gov.cn/WS01/CL1908/168599.html.

ANALYTICAL REPORT ON CHINA'S FOOD AND DRUG SAFETY SITUATION   323

(1)   Bulk daily consumer goods with a relatively high passing rate. The passing rate of dairy products was the highest, at 99.5%, which was followed by grain-processed products, at 98.2%. The passing rate for agricultural products such as meat, eggs, vegetables, and fruit was 98.0%, and that for edible oil, grease, and oil products was 97.8%.

(2)   For infant formulas with a high degree of social attention, according to the random check results, only 0.9% of the samples did not meet national food safety standards, and 0.4% of the samples met the national standards but did not meet the values listed on the label.

(3)   For stores of large manufacturing enterprises and operational groups, the passing rates of the samples were 99.0% and 98.1%, respectively, which were higher than the general passing rate by 2.2 and 1.3 percentage points, respectively.

In general, the passing rates of random samples of nine food categories—condiments, beverages, fruit products, egg products, aquatic products, starch and starch products, bean products, health food, and food additives—increased year by year from 2014 to 2016. The samples of the three categories with a high degree of social attention passed the random checks in all three years, including checks for melamine in infant formula food products, the aflatoxin B1 in wheat powder, and Sudan Dyesin egg products. At the same time, the passing rate of random checks for the aflatoxin B1 in peanut oil, the aerobic bacterial count in dried fruit products, and sodium cyclamate in fermented flour products increased year by year. The results of the random check on various food products in the first quarter of 2017 are listed in Table 15.1.

TABLE 15.1   Results of a Random Check on Various Food Products in the First Quarter of 2017
Unit: Batch, %

No.	Food category	Sample number	Qualified sample number	Unqualified sample number	Sample passing rate
1	Grain-processed products	22925	22680	245	98.9
2	Edible oil, grease, and oil products	12439	12168	271	97.8
3	Condiments	15830	15502	328	97.9
4	Meat products	21654	21210	444	97.9
5	Dairy products	7385	7284	101	98.6
6	Beverages	18217	17510	707	96.1

TABLE 15.1 Results of a Random Check on Various Food Products in the First Quarter (*cont.*)
Unit: Batch, %

No.	Food category	Sample number	Qualified sample number	Unqualified sample number	Sample passing rate
7	Instant food products	4212	4067	145	96.6
8	Biscuits	2391	2342	49	98.0
9	Canned products	2137	2095	42	98.0
10	Frozen beverages	1323	1274	49	96.3
11	Quick-frozen food	6195	6138	57	99.1
12	Potatoes and puffed food	3258	3185	73	97.8
13	Candies	4582	4511	71	98.5
14	Tea and related products	6230	6177	53	99.1
15	Alcoholic beverages	13041	12582	459	96.5
16	Vegetable products	9922	9456	466	95.3
17	Fruit products	4987	4801	186	96.3
18	Roasted seeds and nuts	5389	5216	173	96.8
19	Egg products	1212	1202	10	99.2
20	Cocoa and baked coffee products	255	2550	0	100.0
21	Sugars	1409	1371	38	97.3
22	Aquatic products	6556	6348	208	96.8
23	Starch and starch products	3978	3629	349	91.2
24	Cakes and pastries	18204	17456	748	95.9
25	Bean products	5559	5463	96	98.3
26	Bee products	1937	1895	42	97.8
27	Health food	2425	2397	28	98.8
28	Special food products	634	634	0	100.0
29	Special formula food for medical purposes	24	24	0	100.0
30	Infant formula food products	1715	1705	10	99.4
31	Catering food products	34460	33276	1184	96.6
32	Food additives	1038	1035	3	99.7
33	Edible agricultural products	64222	63174	1048	98.4
34	Others	4384	36	2	99.5
Total		306183	298498	7685	97.5

ANALYTICAL REPORT ON CHINA'S FOOD AND DRUG SAFETY SITUATION

TABLE 15.2   Drug Inspections Completed in 2016

Inspection work	Number of inspected enterprises/drug categories	Number of teams dispatched	Number of people dispatched
Inspection of the registered drug production sites	34	43	178
Drug GMP certification inspection	16	16	47
Drug GMP tracking inspection	204	197	704
Drug air transport inspection	39	39	155
Overseas production site inspection of imported drugs	7	7	31
Drug circulation inspection	50	50	77
International observation inspection	81	81	85
Total	431	433	1277

1.4   *Drug Inspection*[6]

Drug inspections included the inspection of registered drug production sites, drug GMP certification inspection, drug GMP tracking inspection, drug flying inspection, overseas production site inspection of imported drugs, drug circulation inspection, and international observation inspection, totaling 434 items. The inspection scales, the number of inspection teams, and the number of people dispatched are listed in Table 15.2.

For site inspections, 42 reports were completed in total, including eight reports about inspections that resulted in the discovery of unqualified sites and registration applications canceled by enterprises. Sixteen drug GMP certification inspections were completed, and sixteen site inspection reports were received, fourteen of which were reviewed; twelve drug production enterprises

---

6   The data in this section are from *The 2016 Drug Inspection Report*, http://www.sda.gov.cn/WS01/CL0844/173310.html.

passed the drug GMP certification inspection but two enterprises did not pass, and the certification procedures were suspended for another two enterprises since the related registration approval certificates were not submitted. Among the 204 drug GMP tracking inspections, 2,260 flaws were identified, including 22 serious flaws, 212 major flaws, and 2,026 common flaws. The number of flaws was higher than in 2015. In the drug flying inspections in 2016, many issues were found in terms of traditional Chinese medicines and biochemical drugs. For fourteen enterprises, the recommendation was made to revoke the drug GMP certificates; ten enterprises were recommended for registration and investigation, and the problematic products of seven enterprises were recalled. At the overseas production site inspections of imported drugs, three categories of drugs did not pass the inspections, and eight categories of drugs were rejected or had their import registration certificates recalled by the enterprises. Another 21 categories of drugs were covered by the overseas inspection plan in 2017.

In general, efforts in drug inspection improved in 2016 and some achievements were made, promoting the standardization of the drug market.

1.5 Food and Drug Complaints and Reporting

In 2016, the food and drug administrations at all levels received 577,915 food and drug complaints; 22,479 of them were filed and 20,988 of them were settled. The administrations received 26,966 health food complaints, with 640 of them filed and 705 of them settled. The administrations received 49,354 drug complaints, with 4,144 of them filed and 4,880 of them settled.[7] The reports on food and drugs indicated that the people's sense of safety about and satisfaction with food and drugs could be further improved, which should be a focus in future work.

2 Major Issues Regarding Food and Drug Safety in Our Country and an Analysis

2.1 Overuse of Food Additives

According to data from the random check by the China Food and Drug Administration in 2016, among the cases of non-compliance noted in food inspections, the overuse of food additives accounted for 33.6%, to which close

---

7 The data are from *The 2016 Food and Drug Supervision Statistical Yearbook.*

ANALYTICAL REPORT ON CHINA'S FOOD AND DRUG SAFETY SITUATION   327

attention should be paid. According to the report of the General Administration of Quality Supervision, Inspection, and Quarantine of the People's Republic of China in April 2017, overuse of additives was mostly detected in imported leisure food and beverages; for example, the carnauba wax and sorbitol contained in the "wonderful leisure cheese bar" (jelly flavor) imported from Lithuania were out of range, and this was also true for the penicillin bacterium contained in Italian Eyrie gorgonzola. All products containing additives out of limits or ranges are disqualified products and should be returned or destroyed to prevent them from flowing into the market.

2.2   *Microorganism Pollution*
According to the results of the random check in 2016, microorganism-polluted samples accounted for 30.7% of all samples, and samples polluted by invasive organisms accounted for 25.6% of the polluted samples. In 2016, imported milk products from Germany, France, Denmark, and New Zealand were destroyed due to out-of-range levels of flora and acidity or packages or additives that did not conform to standards. For example, in May 2016, the Certification and Accreditation Administration of the People's Republic of China published on its official website that the Holle milk powder made by Australian manufacturer Agrana had been suspended. In September 2016, the room-temperature milk made by the famous German milk producer Hochwald, established in 1932, was recalled throughout Germany due to bacterial contamination; and infant milk powders and food products made by an 80-year-old Austrian company were also found to be contaminated.

2.3   *Quality Indicators Not Meeting Standards*
Samples with quality indicators that could not meet standards accounted for 17.5% of the non-compliant samples, and the quality and safety of food products purchased online were worse. In March 2016, the 3.15 Gala of CCTV revealed that some illegal food workshops had joined the Eleme food delivery platform, which had extremely bad hygienic conditions. Some producers and operators would provide consumers with insufficient, exaggerated, or false information when promoting food products. When performing their management obligations, the food delivery platforms also had many issues, such as insufficient or incomplete disclosure of information.

2.4   *Heavy Metal Pollution*
Samples polluted by heavy metals accounted for 8.2% of the non-compliant samples. On November 23, 2016, many citizens of Beijing found that the fish

tanks in many supermarkets had been emptied, and a message circulated on the Internet stated that the fresh fish in supermarkets had been removed due to the pollution of the water in Beijing. The government demonstrated that the passing rate during a random check of aquatic products in Beijing was more than 90%, but this still meant that 10% of aquatic products could not meet standards. For supermarkets, faced with intensified random checks, 10% was still a high probability of risk and they would never take that risk. Therefore, removing all of the fresh fish was a countermeasure taken by supermarkets to combat strict supervision in order to avoid punishment.

2.5 Residue of Veterinary Drugs Not Meeting the Requirements

Samples containing non-compliant residue of veterinary drugs accounted for 5.5% of non-compliant samples. On August 24, 2017, the police department of Shouguang City received a report from villagers that their sheep had died after eating some fistular onion leaves. According to the investigation, the problematic fistular onions had been spread with phorate pesticide one month before they were sold. If these toxic fistular onions, totaling 26,000 kilograms, had gotten onto the market and made their way to people's dinner tables, there would have been unbearable consequences.

2.6 Biotoxin Pollution

The samples polluted by biotoxin accounted for 1.1% of the non-compliant samples. In February 2016, some media reported that an expert from the School of Public Health of Fudan University found that one or several antibiotics were detected in the urine of 79.6% of children of school age. Researchers also found in the bodies of children some antibiotics that had not been used clinically for years but still existed in the environment and in food products. The major causes of such problems were the pollution of sources, including the pollution of soil and water sources, which may lead to the accumulation of heavy metals and organic matter in plants and animals, and the overuse of veterinary drugs, which may lead to residues of veterinary drugs out of the prescribed limits. Furthermore, the production and operational processes were not managed properly; for example, the environmental and hygienic conditions during production, transportation, and storage were not controlled well, the production processes were not designed reasonably, and no factory inspection was carried out.

3 Policy Suggestions and Tendency Analysis

3.1 *Fully Implement the Entity Responsibilities of Enterprises*

According to the results of the food inspection, improper management of production and operations can lead to food safety problems. Food safety supervision departments should urge food producers and operators to fulfill their legal responsibilities and obligations to make sure that production processes meet the relevant standards and codes, and to guarantee that the data and information linked to each one are true, reliable, and traceable. At the same time, food production enterprises bearing entity responsibilities should assign specific food safety managers and establish complete systems of food safety management to actively supervise products on the market, report those with safety risks, and recall any problematic products. If food enterprises can strictly follow industry rules and regulations from the very beginning, then food safety incidents will be greatly reduced.

3.2 *Conform Our Food Safety Standards to International Standards as Soon as Possible*

Food safety standards are the bottom line of food safety, and they determine the guarantee of food safety. Studying the advanced standards of foreign countries is of great importance to our own food safety standards. We should pay close attention to the development of international standards and establish a system of the strictest food safety standards based on the actual conditions and existing resources of our country. For example, we should encourage enterprises to formulate their own standards that are higher than national and local standards, and likewise we should encourage industry associations to formulate group standards that are higher than national standards. At the same time, national food safety standards and other related standards should be published on network platforms, and a convenient search platform should be established to help enterprises and consumers make inquiries.

3.3 *Improve Laws and Regulations*

Rules and regulations are the guardians of an industry, and can ensure the normal operations of the entire industry. We should establish and improve a legal system with food safety law as the core, supplemented by other laws, regulations, and standards, and we should adjust and supplement the existing legal system through actual implementation.

3.4 *Strictly Control Sources*

Food safety issues caused by pollution at the source accounted for the highest proportion of all food safety issues, especially in the case of residues of veterinary drugs and heavy metal pollution. We recommend conducting comprehensive governance focusing on residues of veterinary drugs and heavy metal pollution. High-efficiency, low-toxicity, and low-residue veterinary drugs should be developed to replace those with high toxicity and residues in order to reduce the residues of veterinary drugs. To deal with heavy metal pollution, we should explore the distribution of soil pollution and regulate the classification of polluted cultivated land. In addition, we should establish and improve the system of slaughter management, strengthen supervision and governance over grain quality and safety, and accelerate the mechanism of long-term operations in regions with tracking systems for meats and vegetables.

3.5 *Conduct Strict Process Supervision and Control*

Negligence in food processing is another major cause of food safety issues. For the catering industry, we should integrate existing resources to establish a system for the display of information regarding permissions for uniform food production and operations throughout the country and promote a transparent kitchen program in catering service units with permits. Processing enterprises should scrupulously inspect the sites of production and operation based on the classification of the food production and operation risks. Site inspections should cover all producers and operators based on the principle of two-random and one-disclosure, focusing on rural areas, schools, kindergartens, small workshops, small restaurants, and cold chain storage and transportation, as well as those food producers and operators with high risks. We should supervise and control special food products strictly and crack down on false advertisements for health food, commercial fraud incidents, and cheating of consumers. New business patterns, such as Internet food operations and online ordering, should be strictly controlled in order to review the operational qualifications of network platforms and improve the mechanisms for online complaints and the protection of post-sales rights. Safety supervision and the control of imported and exported food products should be strictly carried out so as to promote the construction of model processing sites for special food products.

3.6 *Strengthen Sampling Inspections*

Sampling inspection is an effective measure for preventing food safety issues in production and sales. We recommend establishing sampling inspection plans at the national, provincial, municipal, and county levels to cover food products of all types by focusing on the residue of veterinary drugs in food products and disclosing the results of sampling inspections to the public promptly. The sampling inspection for food safety should be considered the key task in the work of examining food safety.

3.7   *Strictly Punish Illegal Activities*

Strict punishment is an important guarantee of food health and safety. In recent years, many food safety issues have arisen, such as the overuse of food additives, using recycled food as raw material, and using industrial alcohols to produce alcoholic beverages. To deal with the outstanding food safety risks and common issues in the industry, we recommend establishing food safety supervision and inspection teams and building a working system where inspections have a guiding function, integrating risk prevention, case investigation, administrative punishment, and case transfer. Public security organs at all levels should strengthen their capacity to crack down on food safety crimes, improve the engagement between administrative law enforcement and justice, and establish a cooperative mechanism for evidence recognition, evidence transfer, the application of laws, and food inspection and certification.

3.8   *Improve the Capacity for Technical Support*

The improvement of risk monitoring and assessment capacities is of great importance in the prevention of food safety issues. Foodborne diseases and food pollutants are important causes of food safety issues. It is possible to establish a mechanism for sharing monitored data that can track foodborne diseases, food pollutants, and toxic substances in food and play an active role in promptly dealing with related food safety issues. Food safety issues may occur and spread in a short period of time; thus, we recommend improving the system for assessing food safety risks and risk exchanges, which are of great importance for the prevention of food safety incidents. At the same time, we should accelerate the construction of a system of food safety inspection and testing at the national, provincial, municipal, and county levels, to affirm the importance of food safety issues in an all-round way, to promote the capacity for intelligent monitoring and governance in terms of food safety, and to strengthen the capacities for monitoring and emergency response at the grassroots level.

3.9 Accelerate the Formation of Professional Inspector Teams

Professional inspector teams have professional knowledge and ample capacity for dealing with practical issues. The acceleration of the formation of these teams can promptly identify food safety issues and prevent such issues from occurring. We recommend establishing a professional inspector system based on existing resources to define the requirements for qualification, inspection obligations, training management, and performance examination, as well as establishing an inspector training system to strengthen the design of professional training and teaching materials for inspectors and to establish inspector training bases. Various measures should be taken to encourage talents to move to the front line.

3.10 Accelerate the Formation of the Pattern of Joint Governance in Society

If the whole population participates in the fight, a crackdown on illegal activities and crimes affecting food safety can be carried out to the fullest. We recommend improving the system for the disclosure of food safety information to inform people of food safety information at any time; we also recommend keeping the reporting channels unblocked in order to encourage employees of food production and operation enterprises to report illegal activities, and we should reward such whistleblowers while protecting their safety. At the same time, we should strengthen the guidance of public opinion in order to encourage the news media to supervise food safety issues and respond promptly to concerns in society. We should strengthen the protection of the rights and interests of consumers, improve their consciousness about food safety and their capacity for self-protection, and enhance scientific publicity to improve the entire population's scientific literacy regarding food safety.

References

Arrangement of Key Food Safety Work in 2017. http://www.sda.gov.cn/WS01/CL1605/171683.html.

"Press Conferences for Food Safety Random Check Information in 2016 and the Random Check Plan in 2017." Official website of the China Food and Drug Administration. http://www.sda.gov.cn/WS01/CL1908/168599.html.

"Record of the Press Conference for the 2016 Drug Inspection Report by the China Food and Drug Administration." http://www.sda.gov.cn/WS01/CL1909/173318.html.

The 13th Five-Year Plan for National Food Safety. Website of the Central Government. http://www.gov.cn/zhengce/content/2017-02/21/content_5169755.htm.

The 2016 Drug Inspection Report. http://www.sda.gov.cn/WS01/CL0844/173310.html.

The 2016 Food and Drug Supervision Statistical Yearbook. http://www.sda.gov.cn/WS01/CL0108/172895.html.

CHAPTER 16

Analytical Report on Environmental Protection in China in 2017

Jia Feng,[1] Yang Ke,[2] Tian Shuo,[3] Huang Jingyi,[4] and Zhou Liantong[5]

Abstract

Since the 18th National Congress of the CPC, the Central Committee of the CPC with President Xi Jinping as the core has conducted a series of fundamental, far-sighted, and creative tasks. As a result, the environmental protection of our country witnessed a historical, revolutionary, and complete change from a recognition of environmental issues to practical action, and the construction of an ecological civilization has also seen unprecedented change. The 19th National Congress of the CPC has marked the new age of socialism with Chinese characteristics, and many new concepts, requirements, targets, and plans have been made for the construction of an ecological civilization and for environmental protection. The concept that clean, clear water and lush mountains are invaluable assets will be firmly established and implemented in the whole society, and the basic national strategy of energy saving and environmental

1 Jia Feng, director and research fellow at the Center for Environmental Education and Communications of the Ministry of Ecology and Environment, and part-time professor at the Chinese Academy of Governance, with research interests in environmental publicity and education, environmental public relationships, and new media transmission.
2 Yang Ke, deputy director and associate research fellow of the Administrative Office of the Center for Environmental Education and Communications of the Ministry of Ecology and Environment, and deputy director of the Institute for Environmental Public Relationships and Strategic Transmission, with research interests in environmental publicity and education, environmental public relationships, and new media transmission.
3 Tian Shuo, engineer at the Center for Environmental Education and Communications of the Ministry of Ecology and Environment, and assistant director of the Institute for Environmental Public Relationships and Strategic Transmission, with research interests in environmental publicity and education, environmental public relationships, and new media transmission.
4 Huang Jingyi, engineer at the Center for Environmental Education and Communications of the Ministry of Ecology and Environment, and project director of the Institute for Environmental Public Relationships and Strategic Transmission, with research interests in environmental publicity and education, environmental public relationships, and new media transmission.
5 Zhou Liantong, engineer at the Center for Environmental Education and Communications of the Ministry of Ecology and Environment, and project director of the Institute for Environmental Public Relationships and Strategic Transmission, with research interests in environmental publicity and education, environmental public relationships, and new media transmission.

© KONINKLIJKE BRILL NV, LEIDEN, 2022 | DOI:10.1163/9789004500723_017

protection will be constantly promoted. Green development modes and lifestyles will be further popularized. The belief in constructing a beautiful China will be firmly upheld, and the people will live and work in a better environment. China will make a new contribution to the ecological safety of the world.

Keywords

ecological civilization – environmental protection – environmental management

1 The General Situation of Environmental Protection in China

1.1 *The Domestic Situation*

Ecological environmental protection has experienced unprecedented new changes and met new opportunities. Since the 18th National Congress of the CPC, the Central Committee of the CPC with President Xi Jinping as the core has conducted a series of fundamental, far-sighted, and creative tasks. As a result, the environmental protection of our country witnessed a historical, revolutionary, and overall change from recognition to practice, and significant progress has been made in constructing an ecological civilization, which has entered a stage characterized by the sharpest consciousness, greatest efforts, most practical measures, fastest progress, and best effects. In short, the following five unprecedented changes have occurred. (1) The depth of ideological understanding is unprecedented. The consciousness and initiative of the whole country and the whole Party in implementing the concept of green development have significantly improved, and ignorance of ecological environmental protection has been almost completely corrected. (2) Current efforts to control pollution are unprecedented. Major action plans to prevent the pollution of air, water, and soil have been issued and implemented to declare war on pollution. (3) The intensity of the establishment of the new system is unprecedented. The Central Leading Group for Comprehensively Deepening the Reform reviewed and approved more than 40 reform plans for ecological civilization and environmental protection, significantly promoting green development and the improvement of the environment. (4) The stringency of supervision and law enforcement is unprecedented. Several laws have been revised, including the environmental protection law, the air pollution prevention and control law, the water pollution prevention and control law, the environmental impact assessment law, the environmental protection tax law, and the nuclear safety law. In addition, the soil pollution prevention and control law is under legislation review in the Standing Committee of the NPC. These laws and mechanisms have played an active role in promoting enterprises' compliance with laws. (5) The speed of environmental quality improvement is unprecedented. In 2016, the average concentrations of PM2.5 in the Beijing–Tianjin–Hebei Region, the Yangtze River Delta, and the Pearl River Delta were reduced by more than 30% compared to 2013. The proportion of the nation's territory afflicted by acid rain was reduced from a historical high of 30% to 7.2%, along with a reduction in the degree of pollution. The proportion of state-controlled section I to III surface waters was increased to 67.8%. The rate of forest coverage improved from 16.6% at the beginning of the twenty-first century to about 22%. All of these achievements reflect the historical changes of the Party and the country since the 18th National Congress of the CPC, and they have bolstered confidence and laid a solid foundation for further improvements in ecological environmental protection.

With the constant growth of the general economy, the growth rate of new pollutants remains at a high level, leading to huge environmental pressure. In 2016, the economy of China witnessed slow yet stable development in a good way. Development has entered a normal pattern, and all systems, including the economy, have witnessed a series of major changes, restructuring the motivation, industries, elements, and growth modes of China's economic development. The economy of China has entered an important period of time featuring innovative, cooperative, and green development, but there is a conflict between the new and old growth modes due to the slowdown of economic growth and the task of stabilizing growth, which is worth our close attention. In 2016, the judgment issued at the Central Economic Work Conference on ecological environmental protection declared that the ecological environment had improved for good and that the initial effects of green development could be seen.[6] In some regions of eastern China, stable economic growth poles have been formed, where the environmental quality is becoming good, the relationship between the environment and development has been further unified, and society is moving forward to an innovative and green stage of development. However, in the west of China and the northeast of China, which are dominated by traditional industries, there is still much pressure in terms of regional economic development and environmental improvement. Investments in projects linked to the heavy chemical industry have been increasing in the middle and western regions of China. The northeastern part of China has lagged behind in terms of economic development, and the environmental quality is not good enough, whereas the relationship between economic development and the environment has obviously been changing.[7]

---

6 "The Central Economic Work Conference Was Held in Beijing and Xi Jinping and Li Keqiang Delivered Keynote Speeches," http://finance.people.com.cn/n1/2016/1216/c1004-28956355.html.

7 Chen Jining, "Improving the People's Sense of Gain with Environmental Quality Improvement and Welcoming the 19th National Congress of the CPC with Good Achievements—Speech

ANALYTICAL REPORT ON ENVIRONMENTAL PROTECTION IN CHINA IN 2017   337

The concept of green development has been widely accepted, and the people have a strong desire to improve environmental quality. With the improvement of material lives and consumption, the people's expectations have turned from food and shelter to environmental protection and from subsistence to ecology, reflecting their urgent need for quality ecological products and an excellent ecological environment. The conflict between such needs and the limited carrying capacity of the ecological resources and environment, the insufficient public ecological products, and the grave situation of ecological environmental protection has become more predominant. The people's sense of happiness is more closely related to the ecological environment. People cannot tolerate damage to the ecological environment any longer and have proposed higher standards for environmental quality. No matter how well the economy develops, without clean air and water and a beautiful ecological environment, people will still complain.

1.2   *The International Situation*

The system of global governance and the reform of the international order have been promoted at a faster speed. The world is in a period of great development, change, and adjustment. With the development of diversification, economic globalization, the informatization of society, and cultural diversification, connections with and dependences on different countries have been deepened with outstanding uncertainties. Protecting the ecological environment, dealing with climate change, and ensuring energy and resource safety are the common challenges the world faces.

The environmental issue is a hotspot throughout the world. In May 2016, the 2nd United Nations Conference on Environment and Development (UNCED) was held; its theme was "Realizing the Environmental Targets in the 2030 Agenda for Sustainable Development." The conference focused on the challenges in terms of environment and sustainable development in the world to promote the implementation of the achievements of the Paris UN Climate Change Conference concerning key environmental topics, such as air pollution, the illegal trading of wild animals and plants, ocean environmental protection, and chemicals and waste.[8]

Climate change is a major crisis and a serious challenge to mankind. On January 18, 2017, the World Meteorological Organization (WMO) issued a bulletin, confirming that 2016 was the hottest year in history according to meteorological records. The average carbon dioxide concentration globally reached a new high, crossing the alarming line of 400 ppm. The sea ice area at

---

Delivered at the National Working Conference on Environmental Protection in 2017," http://www.zhb.gov.cn/xxgk/hjyw/201701/t20170125_395251.shtml.

8   "Disclosure! Top 10 Environmental Hot Button Issues in the World in 2016," http://www.sohu.com/a/132422978_383714.

the North Pole decreased to its minimum value since 1979, when recordkeeping began. The albinism of coral reefs due to high ocean temperatures expanded. Millions of people were affected by extreme weather conditions such as floods, heat waves, and tropical cyclones. Global warming has increased the risks that nature faces and those that social and economic systems face as well, and it has generated various new risks. The increase in temperatures worldwide has also led to an increase in the number of days of stable and static weather in the north of China, which caused frequent occurrences of heavy pollution weather and poor air quality. On October 5, 2016, the EU and seven of its member countries officially submitted a letter of approval of the Paris Climate Accord, increasing the number of contracting parties to 74 and enhancing the proportion of greenhouse gas emissions attributable to the contracting parties to 58.82% of the total global amount. The conditions for the effectiveness of the Accord were finally met. Ban Ki-moon, the United Nations Secretary General, announced that the Accord had officially become effective on November 4, 2016.

Many countries are facing air pollution control problems. In the fall and winter of 2016, besides China, many countries experienced serious pollution weather to different degrees, including the UK, France, Italy, Spain, India, Iran, and Indonesia. According to a report by the World Health Organization (WHO), *Air Pollution: Global Assessment Exposure and Disease Burden*, 92% of the world's population were living in areas where the air quality did not meet the safety standard established by the WHO. Although many countries have taken different measures to control emissions, there is still a long way to go to realize a general improvement worldwide.

It is necessary to make clean energies dominant, but the environmental policies of Western countries are not stable. To reduce carbon emissions and deal with climate change, all coal-fired power plants in the UK will be fully shut down by 2025. On September 29, 2016, China, the UK, and France signed a final agreement to launch the Hinkley Point Nuclear Power Plant project, marking the fact that the UK restarted its nuclear power industry after more than 20 years. It is estimated that the first unit will be put into operation by 2025.[9] The environmental policies of the United States have been complicated. On March 1, 2017, Trump announced that the Environmental Protection Agency (EPA) would lay off one-fifth of its employees and stop more than 10 core projects. On March 28, 2017, Trump signed an administrative order to "suspend, alter or abolish" the Clean Power Plan of the Obama administration. On June 1, 2017, the United States announced that it was leaving the Paris Climate Accord. We do not know how the energy and environmental policies of the United States will change in the future.

---

9 "Road to Re-Starting Nuclear Power in the UK," http://finance.ifeng.com/a/20161010/14925600_0.shtml.

China has become an important worldwide participant, contributor, and leader in the building of an ecological civilization. While actively solving its own environmental issues, China has actively participated in the environmental protection of the world. To date, China has been approved to participate in more than 30 multilateral conventions or agreements related to the ecological environment, and it has issued the *National Plan for China to Implement the 2030 Agenda for Sustainable Development*. With respect to the millennium targets of the UN, China has had the best effect overall and has made the largest contribution to the world, as has been widely recognized. Under the framework of the *Montreal Protocol on Substances That Deplete the Ozone Layer*, the substances that deplete the ozone layer eliminated by China accounted for more than half of the total amount eliminated by all developing countries. To deal with climate change, China has actively promoted the effectiveness of the *2030 Agenda for Sustainable Development* and the Paris Climate Accord, and it has played an important role as the largest developing country in the world. China has guided the issuance of the *G20 Action Plan on the 2030 Agenda for Sustainable Development* and has introduced sustainable development and green finance into the plan for the first time. In September 2017, at the 13th Contracting Party Conference of the United Nations Convention to Combat Desertification, China proposed to establish a mechanism for cooperation on the prevention of desertification under the Belt and Road Initiative, providing a platform for countries along the route of the initiative. International cooperation on the protection of the ecological environment has become both a necessary support and a guarantee for the green Belt and Road Initiative.[10]

China's building of an ecological civilization has provided the world with its unique Chinese Wisdom and Chinese Plan. In contrast to the ever-changing environmental protection policies in some major countries, China has spared no effort in promoting the building of an ecological civilization coupled with green and sustainable development of the country. The building of an ecological civilization could reflect Chinese voices, original creations, and expressions, and it might contain the ancient ecological wisdom of the Chinese civilization, providing systematic theories, methods, and policy experiences for the transformation from an industrial civilization to an ecological one, while showing great vitality throughout the world. In 2016, the United Nations Environment Programme (UNEP) issued a report entitled "Clear, Clean Waters and Lush Mountains Are Invaluable Assets: China's Strategies and Actions for an Ecological Civilization," and Erik Solheim, the deputy secretary general of the UN and the executive director of UNEP, said, "China's ideas and experiences regarding the

---

10   Shi Feng et al., "Situation and Challenges for International Cooperation for Environmental Protection during the 13th Five-Year Plan," *Environmental Protection Science*, 2016(1).

building of an ecological civilization have provided the world with important lessons for sustainable development, contributing China's solutions."

2 The Quality of China's Environment from 2016 to 2017

Since 2016, China has achieved unprecedented speed in improving the quality of its environment. However, the outlook for its level of environmental protection has not been optimistic. In particular, the control of air pollution has been traversing a key period of a huge burden, and imbalances among cities continue to exist.

2.1 *The Quality of the Air Environment*
In 2016, the general air quality in urban areas was improved over that in 2015. The concentrations of major pollutants in key regions witnessed a year-on-year reduction, but some regions, especially northern China, were still subject to serious air pollution in the fall and winter. In 2016, 84 of the 338 cities at the prefecture level and above met the air quality standard, accounting for 24.9%, with a year-on-year increase of 3.3 percentage points. The ratio of days with good air quality in the 338 cities was 78.8%, with a year-on-year increase of 2.1 percentage points. The average PM2.5 concentration was 47 $\mu g/m^3$, with a year-on-year reduction of 6.0%, and the average PM10 concentration was 82 $\mu g/m^3$, with a year-on-year reduction of 5.7%. Among the first 74 cities implementing the new air quality standard in the Beijing–Tianjin–Hebei Region, the Yangtze River Delta, the Pearl River Delta, and the municipalities, provincial capitals, and individual cities under the plan, the ratio of days with good air quality was 74.2%, with a year-on-year increase of 3.0 percentage points. The average PM2.5 concentration was 50 $\mu g/m^3$, with a year-on-year reduction of 9.1%, and the average PM10 concentration was 85 $\mu g/m^3$, with a year-on-year reduction of 8.6%.[11] The related data are shown in Figure 16.1.

From January to September 2017, the general air quality in the 338 cities at the prefecture level and above improved, and the concentrations of atmospheric particulates in key regions continuously decreased. The average PM2.5 concentration was 41 $\mu g/m^3$, with a year-on-year reduction of 2.4%, and the average PM10 concentration was 72 $\mu g/m^3$, with a year-on-year reduction of 2.7%. The ratio of days with good air quality was 79.4%, decreasing by 2.2 percentage points from 2016. However, the outlook for air quality in key regions, especially in northern China, was still not optimistic. From January to September 2017, the ratio of days with

---

11   Ministry of Environmental Protection, "China Environmental Status Communiqué 2016," June 5, 2017.

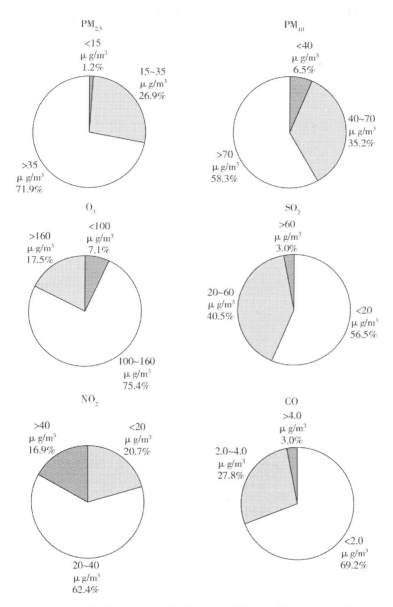

FIGURE 16.1 The Proportion of Indicators in Different Concentration Ranges in 338 Cities at the Prefecture Level and Above in 2016
SOURCE: MINISTRY OF ENVIRONMENTAL PROTECTION, "THE 2016 CHINA ENVIRONMENTAL STATUS BULLETIN," JUNE 5, 2017

good air quality in the Beijing–Tianjin–Hebei Region, the Yangtze River Delta, and the Pearl River Delta decreased to 52.6%, 74.3%, and 86.4%, respectively, with year-on-year reductions of 8.7, 0.5, and 3.8 percentage points.[12]

2.2 *The Quality of the Water Environment*

In 2016, the state-controlled section ratio of surface water that met or surpassed the Class III standard of water quality (i.e., the standard for good water quality) was 67.8%, while the section ratios of water rated as Class IV, Class V, or Below Class V (i.e., water not fit for use) were 23.7% and 8.6%, respectively. Compared to 2015, the ratio of water rated as Class I to Class III increased by 3.3 percentage points, while water rated Below Class V increased slightly by 0.2 percentage point. In cities at the prefecture level and above with monitoring programs, 93.6% of the surface sources of drinking water met the quality standards, with a year-on-year increase of 1.0 percentage points, and 85.0% of the underground sources of drinking water met the quality standard, with a year-on-year reduction of 1.6 percentage points.[13] In general, the quantity of surface water has been improving stably, with a high rate of compliance, but the poor environmental quality of some water has led to a decline in the quality of water sources (see Figure 16.2). In the first half of 2017, the quality of the water environment throughout the country was improving, but the work in this aspect was not balanced among the different provinces (autonomous regions and municipalities), and it was hard for some regions to reach the 2017 targets for water quality. The ratio of surface water that met or surpassed the Class III quality standard (i.e., good water quality) was 70% (the target for 2017 was 68.3%), with a year-on-year increase of 1.2 percentage points. The ratio of water rated Below Class V (i.e., not fit for use) was 8.8% (the target for 2017 was 8.4%), with a year-on-year reduction of 1.7 percentage points.[14]

In 2016, the quality of the water of the seas, except the offshore areas, was good, and the water quality of the offshore areas was normal and stable. The ratio of good (Class I and II) water in the offshore areas was 73.4%, with a year-on-year increase of 2.9 percentage points. The polluted sea areas were

---

12 Ministry of Environmental Protection, "Report on the Conditions of Air Quality of Key Regions and 74 Cities in September 2017 and from January to September 2017," official website of the Ministry of Environmental Protection, http://www.mep.gov.cn/gkml/hbb/qt/201710/t20171028_424246.htm, 2017-10-29.

13 Ministry of Environmental Protection, "China Environmental Status Communiqué 2016," June 5, 2017.

14 Ministry of Environmental Protection, "Report on the Quality of Water and Water Quality Reduction Sections of All Provinces (Autonomous Regions and Municipalities) in the First Half of 2017," official website of the Ministry of Environmental Protection, http://www.mep.gov.cn/gkml/hbb/qt/201708/t20170814_419655.htm, 2017-10-28.

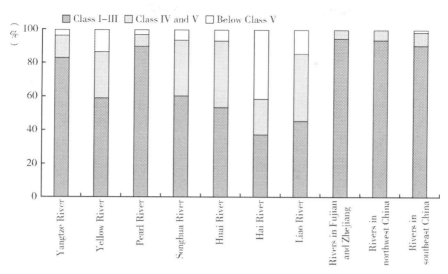

FIGURE 16.2　Water Quality in the Seven Major River Basins, the Zhejiang–Fujian Rivers, the Northwestern Rivers, and the Southwestern Rivers in 2016
SOURCE: MINISTRY OF ENVIRONMENTAL PROTECTION, "THE 2016 CHINA ENVIRONMENTAL STATUS BULLETIN," JUNE 5, 2017

concentrated in the Gulf of Liaodong, the Gulf of Bohai, the Yangtze Estuary, and the Pearl River Estuary and the offshore areas in Jiangsu, Zhejiang, and Guangdong. The major over-limit factors were mineral nitrogen (spot over-limit rate was 23.3%) and labile phosphate (spot over-limit rate was 10.1%). In the four major sea areas, the water quality in the offshore area of the Bohai Sea was normal, the quality in the offshore areas of the Yellow Sea and the South Sea was good, and that in the offshore area of the East Sea was poor. Among the nine important gulfs, the Gulf of Beibu had good water quality; the Gulf of Liaodong, the Yellow River Estuary, and the Gulf of Jiaozhou had normal water quality; the Gulf of Bohai and the Pearl River Estuary had poor water quality; and the Yangtze Estuary, the Gulf of Hangzhou, and the Minjiang Estuary had very poor water quality. Compared to the previous year, the water quality of the Gulf of Liaodong and the Pearl River Estuary was getting better, the water quality of the Minjiang Estuary was getting worse, and the water quality of other gulfs had not changed too much.[15]

15　Ministry of Environmental Protection, "China Environmental Status Communiqué 2016," June 5, 2017.

2.3 The Quality of the Soil Environment

From 2005 to 2013, the national soil pollution survey was conducted in our country for the first time, enabling us to get a handle on the overall conditions of soil pollution in China.[16] The survey results showed that soil pollution in our country was less than optimal and the soil in some areas was seriously polluted. In addition, the quality of the soil environment of cultivated lands was a major concern, and the pollution of abandoned industrial lands was very noticeable. The general spot over-limit rate of the soil nationwide was 16.1%, whereas the spot ratios for slight, light, moderate, and heavy pollution were 11.2%, 2.3%, 1.5% and 1.1%, respectively. Most of the pollutants were inorganic materials (see Table 16.1) and organic materials (see Table 16.2). The ratio of compound pollution was small. Human activity in the industrial and mining industry and agriculture as well as the high background value of the soil environment were the major causes of soil pollution or over-limit pollution. In terms of the distribution of pollution, the soil pollution in southern China was heavier than that in northern China. Soil pollution in the Yangtze River Delta, the Pearl River Delta, and the old industrial bases in northeastern China was prominent. The issue of heavy metal over-limit pollution of the soil in southwestern and central southern China was widespread. The amounts of four pollutants, namely, cadmium, lead, arsenic, and mercury increased from northwest to southeast and from northeast to southwest.

2.4 The Quality of the Natural Ecological Environment

According to the results of the 8th National Forest Resources Inventory (2009 to 2013),[17] the forest area of China was 208 billion hectares with a forest coverage rate of 21.63%. In 2016, the grassland area of China was close to 400 million hectares, accounting for 41.7% of the national territorial area. In China, 2,750 nature reserves of different types and at different levels were built, accounting for 14.88% of the total land area of China. In addition, there were 446 nature reserves at the national level, accounting for 9.97% of the total land area of China. A network of nature reserves with complete types, a reasonable layout, and complete functions has been established.[18]

In 2015,[19] among 2,591 counties, those with an excellent or good quality of ecological environment accounted for 44.9%, which were mainly distributed

---

16 Ministry of Environmental Protection and Ministry of Land and Resources, "Bulletin of the National Soil Pollution Survey," April 17, 2014.

17 As of June 2017, the results of the 8th National Forest Resources Inventory (2009–2013) were still the most recent, so they were used again.

18 Ministry of Environmental Protection, "China Environmental Status Communiqué 2016," June 5, 2017.

19 Limited by the duration of the data collection, the assessment of the quality of the ecological environment lagged behind by one year.

TABLE 16.1   Inorganic Soil Pollutant Over-Limits in China
Unit: %

Type of pollutant	Spot over-limit rate	Ratio of pollution spots of different degrees			
		Slight	Light	Moderate	Heavy
Cd	7.0	5.2	0.8	0.5	0.5
Hg	1.6	1.2	0.2	0.1	0.1
As	2.7	2.0	0.4	0.2	0.1
Cu	2.1	1.6	0.3	0.15	0.05
Pb	1.5	1.1	0.2	0.1	0.1
Cr	1.1	0.9	0.15	0.04	0.01
Zn	0.9	0.75	0.08	0.05	0.02
Ni	4.8	3.9	0.5	0.3	0.1

SOURCE: THE MINISTRY OF ENVIRONMENTAL PROTECTION AND THE MINISTRY OF LAND
AND RESOURCES, "BULLETIN OF THE NATIONAL SOIL POLLUTION SURVEY," APRIL 17, 2014

TABLE 16.2   Organic Soil Pollutant Over-Limits in China
Unit: %

Type of pollutant	Spot over-limit rate	Ratio of pollution spots of different degrees			
		Slight	Light	Moderate	Heavy
666	0.5	0.3	0.1	0.06	0.04
DDT	1.9	1.1	0.3	0.25	0.25
PAH	1.4	0.8	0.2	0.20	0.20

SOURCE: THE MINISTRY OF ENVIRONMENTAL PROTECTION AND THE MINISTRY OF LAND
AND RESOURCES, "BULLETIN OF THE NATIONAL SOIL POLLUTION SURVEY," APRIL 17, 2014

on the south side of the Qinling Mountains: the Huaihe River, the Great
Khingan, and the Lesser Khingan in northeastern China, and the Changbai
Mountains. Counties with an ordinary quality of ecological environment
accounted for 22.2%, which were mainly distributed on the North China Plain,
the middle and western areas of the Northeastern Plain, the middle area of
Inner Mongolia, the middle part of the Qinghai–Tibet Plateau, and the northern part of Xinjiang. Counties with a poor quality of ecological environment
accounted for 32.9% and were mainly distributed in the western part of Inner

Mongolia, the northwestern part of Gansu, the northern part of the Qinghai–Tibet Plateau, and most areas in Xinjiang.[20]

2.5 The Quality of the Acoustic Environment

In 2016, the average level of the quality of the acoustic environment of 322 cities at the prefecture level and above in daytime was Class II, with an equivalent level of sound measuring 54.0 dB. First-class cities accounted for 5.0%, with a year-on-year increase of 1.0 percentage points; second-class cities accounted for 68.3%, with a year-on-year reduction of 0.2 percentage points; third-class cities accounted for 26.1%, with a year-on-year reduction of 0.1 percentage points; fourth-class cities accounted for 0.6%, with a year-on-year reduction of 0.3 percentage points; and no fifth-class cities were included (see Figure 16.3).[21]

In 2016, the average level of road traffic noise in cities throughout China in the daytime was Class I, with an equivalent sound level measuring 66.8 dB, as shown in Figure 16.4. In all cities, the average rate of compliance of daytime monitoring points was 92.2%, and the nighttime rate of compliance was 74.0%, with a year-on-year reduction of 0.2 percentage points and 0.3 percentage points, respectively. The average rates of compliance and the quality of the regional and road traffic acoustic environments of municipalities and provincial capitals were all lower than the average level of China.[22]

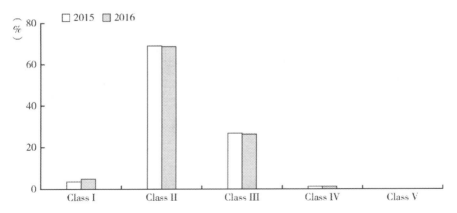

FIGURE 16.3 Ratios of Average Levels of the Quality of the Daytime Acoustic Environment in Cities Nationwide, 2015–2016

20 Ministry of Environmental Protection, "China Environmental Status Communiqué 2016," June 5, 2017.
21 Ibid.
22 Ibid.

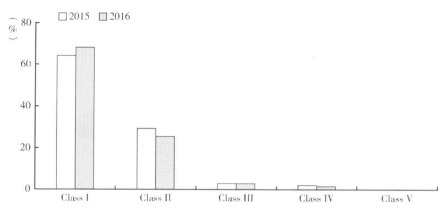

FIGURE 16.4　Ratios of Average Levels of the Quality of the Daytime Traffic Acoustic Environment in Cities Nationwide, 2015–2016
SOURCE: "CHINA ENVIRONMENTAL STATUS BULLETIN 2016," JUNE 5, 2017

2.6　Solid Waste

In 2015, the total amount of ordinary industrial solid waste generated by 246 large and medium-sized cities was 1.91 billion tons, including the comprehensive utilization amount of 1.18 billion tons, accounting for 60.2%, and disposal and storage amounts of 440 million tons and 340 million tons, accounting for 22.5% and 17.3%, respectively. The discarded amount was 170,000 tons. The top three provinces in generating ordinary industrial solid waste were Shanxi, Inner Mongolia, and Liaoning.

The national output of hazardous industrial waste amounted to 28.018 million tons, including the comprehensive utilization amount of 13.727 million tons, accounting for 48.3%, and disposal and storage amounts of 12.543 million tons and 2.167 million tons, accounting for 44.1% and 7.6%, respectively. The top three provinces in generating hazardous industrial waste were Shandong, Hunan, and Jiangsu.

The total amount of China's medical waste was 697,000 tons, with a disposal amount of 695,000 tons, and the disposal rates of medical waste in most cities could reach 100%. The top three provinces in generating medical waste were Shandong, Zhejiang, and Jiangsu.

The total amount of household waste in China was 185.64 million tons, with a disposal amount of 180.695 million tons and a disposal rate of 97.3%. The city that generated the most household waste was Beijing, at an amount of 7.903

million tons, followed by Shanghai, Chongqing, Shenzhen, and Chengdu, at 7.899, 6.26, 5.748, and 4.675 million tons, respectively.[23]

2.7 *Nuclear Energy and Radiation*

The year 2016 saw fairly high radiation safety levels across the country. The level of environmental ionizing radiation was within the normal range of background radiation, and the environmental electromagnetic radiation was lower than the electromagnetic environmental control threshold specified by the national government. The individual annual effective dose caused by the operation of nuclear power bases was far below the dose constraint value specified by the national government. No safety incident or accident at a level of Class 2 or above, as specified in the International Nuclear Event Scale (INES), occurred at any of the types of civil nuclear facilities and programs. As of the end of December 2016, there were 35 operating nuclear powered units, 21 nuclear power units under construction, and 19 research reactors for civil purposes (critical facilities) in China. Good, safe operation records have been maintained for the operating nuclear power units, the quality of the nuclear power units under construction was under control, and the operation of civil research reactors (critical facilities) was good.[24]

3 Prominent Issues of Environmental Protection

Since the 18th National Congress of the CPC, the quality of the environment has improved at an unprecedented speed, but pollution issues due to extensive, long-term development could hardly be eliminated immediately. The degree of improvement in the quality of the environment could not meet the needs of the people for a better life. In 2017, China's ecological system was stable in general and the quality of the environment was getting better nationwide in general. However, some areas witnessed degeneration in terms of some characteristic pollutants in certain periods of time. The situation of environmental protection was still severe.[25] The ecological environment has become

---

23 Ministry of Environmental Protection, "Annual Report on the Control of Environmental Pollution Caused by Solid Waste in Large- and Medium-Sized Cities in 2016," November 22, 2016.

24 Ministry of Environmental Protection, "2016 Annual Report of the National Radiation Environment," August 21, 2017; National Nuclear Safety Administration, "2016 Annual Report of the National Nuclear Safety Administration of the People's Republic of China," July 12, 2017.

25 Chen Jining, "Improving the People's Sense of Gain."

a shortcoming of national development and a sore spot in people's quality of life. We still have a long way to go in the area of environmental protection.

3.1 The Improvement of Environmental Quality in Major Fields Such as Water, Air, and Soil Was Insufficient

In terms of air quality, pollution was still severe: the air quality was not ideal, and there was a large gap between the expectations and requirements of the people. In 2016, only 84 of the 338 cities in China could meet the environmental quality standard for the whole year, accounting for 24.9%. The average PM10 concentration in the country was 82 $\mu g/m^3$, which was higher by 17.1% than the standard of 70 $\mu g/m^3$. The average PM2.5 concentration in the country was 47 $\mu g/m^3$, which was higher by 34.3% than the standard of 35 $\mu g/m^3$. Air quality during the fall and winter seasons did not see much improvement. Pollution in key regions and periods worsened. Weather associated with heavy pollution could be seen more frequently in northern China in the fall and winter, especially in the Beijing–Tianjin–Hebei Region and the surrounding area. From 2016 to 2017, many areas saw heavy large-scale pollution that lasted a long time during the fall and winter periods, seriously affecting the lives of the people.

In terms of water quality and soil quality, large areas of industrial seepage occurred in northern China, and waste ships from Jiaxing dumped waste illegally into the Yangtze River; all of these pollution incidents indicated that water and soil pollution was still severe. Issues in the ecological environment along the Yangtze River Economic Belt were prominent, with obvious weaknesses and huge burdens on governance, improvement, and restoration: insufficient infrastructure facilities and the intensified layout of the heavy chemical industry have led to high environmental risks, non-point source pollution was prominent in rural areas, and the shoals and wetlands providing services for the ecological system were damaged.

In terms of ecological environmental protection, the general level of the quality of the ecological system was relatively low. In some areas, the fragmentation of ecological spaces worsened and the ecological system degenerated. The rate of reduction of biological diversity has not been controlled effectively. Typical diversity-related incidents, such as the serious damage to the ecological environment of the national nature reserve in Qilianshan, indicated that efforts to protect the ecological environment were still insufficient.

In terms of controlling pollution by enterprises, there were still some problems with legal and standard-compliance emissions. Some enterprises did not have a sufficient awareness of compliance with the law and were reluctant to improve the environment and thus did not make modifications promptly. Some of them even stopped their pollution control facilities without permission or produced emissions beyond the legal limits or without permission. Pressure to comply with environmental protection standards was not effectively transferred to enterprises. In some places, measures for the protection of the ecological environment were not fully implemented, and the efforts made in the name of environmental protection were not enough.

In general, environmental protection was still in a stage with a heavy burden to bear. A fundamental improvement in the quality of the environment is a long-term process. We must prepare for a long-term battle to improve the quality of the environment with regard to water, air, soil, and other aspects.

3.2 The Period of Social Transformation Coexisted with That of Environmental Sensitivity, and Environmental and Social Risks Frequently Overlapped

Structural transformation for industries, energy sources, and transportation should be further strengthened. The proportion of the heavy chemical industry in the industrial structure was high; an energy structure dominated by coal could hardly be changed in the short term; and a transportation structure dominated by roads could be preserved in the national economy for a long time. Environmental problems that had been masked by high economic growth began to appear with the reduction of the rate of growth.

During the parallel advancement of industrialization and urbanization, the ecological environment has become more and more related to people's sense of happiness and of gain. A high-incidence period of environmental issues and a period of updating the public's environmental awareness overlapped, leading to a closer relationship between the environment and people's quality of life. The public concern caused by environmental pollution has become a risk and a sore spot related to the health of the public. The environmental influence of public facilities in cities and industrial facilities for waste disposal, the construction of the chemical industry, and the disposal of hazardous waste and cleanup of polluted land have become social focus points. The close relationship between ecology and resources could be fractured by small impacts. Environmental issues and incidents have become tests for local party committees and governments in terms of political achievements, capacity for governance, image, and credibility.

3.3 The Mechanisms of Environmental Protection and Governance Could Not Meet the Requirements for New Tasks in the New Situation

Since the 18th National Congress of the CPC, the Central Committee of the CPC has attached great importance to the construction of an ecological civilization. Among the 38 meetings of the Central Leading Group for Comprehensively

Deepening the Reform, reform of the system of ecological civilization was mentioned 20 times, and outstanding achievements have been made in that reform. According to the decision of the Central Committee of the CPC and the State Council, the system of environmental protection and governance was initially adjusted and improved, promoting the healthy development of environmental protection undertakings.

The complicity and severity of China's environmental pollution control are unprecedented in the world. A single control mode basically could not eliminate all of the issues. Control over several pollution factors could not meet the requirements of governance. Therefore, pressure must be applied level by level to implement the strictest possible environmental protection system, establish a standardized mechanism of incentives and limitations, accelerate the transformation of the methods and system of environmental protection and management, and form a system of environmental governance that integrates the governments, enterprises, and the public.[26]

The current mechanism of environmental protection could not fully meet the requirements for the new tasks in the new situation. Compared to the reform of the economic system, the reform of the system for an ecological civilization lagged behind, and the problems in the reform could not be resolved immediately. With the deepening of the reform, we met more difficulties and problems. For some reforms, we have no example to follow. The establishment of entity functions and the balance sheet of natural resources are innovative measures. The reform of the ownership system of natural resources was in the pilot stage, with huge difficulties in determining ownership. In addition, some reforms have been hindered by the slow revisions of laws and regulations, and it is hard to integrate the systems and mechanisms. Regarding ecological protection and environmental governance, the issues caused by the overlapping of the functions of different departments have not been resolved, leading to issues of overlap between the central and local governments, insufficient law enforcement guarantees, and focusing on approval without considering supervision. The relationship between development and environmental protection has not been clearly defined. Governmental supervision has been fully strengthened, but the market function has not been used to a sufficient degree.

---

26   Wu Shunze, "Eight Challenges for Environmental Protection during the 13th Five-Year Plan," http://www.h2o-china.com/column/154.html; Chen Jining, "Improving the People's Sense of Gain."

The mechanism of incentives should be further established and improved in the reform.[27]

3.4 Public Participation in Environmental Protection Was Insufficient, and a Joint Force Has Not Been Formed to Push Green Production and Lifestyle Reform Forward

With the building of a moderately prosperous society, the ecological environment has become more and more important to the happiness of the people. The requirements of the people for clean air, good water, safe food, and a beautiful environment have become more and more urgent, and their recognition of the relationship between economic development and environmental protection has been changed profoundly. The concept of green development has been widely accepted. The public is the fundamental beneficiary in the construction of an ecological civilization and a beautiful China, as well as the elimination of outdated capacity, industrial structural updating, and green economic transformation. Effective public participation can promote green development and the updating of the economy. At present, public participation in environmental protection is still in the incubation stage, the related systems and standards are not complete, and some local governments and enterprises have not paid sufficient attention to public participation or are reluctant to accept the supervision of the public. In addition, environmental information is not fully disclosed, and a joint force has not been formed to push forward green production and a reform of contemporary lifestyles.

4 New Progress in Environmental Protection

4.1 Thoroughly Implement Action Plans for Pollution Prevention and Control for Air, Water, and Soil to Improve the Overall Quality of the Environment[28]

In 2017, the Ministry of Environmental Protection implemented action plans for pollution prevention and control of the air, water, and soil to achieve full supervision over environmental protection on the part of the central government.

In terms of air pollution control, efforts were made to solve the pollution caused by coal, especially during the winter periods when heat is supplied

---

27   Record of the 6th News Conference of the 19th National Congress of the CPC (full text), the official account of China Environmental Education and Communications, http://mp.weixin.qq.com/s/_SLj2XEUhuzbkjLI9wvREw##, October 26, 2017.

28   Chen Jining, "Improving the People's Sense of Gain."

in northern China. In the industrial field, specific environmental protection programs were launched in key industries to firmly shut down the polluting enterprises. In promoting the adjustment of the industrial structure, overcapacity in the iron and steel industry in key areas such as the Beijing–Tianjin–Hebei Region was reduced in a faster way. In terms of automobile control, heavy-polluting vehicles were basically eliminated, old automobiles were eliminated in a faster way, clean-energy vehicles were promoted, and gasoline and diesel vehicles meeting the China VI Emission Standard were used in key areas. At the same time, weather conditions that promote heavy pollution were dealt with in a more scientific and accurate way.

In terms of water pollution control, pollution control plans were issued for key bodies of water. A joint pollution prevention and control system for regions, water bodies, and seas was established. The construction of the standardization of drinking water sources was strengthened to identify the safety risks of underground sources of drinking water near chemical industry enterprises and to ensure the safety of drinking water. Good bodies of water were protected, underground water pollution was prevented, and foul-smelling bodies of water in cities were controlled. Livestock breeding areas were defined throughout the country to implement a pilot program for the comprehensive utilization of livestock and poultry excrement.

In terms of soil pollution control, in 2017, the Ministry of Environmental Protection started to create the *Action Plan for the Prevention and Control of Soil Pollution* (called the "Ten Clauses of Soil" for short), proposed some solutions for major targets, and signed soil pollution control target contracts with the people's governments at the provincial, autonomous region, and municipal levels. The nationwide soil pollution survey was fully launched. The legal and standard systems for soil pollution prevention and control were improved to conduct a survey and assessment of the soil environment of land to be developed. Comprehensive control plans were made for 138 key regions in order to prevent heavy metal pollution.

In addition, the Ministry of Environmental Protection promoted constant improvement of the quality of the ecological environment by deepening and implementing the reform in the field of ecological environment, strengthening the establishment of environmental laws, and promoting green production and lifestyles.

4.2 Prevent and Eliminate the NIMBY Environmental Risks by Implementing Comprehensive Measures and Addressing Both Symptoms and Root Causes

During the stage of economic and social transformation, NIMBY ("not in my backyard") issues related to the environment were prominent. With the attention and practice of governments at all levels, an effective mechanism that can be used to prevent and resolve environmental NIMBY issues was established.

First, the system for the disclosure of decision-making information should be improved to strengthen efforts regarding the disclosure of information and to ensure the public's right to know. Second, the channels that enable the public to participate in environmental protection should be expanded. By holding roundtable meetings, workshops, and seminars, the environmental protection departments have listened to the opinions of people from all walks of society and have promptly accepted their claims and resolved the issues of the public through administrative reviews, the 12369 environmental protection hotline, and environmental letters and visits. The public can monitor pollution in their areas and express their opinions by taking part in environmental publicity activities and activities regarding the opening of facilities concerned with environmental protection. Third, some provinces and cities have innovated new methods to guide the public in participating in the mediation of conflicts caused by environmental pollution. In practice, some provinces and cities have worked directly with environmental protection organizations to establish commissions for joint green construction to resolve NIMBY dilemmas. Fourth, claims for benefits should be responded to in a scientific and reasonable way. A compensation, insurance, and return mechanism should be established in the decision-making stage of any project in a timely manner according to law, so as to improve mediation and judicial remedies and resolve conflicts.

In general, great importance was given to NIMBY issues in 2017, and a good situation with prescribed rules and solutions was attained.

4.3 Define the Direction of the Reform of the Environmental Protection System and Steadily Push It Forward

At present, the construction of a system for an ecological civilization has been accelerated, and more efforts have been made to reform the system of environmental governance. According to the reform spirit and requirements of the national government, the reform of the system of environmental protection and governance has been advancing steadily. The purpose of the reform was to preserve the issue-oriented approach and use innovative environmental governance measures to optimize the functional configuration of different departments, define the functional relationship among the various departments, highlight uniform supervision and law enforcement regarding the environment, and define the supervisory obligation of governments at all levels to conduct environmental protection supervision from a system of environmental protection and governance with complete functions, clear levels, consistent rights and obligations, and a high degree of operational efficiency.

To promote the modernization of the national system of and capacity for governance regarding ecological environmental protection, in September 2016 the General Office of the CPC Central Committee and the General Office of the State Council issued the *Guiding Opinions on the Pilots of Reform of a System for the Vertical Management of Supervision and Law Enforcement for the Environmental Protection Organs below the Provincial Level*, and a good pattern with a combination of spots and areas and echelon promotion has been formed. A new system for the management of environmental protection has been basically established at the local level, and vertical reform should be completed by the end of June 2018.[29] The system of environmental supervision was improved to strengthen the supervisory force over environmental protection. In 2017, central supervision over environmental protection covered all of the provinces, autonomous regions, and municipalities in China, focusing on environmental issues that are the object of the close attention of the central government, fierce feedback from the public, and bad social influences. Close attention has been given to water bodies in key regions with a damaged ecology and either a low-quality environment or inaction or negligence on the part of local governments. The determination to correct environmental problems and implement the environmental protection policies of the central government has played an important role in environmental protection, and it has achieved a good effect that resulted in the recognition of the public, affirmation of the government, support from the local government, and solutions to the problems. Some provinces, autonomous regions, and municipalities have established corresponding systems of environmental supervision at the provincial level, forming a tendency toward strict law enforcement and supervision at different levels, with full coverage and long-term effects.

4.4 The Initial Effect of the Participation of Multiple Social Subjects in Environmental Control Has Been Seen

Environmental protection departments in all places have paid attention to the role of the multiple participants of the society in environmental protection, to

---

29   "The 4th Plenary Session of the Central Leading Group for Comprehensively Deepening the Reform Was Held by the Ministry of Environmental Protection in 2017," official website of the Ministry of Environmental Protection, http://www.zhb.gov.cn/gkml/hbb/qt/201709/t20170906_421023.htm.

ensure the public's right to know, to participate, and to supervise. In particular, the active roles of the social environmental organizations and the functions of supervision and publicity of news media have been fully utilized.

In March 2017, according to the *Opinions on Reforming the System of the Management of Social Organizations to Promote the Healthy and Orderly Development of Social Organizations* issued by the General Office of the CPC Central Committee and the General Office of the State Council, the Ministry of Environmental Protection and the Ministry of Civil Affairs jointly issued the *Guiding Opinions on Strengthening the Development of the Guidance and Management of the Standardization of the Social Organizations of Environmental Protection* to guide the environmental protection departments and civil affairs departments at all levels in order to strengthen the development of the guidance and management of the standardization of the social organizations of environmental protection. In May 2017, the Ministry of Environmental Protection, the Ministry of Housing, and Urban-Rural Development jointly issued the *Guiding Opinions on Promoting the Opening of Environmental Protection Facilities and City Sewage and Waste Treatment Facilities to the Public*, requiring the environmental protection departments and housing and urban-rural development departments in all places to open the facilities for environmental supervision, sewage treatment, waste treatment, and hazardous waste and used electronics to the public regularly; to provide a platform for the public to understand, support, and take part in environmental protection activities; and to perform their environmental obligations. The related departments have held training classes to improve the capacities of environmental protection organizations in organizing and participating in environmental protection activities. In addition, small-amount funding programs have been launched to provide various environmental protection organizations with more public spaces and resources.

After a period of cultivation and guidance, a pattern of joint governance for environmental control has been initially formed. Environmental protection organizations and the public have actively participated in the supervision of information disclosure and the promotion of green lifestyles. The new media has created a good atmosphere for public opinion by publicizing positive cases and analyzing negative ones. The governments, public, environmental protection organizations, and news media can supervise and promote each other to realize green development.

5 New Fields and Topics for Environmental Protection

At present, China is in a key phase of building a moderately prosperous society in all respects and starting a new journey of the construction of a modernized socialist country, and ecological environmental protection has met unprecedented challenges. With the deepening of the governing idea of the governments at all levels for environmental protection, the construction of an ecological civilization and ecological environmental protection will be accelerated, the outlook on green development will be changed profoundly, and the deepened reform of ecological environmental protection, revitalization of rural areas, protection of the mother river, control of soil pollution, and the joint governance of multiple elements have become the new fields and topics of environmental protection.

5.1 Thoroughly Implementing the Reform of Ecological Environmental Protection

Since the 18th National Congress of the CPC, among the 38 meetings of the Central Leading Group for Comprehensively Deepening the Reform, the reform of the system for an ecological civilization was mentioned on 20 occasions, and outstanding achievements have been made in the reform. President Xi Jinping promoted an important measure for the reform of the system for an ecological civilization, namely, central supervision over environmental protection.

The pilot program for central supervision of environmental protection was started at the end of 2015, and by the end of September 2017 it covered all 31 provinces, autonomous regions, and municipalities. The effects may be summed up thus: (1) The consciousness of strengthening ecological environmental protection and promoting green development has been strengthened. The consciousness and initiative of the whole country and the whole Party in implementing the concept of green development have significantly improved, and the people's ignorance of ecological environmental protection was corrected to a great degree. (2) Prominent environmental issues have been resolved for a great number of people. During the four central supervisory actions over environmental protection, 135,000 reports from the public were received, which have basically been settled. About 80,000 reports concerning waste, oil fumes, odors, noise, polluting enterprises, and foul-smelling waters have been well resolved and highly praised by the public as well. (3) Central supervision over environmental protection has promoted the transformation and updating of local industrial structures. Many places promoted green development and structural reform on the supply side, strengthened the pollution control of enterprises, internalized environmental costs, and punished polluting enterprises, thus resolving the problem of "bad money drives out good money" in some places in a good way. These places have also significantly improved the benefits of industrial development and expanded its scale; moreover, they have given play to the positive driving role of the optimization of the economic structure while improving the quality of the environment.

(4) The improvement of local environmental protection and the mechanism for an ecological civilization have been effectively promoted. The construction and improvement of legal systems have been accelerated in all places to further promote the building of an ecological civilization and green development.

5.2 Improving the Long-Term Mechanism for Strict Law Enforcement regarding the Environment

To promote the building of an ecological civilization and environmental protection undertakings, we need to integrate the building of an ecological civilization into the legislation; in particular, a long-term mechanism should be established for environmental law enforcement. The achievements and experiences of central supervision over environmental protection show that the deepening of the reform in the field of ecological environmental protection will improve the long-term mechanism for strict enforcement of environmental laws. From supervision over enterprises to supervision over governments, central supervision over environmental protection has created a powerful deterrent force, forming a new situation for the implementation of the same obligations for the Party as for governments and dual responsibilities for one post, and promoting a new pattern with integrated coordination and joint governance of multiple departments. The effect of central supervision over environmental protection was obtained through six practices: (1) Upholding the idea of putting people first to deal with matters related to the people preferentially. (2) Steadily strengthening consciousness of the need to maintain political integrity, think in big-picture terms, uphold the leadership core, and keep in alignment. (3) Paying close attention to the Party committees and governments. (4) Focusing on issues. (5) Disclosing information fully and publicizing the reported issues in society. (6) Claiming accountability seriously. Through the institutional arrangement for strict law enforcement, the wrong understanding held by some officials about environmental law enforcement can be corrected, and any acts damaging the ecological environment must be firmly stopped and punished so as to create a social atmosphere in which nobody will dare to damage the ecological environment.

In addition, the reform of the system of vertical management of supervision and law enforcement for environmental protection organs below the provincial level has been promoted steadily, the implementation of the system of emission permissions has been accelerated, a pilot program for the reform of the compensation system for damages to the ecological environment has been launched, and a series of reform measures, such as the issuance of the *Implementation Plan for Constructing a Network of Supervision over the Ecological Environment* (2016–2020), have been taken. All of these have provided powerful support for strengthening strict enforcement of environmental laws.[30]

5.3 Implementing the Rural Revitalization Strategy to Improve the Ecological Environment in Rural Areas

The improvement of the ecological environment in rural areas is closely related to the basic aspects of people's lives. Governments at all levels have implemented comprehensive measures to improve the environment in rural areas, benefiting 110,000 villages and a rural population of about 200 million. However, in general, the efforts and funds that were directed toward preventing pollution in agricultural and rural areas were insufficient. Compared to the prevention and control of pollution in urban areas, the attention paid to pollution control in rural areas in these years has not been enough, and this has become a weakness in ecological environmental protection and the construction of an ecological civilization.

In the future, we should strengthen supervision over and control of ecological environmental protection in rural areas and prevent urban pollution from being transferred to rural areas. Great efforts should be made in preventing pollution caused by livestock breeding, recycling abandoned materials, disposing waste in rural areas through classification, utilizing straw comprehensively, and preventing pollution caused by pesticides and chemical fertilizers. We should strive to further improve the ecological environment in rural areas and meet the needs of the people in rural areas for a good ecological environment.

5.4 Protecting the Mother River and Repairing the Ecological System of the Yangtze River

In January 2016, at the forum for promoting the development of the Yangtze River Economic Belt, President Xi Jinping emphasized that to develop the Yangtze River Economic Belt, we should put ecology and green development first and make repairing the ecological environment of the Yangtze River the top priority to ensure its grand protection without conducting grand development. To strengthen the macro design for the ecological environmental protection of the Yangtze River Economic Belt, the *Ecological Environmental Protection Plan for the Yangtze River Economic Belt* was issued in July 2017.

30　Li Ganjie, "The Construction of a Beautiful China Is Widely Accepted and Steadily Advanced," http://www.zhb.gov.cn/gkml/hbb/qt/201709/t20170927_422373.htm; Chen Jining, "Improving the People's Sense of Gain."

The contents of the plan could be summarized as: Three Waters, Four Steps, and Five Constructions.[31]

"Three Waters" means that water resources, water ecology, and the water environment should be improved at the same time, so as to use the water resources to restore and protect the water ecology and improve the water environment.

The Four Steps are as follows: (1) The coordination of upstream and downstream should be ensured. (2) Key areas, such as Lake Boyang, Lake Dongting, and the Yangtze Estuary should be focused on. (3) Major projects for ecological environmental protection and environmental control should be implemented. (4) The reform and innovation of related systems and mechanisms should be conducted.

The Five Constructions include (1) A harmonious Yangtze River area should be built through the scientific development and utilization of water resources. (2) A clean Yangtze River should be built by strengthening control over the hydrological ecological environment. (3) A healthy Yangtze River should be built by restoring and protecting the hydrological ecological environment. (4) A beautiful Yangtze River should be built by resolving the environmental issues on both banks. (5) A safe Yangtze River should be built by effectively controlling the related environmental risks.

5.5 Thoroughly Implementing the "Ten Clauses of Soil" to Ensure the Safety of Food for the People

The fundamental work of controlling soil pollution should be strengthened. (1) Laws and regulations related to soil pollution control should be improved by designing procedures for the management of the soil environment in agricultural lands and procedures for the management of the soil environment in urban areas. (2) A survey on soil pollution should be actively conducted according to the *Overall Plan for a Detailed Survey of Soil Pollution in China*.

Two key tasks should be promoted actively: (1) Management of the classification of agricultural lands should be undertaken. In Tianjin, Hunan, Hubei, and Liaoning, a pilot project for defining the non-production areas for agricultural products has been launched to implement the *Pilot Plan for Exploring the Implementation of the Crop Rotation System of Cultivated Lands*. (2) Management of access to construction lands should be implemented. The system for the management of information regarding the soil environment in polluted lands in China should be used to share information among different

---

31   Ministry of Environmental Protection, National Development and Reform Commission and Ministry of Water Resources, "The Ecological Environmental Protection Plan for the Yangtze River Economic Belt," July 13, 2017.

departments. In Beijing, Tianjin, Shanghai, and Chongqing, lists of polluted lands have been drawn up and some places have issued lists of enterprises subject to soil environment supervision in order to strengthen law enforcement and strictly control new pollution. In addition, comprehensive pilot programs have been conducted in 6 areas, and technical pilots have been launched in 200 land lots. We should strengthen the target examination and accelerate repair and governance to significantly improve control over soil pollution.

5.6 Promoting the Formation of the Pattern of Joint Governance of Governments, Enterprises, and the Public

At present, the expectations of the public regarding the quality of the environment have exceeded the stages of and resources for economic development and environmental gifts, increasing the public's difficulty in accepting the improvement of the environment.[32] The demand of the public for better environmental quality was not matched by their willingness to participate in environmental protection activities. This situation has generated higher demands for environmental protection work and provided motivation for advancement from another perspective.

The 13th Five-Year Planning Outline has made a comprehensive arrangement for ecological environmental protection, and it has made the promotion of green production and lifestyles and the acceleration of the improvement of the ecological environment the two major tasks for the building of a moderately prosperous society in all respects and in overall development. On May 26, 2017, the Political Bureau of the Central Committee of the Communist Party of China conducted the 41st collective study for the promotion of green development patterns and lifestyles. When hosting the study, Xi Jinping, as the secretary general of the Central Committee of the CPC, emphasized that the promotion of green development patterns and lifestyles is a necessary requirement for the implementation of the new concept of development, and that we must put the construction of an ecological civilization in an important position in relation to the overall work. Furthermore, we must uphold the policy of putting energy conservation and environmental protection first, based on natural recovery, to form a pattern of space, industrial structure, production modes, and lifestyles focusing on energy saving and environmental protection, so as to realize the joint advancement of economic and social development

---

32   Wu Shunze, "Eight Challenges for Environmental Protection during the 13th Five-Year Plan," http://www.h2o-china.com/column/154.html.

and ecological environmental protection and create an excellent working and living environment for the people.[33]

The Report to the 19th CPC National Congress proposed promoting green development. We should accelerate the construction of the legal system and policy guidance for green production and consumption in order to establish and improve an economic system with green, low-carbon development and better circulation. A green technological system of innovation with a market orientation should be built to develop green finance and to enhance the energy saving and environmental protection industry, the clean production industry, and the clean energy industry. A revolution in energy production and consumption should be promoted to build a clean, low-carbon, safe and effective energy system. Utilization of comprehensive saving and circulation of resources should be promoted to implement national water conservation actions, reduce consumption of energy and materials, and realize the reciprocal connection between the production system and the living system. Simple, green, and low-carbon lifestyles should be promoted to oppose luxurious and unreasonable consumption, and energy-saving organs, green households, green schools, green communities, and green traveling should be established.[34]

The year 2017 was of great importance to the acceleration of the construction of an ecological civilization. The blueprint for ecological environmental protection in the new age has been drawn, which should lead people in all industries to strive to build a beautiful China.

References

Chen Jining. "Improving the People's Sense of Gain with Environmental Quality Improvement and Welcoming the 19th National Congress of the CPC with Good Achievements—Speech Delivered at the National Working Conference on Environmental Protection in 2017." http://www.zhb.gov.cn/xxgk/hjyw/201701/t20170125_395251.shtml.

Shi Feng et al. "Situation and Challenges for International Cooperation for Environmental Protection during the 13th Five-Year Plan." *Environmental Protection Science*, 2016(1).

---

33 "Xi Jinping Hosted the 41st Collective Study of the Political Bureau of the Central Committee of the Communist Party of China," http://cpc.people.com.cn/n1/2017/0528/c64094-29305569.html.

34 "During the Opening Ceremony, Xi Jinping Delivered a Report on Behalf of the 18th Central Committee," http://www.china.com.cn/cppcc/2017-10/18/content_41752399.htm, October 19, 2017.

Ministry of Environmental Protection. "China Environmental Status Communiqué 2016," June 5, 2017.

Ministry of Environmental Protection and Ministry of Land and Resources. "Bulletin of the National Soil Pollution Survey," April 17, 2014.

Ministry of Environmental Protection. "Annual Report on the Control of Environmental Pollution Caused by Solid Waste in Large- and Medium-Sized Cities in 2016," November 22, 2016.

Ministry of Environmental Protection. "2016 Annual Report of the National Radiation Environment," August 21, 2017.

National Nuclear Safety Administration. "2016 Annual Report of the National Nuclear Safety Administration of the People's Republic of China," July 12, 2017.

CHAPTER 17

Analytical Report on China's Industrial Labor Force in 2017

Qiao Jian[1] and Liu Xiaoqian[2]

Abstract

Under the historical direction of socialism with Chinese characteristics in the new age in 2017, the employment of workers improved steadily, and the unemployment rate reached the lowest point since the financial crisis. The salaries of workers increased stably. The State Council made greater efforts to deal with salary payments that were in arrears. The social security system basically covered all qualified persons in order to promote the integration of pension insurance throughout the country. Safety in the workplace developed positively and the opinion of the central government indicated the developmental direction regarding this aspect. The total number of labor disputes and the number of people involved decreased, but it was still at the highest historical level. According to the 8th Survey of Employees' Working Conditions, the new generation of migrant workers had become the major workforce and had a higher educational background. The Internet had become an important space for them to obtain information and conduct social interactions, changing their living and working styles. In the *Reform Plan for the Construction of the Industrial Labor Force in the New Age*, the goal to improve the overall quality of the labor force led to a strategic task to establish a labor force with knowledge, skills, and innovations. In this report, we have for the first time analyzed the influence of the sharing economy on the employment relationship and new styles of working.

---

1 Qiao Jian, associate professor and head of the Department of Employment Relations, China University of Labor Relations, mainly engaged in research on labor relations, employee status, and trade unions.
2 Liu Xiaoqian, teacher in the Department of Employment Relations, China University of Labor Relations, mainly engaged in research on labor relations, labor laws, and labor history.

Keywords

new age – survey on the conditions of workers – industrial labor force – sharing economy

1 Current Conditions of the Working Class in the New Age

1.1 Employment Has Increased Stably and the Unemployment Rate Has Reached a New Low since the Financial Crisis

In the first three quarters of 2017, the GDP witnessed a year-on-year increase of 6.9%, with a growth of 0.2 percentage points. The growth of the added value of the industrial enterprises with an annual revenue above 20 million yuan accelerated, and the leading role of the service industry improved. The added value of tertiary industry accounted for 52.9% of the GDP, higher than that of secondary industry by 12.8 percentage points. Imports and exports saw a year-on-year increase of 16.6%.[3]

The employment rate of workers improved while maintaining a stable condition, and many indicators reached historic records. The conditions were reflected in the following aspects: (1) The core indicators of employment were better than those in previous years. From January to September 2017, the number of newly employed people in urban areas reached 10.97 million, with a year-on-year increase of 300,000, close to the annual target of 11 million. At the end of the third quarter, the urban registered unemployment rate was 3.95%, decreasing by 0.09 percentage points year on year, and this was the lowest since the financial crisis in 2008. The unemployment rate from the urban survey issued by the National Bureau of Statistics for 31 major cities was 4.83%, which was also the lowest point since 2012. (2) The employment of key groups was stable and orderly. In 2017, the employment level of the 7.95 million graduates from colleges and universities saw stable growth. The task of worker resettlement as a means to resolve overcapacity was conducted smoothly. More efforts were made to assist the employment of poor groups, and the dynamic zeroing of households without any employed members was realized. (3) The conditions of the market supply and demand and the

---

3 "Press Conference Held by the Information Office for the National Economic Operation in the First Three Quarters," www.gov.cn, October 19, 2017.

jobs provided by enterprises improved constantly. According to data regarding market supply and demand provided by public employment service agencies in 100 cities, the job vacancies-to-seekers ratio in the third quarter of 2017 was 1.16, a new historical high. The monitoring data of 50,000 enterprises and 27 million employment positions showed that the number of positions witnessed an increase in seven of the first nine months.[4] In May 2017, the International Institute for Management Development published its latest ranking of global competitiveness, and China had the top-ranking employment indicator.

New progress was made in employment for the following reasons: (1) The stabilization and expansion of employment became the major target for macro regulation to implement the Employment Priority Strategy. (2) The employment flexibility resulting from economic growth improved significantly. For each percentage point of GDP growth from 2012 to 2016, 1.72 million non-agricultural workers found jobs. In particular, the rapid development of tertiary industry and the emergence of new industries, business patterns, and employment methods have improved the effect of the driving force of economic growth on employment. In 2016, more than 600 million people in China joined in the sharing economy, with about 5.85 million people working for sharing economy platforms, an increase of 850,000 people over the previous year. (3) The dividends of reform were unleashed. Governments at all levels continued to improve the reform by delegating powers, streamlining procedures, and changing administrative approval systems to promote the Mass Entrepreneurship and Innovation initiative and the development of new industries, business patterns, and business modes, creating a lot of jobs. (4) The active employment policies promoted employment work significantly.

1.2 *The Wages of Employees Increased in a Steady Manner, and the State Council Issued Documents to Comprehensively Manage Unpaid Wages*

From January to September 2017, the per capita disposable income of national residents was 19,342 yuan, with a year-on-year increase of 7.5%. The per capita disposable income of urban residents was 27,430 yuan, with a year-on-year increase of 6.6%. At the end of the third quarter, the total number of members of the rural labor force working in cities had reached 179.69 million, with a year-on-year increase of 3.2 million or 1.7%. The average monthly income of

---

4 "Press Conference of the 3rd Quarter of 2017 Held by the Ministry of Human Resources and Social Security," official website of the Ministry of Human Resources and Social Security, November 1, 2017.

those laborers was 3,459 yuan, increasing by 7.0%, or 1.1 percentage points on a year-on-year basis.

In terms of minimum wages, as of the end of October 2017, 17 regions throughout China had adjusted the minimum wage standard, with an average growth rate of 10.4%. For example, Shanghai had the highest minimum monthly salary, 2,300 yuan, and Beijing had the highest minimum hourly salary, 22 yuan. The scale of adjustment of the minimum salary in 2017 was expanded, but the growth rate was still small, given the huge downward economic pressure and the difficulties that enterprises faced in operations. Salary guidance lines were issued in 19 regions with the baseline at about 8%.

In terms of unpaid wages, the total amount of unpaid wages in 2016 was 27.09 billion yuan, with an increase of 0.3% over the previous year; 2.369 million migrant workers were affected, but this number had decreased by 14.1% over the previous year. The proportion of migrant workers with unpaid wages was 0.84%, decreasing by 0.15 percentage points over the previous year. However, the average unpaid wages for each migrant worker was 11,433 yuan, increasing by 16.8% over the previous year. In terms of industries, the proportions of migrant workers with unpaid wages in the manufacturing industry, construction industry, wholesale and retail industry, and the transportation, storage, and postal industry were 0.6%, 1.8%, 0.2%, and 0.4%, decreasing by 0.2, 0.2, 0.1, and 0.3 percentage points over the previous year, respectively. The proportions of migrant workers with unpaid wages in resident service, repairing service, and other service industries increased to some extent, which was 0.6% in 2016, a rise of 0.3 percentage points over the previous year.[5]

To deal with the problem of unpaid wages, in February 2017, Premier Li Keqiang hosted an executive meeting of the State Council to conduct specific controls and supervisory programs to expose a group of typical cases, to strictly investigate the illegal activities related to unpaid wages, and to firmly crack down on the crimes of unpaid wages, and especially, to deal with unpaid wages resulting from the delay in price payments of projects that governments had invested in.[6] In July, the Ministry of Human Resources and Social Security issued the *Three-Year Action Plan for Dealing with Salary Arrears and Ensuring Payment (2017–2019)*, making it a requirement to reduce the proportion of migrant workers with unpaid wages year by year and to eliminate the

---

5 National Bureau of Statistics, "The 2016 National Report on Migrant Worker Monitoring and Survey," official website of the National Bureau of Statistics, April 28, 2017.

6 "Supervision of the State Council on the Salary Arrears for Migrant Workers: Black List," *China Youth Daily*, February 14, 2017.

unpaid wages for migrant workers by 2020 by focusing on the issue of unpaid wages in the field of engineering construction.[7] In September, the Ministry of Human Resources and Social Security issued the *Interim Measures for the Administration of the "Blacklist" of Arrears of Migrant Workers' Wages* in order to include on the unpaid wages "blacklist" all employing units and employers who deducted or delayed the salaries of migrant workers for any reason until the amount in arrears crossed the threshold of the crime of refusing to pay labor remuneration, or who caused group events, extreme events, and a serious adverse social impact due to their illegal behavior regarding migrant workers' unpaid wages.[8] The Finance and Economic Commission of the NPC has recommended that the related departments strengthen their surveys and revise their drafts to include the modification of the *Labor Contract Law* in the legislation planning of the next Standing Committee of the NPC.[9]

1.3 *The Social Security System Has Basically Covered All Qualified People, Promoting the Nationwide Integration of Pension Insurance*

The coverage of social insurance expanded continuously. By the end of September 2017, the participants in basic pension insurance, basic health care insurance, unemployment insurance, work-related insurance, and maternity insurance had reached 905 million, 1,129 million, 186 million, 224 million, and 190 million, respectively,[10] witnessing year-on-year increases. From January to September 2017, the total income of the five major social insurances reached 4.7 trillion yuan, with a year-on-year increase of 37.7%, and the total amount of expenditures reached 4.02 trillion yuan, with a year-on-year increase of 34%. The achievements made by our country in expanding the coverage of social insurance have been highly recognized by the international community. In November 2016, the International Social Security Association (ISSA) awarded the Chinese government its Outstanding Achievement in Social Security award.

---

7   Ministry of Human Resources and Social Security, "Resolve Salary Arrears for Migrant Workers in 3 Years," *People's Daily* (Overseas), July 18, 2017.

8   "Employers Deferring Salaries for Migrant Workers Will Be Included on the Black List," *People's Daily* (Overseas), October 10, 2017.

9   "Report of the Finance and Economic Commission of the NPC on the Review of the Proposals Made by the Presidium of the 5th Session of the 12th NPC," www.npc.gov.cn, November 4, 2017.

10 "Press Conference of the 3rd Quarter of 2017 Held by the Ministry of Human Resources and Social Security," the official website of the Ministry of Human Resources and Social Security, November 1, 2017.

The benefits of workers steadily improved. The basic monthly pension for enterprise retirees increased from 1,686 yuan in 2012 to 2,362 yuan in 2016, with an annual average increase of 8.8%, which increased at the average rate of 5.5% in 2017. The minimum level for the fundamental pension of the basic pension insurance for rural and urban residents increased from 55 yuan to 70 yuan per month, and the per capita pension reached about 120 yuan. The subsidy for the basic health care insurance of urban and rural residents increased from 420 yuan in 2016 to 450 yuan in 2017.[11]

At present, the major issues for social insurance are the following: (1) The imbalance between income and expenditures. In recent years, the growth rate of expenditures from the social insurance fund has been higher than the income growth rate. In some integrated areas, especially in the middle and western regions of China, the current receipts of pension funds cannot cover expenditures, and financial subsidies and surplus retained from previous years should be used to ensure the payment of pensions. (2) The suspension or reduction of contributions is serious. In recent years, more than 30 million participants opted to stop contributing to the pension insurance, and the people actually making contributions only account for 85% of those participating in employee pension insurance. Some employers report a false contribution base or number of participants to avoid or delay contributions. (3) The rate of the basic pension insurance is too high. (4) The retirement age of urban workers is too low, leading to an increase in the dependency ratio. At present, the actual retirement age of urban enterprise workers is only 54, with an average life span of more than 20 years after retirement, but the minimum contribution period of pension insurance is only 15 years. An obvious imbalance can be seen between contributions and benefits. (5) The pressure to reduce the social insurance premium rate and the associated risks have increased. At present, many enterprises and governments would like to reduce the burdens on enterprises as soon as possible and lower the social insurance premium rate. However, because the funds received for pension insurance and health care insurance cannot cover expenditures, the reduction of the premium rate would further increase the pressure on the imbalance between receipts and payments and widen the gap between receipt and payment of the funds in the future. (6) No institutional guarantee has been provided for the long-term nursing of disabled or semi-disabled people, affecting the guarantee of life for more than 35 million people.

---

11 "Bulletin of the Ministry of Human Resources and Social Security on the Progress of Social Affairs Work in the 2nd Quarter of 2017," www.china.com.cn, July 28, 2017.

1.4 Safety in the Workplace Was Developing in a Good Way, and the Central Government Has Indicated the Direction That Further Development Should Take

In December 2016, the Central Committee of the Communist Party of China and the State Council issued the *Opinions on Promoting the Reform and Development of Safety in the Workplace* (hereinafter the Opinions). This is the first outline document issued by the Central Committee of CPC and the State Council concerning safety in the workplace since the founding of the new China. The Opinions stated that the red line that "development must not be realized at the cost of safety" should be upheld, specifying a system for the accountability of safety in the workplace and making it a requirement to (1) establish a mechanism whereby enterprises are responsible for implementing the entity responsibilities for safety in the workplace, (2) establish a system to supervise the correction of any identified problems, (3) establish a system to ensure that the supervisors of safety in the workplace can perform their obligations according to law, and (4) implement the one-vote veto system for major safety risks. The Opinions recommended modifying the related articles of the Criminal Law to include illegal activities that may easily lead to major accidents involving safety in the workplace during production and operations. After implementing the Opinions, supervision and law enforcement have been reinforced in all places and punishments have also improved. In the first three quarters of 2017, onsite inspections, administrative punishments, and the number of punishments witnessed year-on-year increases of 10.5%, 36.2%, and 73.1%, respectively, and the pre-supervision fines amounted to 1.49 billion yuan, with a year-on-year increase of 123%. The above measures were the major reasons for the good situation of safety in the workplace in 2017.

In the first three quarters of 2017, 36,000 safety incidents occurred in China, leading to 26,000 deaths, with year-on-year decreases of 26.3% and 19%, respectively. These incidents included 21 major accidents with 293 deaths, decreasing by 3 accidents and 66 deaths on a year-on-year basis, forming a pattern of double reductions in terms of the number of accidents and of deaths.[12] However, some industries and fields still have many major accidents, such as the road transportation and coal mining industries. From January to September 2017, in the road transportation and coal mining industries, 17 major production

---

12 "The General Situation of Safety in the Workplace Was Getting Better Stably in the First Three Quarters," official website of the State Administration of Work Safety, October 23, 2017.

and operational fire accidents occurred, accounting for 81% of the total number of major accidents in the first three quarters. The frequent occurrences of major accidents in the coal mining industry were caused by the that fact that some enterprises were producing beyond their capacity, given the constant increase in the price of coal since the second half of 2016.

In November 2017, to further promote the reform of delegating powers, streamlining administration, and optimizing services and to stimulate the innovative and creative vitality of the market and the society,[13] the *Law of the People's Republic of China on the Prevention and Control of Occupational Diseases* was amended at the 30th Session of the 12th Standing Committee of the NPC for the third time, relaxing the qualification criteria of the medical organizations providing occupational health inspections as well as the restrictions on the number of medical practitioners for occupational disease diagnosis.[14]

1.5 The Total Number of Labor Disputes and People Involved Has Been Reduced, but It Remained at a Historically High Level

In 2016, the labor dispute mediation and arbitration organizations in China resolved 1.771 million labor disputes, with a year-on-year increase of 2.9%. These disputes involved 2.268 million workers, decreasing by 2.1% year on year, and an amount of 47.18 billion yuan, increasing by 29% year on year. The success rate of mediation cases was 65.8%, and the settlement rate of arbitration cases was 95.5%.[15] In the first half of 2017, labor dispute mediation and arbitration organizations in different places dealt with more than 800,000 labor dispute cases, involving more than 900,000 people. Despite the year-on-year reduction, the number was still the second-highest in history.

For example, in Beijing, in the first half of 2017, the arbitration organizations of the whole city received 38,191 labor dispute cases, decreasing by 10.2% year on year; 13,996 workers were involved, with a year-on-year decrease of 21.3%. In general, the number of cases decreased to some extent. However, in terms of the cases received in the past 5 years, the total number of arbitration cases was only lower than that in 2016, and it remained at a high level without a tendency

---

13   "Explanation of the Amendments (Drafts) of 11 Laws Including the Accounting Law of the People's Republic of China," www.npc.gov.cn, November 4, 2017.

14   "Decision of the Standing Committee of the NPC on Modifying 11 Laws Including the Accounting Law of the People's Republic of China," www.npc.gov.cn, November 4, 2017.

15   "Statistical Bulletin on the Development of Human Resources and Social Security Undertakings in 2016," official website of the Ministry of Human Resources and Social Security, May 31, 2017.

toward significant reduction. With the progress of the industry still in a phase of transformation and updating, the uncertainties of labor relationships and the factors leading to the rebound of labor disputes still existed. The major features of the dispute cases in Beijing are as follows: (1) The base number of the cases was still large. The arbitration organizations of the city would accept more than 6,300 cases every month, and the total number of cases remained high in the same period in recent years. (2) The number of labor dispute cases for migrant workers increased by 8.7% on a year-on-year basis, accounting for 14.1% of the total number of cases. (3) The disputes were mainly about remuneration, economic compensations for terminations of labor relationships, and the compensation for social insurance. Disputes over remuneration were common for private enterprises, and disputes over salaries and overtime payments not only accounted for more than 70% of the disputes related to private enterprises but also for 54.9% of all remuneration disputes throughout the city. (4) The cases became more and more complicated, and the claims of the related parties were diversified, increasing the difficulty in reviewing those cases. (5) The number of cases of collective disputes diminished significantly on a year-on-year basis. The number of collective dispute cases and the number of workers involved in the first half of the year decreased by 8.0% and 21.3%, respectively. In particular, the number of cases concerning collective disputes involving more than 30 people and the number of workers involved decreased by 50.8% and 48.0%, respectively.

...

2 Current Conditions of Labor Relationships in the Sharing Economy

The Internet has permeated into all aspects of daily activity, profoundly changing the lifestyles and economic structure of the whole society. According to the report of the State Information Center, in 2016, the volume of market trading of the sharing economy of China was about 3,452 billion yuan, increasing by 10.3% over the previous year. Correspondingly, the number of service providers in the sharing economy in 2016 was about 60 million, and the number of the people working for sharing economy platforms was about 5.85 million.[16]

---

16 State Information Center, "2017 Annual Report on China's Sharing Economy," www.ccioa .com.cn, March 2, 2017.

2.1 The Sharing Economy Has Brought Various Forms of Flexible Employment

The digital technologies represented by the Internet have become an important driving force promoting the updating of consumption habits, economic and social transformation, and the formation of the new competitiveness of the country. According to the report, in the first half of 2017, commercial trading apps in China witnessed a rapid development, and the volume of users of online shopping, online take-out services, and online traveling bookings increased by 10.2%, 41.6%, and 11.5%, respectively. As of June 2017, the volume of the users of sub-fields of public services had witnessed increases, and the volumes of users of online education, online taxi hailing, online tailored taxi service / fast vehicle service and bike sharing had reached 144 million, 278 million, 217 million, and 106 million, respectively.[17] For example, the online take-out service witnessed the highest growth rate among the business trading Apps, accompanied by the rapid growth of the members of food delivery.

While increasing the number of practitioners, the sharing economy has also promoted more diversified forms of employment. In addition to typical full-time employees, there are part-time workers, non-full-time workers, and independent contractors. All of these forms of employment share the same features, namely, flexible work and a piecework system for salaries.

Thanks to the development of information technologies, employers do not need to provide concentrated workplaces, giving more freedom to workers. Employers can use contracting and cooperation agreements to effectively control labor costs and reduce their responsibilities, and the piecework system for salaries has become popular. This has provided workers with the opportunity to make more money by working harder, but could cause some problems. First of all, workers have to take certain market operation risks, and second, they have no guarantees. If they cannot work due to disease or family reasons, their income will drop to zero, without any sick leave wages or paid time off. In addition, if workers cannot adjust their working conditions, their physical condition and family life will be affected, and the quantity and quality of employment in the whole society will also be affected accordingly, leading to improper competition factors and impacting the labor cost of normal labor relationships.

---

17   China Internet Network Information Center, "The 40th China Statistical Report on Internet Development," www.ccioa.com.cn, August 4, 2017.

The new information technologies have posed challenges to the traditional salary system of working hours, and it is not clear how to meet such challenges. However, in the sharing economy, given the establishment of big data platforms, such platforms can handle the working hours of workers accurately. If online platforms can effectively use their data systems and data accumulation and analysis to reasonably arrange and guide the service time of workers, they can increase standardization of the ever-growing flexible employment system.

2.2 New Patterns of Employment Have Made Labor Relationships Unclear

The employment pattern of sharing economy enterprises, producing values based on online platforms, is not the traditional "company + employee" model but the "platform + individual" model. The platforms could provide technical services and resource-scheduling services to ensure that various services can be provided. This innovative model has changed the definition of working hours, workplaces, and working methods in the modern era of mechanical industry.

The outstanding feature of the new pattern of employment is the unclear labor relationship. Workers in the platform economy are often called independent contractors or business partners; this arrangement has replaced the traditional labor system, which has employer-employee relations as its basic principle and the labor contract as its core. It has become a common problem in many countries to adapt labor laws to apply to such workers. The companies possessing platforms consider these practitioners as business partners and independent contractors, but not workers in the legal sense, and they make cooperation agreements with them. However, with the development of the sharing economy, many practitioners have made the sharing economy their major source of income, and more and more practitioners from different industries are requesting confirmation of their labor relationships. In such labor disputes, the practitioners claim that they are subject to the management of the employers and that they follow the rules of the employers and provide services that are integral parts of the employers' businesses, so the relationship between them and the employers should be a labor relationship. The employers deny the existence of a labor relationship on the basis of the cooperation agreements and defend that position on the basis of their management of the working process. For example, in 2014, when judging a labor dispute involving a substitute driving service company, the employer said that practitioners were free to select their working hours and places and to determine when to take breaks without being controlled or managed by the company, and that because drivers were collecting fees directly from clients without being paid by the company, they should pay an information service fee to the company. In the end, the court did not confirm the labor relationship.[18] However, in 2016, when judging who was liable to provide compensation following a traffic accident caused by car sharing, although the labor relationship between the substitute driving service company and the driver was not confirmed, the court determined that the company "as the platform provider should audit the vehicles on the platform, and that the company has defined operation regions for the driver, so there was a managing-managed relationship between the two parties." Finally, the court judged that the company should assume joint and several liability.[19] In judicial practices in foreign countries, such a problem has also arisen. For example, Uber faces claims regarding labor relationship confirmation in the United States and in the UK that have not been judged yet.

2.3 Advances in Information Technologies Have Eroded the Boundary between Life and Work

With the development of information technologies, working hours and locations have become more and more flexible. However, with the convenience of communication and the accuracy of positioning that are realized through new information technologies, the personal time of workers has been reduced due to the mixture of work and life. At present, the long working time and high working pressure of technical workers on the Internet has become a common motif of workplace culture. The root cause is market pressure. Most Internet enterprises are obtaining market shares by providing round-the-clock services, setting high requirements for the number of hours that workers are expected to put in. To catch up with schedules and deal with various emergencies, enterprises have to provide solutions promptly; otherwise, they would be eliminated. In a flat management system, such pressure could be directly transferred to grassroots employees.

---

18   "Paper of Civil Judgment of the 1st Trial of the Labor Dispute between Wang Zheshuan and Beijing Yixin Yixing Auto Technological Development Service Co., Ltd.," Beijing Shijingshan District People's Court [2014] Shi Min Chu Zi No. 367; judgment date: December 15, 2014.

19   "Paper of Civil Judgment of the 2nd Trial of a Traffic Accident Liability Dispute between Xu Xiaoyin and Beijing Yixin Yixing Auto Technological Development Service Co., Ltd.," Beijing No. 3 Intermediate People's Court [2015] San Zhong Min Zhong Zi No. 04810; judgment date: May 27, 2016.

As for the service practitioners in the sharing economy, their lives have been totally integrated with their work due to methods of real-time communication. For example, online car-hailing drivers have to stay online to avoid missing out on clients, but they are not paid for the time they spend waiting. Yet when they are on standby, their time is not considered leisure time, since they are subject to high mental pressure even though they are not working. The long working hours have significantly influenced the personal health and life of workers, and the frequency of deaths and depressive disorders due to overwork has become a social problem worth our attention. We can say that information technologies have made the working process more intelligent and have improved the efficiency of work, but they have not freed the laborers and have even expanded their work, dipping into the time that workers dedicate to their personal lives.

2.4 Uncertainties in Work and Employment Have Increased

The rapid changes of the market and technologies have also influenced employment relationships. From a long-term perspective, technical development will significantly improve the convenience and comfort of the lives of the people. However, from the short-term perspective, rapid technical development will generate an uncertain influence on employment due to the replacement of human labor by automation and AI. AI and machine learning abilities indicate that science and technology are obtaining a cognitive competence that used to be considered the unique capacity of human beings. In terms of complicated tasks, robots are surpassing humans. As time goes by, robots will become more capable and cheaper. In this process, options for new jobs should be explored in order to give play to the unique creativity of human beings, and a good training system and social security system will be needed to complete the transformation and transition. To determine what jobs are suitable for robots and humans may become an important problem for labor and employment in the future.

3 Current Conditions of the Industrial Labor Force and Contents of the Reform Plan

In the new historical stage of socialism with Chinese characteristics, labor relationships under the "new normal" economic conditions are becoming more and more flexible, and new changes have occurred in the labor force. Therefore, in 2017, the All China Federation of Trade Unions (ACFTU) conducted the 8th

Survey of Employees' Working Conditions, covering 15 provinces, to summarize the current features and development of the labor force and provide theoretical support for the construction and reform of the labor force.

3.1 New Changes to the Labor Force

For example, in Guangdong, in terms of labor distribution, the Pearl River Delta is still the major employment area, but the proportion of workers in other areas has been increasing. Growth of practitioners in the manufacturing industry has slowed down, while practitioners in the service industry have witnessed a rapid growth. In Guangdong too, where the manufacturing industry is fundamental to the economy, the source structure of the labor force has changed, and the tendency to employ local people has become greater. The numbers of employees in the public sector units and enterprises invested in Hong Kong, Macau, and Taiwan have diminished in number, and those of the employees in foreign-invested enterprises and private enterprises have increased rapidly. The educational backgrounds of the workers have changed greatly. The average period of education of workers was 13.2 years, higher than that in 2012 by 0.5. The degree of education of manufacturing workers has seen an obvious increase. In terms of the composition of the labor force, the new generation of migrant workers has become the major workforce, and they have a higher educational background. The Internet has become an important space where they can obtain information and conduct social interactions, significantly changing their styles of living and working. In addition, new business patterns have provided workers with new developmental opportunities, changing their concepts of employment and weakening their consciousness of solidarity.

In Zhejiang, the labor force has distinct regional characteristics. At present, Zhejiang has an industrial labor force of about 20 million workers, including about 14 million in secondary industry and nearly 5 million in tertiary industry. Workers aged 35 and below accounted for 50%, and those with an educational background of junior high school and below also accounted for 50%. Nearly 80% of workers are employed in the manufacturing industry, nearly 80% of them are migrant workers, and nearly 80% of them are concentrated in the industrial cluster districts. At the end of 2015, the average educational period of the new workers was 13.5 years, and the total number of highly skilled talents at the end of 2016 was 2.45 million. In the industrial labor force in the new age, migrant workers have become the major force. Workers in the downstream service industry of the new economic system have become a new force, and various workers in fields related to knowledge, technology, and innovation, as well as compound-type high-skill workers, have become the leading force.[20] The skills and quality of the industrial labor force in Zhejiang have been improving, the regional distribution has been aggregating, the degree of organization has been improving, and the influence of new elements has been increasing, fully reflecting the characteristics of Zhejiang, namely, private economy, industry-city integration, industrial clusters, Internet+, and AI+.

In Henan, by the end of 2016, the labor force totaled 28.05 million, increasing by 7.5 million over 2011 with an average annual increase of 1.5 million. The workers accounted for 41.7% of the total labor force of the province, increasing by 0.8 percentage points over 2011. The following features are noteworthy. First of all, after three increases and three reductions, the structure of the labor force has witnessed steady growth. "Three increases and three reductions" means that the proportion of workers in tertiary industry increased while that of workers in primary industry decreased; the proportion of workers in the non-public sector increased while that of workers in state-owned and collective enterprises decreased; and the proportion of workers in emerging industries and new economic business patterns increased while that of workers in the traditional manufacturing industry diminished. At the end of 2016, the proportions of workers in the three industries were 38.4%, 30.6%, and 31%, respectively. Compared to 2011, the proportion of workers in tertiary industry had increased by 4 percentage points, the proportion of workers in primary industry had decreased by 4.7 percentage points, and the proportion of workers in secondary industry had not changed too much. Second, two major forces had obvious features and were changing constantly: the new generation of workers has become the major labor force, while migrant workers have become the major component of the industrial labor force. According to a survey, workers aged 40 and below accounted for 58.7% and those aged 40–50 accounted for 30%. By the end of 2016, 28.76 million rural laborers in Henan had moved to cities, including 17.09 million who had moved within the province. Most new-generation workers are the only child in their families and they have high educational backgrounds, high occupational expectations, high requirements for mental and material enjoyment, and low working tolerance in terms of personalities, values, and outlook on life. The profile of the new generation of migrant workers has changed from farmers to workers; from

---

20   Zhejiang Provincial Federation of Trade Unions, "Embodying Zhejiang Industry Characteristics, Showing Features of Industrial Labor Force, and Integrating Elements and Claims of Trade Unions," materials for the Theory and Policy Research Meeting of ACFTU, September 2017.

making money in the city and going back home for development to seeking jobs, experiencing life, and pursuing dreams in cities; and from endurance to pursuit of equal rights. Finally, the degree of freedom of employment for workers has increased, showing a more flexible pattern. Small and medium-sized enterprises and tertiary industry have become the major force providing jobs. New industries, new business patterns, and new models have witnessed rapid development. New patterns of employment have provided workers with new options and generated new features such as unfixed workplaces, more flexible working hours, and diversified service subjects. The workers' concept of employment has been changing. They have paid more attention to their working environment, benefits, occupational stability, and developmental opportunities for the future. Seeking jobs online has become the first choice for workers, especially young people who are looking for jobs. Migrant workers prefer to work in their hometowns, and some of them have changed from indus-trial laborers into business workers. In the first half of 2017, 137,200 migrant workers returned to their hometowns to start their own businesses, and 76,700 enterprises were established, providing jobs to 1.1494 million people.[21]

In Beijing, reducing the non-capital functions and establishing a sophisti-cated economic structure has brought distinct changes to the structure of the labor force. The year 2013 was a turning point for workers in the manufacturing industry, whose numbers had been increasing annually but began to decline year by year. In 2016, the number of workers in the manufacturing industry decreased by 204,000 over 2012. The number of workers in the wholesale and retail industries in 2016 was 700,000, decreasing by 6,000 over the previous year. During the adjustment, Beijing also made great efforts to develop the high-end production service industry, and the number of workers in tertiary industry accounts for 80.1% of the total number of workers. The information transmis-sion, software, and information technology industries as well as the scientific research and technical service industries have witnessed rapid growth in terms of number of workers for nearly 10 years, providing a sufficient guarantee of talent for the establishment of scientific and technological innovation centers in Beijing. In 2016, the number of workers in the above two industries reached 680,000 and 638,000, increasing by 32.8% and 28.9%, respectively, over 2012. In addition, the online-hailing economy witnessed a rapid increase in the number of its employees. As of 2016, the number of registered drivers of Didi

---

21 Liu Xuefeng, "New Tendencies and Features of the Development of the Labor Force," materials for the Theory and Policy Research Meeting of ACFTU, September 2017.

Chuxing in Beijing had reached 1 million. Nearly 100,000 workers (including part-time workers) were on the 58 platform of Beijing, including about 10,000 full-time workers. Baidu Takeaway had about 20,000 employees in Beijing, and FlashEx had more than 100,000 deliverymen in Beijing. In addition, based on the Going-Out developmental strategy, more and more foreign companies have established themselves in Beijing with plans for expansion, and the number of employees at those companies also increased rapidly. In general, the employment situation of workers in Beijing has remained stable. According to the survey, 77.3% of workers said that they had not been laid off, nor had they had to wait long for a job, nor had they experienced resettlement in the past five years; 60.7% of them were not concerned about unemployment. Incomes and guarantees for workers have been improving steadily.

3.2 New Issues for the Building of the Labor Force

In this survey, we also found some typical new issues and conditions at the national or regional level. (1) More labor disputes occurred during the downturn of the economy. Salary arrears was the most important reason. Labor disputes caused by unpaid wages in some provinces accounted for about 70% of the total number of labor disputes. Other major causes of labor disputes included the suspension of contributions to social insurance and housing provident funds, and the consolidation, transfer, and personnel reduction caused by the transformation and updating of enterprises. The group, industrial, and chain features of the disputes were prominent, and some strikes were not justifiable. (2) The guarantee of the rights and interests of employees should be further improved. In particular, in the new business patterns, labor relationships have not been defined clearly, generating a blind spot in guaranteeing the rights and interests of employees. According to the survey, most online-hailing platforms have not signed labor contracts with their workers, and most of the sharing economy platforms believe that the relationship between them and their workers is a cooperative relationship and not an employment relationship. Workers were in a position of disadvantage and had no voice in terms of making rules for salary and benefits, and government supervision of the platforms should be further improved.[22] The right of the employees to rest can hardly be ensured, and overtime compensation is not enough in some industries.

---

22 Research Office of Beijing Federation of Trade Unions, "Strengthening Right Protection Services, Streamlining Development Channels, and Building a Labor Force Meeting the Functional Positioning of Capital," materials for the Theory and Policy Research Meeting of ACFTU, September 2017.

(3) There are barriers to the social mobility of the labor force, such as identity rights, children's education, medical resources, and city public services. (4) The social values of the workers have diversified in the transformation period. Especially, the development of mobile network media has generated a diversified media transmission pattern, and the Internet, smartphones, microblogs, and WeChat have established more convenient platforms for the transmission of information, thus increasing the channels by which employees are able to obtain information and improving the diversity of social values. (5) There are a lot of difficulties for new migrant workers seeking to become citizens under the obvious influence of the system of the transformation of costs, the qualities of the migrant workers, and the traditional household register system. (6) The scale of non-formal employment has expanded, and some workers are facing job instability. Such jobs usually had unofficial labor relationships (no contract or no valid contract, temporary employment, and salaries determined randomly), were not supervised by governments, and had low-level employment features and positions, such as labor dispatching, outsourced employees, student workers, and casual labor.[23] (7) The sharing economy based on the Internet has created wholly new forms of working, which are reflected in terms of employment fields, techniques, methods of organization, and concepts of working, and the labor force is being shaped in a new way. Therefore, deep research and rules are needed in this aspect.

3.3 Main Contents of the Reform Plan for the Construction of an Industrial Labor Force

In May 2015, the State Council issued *Made in China 2025*. This document was the great blueprint for the Manufacturing Power Strategy at the national level, which is of great importance to the "new normal" economic conditions, the promotion of stable growth, the adjustment of structure, and the transformation of economic methods. However, the document also pointed out that the total working age population is decreasing, the advantage of low-cost labor is vanishing rapidly, and the overall qualities and skills of the industrial labor force are not high enough, limiting the realization of the target of the Manufacturing Power Strategy. Therefore, in April 2017, the Central Committee of the Communist Party of China and the State Council issued the *Reform Plan*

---

23   Wu Guozhang, "New Changes, New Issues, and New Conditions of the Labor Force in Guangdong and Related Countermeasures and Suggestions," materials for the Theory and Policy Research Meeting of ACFTU, September 2017.

for the Construction of an Industrial Labor Force in the New Age (hereinafter the Plan), making improvement of the overall quality of the labor force a strategic task to be accomplished by establishing a labor force with knowledge, skills, and innovations, and fully motivating front-line workers, manufacturing workers, and migrant workers.

This is the first time in the history of the Party and our country that a plan was made and implemented to make specific arrangements for the construction of the industrial labor force. In the Plan, 25 reform measures[24] were proposed under five headings, namely: strengthening and improving the political and ideological construction of the industrial labor force, establishing a system of skills formation for the industrial labor force, using the Internet to promote the construction of an industrial labor force, innovating the developmental system for the industrial labor force, and strengthening the support and guarantees for the construction of that labor force. This program involved systems and mechanisms related to ideological guidance, skill improvement, functions, and support and guarantees.

First of all, we should strengthen and improve the ideological and political construction of the industrial labor force. President Xi Jinping pointed out that we should not forget that the fundamental policy of the Party is to wholeheartedly depend on the working class. This policy should be implemented in all aspects related to economic, political, cultural, social, and ecological construction and Party building, as well as the entire processes of policy making and promotion, and should be reflected in all links of the production and operation of enterprises. In the Plan, reform measures have been proposed to strengthen and improve the ideological and political construction of an industrial labor force, involving the Party in forming an industrial labor force, supplying ideological and political guidance, and promoting labor union reform.

Second, we should build a high-quality manufacturing labor force that can meet the requirements of *Made in China 2025*. In the Plan, six major measures were proposed to establish a system of skill formation for the industrial labor force: (1) We should improve the modern system of occupational education by strengthening the organic connections among occupational education, continuing education, and general education; upholding the integration of production and teaching, cooperation between schools and enterprises, the combination of workers and students, and the mixture of knowledge and

---

24   Unless specified otherwise, the data in this section are from Li Yubin: *New Mission and Burden—Interpretation of the Reform Plan for the Construction of an Industrial Labor Force in the New Age*, China Worker Press, 2017.

practical experiences; and innovating the occupational educational modes at all levels. (2) We should reform the system of occupational skill training; promote the reform of marketing, socializing, and diversifying the occupational training courses; and establish a skill training mechanism with equal competition among various training organizations, the independent participation of the industrial labor force, and the services purchased by governments. (3) We should coordinate the development of vocational school education and occupational training, establish a system of occupational education and training with large coverage, various forms, standardized operations, and the joint participation of the industry, enterprises, schools, and social forces; and promote the vertical connection and horizontal recognition of diploma and non-diploma forms of education. (4) We need to improve the skills evaluation method for the industrial labor force, optimize the classification standards for occupational skills, improve the policies of classification certification for occupational skills, and guide and support enterprises, industrial organizations, and social organizations in conducting skills evaluation independently. (5) We should implement the national plan for the revitalization of highly skilled talents, innovate cooperative training modes, and build model training bases for highly skilled talents in large backbone enterprises in order to cultivate more highly skilled talents. (6) We should promote the integration of migrant workers into cities, stabilize their jobs, and implement an action plan for improving the education and capacity of migrant workers as well as a plan for improving their occupational skills.

Third, we should innovate the developmental system for the industrial labor force. In the Plan, six types of measures were proposed: (1) We should expand the developmental spaces for the industrial labor force and reform the dual-rail management system that separates enterprise staff management from labor management. (2) We should ensure the smooth flow of the channels for the industrial labor force, improve the public employment service system, and enhance the efficiency of human resource allocation for them. (3) We should innovate the skills-oriented incentive mechanism and establish an incentive system integrating cultivation, examination, utilization, and benefits to make it possible for more productive workers and skilled workers to earn more. A system should be established to allow technical workers to participate in the elements and distribution of the achievements of innovation, and to increase the proportion of the industrial labor force in the evaluation of working models and advanced representatives. (4) We should improve the labor and technical system of competition by establishing a mechanism for labor and skills competition based on job training and technical competition, with competitions in national and industrial occupational skills as the main body, and domestic and international competitions as supplementary ones. (5) We need to improve support for the industrial labor force's innovation and efficiency, deepen mass technological innovation activities, carry out a summary of the naming and promotion activities in advanced operation methods, and promote qualified industrial enterprises to establish employee innovation studios, model labor innovation studios, and skill master studios. (6) We should organize the industrial labor force so that they can participate in the "Going-Out" strategy and the construction of the Belt and Road Initiative, so as to strengthen their international exchanges and cooperation with respect to the acquisition of skills.

Fourth, we should use the Internet to promote the construction of an industrial labor force by implementing three major measures: (1) We should renovate the network carrier for the construction of the industrial labor force and establish and improve the basic database for that labor force. (2) We should establish some online learning platforms to integrate the lifelong learning of the industrial labor force into the stockpiling of information in urban and rural areas. (3) We should promote Internet+ services and establish the Employee Home on the Internet.

Fifth, we should make more efforts to craft policies that safeguard the rights and interests of the industrial labor force. The Plan calls for strengthening the legal guarantee for the construction of the industrial labor force, improving the financial input mechanism, establishing a mechanism for diversified social input, enhancing the mechanism to ensure economic benefits to the industrial labor force, deepening research on theories and policies for the construction of the industrial labor force, and creating a social atmosphere that respects laborers, admires skills, and encourages different types of creativity.

References

Central Committee of the Communist Party of China and the State Council. "Reform Plan for the Construction of an Industrial Labor Force in the New Age," April 2017.

Li Yubin. *New Mission and Burden—Interpretation of the Reform Plan for the Construction of an Industrial Labor Force in the New Age*. China Worker Press, 2017.

Materials of the Theory and Policy Research Meeting of ACFTU, September 2017.

National Bureau of Statistics. "The 2016 National Report on Migrant Worker Monitoring and Survey." Official website of the National Bureau of Statistics, April 28, 2017.

"Press Conference Held by the Information Office for the National Economic Operation in the First Three Quarters." www.gov.cn, October 19, 2017.

"Press Conference of the 3rd Quarter of 2017 Held by the Ministry of Human Resources and Social Security." Official website of the Ministry of Human Resources and Social Security, November 1, 2017.

Report to the 19th CPC National Congress, October 2017.

CHAPTER 18

Analytical Report on Rural Household Development in China in 2017

Peng Chao[1] and Zhang Xiaorong[2]

Abstract

With the implementation of a series of policies related to agriculture, rural areas, and rural residents, the production and living conditions of farmers have improved significantly. Understanding the current conditions of farmers could help us to better evaluate the effects of the policies and lay a policy foundation for the development of agriculture in the future. In this report, we have used data from the fixed observation points in rural areas nationwide to analyze the current production and living conditions of farmers from the perspective of rural households and different agricultural operational methods. The details of the analysis include the educational backgrounds of householders, the working time of householders, the skills training of householders, household income and expenditure, the land conditions of households, and the output of agricultural products.

Keywords

farmers – income and expenditure – land conditions

The Report to the 19th CPC National Congress pointed out that we should "establish a modern agricultural and industrial system, production system, and operational system; improve the system of agricultural support and protection; develop various operations with appropriate scales; forge new agricultural operational subjects; improve the socialized service system for agriculture; and realize the organic connection between agricultural households with combined

---

1 Peng Chao, deputy director and associate research fellow of the Management Department of Rural Fixed Observation Points of the Research Center for Rural Economy.
2 Zhang Xiaorong, postgraduate of Renmin University of China and research assistant of the Research Center for Rural Economy, with the research fields of agricultural policies and rural household economy.

© KONINKLIJKE BRILL NV, LEIDEN, 2022 | DOI:10.1163/9789004500723_019

occupations and modern agricultural development." At present, the operational subject of the new agriculture and the traditional rural household cannot exist at the same time, and the policies formulated by the government are not specific enough. For example, for the system of high-standard farmland implemented by the agricultural departments, given the huge construction input, some local governments have to borrow from banks to construct high-standard farmlands, but they have failed to define who shall repay the loans. Therefore, we should break down the existing subjects of production and operations and conduct the analysis in terms of labor supply and amounts of fixed assets in order to provide a data reference for making agricultural policies. Specifically, in this report, we have analyzed three groups to provide solid reference data for making policies, namely, rural households with combined occupations (working without hiring laborers), farming-only households (not working and not hiring laborers), and family farms (not working and hiring laborers).

The data used herein are from the fixed observation points in rural areas nationwide in 2016. The survey subjects of the fixed observation points of the Ministry of Agriculture are distributed in 31 provinces (autonomous regions and municipalities), excluding Hong Kong, Macau, and Taiwan, covering 355 counties (county-level cities and districts), and 360 administrative villages. A total of 23,000 rural households were surveyed in 2016.

1 Basic Conditions of Rural Households

According to the survey, the ages of the householders of rural households were relatively high, with an average age of 56. Most householders were aged 50–59, accounting for 30.49% of the total samples; householders aged 60–69 accounted for 28.59%; and those aged 40–49 accounted for 22.41% (see Figure 18.1).

In terms of gender, most of the householders were males. Male accounted for 91.73% of householders and females only accounted for 8.27%. In terms of educational background, most householders had a junior high school education or below, accounting for 91.18% of the total samples. To be specific, householders with no schooling accounted for 1.85%, those with a primary school education accounted for 42.91%, and those with a junior high school education accounted for 46.42%. In addition, some householders had higher educational backgrounds, but the proportion was relatively low. Householders with a college education or above accounted for only 0.67% (see Figure 18.2).

In terms of political status, only a few householders were CPC members; in contrast, 16.04% of rural households contain CPC members, and 83.96% of them only contain ordinary people. In terms of ethnic groups, few rural

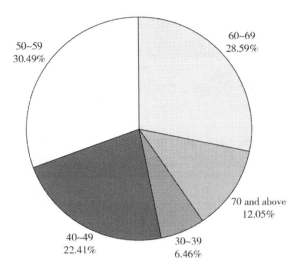

FIGURE 18.1   Householder Age Distribution

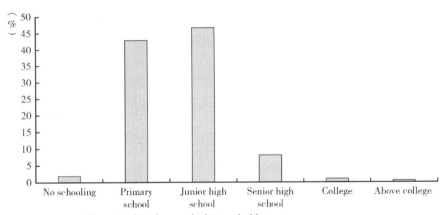

FIGURE 18.2   Educational Background of Householders

households were from minority groups; in fact, only 11.79% of rural households included members of minority groups. In addition, households with members working as village cadres accounted for 4.17% (see Figure 18.3).

The data showed that the average number of permanent residents of each household was four. Households with less than three permanent residents accounted for 49.08% of the total samples, and those containing four to six permanent residents accounted for 46%. Furthermore, the average housing area of each household measured 158.59 square meters. In terms of the cultivated land of the rural households, the households with more than 5 *mu* (about 3,333 square meters) of cultivated land (including contracting farmland, flexible

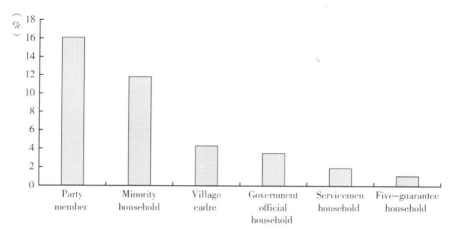

FIGURE 18.3   Family Characteristics of Rural Households

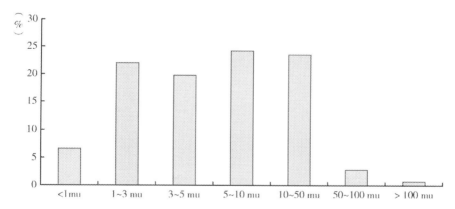

FIGURE 18.4   Distribution of Farmland Area of Rural Households

farmland contracted from village committees, and subcontracting farmland) at the end of the year accounted for 51.36% of the total sample (see Figure 18.4).

It was common for rural residents to work part-time. Among the rural residents working part-time locally, those who worked for less than one month accounted for 25.96% of the total sample, and those who worked for less than 3 months accounted for 51.14% (see Figure 18.5). By contrast, their working time in other places was longer than the local working time, and 55.22% of rural residents work for more than 10 months in other places (see Figure 18.6).

At present, the family expenditures of the rural households surveyed at the fixed observation points are mainly spent on the following aspects: operational expenditures of the household, productive fixed-asset expenditures, non-operational investments of the household, taxes paid to governments,

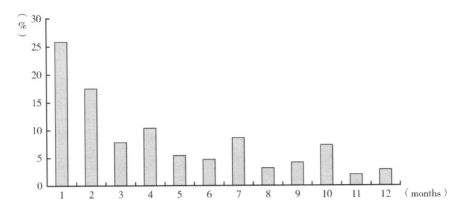

FIGURE 18.5   Local Working Time

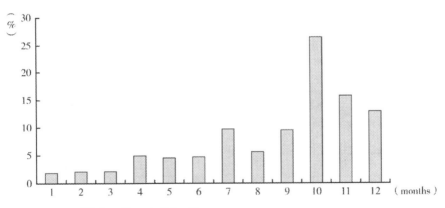

FIGURE 18.6   Working Time in Other Places

collective expenditures submitted to village committees, consumption expenditures for living necessities, and other non-loan expenditures. The consumption expenditures for necessities of life include expenditures on food, clothing, housing, fuel, articles, insurance, life services (including medical fees), cultural services (including educational tuitions), traveling, transportation, and communication and other items. In 2016, the average total expenditure of the surveyed rural households was 50,061.61 yuan, including a total amount of 31,681.24 yuan for expenditures on necessities, accounting for 63.28% of total household expenditures. Among the expenditures on necessities, the major item is food, which accounted for 32% of the total. In addition, expenditures on life services, cultural services, and transportation and communication each accounted for about 8% of the total expenditures on necessities, and traveling expenditures accounted for 1% (see Figure 18.7).

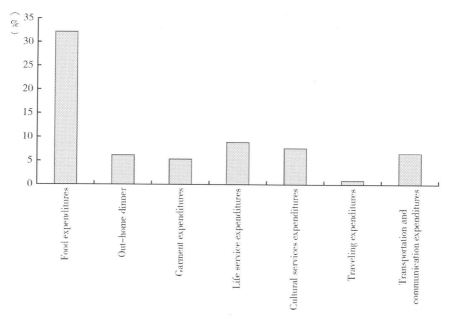

FIGURE 18.7   Proportion of Total Expenditures Spent on Necessities

2   The Status of Different Production and Operational Subjects

Through crop diversification, the industrialization of agriculture, and non-agricultural jobs, rural residents have realized a level of household accumulation that cannot be achieved under man-made restrictions. At the same time, differences among rural households in terms of technical skills and capacity for market participation have led to a great difference in income structure and employment structure, which diversifies the rural households through the circulation of self-accumulation. Rural household differentiation is a process through which the rural households in a given area are differentiated by becoming rural households of homogeneous operations or heterogeneous rural households operating in agriculture, industry, or commerce. Pure rural households differentiate into rural households with combined occupations and non-agricultural households, forming a pattern of coexistence and constant mutual involvement between farming-only households, rural households with combined occupations, and non-agricultural households.

Therefore, in this report, we have divided the surveyed rural households into three groups according to the existing documents and according to working time and the time spent on hiring others during production and operations: rural households with combined occupations, farming-only households, and family farms. Rural households with combined occupations provide laborers to other rural households while operating their own businesses without hiring others. During production and operations, farming-only households neither provide laborers to others nor do they hire others to aid the household. Family farms do not provide laborers to others, but they hire other laborers. At the time of the survey, among all of the samples, there were 9,272 rural households with combined occupations, 9,655 farming-only households, and 541 family farms (see Table 18.1).

TABLE 18.1   Classification of Rural Households

Type	Work or not	Hire laborers or not	Sample number
Rural households with mixed occupations	Yes	No	9272
Farming-only households	No	No	9655
Family farms	No	Yes	541

2.1   *Personal Characteristics of Householders*

Householders differed by type, but the age distribution was basically the same. Most householders of rural households with combined occupations were more than 50 years old, accounting for 71% of the total sample, where the householders of rural households with combined occupations aged 40–49 accounted for 23%, those aged 50–59 accounted for 33%, and those aged 60–69 accounted for 30%. As for farming-only households, householders aged over 50 accounted for 73% of the total sample, while householders of farming-only households aged 40 and below accounted for 7%, those aged 40–49 accounted for 21%, those aged 50–59 accounted for 26%, those aged 60–69 accounted for 29%, and those aged 70 and above accounted for 18%. Most of the responsible people on family farms were more than 50 years old, accounting for 75% of the total sample; the responsible people aged 40–49 accounted for 18%, those aged 50–59 accounted for 27%, those aged 60–69 accounted for 27%, and those aged 70 and above accounted for 21% (see Figure 18.8). Therefore, most of the householders/responsible people had higher ages and only a few young people opted to pursue agriculture.

In terms of educational background, most householders have been educated, but most of them only had a junior high school education, while a smaller portion had received only a primary school education. The educational backgrounds of householders varied. Most of the responsible people on family farms had a junior high school education, accounting for 37%, or a primary

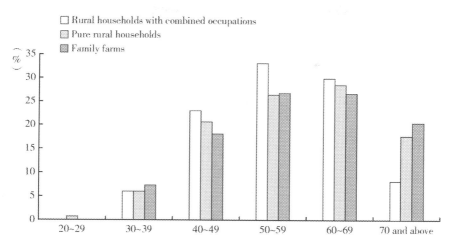

FIGURE 18.8   Age Structure of Rural Householders according to Type

school education, accounting for 31%; in the rural households with combined occupations, householders with a junior high school education accounted for 48% and those with a primary school education accounted for 42%; and as for the farming-only households, householders with a primary school education accounted for 42% and those with a junior high school education accounted for 41% (see Figure 18.9).

2.2 Family Characteristics

In terms of political status, the proportion of rural households containing party members was relatively high. Among rural households with combined occupations, the party-member households accounted for 16.16%; the proportion in farming-only households was 16.14% and in family farms 17.5%. Pure rural households that included government officials accounted for 4.41%, while the proportion on family farms was 3.75%. Rural households with combined occupations that included village cadres accounted for 4.4%, while the proportion on family farms was 4.17%. In addition, households that included revolutionary martyrs and servicemen and households enjoying the five guarantees accounted for 1.7% and 1%, respectively (see Figure 18.10).

In general, the average number of permanent residents in rural households was four, and the different types of rural households were not so different in this respect. For example, the number of permanent residents on family farms was the highest, at 4.28 people, and the numbers for rural households with combined occupations and farming-only households were close—3.7 and 3.6 people, respectively. The number of laborers in rural households of different types were quite different. Rural households with combined occupations and

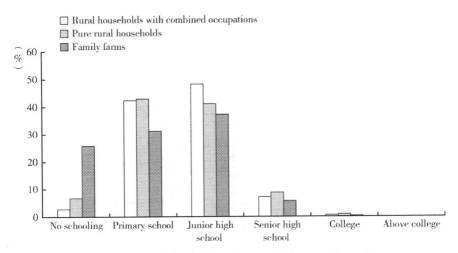

FIGURE 18.9   Educational Background of Rural Householders according to Type

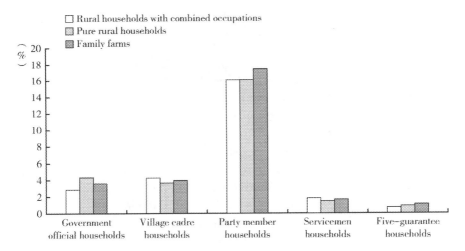

FIGURE 18.10   Status of the Members of Rural Households

farming-only households had more laborers (10.46 and 8.19, respectively), in each case twice the number of permanent residents. However, on family farms, the number of laborers was less than that of the permanent residents, with an average value of 2.59 people (see Figure 18.11). Furthermore, the time spent living at home varied among rural households. Members of rural households with combined occupations spent the most time at home, 330 days per year; the number for farming-only households was 281 days, and for the responsible people on family farms, 248 days.

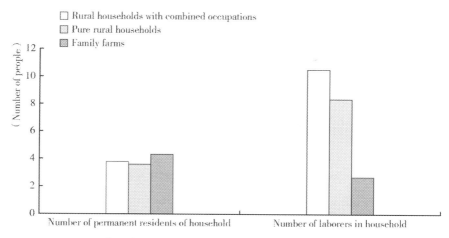

FIGURE 18.11   Number of Permanent Residents and Laborers in Rural Households

In each type of rural household, certain householders were religious, but the proportions were no higher than 20%. Looking at the various types of rural households, religious householders on family farms accounted for 15.83%, which was the highest among the three types of rural households, and in fact higher than the sum of the other two types. Rural households with combined occupations contained the lowest proportion of religious householders, accounting for only 3.61% of the total samples (see Figure 18.12).

2.3   *Incomes*

The total annual income of the households surveyed at the observation points included household operating income, salary income, leasing income, interest income, dividend income, land requisition compensation, government subsidies, and pension benefits. The average annual income of rural households with combined occupations was 60,495.1 yuan; the number for farming-only households was 70,941.2 yuan, and for family farms 101,656.8 yuan.

In general, most of the rural households had an income between 10,000 and 100,000 yuan. Among rural households with combined occupations, rural households with an annual income of 10,000 to 50,000 yuan formed the largest proportion, 49.85%; these were followed by rural households with an annual income of 50,000 to 100,000 yuan, accounting for 35.15%. Among farming-only households, those with an annual income of 10,000 to 50,000 yuan were in the majority, 41.79%; they were followed by farming-only households with an annual income of 50,000 to 100,000 yuan, accounting for 35.80%. Among family farms, conditions were different from both the rural households with

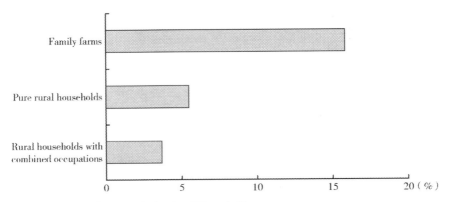
FIGURE 18.12   Religious Belief in Rural Households

combined occupations and farming-only households; the rural households with an annual income of 50,000 to 100,000 yuan made up the largest proportion, 39.04%, and they were followed by those with an annual income of 10,000 to 50,000 yuan, accounting for 37.37%. However, a small number of rural households had relatively high incomes. For example, about 0.3% of rural households with combined occupations and 0.73% of farming-only households had an income of more than 500,000 yuan, and the proportion for family farms was 3.13% (see Figure 18.13).

Annual household income included government subsidies, such as the subsidy for returning grain fields to forestry or grasslands, and agricultural subsidies (direct grain subsidy and subsidy for growing superior grain cultivars). The average government subsidy for rural households with combined occupations was 1,112.81 yuan, that for farming-only households was 883.23 yuan, and that for family farms was 4,370.65 yuan (see Figure 18.14).

2.4   Expenditures
2.4.1   Total Household Expenditures
In terms of total household expenditures, the amount for family farms was the highest, with an average value of 76,447.98 yuan; farming-only households were second at 48,826.58 yuan, and rural households with combined occupations spent 43,450.85 yuan (see Figure 18.15).

2.4.2   Total Expenditures on Living Necessities
For farming-only households, the ratio of expenditures on necessities of life to total household expenditures was relatively high, at about 70.58%; the proportion for rural households with combined occupations was 63.42% and that for family farms was 47.99% (see Figure 18.16).

ANALYTICAL REPORT ON RURAL HOUSEHOLD DEVELOPMENT IN CHINA

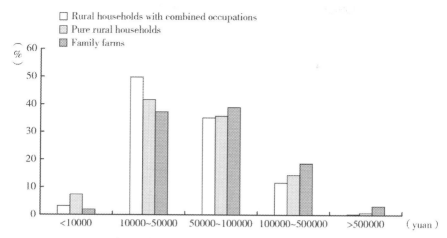

FIGURE 18.13   Annual Household Income

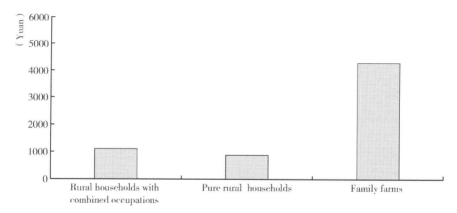

FIGURE 18.14   Government Subsidies

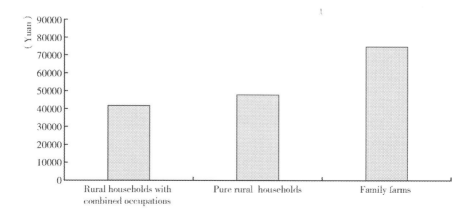

FIGURE 18.15   Total Household Expenditures

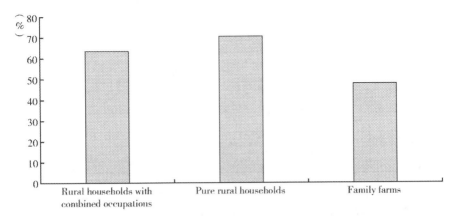

FIGURE 18.16   Proportion of Total Household Expenditures Spent on Necessities of Life

2.4.2.1   Food Expenditures

The proportion of food expenditures in the total expenditures of rural households was relatively small, which was 22.02% for farming-only households, 20.68% for rural households with combined occupations and 15.1% for family farms. In addition, the proportions of food expenditures in the expenditures on living necessities of the three types of rural households were not very different, which were 32.61% for rural households with combined occupations, 31.19% for farming-only households and 31.47% for family farms. Furthermore, we subdivided the food expenditure indicator at the observation points, and the proportions of the expenditures on eating-out were similar for the rural households with combined occupations and the farming-only households, which were 20.22% and 20.59% respectively, with an amount difference of about 300 yuan. The proportion for family farms was 18.86% (see Figure 18.17).

2.4.2.2   Expenditures on Entertainment

Among life expenditures, the proportion of food expenditures was relatively high, followed by life services expenditures, cultural services expenditures, garment expenditures, and transportation and communication expenditures, where the life services expenditures, cultural services expenditures, and traveling expenditures served as indicators for improving living standards and entertainment. In general, expenditures on entertainment on family farms were higher than those of rural households with combined occupations and farming-only households.

For the three types of rural households, food expenditure accounted for about 30% of their life expenditures. In terms of amount, the expenditure of family farms was relatively high. The average food expenditure of rural

ANALYTICAL REPORT ON RURAL HOUSEHOLD DEVELOPMENT IN CHINA 399

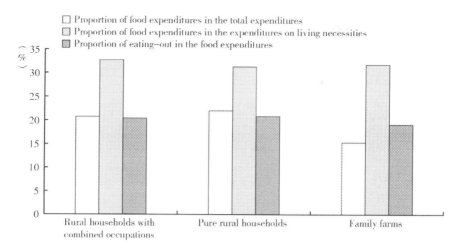

FIGURE 18.17   Proportion of Total Household Expenditures Spent on Food

households with combined occupations was 8,986.97 yuan, that of farming-only households was 10,759.44 yuan, and that of family farms was 11,546.09 yuan. The proportion of life services expenditures in the total expenditures on necessities of life on family farms was relatively high, at 10.64%. The life services expenditures of family farms were 3,905.02 yuan, which was higher than that of rural households with combined occupations by about 1,500 yuan. The life services expenditures of rural households with combined occupations amounted to 2,441.32 yuan, accounting for 8.85% of the total expenditures on life's necessities. The life services expenditures of farming-only households were 3,097.5 yuan, accounting for 8.99% of the total expenditures on life's necessities. In terms of cultural services expenditures, the difference among the three types of rural households was not big, and they accounted for about 8% of the total expenditures on life's necessities. In addition, for all three types of rural households, the proportion of expenditures on transportation and on communication and traveling in the total amount of expenditures on life's necessities was relatively small (see Figure 18.18). For example, the expenditure on transportation and communication accounted for about 6% of the total amount of expenditures on life's necessities. The amount of these expenditures for rural households with combined occupations was 1,730.17 yuan, that for farming-only households was 2,230.36 yuan, and that for family farms was 2,295.83 yuan. According to statistics, the expenditures on traveling for the three types of rural households were all lower than 1,000 yuan: 566.53 yuan for family farms, 435.69 yuan for farming-only households, and 204.25 yuan for rural households with combined occupations.

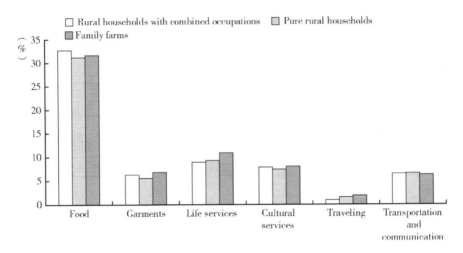

FIGURE 18.18   Proportions of Expenditures on Life's Necessities

2.5   Land Conditions

Figure 18.19 summarizes the cultivated land areas of rural households at the end of the year. Family farms had the largest area of cultivated land at the end of the year, which was 14.298 *mu* (about 9,532 square meters); the number for rural households with combined occupations was 8.938 *mu* (about 5,959 square meters), and that for farming-only households was only 2.38 *mu* (about 1,587 square meters). In terms of the area of farmland, in general, most of the rural households had more than 5 *mu* (about 3,333 square meters) of farmland, including 4,424 rural households with combined occupations, 1,239 farming-only households, and 276 family farms; this was followed by the rural households with 1–3 *mu* (667–2,000 square meters) of farmland, including 2,036 rural households with combined occupations, 830 farming-only households, and 82 family farms. Only a few rural households had less than 1 *mu* (667 square meters) of farmland, including 573 rural households with combined occupations, 327 farming-only households, and 5 family farms. Furthermore, according to the number of land lots operated at the end of the year, the average number of land lots operated by rural households with combined occupations was 4.46, the number for farming-only households was 1.34, and that for family farms was 4.27. See Figure 18.20 for the distribution.

2.6   Housing Conditions

The three types of rural households did not show much difference in terms of housing area. The average housing area for rural households with combined occupations was 148.13 square meters, that for farming-only households was

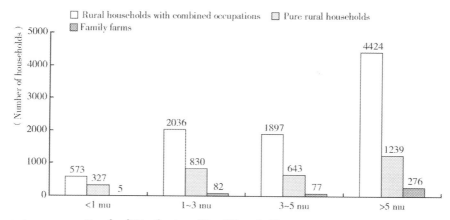

FIGURE 18.19   Farmland Distribution of Rural Households

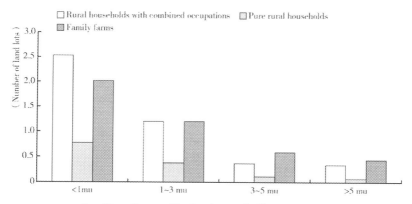

FIGURE 18.20   Land Lots Operated by Rural Households

166.16 square meters, and that for family farms was 155.8 square meters. Most of the rural households with combined occupations were living in one-story houses built with bricks, while most of the farming-only households were living in buildings and most of the responsible people of family farms were living in one-story houses built with bricks. About 33.73% of rural households with combined occupations, 48.86% of farming-only households, and 33.5% of the responsible people of family farms were living in buildings. About 54.33% of rural households with combined occupations, 40.66% of farming-only households, and 74.68% of the responsible people of family farms were living in one-story houses built with bricks (see Figure 18.21).

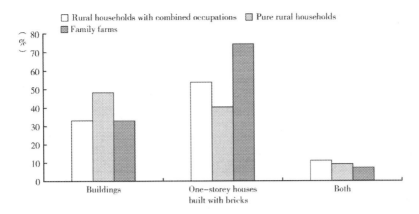

FIGURE 18.21   Types of Housing for Rural Households

2.7   *Other Conditions*
2.7.1   Crop Output

As for the planting of crops, in terms of total area, rural households with combined occupations devoted the largest area to the three main grain crops, followed by farming-only households. In terms of the proportions of the three major grain crops sown by rural households, the proportion of corn was the highest for all three types of rural households. The area used for planting corn by rural households with combined occupations, farming-only households, and family farms was 5,625 *mu* (3,750,019 square meters), 1,607 *mu* (1,071,339 square meters), and 249 *mu* (166,001 square meters), respectively. In terms of the planting of rice and wheat, for rural households with combined occupations and family farms, more space was given to rice than to wheat, but for farming-only households it was just the opposite (see Figure 18.22).

In terms of the average yield per *mu*, corn had the highest yield, and the corn yield for family farms was the highest among the three types of rural households—744.93 kilograms per *mu*. The average yield of rice was essentially the same for all three types of rural households, but the average wheat yield differed widely among the three types of rural households. For example, the wheat yields for rural households with combined occupations and farming-only households were close, at 381.42 and 405.52 kilograms, respectively, but the number for family farms was only 295.13 kilograms (see Figure 18.23).

In terms of the sale of grains (including wheat, corn, and rice), the three types of rural households were quite different. Family farms ranked first in terms of amount of grain sales, quantity of grain sales, and the total amount of agricultural products sold, followed by rural households with combined occupations and finally the farming-only households. In general, family farms had

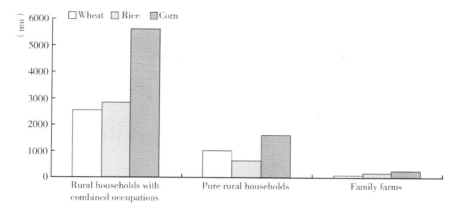

FIGURE 18.22   Main Grain Crops Planted by Rural Households

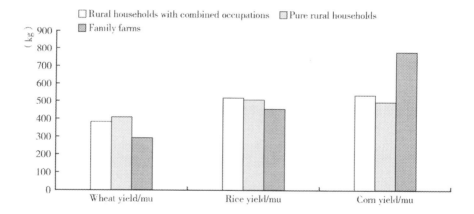

FIGURE 18.23   Average Yields of Main Grain Crops

the smallest area for the planting of grain but the highest grain output and sales, while rural households with combined occupations had the largest area for planting grain but lagged behind the family farms in terms of grain output and sales.

2.7.2   Fixed Assets for Rural Households

The productive fixed assets include draught animals, breeding stock, and product stock; large- and medium-sized iron and wooden farm tools; agricultural, forestry, animal husbandry, and fishery machines; and industrial machines, transportation machines, production houses, and fixed assets for facility agriculture. At the end of the year, the average value of the productive fixed assets held by rural households with combined occupations was 14,190.74 yuan, that for farming-only households was 11,268.17 yuan, and that for family farms was 44,401.46 yuan. In general, most rural households had fixed assets of less than 10,000 yuan, while a lesser proportion had fixed assets between 10,000 and 50,000 yuan.

3   Conclusion

In this report, based on data from the fixed observation points of the Ministry of Agriculture, we divided the rural households into three types according to their working and hiring conditions, namely, rural households with combined occupations, farming-only households, and family farms. In addition, we used the general samples and the small samples of the three types of rural households to analyze individual and family characteristics, land operations, crop output, income, fixed assets, and housing conditions among rural households.

In terms of life expenditures, expenditures on food made up the largest proportion of spending on life's necessities for rural households, while expenditures on entertainment (expenditures on traveling, life services, and cultural services) only accounted for a small part of expenditures on life's necessities. All three types of rural households had relatively low expenditures on entertainment. Expenditures for entertainment on family farms were higher than those of both rural households with combined occupations and farming-only households.

In terms of the personal characteristics of rural householders, the age structures were similar, with an average age of 55 to 57. In addition, most of the rural householders had received a primary school education and a few of them had received a senior high school education or above. In terms of family members, most of the rural households in the samples were ordinary households that did not include any government officials, servicemen, or party members. Family farms had the greatest number of permanent residents, followed by farming-only households and rural households with combined occupations. In terms of stay-at-home time, members of family farms spent more time outside their home, while members of rural households with combined occupations spent the shortest time at home. In addition, family farms had more religious members. In terms of crop planting and output, family farms had the highest average yield and grain income. In terms of fixed assets, rural households did not have too many fixed assets, and the values of the fixed assets held by most rural households were lower than 50,000 yuan. As for housing conditions, the dimensions of the housing area for the three types of rural households were similar, but they had different living conditions. For example, most responsible people on family farms and in rural households with combined occupations were living in one-story houses built brick, while most of the farming-only households were living in buildings.

According to the above analysis, for agricultural development in the future, we should promote the citizenization of rural households with combined occupations and find ways to encourage them to transfer their farmlands to family farms or cooperatives, such as changing the agricultural subsidies for rural households with combined occupations to social insurance. Next, we should promote the self-development of farming-only households, by strategies such as providing them with generalized preference subsidies. Finally, we should form plans to develop the family farms, such as providing them with project-specific subsidies and accurate subsidies to promote their marketization, so as to expand their scale of operation, improve their competitiveness, and enhance their living standards and comfort.

References

Chen Chunsheng. "Evolution Logics and Classification of the Rural Households in China." *Issues in Agricultural Economy*, 2007(11).

Du Zhixiong and Xiao Weidong. "Actual Conditions and Policy Supports for the Development of Family Farms: International Experiences." *Reform*, 2014(6).

Eswaran, M., and Kotwal, A. "Access to Capital and Agrarian Production Organization." *The Economic Journal*, 1986, 96(382).

Huang Zongzhi. "Is the Family Farm the Developmental Road for Agriculture in China?" *Rural China*, 2014(1).

Li Xianbao and Gao Qiang. "Behavioral Logics, Differentiation Results, and Development Prospects—Survey on the Differentiation Behaviors of Rural Households in China since 1978." *Issues in Agricultural Economy*, 2013(2).

Zhang Liyao. "Research on the Economic Classification of Rural Households and the Influential Factors—Analysis Based on the Survey Data from the Fixed Observation Points in Rural Areas in Guangzhou." *Southern Rural*, 2010(2).

Zhu Qizhen. "New Occupational Farmers and Family Farms." *Journal of China Agricultural University* (Social Sciences Edition), 2013(2).

CHAPTER 19

Analytical Report on Newly Established Small and Micro-Enterprises in China in 2017

Zhang Jiurong,[1] Lyu Peng,[2] and Jin Zhaohui[3]

Abstract

In this report, we have described the development of small and micro-enterprises in China since the reform of the commercial affairs system. According to the macro data provided by the State Administration for Industry and Commerce, new private enterprises and individual businesses have witnessed rapid development. Based on the micro survey of Vitality on the Anniversary of 10,000 New Small and Micro-Enterprises in 100 Counties in China conducted by the China Private-Owned Business Association (CPBA) in 2015, we have reported the vitality, rate on the anniversary of opening, operating income, profits, and job creation of new small and micro-enterprises. In this report, we have also reflected on the issues of new small and micro-enterprises in terms of financing, costs, and the environment of business operations, and we have put forward some policy suggestions.

Keywords

new small and micro-enterprises – vitality survey – reform of the commercial affairs system

1 Basic Conditions of the Survey

The tracking analysis of the development of new small and micro-enterprises was not only an important part of market supervision and control but also a reflection of the vitality of the innovation and starting up of businesses across the whole society. With the great efforts made in promoting the reform of the commercial affairs system and the reform of delegating powers, streamlining administration, and optimizing services, market vitality has been effectively

---

1 Zhang Jiurong, China Private-Owned Business Association.
2 Lyu Peng, the Institute of Sociology, the Chinese Academy of Social Sciences.
3 Jin Zhaohui, China Private-Owned Business Association.

© KONINKLIJKE BRILL NV, LEIDEN, 2022 | DOI:10.1163/9789004500723_020

activated. A key sign of this vitality was the rapid growth in the number of small and micro-enterprises. From March 2014 to August 2017, newly registered market entities reached 55.117 million, accounting for 59.07% of all market entities, and they have played an important role in promoting economic development, creating jobs, and maintaining social stability. Most of the new enterprises were private small and micro-enterprises. Therefore, facilitating the innovation and development of small and micro-enterprises meant promoting the innovation and development of private small and micro-enterprises. What about the conditions of the small and micro-enterprises registered in the three years since the reform of the commercial affairs system? What were their difficulties and problems during development? How could we further promote the reform of delegating powers, streamlining administration, and optimizing services based on these difficulties and problems?

For this purpose, since August 2015, in cooperation with the delegation from the State Administration for Industry and Commerce, the China Private-Owned Business Association (CPBA) has carried out a survey of Vitality on the Anniversary of 10,000 New Small and Micro-Enterprises in 100 Counties in China throughout the country, with the support of local private-owned business associations. The survey covered 100 counties (districts) in 31 provinces, autonomous regions, and municipalities, so a survey point was set in each province to ensure the comprehensiveness of the survey. The CPBA established 100 grassroots survey working points at the county-level associations of the 31 provinces according to a ratio of 5:3:2 and based on the levels of economic development and the total number of enterprises in eastern, central, and western China (the quantity of those distributed in northeastern China was estimated according to the figures from the central region). The surveyed enterprises were randomly selected from the enterprise information database of the State Administration for Industry and Commerce, and the total amount of samples for each year was 40,000, or 10,000 per quarter. To help the surveyed enterprises fill in the questionnaires, an online survey system was developed.

As of the end of September 2017, the CPBA had completed 10 major questionnaire surveys that were conducted once per quarter on 10,000 enterprises each time. All in all, 100,000 small and micro-enterprises were surveyed and 13 survey reports were completed.[4] In this report, we present the main contents and results of the survey to encourage members of all walks of society to pay

---

4 If the object of analysis is a quarter of a given year in the report, the sample size is the 10,000 enterprises surveyed in that quarter. If the object of the analysis is a given year, the sample size is the 40,000 enterprises surveyed in the four quarters of that year. If the object of the analysis is N quarters, the sample size is N × 10,000 enterprises.

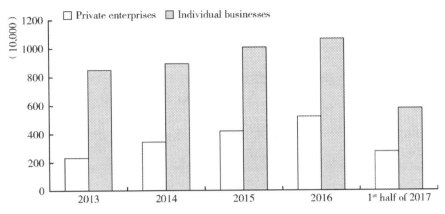

FIGURE 19.1   The Number of New Private Enterprises and Individual Businesses Nationwide (2013–First Half of 2017)

more attention to the development of small and micro-enterprises and to create a good business environment.

2   Macro Conditions of the New Small and Micro-Enterprises in China

Since the reform of the commercial affairs system, various market entities, especially private-owned businesses, have witnessed rapid development. We can see the general situation through the macro data provided by the State Administration for Industry and Commerce.

First of all, we can see the absolute quantity and growth rate of new private enterprises and individual businesses. Most new private enterprises were small and micro-enterprises, and most individual businesses were conducting small-scaled production and operation activities. Some scholars also considered individual businesses to be small and micro-enterprises. From Figure 19.1, we can see that from 2013 to 2016, the numbers of newly established private enterprises and newly registered individual businesses have been increasing. In 2016, the number of new individual businesses was 10,689,489, an increase of 25.3% over 8,530,240 in 2013. In 2016, the number of new private enterprises was 5,228,241, which was 2.2 times the number of 2,327,261 in 2013 (see Figure 19.1).

Second, we can trace the year-on-year growth rate of new private enterprises in 2016. Table 19.1 shows that the year-on-year growth rate of new private enterprises nationwide reached 24.14%. The top three administrative zones at the provincial level were Tibet, Jilin, and Xinjiang, with growth rates of 54.09%, 47.07%, and 32.33%, respectively. Yunnan, Guangxi, and Beijing were at the bottom, with growth rates of 1.89%, 6.93%, and 8.95%, respectively.

REPORT ON NEWLY ESTABLISHED SMALL AND MICRO-ENTERPRISES 409

Finally, we can chart the increase in the number of new enterprises per 10,000 people nationwide. Although the two statistical calibers are not totally the same, most of the new enterprises are private small and micro-enterprises. According to Table 19.1, based on the data in 2016, the number of new enterprises per 10,000 people was 39.27. In terms of provinces, Heilongjiang (17.2), Hunan (19.63), and Xinjiang (21.79) were at the bottom, while Shanghai (122.01), Beijing (105.91), and Guangdong (72.06) were at the top.

3 Analysis of the Results of the Survey

3.1 *Vitality and Active Index*
The indicators of the survey of Vitality on the Anniversary of 10,000 New Small and Micro-Enterprises in 100 Counties in China were divided into three categories. The first category indicates whether an enterprise is alive; the second category indicates the vitality of the live enterprise; and the third category indicates the difficulties encountered by the enterprise in operations, so as to better understand the needs of enterprises. See Table 19.2 for details.

During the calculation, the vitality of an enterprise was quantified according to the opening conditions, income conditions, and production and operations of the enterprise. The method of equal probability was used for quantification: the vitality of any activity is P, and P is determined by whether the enterprise has income and by the number of its production and operation activities (N). The algorithm is thus: vitality $= 1-P^\wedge[N^\wedge(1/2)]$. According to the values calculated using the algorithm, the degree of vitality of the enterprises can be divided into five categories, namely, no vitality (unopened enterprises), low vitality (opened enterprises without any production or operations), low to middle vitality (enterprises with a degree of vitality from 0.5 to 0.6), middle to high vitality (enterprises with a degree of vitality from 0.6 to 0.7), and high vitality (enterprises with a degree of vitality at or above 0.7).

From the statistics and calculations for the survey samples, we can see the vitality of new small and micro-enterprises on the anniversary of each of the past three years and the vitality curve formed from the results of the 10 surveys.

Figure 19.2 depicts the proportion of new small and micro-enterprises with different levels of vitality in the third quarter of 2016. From the figure, we can see that enterprises with a middle to high degree of vitality and above accounted for 45.2%, an increase of 2.0 percentage points over the second quarter of 2016. The results of all the surveys were slightly different with regard to values.

The activity index was determined based on six indicators, namely, enterprise opening rate, proportion of enterprises with activities, average number of employees, average operating income, average tax, and proportion of profitable

TABLE 19.1   Number of New Enterprises per 10,000 People Nationwide and Year-on-Year Growth Rates of New Private Enterprises by Province (2016)

Unit: Number, %

Province	Number of new enterprises per 10,000 people	Year-on-year growth rate of new private enterprises
Heilongjiang	17.20	23.08
Hunan	19.63	24.19
Xinjiang	21.79	32.33
Guangxi	22.01	6.93
Shanxi	23.87	28.97
Henan	24.25	28.45
Gansu	24.60	23.41
Yunnan	24.81	1.89
Jiangxi	25.03	26.11
Sichuan	26.07	25.91
Inner Mongolia	26.33	17.58
Guizhou	26.53	22.52
Liaoning	26.56	19.96
Shaanxi	27.43	16.76
Jilin	28.18	47.07
Qinghai	29.93	29.14
Anhui	30.04	32.27
Hebei	33.00	32.10
Hainan	34.19	18.82
Hubei	34.41	21.69
Tibet	41.82	54.09
Ningxia	42.40	10.94
Chongqing	43.54	12.06
Zhejiang	51.40	28.80
Fujian	51.57	23.98
Shandong	52.50	27.21
Jiangsu	63.67	27.23
Tianjin	68.87	28.47
Guangdong	72.06	28.86
Beijing	105.91	8.95
Shanghai	122.01	17.69
Whole country	39.27	24.14

TABLE 19.2　　Important Indicators

Name of indicator	Description
Basic enterprise information	Obtained from the registration database of market entities
Operation status	Reflects whether the enterprise is alive
Employees	Reflects the vitality of the live enterprise
Operating income	
Taxation	
General situation of operations	
Operation activities	
Activities conducted through the Internet	
Difficulties encountered by the enterprise in operations	Understanding enterprise needs

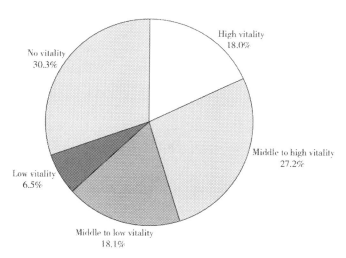

FIGURE 19.2　　Proportions of New Small and Micro-Enterprises with Different Degrees of Vitality in the Third Quarter of 2016

enterprises. Indicators were weighted according to the relative importance of issues in the analysis before determining the compound index. Figure 19.3 plots the activity indexes of new small and micro-enterprises in each quarter from the second quarter of 2014 to the third quarter of 2016. The overall trend is basically the same as that of the Purchasing Managers' Index (PMI) of the manufacturing industry in China.

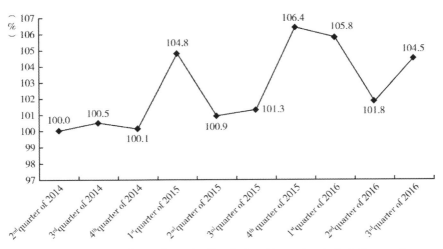

FIGURE 19.3 Activity Indexes of New Small and Micro-Enterprises in Each Quarter since the Second Quarter of 2014

3.2 *Anniversary Operations of New Small and Micro-Enterprises*

According to the survey, the average percentage of new small and micro-enterprises that are still in operation by their one-year anniversary was 70.3%. Enterprises established in the third quarter of 2014 witnessed the highest opening rate of 72.3% on the first anniversary after opening. Enterprises established in the second quarter of 2015 saw the lowest opening rate, 68.8%. See Figure 19.4 for details.

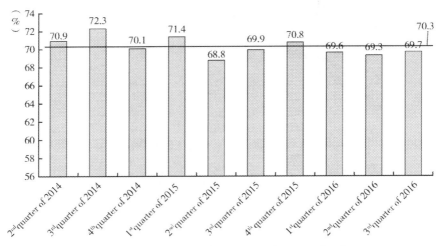

FIGURE 19.4 Rates on the Anniversary of the Opening of New Small and Micro-Enterprises in Each Quarter since the Second Quarter of 2014

REPORT ON NEWLY ESTABLISHED SMALL AND MICRO-ENTERPRISES   413

TABLE 19.3   Reasons for the Failure to Open or the Suspension of New Small and
             Micro-Enterprises in the Third Quarter of 2016, by Percentage

Unit: %

Reason for not opening or for suspension	Proportion	Reason for not opening or for suspension	Proportion
Poor industry conditions, no business	24.00	Internal adjustment of the enterprise	7.80
Personal reasons of bosses	20.60	Low profit and high loss	6.10
Insufficient funds or financing difficulties	18.60	Recruitment difficulties, shortage of personnel and technologies	8.20
Fierce market competition and low competitiveness	11.40	Other	8.20

According to the survey, about 30% of enterprises did not operate normally and either did not open or were suspended. The major issues affecting such enterprises included poor industrial conditions, no business, personal reasons of bosses, insufficient funds, financing difficulties, fierce market competition, and low competitiveness. For example, in the survey in the third quarter of 2016, the above issues accounted for more than 70% of the issues reported by enterprises that did not open (see Table 19.3). Therefore, to improve the opening rate of small and micro-enterprises, we can study these issues to find ways to overcome the difficulties that new small and micro-enterprises may encounter during the early stage of development.

3.3   *Income and Profits on the Anniversary of the Operations of the New Small and Micro-Enterprises*

According to the survey, more than 80% of the enterprises that opened had an operating income, and more than 20% of them earned a profit. Despite the poor economic situation, the operations of new small and micro-enterprises were good. As shown by survey data from the third quarter of 2016, 78.8% of the enterprises in operation had an operating income, and the proportion of those enterprises was basically the same as in the second quarter of 2016. Enterprises with profits or even profits and losses accounted for 65.4%, whereas enterprises with profits accounted for 20.4%. The data showed that the profitability of enterprises that have undergone corporate overhaul and enterprises with scale expansion were higher than that of the initial business-starting enterprises by

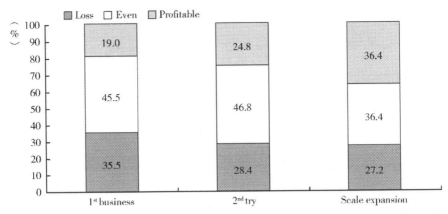

FIGURE 19.5   Profits and Losses among New Small and Micro-Enterprises That Had Opened by the Third Quarter of 2016

5.8 and 17.4 percentage points (see Figure 19.5). This means that the accumulation of experience is very important to business-starting enterprises, and thus the whole society should create an atmosphere that encourages business-starting and innovation.

3.4   *Jobs Provided by New Small and Micro-Enterprises*

According to the survey, after the first anniversary of opening, the average number of employees of the new small and micro-enterprises was higher than that at the opening by 16.9%, and each enterprise could provide jobs for 7.4 people. In the third quarter of 2016, after the first anniversary of opening, the average number of employees of the new small and micro-enterprises was higher than that at the opening by 18.3%, increasing from 6.27 people per enterprise to 7.42. In the third quarter of 2016, full-time employees accounted for 91.6% of the total employees of the new small and micro-enterprises, college graduates of the same year accounted for 7.3%, and reemployed laid-off workers accounted for 6.9%. These enterprises made a great contribution to driving forward the employment of college students and laid-off workers. Retired servicemen accounted for 1.9%, and the proportion of disabled employees was 0.3% (see Figure 19.6).

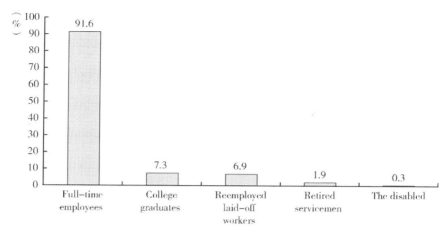

FIGURE 19.6 Proportions of Types of Employees of New Small and Micro-Enterprises in the Third Quarter of 2016

4 Issues That Arose During the Development of Small and Micro-Enterprises

4.1 *High Costs, Fierce Competition, and Financing Difficulties Were Still the Major Problems Encountered by Small and Micro-Enterprises*

According to the survey, the major difficulties for new small and micro-enterprises in operation included: (1) high operation costs, high labor costs, and high rents; (2) fierce competition and low profits; and (3) insufficient funds, insufficient channels of financing, and financing difficulties. The survey in the third quarter of 2016 showed that the above three types of issues accounted for 24.3%, 21.6%, and 19.9% of the total difficulties reported by new small and micro-enterprises, respectively, totaling 65.8% (see Table 19.4). By contrast, an unreasonable threshold of access to an industry or monopoly, as well as difficulties in applying for operating and business certification, only accounted for less than 10%, combined, reflecting that reform has facilitated the market access of enterprises and applications made by the enterprises.

TABLE 19.4 Proportions of Operation Difficulties Reported by Small and Micro-Enterprises in the Third Quarter of 2016

Unit: %

Operation difficulty	First entreprenneurial attempt	Second business-starting	Scale expansion	Total
High operation costs, labor costs, and rent	24.5	23.9	22.6	24.3
Fierce competition and low profits	21.3	23.7	23.1	21.6
Insufficient funds, insufficient channels of financing, and financing difficulties	20.6	16.7	13.0	19.9
Shortage of laborers and recruitment difficulties	8.5	6.6	7.5	8.3
Limited operation locations or lack of suitable locations	7.0	6.3	8.3	7.1
Difficulties in retaining and recruiting professional talents	6.3	6.5	8.9	6.5
Low technical levels and innovation difficulties	4.3	2.7	5.4	4.2
Low operational and management levels, or improper operations and management	3.0	4.4	2.4	3.0
High tax rates and tax burden	1.7	4.6	2.3	1.9
Difficulties in applying for operation and business certification	0.7	0.6	1.2	0.7
Unreasonable threshold for access to industrial operations or monopoly	0.6	0.9	1.2	0.7
Other	1.6	3.1	4.0	1.8

4.2 *The Smaller the Enterprise, the More Difficulties and Problems It Will Encounter*

By analyzing the relationship between the scale of the enterprise and the difficulties it encounters, we found that the smaller the enterprise, the more

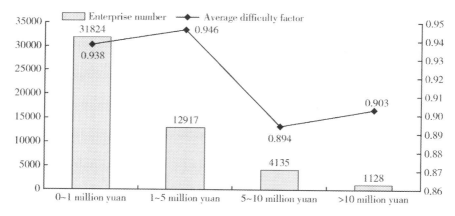

FIGURE 19.7   Relationship between the Scale of an Enterprise and Its Factor of Difficulty

difficulties and problems. For example, the difficulty factor of enterprises with a capitalization between 1 and 5 million yuan was the highest (see Figure 19.7). This means that enterprises that had experienced a period of development would meet the greatest number of difficulties and problems at the initial expansion stage, which is a bottleneck for development.

4.3   New Small and Micro-Enterprises Thought That Enterprise Costs Had Increased

According to survey data from the third quarter of 2017, in the past three years, enterprises witnessed rapid increases in labor cost, logistics cost, and energy cost. Specifically, enterprises that felt that their labor cost had "increased to some extent" accounted for 54.1%; when combined with those feeling that their labor cost had "increased too fast," the total proportion reached 71.5%. Enterprises that felt that their logistics cost and energy cost had increased "to some extent" or "too fast" accounted for 64.5% and 58.9%, respectively. Only 4.8%, 6.4%, and 5.3% of enterprises thought that the above three costs had decreased (the sum of the proportions of those that thought that their costs had decreased "to some extent" or "significantly"). Overall increases in the three major costs have increased the overall input costs of small and micro-enterprises. The government service cost, however, has decreased significantly. Enterprises that felt that the government service cost had decreased "to some extent" or "significantly" accounted for 51.6% (see Table 19.5), indicating that a positive outcome was achieved through the reform of delegating powers, streamlining administration, and optimizing services.

TABLE 19.5 Perception of Costs by Enterprises in the Third Quarter of 2017

Unit: %

Type	Labor cost	Logistics cost	Energy cost	Government service cost	Tax cost	Financing cost
Decreased significantly	0.6	0.6	0.5	24.7	12.3	3.3
Decreased to some extent	4.2	5.8	4.8	26.9	20.7	7.1
No change	23.7	29.1	35.7	40.9	49.2	56.1
Increased to some extent	54.1	51.9	46.9	5.4	14.7	26.5
Increased too fast	17.4	12.6	12.0	2.1	3.2	7.0

4.4 *Opinions of Enterprises on the Business Environment*

According to survey data from the third quarter of 2017, in terms of the opinions of enterprises on the business environment, the satisfaction of enterprises with basic public services was high. Satisfaction with industry and business registration was the highest, reaching 79% for "satisfied" and "very satisfied," combined. Among the nine indicators of the business environment, this is the only one that did not elicit a "very unsatisfied" response from any respondents to the survey. As for the indicators of security environment, power supply, tax declaration, and water supply, the proportions of "satisfied" and "very satisfied," combined, were 68.2%, 68.1%, 67.5%, and 67.2%, respectively (see Table 19.6).

TABLE 19.6 Opinions of Enterprises on Basic Public Services in the Business Environment in the Third Quarter of 2017

Unit: %

Type	Water Supply	Power Supply	Security Environment	Business Registration	Tax Declaration	Basic Education	Health Care Service	Transportation and Traffic	Legal Service
Very satisfied	12.2	12.7	11.9	23.1	13.7	10.2	9.6	9.8	9.8
Satisfied	55.0	55.4	56.3	55.9	53.8	50.1	46.1	47.1	45.1
Average satisfaction	30.6	30.2	31.3	20.8	31.3	37.0	40.7	39.3	43.2
Unsatisfied	1.6	1.1	0.5	0.2	0.8	2.1	2.9	3.1	1.3
Very unsatisfied	0.6	0.5	0.1	0.0	0.5	0.6	0.7	0.6	0.5

The subsistence and development of new small and micro-enterprises are very important. Strengthening the surveys and research on such enterprises—especially with respect to the subsistence and vitality of those that have been established for two or three years—and understanding the causes of their operational difficulties and identifying improvements in the business environment are of great importance to the deepening of the reform and the creation of a business environment that is suitable for business-starting and innovation.

5 Policy Suggestions

In this report, we have fully evaluated the development of new small and micro-enterprises since the reform of the commercial affairs system. According to the survey, although the policy of streamlining administration and delegating powers has improved the sense of gain among owners of small and micro-enterprises, there is still a long way to go to reduce the institutional costs of the enterprises. This reflected the effect of the aforementioned policy and reminded us that the healthy development of small and micro-enterprises can be further improved. Therefore, we have made the following suggestions.

5.1 *The Key Point of the Reform of Delegating Powers, Streamlining Administration, and Optimizing Services Is to Ensure the Subsistence and Good Development of Small and Micro-Enterprises*

At present, the reforms of the administrative approval system and the commercial affairs system have made significant achievements in promoting the registration of new enterprises, but more specific policy support is needed to improve their survival rate. Although the normal operational ratio of the new small and micro-enterprises under the survey was about 70%, these small and micro-enterprises were still within the business-starting period of three years. As time goes by, these enterprises will constantly meet challenges in their development. The development of enterprises in their business-starting stage has special characteristics. The reform of delegating powers, streamlining administration, and optimizing services should help market entities to break the developmental bottlenecks in that period. In recent years, the number of new enterprises has witnessed rapid growth, creating a lot of jobs. However, these new enterprises have to withstand the test of the market, survive after opening, develop after survival, and create more jobs. To do this, the existing policies should be further implemented and related policies and regulations should be improved to provide further support to the new enterprises.

5.2 New Enterprises Have Their Own Features That Deserve Special Attention

At first, the number of new enterprises is huge, and the subsistence of such enterprises is in essence the result of market competition. However, in terms of taxation, finance, industry and commerce, training and employment, and business-starting services, the national government should craft inclusive policies to enable every new enterprise to compete fairly in a relaxed environment. Second, the new small and micro-enterprises are not mature in terms of the market or social and political connections, and compared to mature enterprises, they are weak when faced with difficulties or infringement of their rights and interests. In such cases, special attention is needed from industry associations, chambers of commerce, or even the CPPCC and the NPC to establish smooth channels of expression and correct mechanisms of protection for new enterprises. In terms of legislation, laws and regulations can be issued to protect new enterprises and the "bad" laws limiting their development should be abolished.

5.3 Policy Implementation Should Be Followed by Various Departments, and the Improvement of the Business Environment Should Be Coordinated by Different Departments

To unleash the dividends of the reform of delegating powers, streamlining administration, and optimizing services, including the commercial affairs system, various departments should be coordinated. Except for the industry and commerce administrations, if the policies of some departments with administrative approval rights cannot be connected properly, some new small and micro-enterprises will become businesses without licenses. In this case, a joint force for reform should be formed by various government departments to achieve the best effect. To better complete the reform of delegating powers, streamlining administration, and optimizing services, a comprehensive coordination in the construction of laws is required so as to promote the implementation and continuity of market reform with a legal business environment.

5.4 We Should Create a Policy Environment and an Environment of Cultural and Public Opinion That Encourage People to Start a Second Business after Experiencing Failure

According to the survey, most new small and micro-enterprises were the first businesses started by their owners. In case of failure in starting the business, the business owner was likely to leave the market completely. Great courage is needed to make a second try. As shown by the data, in reality only a few individuals and enterprise owners have tried to start a business more than three times, and the proportion of business owners who made a second try was not high. This situation was caused partially by economic laws and partially by the market environment and public opinion.

We should allow those who failed to start a business, especially their first business, to receive assistance from government agencies and social organizations. Under current social conditions, with many new enterprises and high pressure due to the decline of economic growth and structural adjustment, failure in business-starting could become an aspect of the "new normal" economic conditions. Therefore, related departments should do research on the conditions of those who are trying to start businesses again after an initial failure in terms of taxation, finance, industry and commerce, training and employment, and business-starting services, and establish corresponding supporting policies.

In terms of public opinion, encouraging business-starting has become a consensus, but an atmosphere in which nobody judges anyone based on his or her failures has yet to be created. We should encourage the government media, market media, and even We Media to use methods that are familiar to those starting businesses to establish examples of successful small and micro-enterprises and summarize and disseminate the successful experiences of new enterprises. In particular, we should discover and spread successful methods for second business-starting, summarize related experiences and lessons, and invite those who have succeeded on their second try to tell their stories, so as to create an atmosphere that encourages people to try starting up a business for the second time.

References

Jiang Zhilei. "Research on the Vitality of Small and Micro-Enterprises Based on Big Data." *Research on China Market Supervision*, 2016(5).

Xie Yaping and Huang Meijiao. "Social Network, Business-Starting Learning, and Business-Starting Capacity—An Empirical Study Based on Those Starting Small and Micro-Enterprises." *Studies in Science of Science*, 2014(3).

Yang Wen. "Annual Reports and Enterprise Operation Tendency—Report on the Analysis of the Enterprise Annual Reports Nationwide from 2013 to 2014." *Research on China Market Supervision*, 2016(3).

Zhu Qichang. "What Are Small and Micro-Enterprises?" *Sichuan United Front*, 2012(5).

CHAPTER 20

A Statistical Overview of China's Social Development in 2017

Zhang Liping[1]

1   Economic Development

In 2016, the GDP of China was 74,412.72 billion yuan, a year-on-year increase of 6.7%. The primary, secondary, and tertiary industries boosted the growth of the GDP by 0.3%, 2.5%, and 3.9% respectively. In the first three quarters of 2017, the gross domestic product was 59,328.9 billion yuan, a year-on-year increase of 6.9%.

The total retail sales of consumer goods witnessed a constant increase. In 2016, the total retail sales of consumer goods were 33,231.63 billion yuan, an increase of 10.4% over the previous year. From January to October 2017, the total retail sales of consumer goods were 29,741.94 billion yuan, with a year-on-year increase of 10.3%.

The total retail sales of consumer goods and the growth rates in different provinces varied significantly. In 2015 and 2016, Guangdong, Shandong, Jiangsu, Zhejiang, and Henan were the top five provinces in terms of the total retail sales of consumer goods. In 2016, Chongqing and Guizhou witnessed the highest growth rate in total retail sales of consumer goods, which was higher than 13%; the growth rates in Tibet, Yunnan, Anhui, and Jiangxi also surpassed 12%.

The development of a network economy continued to change how residents consumed. In 2016, online retail sales in China reached 5,155.57 billion yuan, and the retail sales of physical commodities online totaled 4,194.45 billion yuan, increasing by 26.2% and 25.6% over the previous year, respectively. In terms of regions, online retail sales in Guangdong, Zhejiang, Beijing, Shanghai, and Jiangsu were much higher than those in other provinces. In terms of growth rate, online retail sales in Guizhou increased by 55.6% over the previous year, and those of Henan, Jilin, and Anhui also topped 40%.

---

1   Zhang Liping, associate research fellow of the Institute of Sociology, the Chinese Academy of Social Sciences.

© KONINKLIJKE BRILL NV, LEIDEN, 2022 | DOI:10.1163/9789004500723_021

A STATISTICAL OVERVIEW OF CHINA'S SOCIAL DEVELOPMENT IN 2017

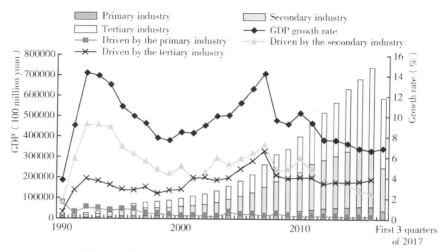

FIGURE 20.1 Growth of the GDP since 1990

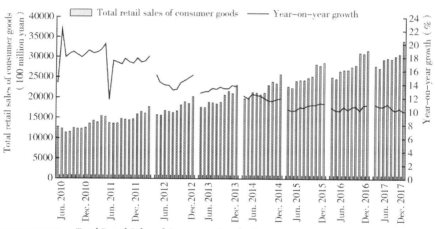

FIGURE 20.2 Total Retail Sales of Consumer Goods since 2010

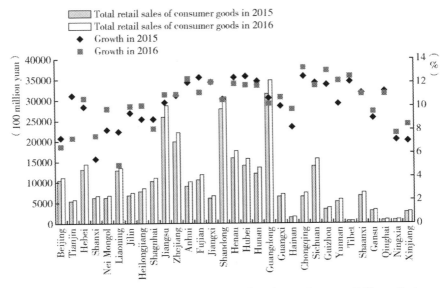

FIGURE 20.3   Total Retail Sales of Consumer Goods and Growth Rates in Different Regions in 2016

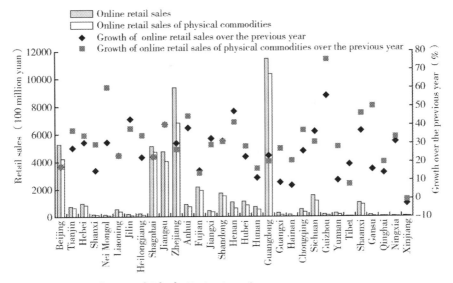

FIGURE 20.4   Online Retail Sales by Region in 2016

2 Population and Employment

With the adjustment of family planning policies, the fertility rate increased from 12.07‰ in 2015 to 12.95‰ in 2016, the mortality rate decreased to 7.09‰, and the natural population growth rate increased from 4.96‰ in the previous year to 5.86‰. The urban and rural structure of the population also changed. By the end of 2016, the total population was 1,382.71 million; the proportion of the urban population increased to 57.35% and that of the rural population decreased to 42.65%.

In addition to the changes in population and in the urban and rural structure, the age structure of the population also changed. In 2016, the population of children was 230 million, increasing by 3.27 million over the previous year; the population of senior citizens aged 65 and above was 150 million, increasing by 5.69 million over 2015; and the working-age population from 15 to 64 started to decrease in 2014 and reached 1,003 million in 2016, a reduction of 870,000 over the previous year. The ratio of population dependency also changed. In 2016, the total ratio of dependency continued to grow to 37.9%, the ratio of the dependency of children increased to 22.9%, and that of the elderly increased to 15%.

The structure of marriages and households of the population also witnessed significant changes. Since the 1990s, the number of registered marriages every year fluctuates, and has shown a tendency to decrease in recent years. By the end of 2016, civil affairs departments and marriage registries at all levels had registered 11.428 million couples according to law, a decrease of 6.7% compared to the previous year. At the same time, the number of divorced people

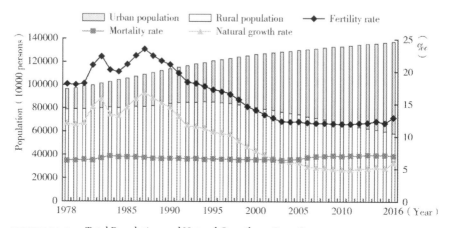

FIGURE 20.5   Total Population and Natural Growth, 1978–2016

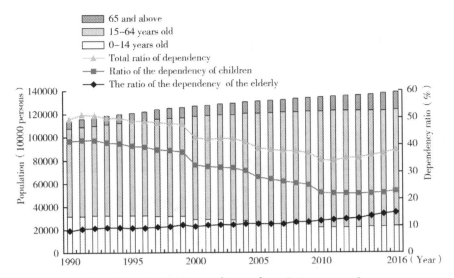

FIGURE 20.6   Population Age Structure and Dependency Ratio, 1990–2016

FIGURE 20.7   Marriages and Divorces, 1990–2016

and the divorce rate were increasing year by year. In 2016, 4.158 million couples divorced according to law, an increase of 8.3% over the previous year. The crude divorce rate was 3.02‰, an increase of 0.2‰ over the previous year.

With the reduction of the fertility level and the increase of the population in motion, the average household size has been decreasing to less than 3.5 people since 2000; it was less than 3 people in 2013 and 3.11 people in 2016, but it increased in 2015.

A STATISTICAL OVERVIEW OF CHINA'S SOCIAL DEVELOPMENT IN 2017 427

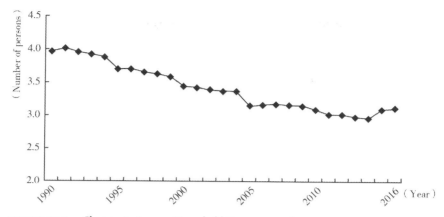

FIGURE 20.8   Changes in Average Household Size, 1990–2016

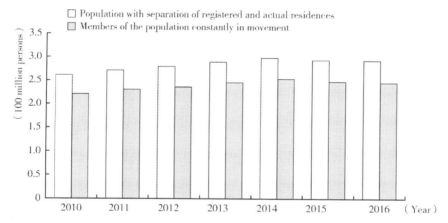

FIGURE 20.9   Members of the Population Constantly in Motion and Those Whose Registered Residence Did Not Match Their Actual Residence, 2010–2016

The increase in the number of members of the population who had been in motion for years was stabilized and even diminished. In 2000, that population was 121 million, and it reached 253 million in 2014 but decreased to 245 million in 2016. The population whose registered residence did not match their actual residences was 144 million in 2000, 298 million in 2014, and 292 million in 2016.

The employed population, urban and rural structure, and industrial structure also changed. In 2016, the employed population was 776.03 million, an increase of 55 million over 2000. In 2000, more than two-thirds of the employed population was rural population, and the ratio decreased to 46.6% in 2016. In terms of industrial structure, the population employed by primary

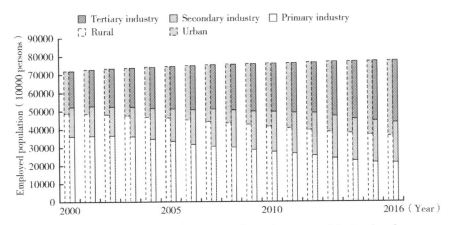

FIGURE 20.10   Urban and Rural Structure and Industrial Structure of the Employed Population, 2000–2016

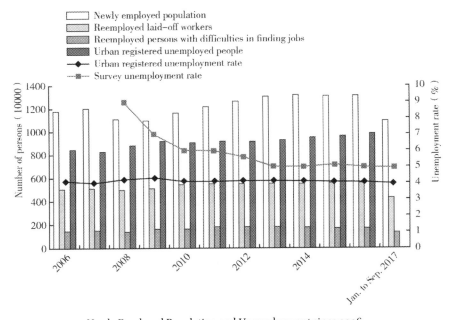

FIGURE 20.11   Newly Employed Population and Unemployment since 2006

industry accounted for 50% in 2000, and those employed by secondary industry and tertiary industry accounted for 22.5% and 27.5%, respectively. In 2016, the population employed by primary industry, secondary industry, and tertiary industry accounted for 27.7%, 28.8%, and 43.5%, respectively.

The situation of employment in our country was basically stable. In 2016, the newly employed population in urban areas was 13.14 million, and the reemployed laid-off workers and the reemployed people with difficulties in finding jobs numbered 5.54 million and 1.69 million, respectively. In 2016, the number of registered laid-off workers in urban areas was 9.82 million, and the urban registered unemployment rate was 4.02%. At the end of the first three quarters of 2017, the registered unemployment rate was 3.95%, which was the lowest it had been since the financial crisis.

3 Life of Urban and Rural Residents

The income of urban and rural residents has kept growing. In terms of income, from 2015 to 2016, the per capita disposable income of urban households increased from 31,194.8 yuan to 33,616.2 yuan; and the per capita net income of rural households increased from 11,421.7 yuan to 12,363.4 yuan. In terms of comparison between urban and rural incomes, with the increase in the income of rural residents, the gap between urban and rural incomes was narrowing, and the growth rate of the per capita net income of rural households was higher than that of urban households.

In terms of resident income, the proportion of income from salaries in 2016 was the highest, at 56.5%; the proportions of net transfer income and net operating income were close, at 17.9% and 17.7%, respectively; and the proportion of net asset income was 7.9%.

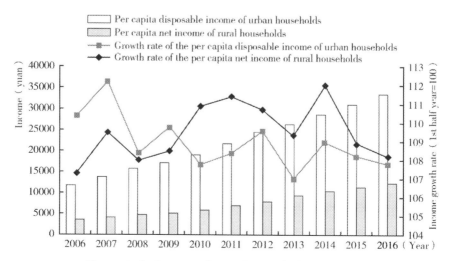

FIGURE 20.12 Changes in the Income and Expenditures of Urban and Rural Residents, 2006–2016

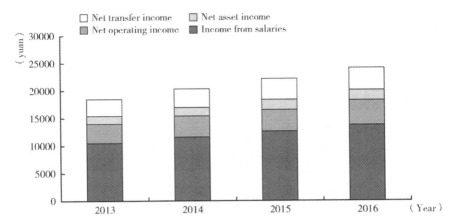

FIGURE 20.13   Per Capita Disposable Income of Residents, 2013–2016

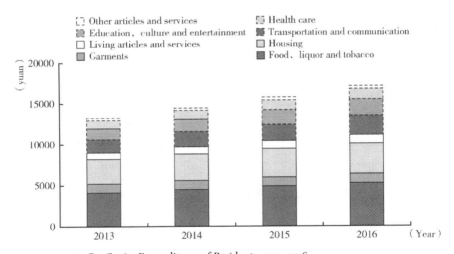

FIGURE 20.14   Per Capita Expenditures of Residents, 2013–2016

The residents' expenditures on consumption also increased to 17,110.7 yuan in 2016. Expenditures on food, liquor, and tobacco accounted for more than 30%, which was the highest proportion; this was followed by expenditures on housing, at 21.9%, and expenditures on transportation and communication as well as education, culture, and entertainment, at 13.7% and 11.2%, respectively.

Progress was made in reducing poverty. In 2016, the size of the impoverished portion of the population decreased to 43.35 million and the incidence of poverty decreased to 4.5%.

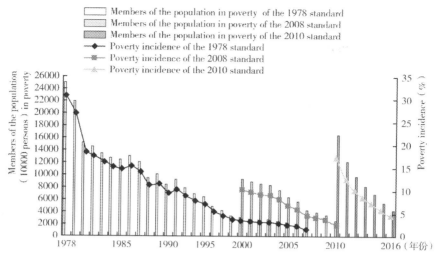

FIGURE 20.15 Impoverished Population and Poverty Incidence, 1978–2016
Note: (1) Standard in 1978: it was called the rural poverty standard from 1978 to 1999, and the absolute rural poverty standard from 2000 to 2007. (2) Standard in 2008: it was called the rural low-income standard from 2000 to 2007, and the rural poverty standard from 2008 to 2010. (3) Standard in 2010: the newly determined standard of rural poverty reduction.

4   Science, Health, Social Security, and Social Services

The input in scientific expenditures continued to increase. The ratio of expenditures on R&D to GDP in 2016 was 2.11%, an increase of 0.38 percentage points over 2010. In total, expenditures on R&D surpassed one trillion yuan in 2012, and 1.5 trillion yuan in 2016 to reach 1.56767 trillion yuan. In expenditures on R&D, the input ratios for fundamental research, applied research, and the development of experiments were 5.3%, 10.2%, and 84.5%, respectively.

The amount and structure of total health care expenditures continued to change. The proportion of total health care expenditures in the GDP was higher than 5% in 2009, reached 5.98% in 2015, and surpassed 6% to reach 6.23% in 2016. In 2016, total health care expenditures reached 4,634.48 billion yuan, in which government health expenditures, social health expenditures, and personal health expenditures in cash accounted for 30.0%, 41.2%, and 28.8%, respectively. Compared to the previous year, the ratio of social health expenditures continued to increase, while the proportions of personal and government expenditures decreased to some extent.

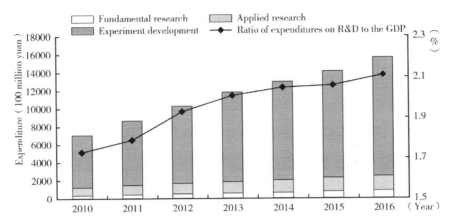

FIGURE 20.16 Inputs in Research and Development (R&D), 2010–2016

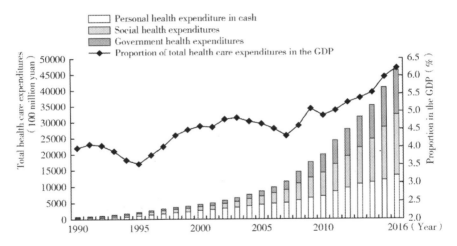

FIGURE 20.17 Total Health Care Expenditures, 1990–2016

Medical conditions improved significantly. The number of medical personnel for each 1,000 people in urban areas increased from 5.82 in 2005 to 10.79 in 2016, and the number in rural areas increased from 2.69 in 2005 to 4.04 in 2016. In terms of regions, in 2016, Qinghai, Beijing, and Xinjiang ranked at the top in terms of the number of medical personnel for each 1,000 people in urban areas, and the numbers in Tianjin, Shanghai, and Zhejiang in rural areas were higher than those of other regions.

With the rapid promotion of the construction of the system of social security, the coverage of various social insurances continued to expand and the

A STATISTICAL OVERVIEW OF CHINA'S SOCIAL DEVELOPMENT IN 2017 433

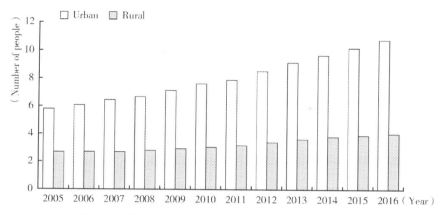

FIGURE 20.18   Number of Medical Personnel for Each 1,000 People, 2005–2016

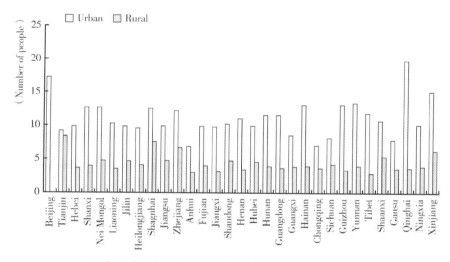

FIGURE 20.19   Number of Medical Personnel for Each 1,000 People in 2016, by Region

number of participants increased year by year. In 2016, the participants in basic pension insurance numbered 887.768 million, and those participating in urban basic health care insurance and urban and rural basic pension insurance were 743.916 million and 508.471 million, respectively. In addition, the participants in unemployment insurance, work-related injury insurance, and maternity insurance also increased to different extents, numbering 180.888 million, 218.893 million, and 184.510 million, respectively. The income and expenditures of the social insurance funds witnessed rapid growth. In 2016, the

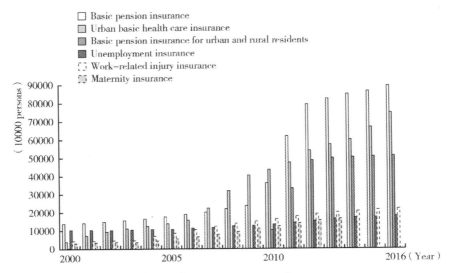

FIGURE 20.20 Participants in Social Insurances, 2000–2016

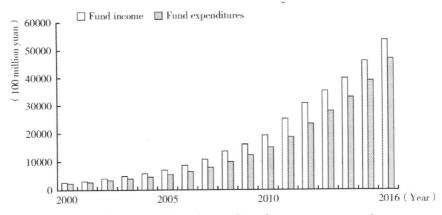

FIGURE 20.21 Fund Income and Expenditures of Social Insurances, 2000–2016

income of the funds of the five social insurances was 5,356.271 billion yuan, and the expenditures were 4,688.843 billion yuan, with an accumulated surplus of 5,953.253 billion yuan.

In terms of social assistance, the number of urban residents enjoying subsistence allowances was stable, with some reduction in recent years, and at the end of 2016, 14.80 million people had received subsistence allowances nationwide. The number of rural residents receiving subsistence allowances increased rapidly from 35.663 million in 2007 to 53.88 million in 2014, and decreased to 45.865 million in 2016. In 2016, the number of extremely impoverished

A STATISTICAL OVERVIEW OF CHINA'S SOCIAL DEVELOPMENT IN 2017

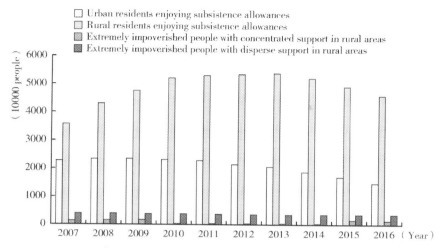

FIGURE 20.22   Social Assistance, 2007–2016

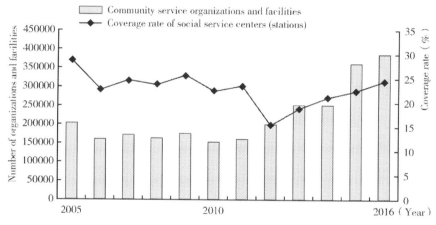

FIGURE 20.23   Community Service Organizations, 2005–2016

people with concentrated support in rural areas was 1.397 million, a decrease of 227,000 over the previous year. In 2016, the number of extremely impoverished people with dispersed support in rural areas was 3.572 million.

Community service organizations and facilities continued to develop, and the coverage of social service centers (stations) has improved greatly. At the end of 2016, there were 386,000 community service organizations and facilities nationwide, an increase of 25,000 over the previous year, and the coverage rate of social service centers (stations) was 24.4%.

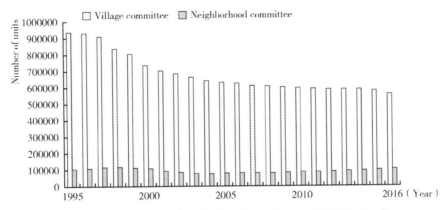

FIGURE 20.24 Changes in the Number of Village Committees and Neighborhood Committees, 1995–2016

The system of community-level self-governance improved gradually. As of 2016, there were 559,000 village committees and 103,000 neighborhood committees nationwide.

References

National Bureau of Statistics. *The 2011 China Statistical Yearbook*, China Statistics Press, 2011.

National Bureau of Statistics. *The 2017 China Statistical Yearbook*, China Statistics Press, 2017.

Website of the Ministry of Human Resources and Social Security of the People's Republic of China. http://www.mohrss.gov.cn/.

Website of the National Bureau of Statistics of the People's Republic of China. http://www.stats.gov.cn/tjsj/.

Index

absolute amount   282, 285
acceptance of death   254–256
acoustic environment   346–347
Action   18, 76, 94, 105–106, 110–114, 128, 159, 194, 240–241, 263, 265, 268, 316, 334–335, 339, 352–353, 367, 383
active users   297
activity index   409
actual employment rate   57
actual working hours   221
added value   4, 47, 365
added value of the industrial enterprises with an annual revenue above 20 million yuan   365
administrative adjudication   138
affluent society   180, 184
aging of the population   86
agricultural household population in urban areas   52
agriculture, rural areas, and rural residents   386
air pollution   19, 335, 337–338, 340, 352
air pollution control   338, 352
anniversary   1–2, 22, 304, 406–407, 409, 412–414
anti-terrorist   139
anxiety over death   254–256
a Population   10, 19–21, 115, 128
asset income   34–36, 43, 429
asset securitization   109–110
assistance for extremely impoverished people in rural areas   288
audio apps   246
average amount of health care insurance reimbursement   292
average annual expenditure   284
average annual income   395
average annual per capita income   152
average carbon dioxide concentration   337
average educational expenditure   98
average housing area   388, 400
average monthly income   25, 62, 221–222, 366
average monthly salary   63, 221
average rate of compliance   346

average sleeping time   228
average unpaid wages   367
average yield per mu   402
awareness rates   183

B2C   181–182, 184–185, 188
basic health care insurance   72–73, 77, 81, 89, 120, 154, 222, 224, 368–369, 433
basic monthly pension   369
basic old-age pension   35
basic pension insurance   35, 72–74, 154, 222, 224, 368–369, 433
Belt and Road Initiative Education Action   94, 105–106
binary communities   287
Biotoxin pollution   328
business   9–10, 23, 46–47, 53, 56, 58, 65–67, 71, 75–76, 101, 113, 129, 138, 140, 148–149, 191–192, 198–200, 203–204, 214, 247, 249, 305, 307, 309, 330, 366, 373–374, 377–380, 406–408, 413–416, 418–421
business arbitration   138
business environment   408, 418–420

C2C   181–182, 184–185, 188
calculated trust   187
central supervision over environmental protection   355, 357–358
charity   71, 86, 90–91, 93, 161–162, 291
charity events   91
charity undertakings   71, 86, 90–91, 93
child enrollment   94, 112
Children's welfare   88
China's Social Conditions   1, 45, 139, 141, 177
China's Urban and Rural Households   33
chronic diseases   126, 292–294
civil disputes   132
clean energies   338
Climate change   337–339
clinics   116–119, 122
collaborative consumption   180–181
Collective Anxiety   296, 304
college education   284–286, 387
college graduates   46, 51–52, 54–56, 58–70, 197–198, 220, 414

commercial medical insurance policies   226
common diseases   226, 228–229
community   2–3, 9, 15, 87, 92, 117, 119, 123,
    132–133, 142–146, 149–150, 180, 187, 212,
    215–216, 234–237, 239, 251, 315, 368,
    435–436
community identity   236–237
Commuting   226–227
commuting time   226–227
complaints and reporting   326
Comprehensive Reform of Public
    Hospitals   121, 124
compulsory education   11, 29, 85, 94, 96, 98,
    101–102, 104–107, 110, 284–285, 306
compulsory education in counties   104–105
consumption   3–4, 7–9, 16–18, 24, 32–33,
    38–42, 44–45, 180–181, 183–184, 187,
    190–191, 193, 195, 200–201, 211–212, 248,
    277, 320, 337, 362, 373, 390, 430
consumption ideology   184
credible society   159
credit filing   101
Crop output   402, 404
crude divorce rate   426

days with good air quality   340
death tax rate   305
degree of satisfaction   60, 230, 238
delegating powers, streamlining
    administration, and optimizing
    services   191, 366, 371, 406–407, 417,
    419–420
dependency   21, 369, 425–426
dependent family members   274
desertification   339
differences with respect to social class   189
difficulty factor   417
difficulty in seeking medical advice   123
digital economy   47
dinner parties   201
disabled children   85, 88, 110
disaster assistance   82, 291
Discipline Innovation and Talent
    Introduction Program for Higher
    Educational Institutions   108
disposal rates   347
dispute mediation   136–138, 371
dividends of reform   366
drinking water   41, 342, 353

dropouts   85, 107
drug distribution certificates   321
Drug inspection   320, 325–326, 332–333
Drug Safety   320–321, 326
drug system   124–125

Ecological Civilization   334–335, 339–340,
    350–352, 354, 357–359, 361–362
ecological environment   27, 111, 336–337,
    339, 344–345, 348–350, 352–353,
    358–361
ecological safety   335
Economic cases involving a large number of
    people   143
economic fairness   165
Economic Poverty   269, 276
economic sustainability   278–279
education   3, 5, 8–12, 19, 22, 28–30, 40,
    42–44, 51, 57, 63–70, 85, 88, 91, 93–114,
    128, 131, 164, 168, 177, 191, 198–199,
    237, 246, 269, 273, 279–282, 284–286,
    295, 305–306, 313, 334, 352, 373, 377,
    381–383, 387, 392–393, 404, 418, 430
educational assistance   86, 290–292
educational background   65, 106, 108, 110,
    165, 215–216, 220, 242, 254, 259–260,
    263, 273–274, 312–313, 364, 377,
    387–388, 392, 394
educational conflicts   111
educational fairness   113, 165
Educational Reform   95–96, 105
educational resources   11, 21, 42, 95–96, 112,
    168–169, 284
education assistance   85
Education Development   95
Education Equality   95
education industry   94, 106, 109–110,
    113–114
education information system   113
emission permissions   358
employed population   4, 23, 427–428
Employment   5, 7–10, 21–22, 24, 27–28, 30,
    33, 42–43, 46–69, 73, 75–77, 84–85,
    112–113, 155–157, 165–166, 169, 181,
    192–198, 209–211, 274–275, 364–366,
    373–374, 376–377, 379–381, 383, 391,
    414, 420–421, 425, 428
employment assistance   52, 84
employment contracts   156

INDEX

439

employment flexibility 366

Employment for College Graduates 46, 54–55, 64

employment index 55–57

employment indicator 366

employment industries 275

Employment Priority Strategy 366

employment quality index 59–60

employment relationships 376

Employment structure 274, 391

Engel coefficient 8, 39, 277–278

enrollment 9, 11–12, 29–30, 51, 56–59, 63, 70, 94, 96–100, 106, 110, 112, 197

enterprise public opinion 297, 300–301

entertainment 8–9, 40, 44–45, 140, 203, 207–209, 211–212, 244–247, 265, 296, 300–301, 309, 314, 398, 404, 430

environmental electromagnetic radiation 348

environmental ionizing radiation 348

environmental law enforcement 358

Environmental Management 335

Environmental Protection 18–19, 54, 91–92, 168, 170, 334–346, 348–363

environmental protection and governance 350–351, 354–355

equal probability 409

equal rights for home tenants and owners 94, 112, 298

Equal rights for renters and homeowners 112

equivalent level of sound 346

expenditure 3, 5, 7–8, 17, 24, 38–40, 78, 80–86, 92, 95, 97–98, 116, 121, 127, 277, 284, 386, 390, 398–399

extremely impoverished people 80–81, 85, 288, 435

extremely impoverished people with concentrated support 435

extremely impoverished people with dispersed support 435

family farms 387, 392–396, 398–405

Farmers 7, 15–17, 25, 35, 127, 274, 287, 378, 386

farming-only households 387, 391–396, 398–402, 404–405

Fee-based access to online content 318

fertility rate 20–21, 425

fixed observation points 386–387, 389, 404–405

flexible employment 43, 55–56, 61–62, 65, 68–69, 77, 85, 373–374

food 7–8, 39–40, 44, 181, 183–185, 201, 246, 277, 279–280, 307, 311, 320–324, 326–332, 337, 352, 360, 373, 390, 398–399, 404, 430

food additive production licenses 321

food additives 321, 323–324, 326, 331

food and drug inspection 320

food and drug registration 322

Food and Drug Safety 320–321, 326

Foodborne diseases 331

food pollutants 331

food production licenses 321

Food Safety 320–323, 329–332

food safety information 332

Food Safety Law 320, 329

food safety risks 331

forest area 344

forest coverage rate 18, 344

fraud 134, 240–241, 250–251, 256, 259–260, 263, 265–266, 300, 302, 330

Gini coefficient 6, 36

global governance 337

government assistance 278–279

government subsidies 286, 395–397

grassland area 344

green development 335–337, 352, 356–359, 361–362

Green development modes 335

green finance 339, 362

green technological system of innovation 362

gross rate of enrollment 96

group activities 250–252, 308

group regulations 309

hazardous industrial waste 347

health 3, 5, 9, 12–14, 20, 28–29, 40, 42, 44, 72–73, 77, 81, 88–89, 91–92, 115–131, 154, 166, 168, 191, 215, 218, 222, 224, 226, 240–241, 245–247, 253–257, 259–260, 268–269, 272–273, 279–280, 283, 292–295, 313, 321–324, 326, 328, 330–331, 338, 350, 368–369, 371, 376, 418, 431–433

440 INDEX

health care   9, 40, 42, 44, 72–73, 77, 81,
  88–89, 91–92, 115–117, 119–122, 124–127,
  154, 166, 168, 191, 218, 222, 224, 259, 269,
  279–280, 283, 292–295, 313, 368–369,
  418, 431, 433
health care insurance   72–73, 77, 81, 89, 92,
  115, 120–125, 127, 154, 222, 224, 259, 283,
  292–295, 368–369, 433
health care insurance systems established for
  the transferee population   293
Health Literacy   115, 125, 130–131
Health Poverty Reduction program
  126–127
Healthy China Strategy   116
Heavy metal pollution   327, 330, 353
hierarchical diagnosis and treatment   122,
  124
high cost of medical treatment   116
high degree of trust   159
High-End Foreign Expert Program   108
higher education   9–12, 29, 51, 57, 65, 67,
  97–98, 101, 103–104, 109, 237
higher educational backgrounds, higher
  incomes, and higher positions   215
higher vocational colleges   65, 97
high-income households   153
homeownership   153–154
homicide cases   133
householders   386–388, 392–395, 404
household poverty   272
household registers   111, 220–225, 238
household waste   347
housing   8, 10, 17, 21, 23–25, 41, 112, 116,
  137–138, 153–154, 179, 181, 186, 188,
  202–203, 222, 224–225, 239, 269–270,
  279–280, 286–287, 290–292, 295, 298,
  304, 313–315, 356, 380, 388, 390, 400,
  402, 404, 430
housing assistance   290–292
housing burden   286
HR market   48–50
Human capital   12, 184, 272–273

ideological and political education system
  for colleges, middle schools, and primary
  schools   102
ideology   184, 300, 302, 306, 314
illegal activities   142–144, 147–148, 331–332,
  367, 370

illegal fund-raising cases   143
illiteracy rate   273
impoverished population   44, 80, 125–127,
  288, 290
impoverished population in particular   80
impoverished portion of the
  population   430
income   1, 3, 6–8, 11–17, 22, 24–25, 29,
  32–38, 42–43, 55, 60, 62–63, 71–74, 80,
  92, 96–97, 108, 116, 119, 121–123, 127,
  152–153, 165–166, 169, 181, 184, 190–191,
  213–215, 221–222, 232–233, 239, 257,
  259–260, 271–272, 276–279, 285, 288,
  295–296, 313, 366, 368–369, 373–374,
  386, 391, 395–397, 404, 406, 409, 411,
  413, 429, 433–434
income gap   6, 22, 24–25, 33, 36–38, 123,
  152–153
individual annual effective dose   348
individual businesses   28, 219, 406, 408
Industrial Labor Force   364–365, 376–378,
  381–384
industry mediation   138
information   5, 40, 47, 66, 68, 77, 91, 101,
  109–111, 113, 117, 130–131, 136, 145–150,
  169, 180–184, 187–188, 192, 202–207,
  212, 216, 235, 238, 242–246, 250–251,
  253–254, 256–257, 260–261, 263, 268,
  296–297, 299, 306, 309–310, 312, 315–
  319, 321–322, 327, 329–330, 332, 352,
  354, 356, 358, 360, 364–365, 372–377,
  379, 381, 384–385, 407
information publicity   101
initial diagnosis   116, 123, 131
initial diagnosis at the grassroots   123
injury cases   133
innovation and education toward starting a
  business   199
innovation services   44
inspector training system   332
integrated discussion system   149
Interlink of Reforms on Health Care
  Insurance, Health Care System and
  System of Drug Circulation   115, 121
international order   337
Internet   9, 66, 91, 101, 129, 143, 146–148,
  161–162, 180, 182, 191, 202, 204–208,
  212, 240–245, 247–251, 253, 255–257,
  259–268, 296–297, 299–300, 303–319,

INDEX

328, 330, 364, 372–373, 375, 377–378,
  381–382, 384, 411
Internet Hot-Button Issues   303
Internet Public Opinion   296–297, 303,
  313–316, 319
Internet users   182, 202, 205–206, 208, 241,
  296, 300, 303–315, 317–319
inter-regional income gap   37

job vacancies-to-seekers ratio   366
joint pollution prevention and control
  system   353

Key Supporting Program for Introducing
  High-End Overseas Scientific and
  Teaching Experts   108
knowledge services   182–184, 186, 190
knowledge-sharing economy   318

labor   5–6, 9–10, 19, 21–22, 27–28, 46, 53, 55,
  58, 63–64, 67–69, 71, 113, 129–130, 135,
  138, 214, 278–282, 300, 302, 364–366,
  368, 371–384, 387, 415, 417–418
labor and technical system of
  competition   383
labor arbitration   138
labor disputes   300, 302, 364, 371–372, 374,
  380
Labor Force   27, 129, 280, 364–366, 376–384
labor market   10, 27–28, 46, 53, 55, 58,
  63–64, 67
Labor Relationships   372–374, 376, 380–381
labor supply-demand relationship   63
laid-off workers   8, 52, 54, 414, 429
law-based governance of the country   158
lawyer mediation   138
left-behind children   11, 85, 88, 110–111
life services   40, 182, 184, 186, 190, 390,
  398–399, 404
living conditions   80, 129–130, 200, 213, 230,
  270, 280–282, 286–287, 304, 386, 405
living environment   41, 287, 362
Locally based policies   287
Longitudinal   58, 193–194, 209–210, 215,
  270
Longitudinal Survey on China's Employment,
  Lives, and Values of College Students and
  Graduates   193–194, 209–210
low-income households   152–153
Low-Rent Housing   286–287, 314

Made in China 2025   101, 191, 381–382
major diseases   83, 125–127, 282, 292–294
major infectious diseases   129–130
making room, adjusting the structure, and
  ensuring linkage   120–121
management of dependent territories   309
"margin subsistence allowance
  households"   270
market entities   9, 407–408, 411, 419
market players   305
market trading   372
Mass Entrepreneurship and Innovation   43,
  47, 198, 366
maternity insurance   12–13, 72–73, 76–77,
  92, 154, 368, 433
medical assistance   78, 81–82, 89, 126–127,
  290–292
medical consortium   121, 123–124
medical waste   347
mental disorders   89–90, 128
mentally handicapped people   89–90
Microblog   205, 297–299, 307, 309, 311–312,
  316
Microorganism pollution   327
middle class   36, 190, 213–215, 238–239, 313
middle-income group   213–214, 239, 296, 313
migrant population   23–24, 125, 127–128
migrant workers   10, 17, 23–25, 46, 51–52,
  55, 65, 128–130, 287, 364, 367–368, 372,
  377–379, 381–383
minimum wage   367
modern system of occupational
  education   382
monitored data   331
monitoring and emergency response   331
moral and legal construction   158
moral education and cultivating civic virtues
  for education   102–103
moral trust   187
mortality rate   14, 425
mortgage slaves   202

National financial expenditure on
  education   97
national identity   158
natural population growth rate   425
natural villages   41–42
nature reserves   344
net asset income   34–35, 43, 429
net enrollment rate   96

442 INDEX

net operating income   429
net transfer income   34–35, 429
network opinions   205
new economic mode   181
newly employed people   48, 365
newly employed population in urban
    areas   428
new rural cooperative health care
    insurance   293
News reporting should demonstrate greater
    political   317
new system of social credit   192
New White-Collar Urban Workers   213–239
NIMBY   353–354
nine-year compulsory education   11, 29, 96,
    104
non-agricultural workers   28, 156, 366
non-point source pollution   349
non-public sector   218–222, 238, 305, 378
Nuclear energy and radiation   348
number of medical personnel for each 000
    people   432–1
number of new enterprises per 000
    people   409, 10, 410
number of new workers   48, 155
number of participants   72, 75, 77, 81, 369,
    433
nursing insurance   72, 75, 93
nursing insurance system   72

occupational diseases   128–130, 371
occupational skill training   383
offshore areas   342–343
one-vote veto system   370
online platforms   146, 183–184, 187–188, 240,
    318, 374
online retail sales   422
operating income   43, 122, 279, 395, 406,
    409, 411, 413, 429
ordinary industrial solid waste   347
Outlook on Consumption   193, 195, 200,
    211
Outlook on Employment   193, 195–196, 211
outlook on green development   357
overcapacity   52–54, 183, 353, 365
Overuse of food additives   326, 331
ownership system   305, 351
ownership system of natural resources   351

parasitic economy   287
Participation   21–22, 30–31, 43, 55, 72, 80,
    87–88, 90, 114, 133, 167–175, 177, 179–182,
    189–191, 193, 195, 202–203, 211, 215, 222,
    224–225, 236–237, 239–241, 250–253,
    268, 314, 352, 355, 383, 391
passing rate of random checks   320, 323
patriotic enthusiasm   158, 300
people looking for jobs   50
people to be recruited   50
people with difficulties in finding jobs   52,
    429
per capita consumption expenditure   7–8,
    38–40
per capita disposable income   3, 6, 13–14, 16,
    24–25, 33–35, 38, 366, 429–430
per capita expenditures   277
per capita housing construction area   41
per capita income   6, 35, 38, 152, 276–277
per capita living area   230
per capita living area of residences   230
per capita net income   34, 116, 119, 429
per capita subsistence allowances   79–80
perception   240–241, 249–250, 254, 263, 265,
    268, 315, 418
personal health expenditure   116
personal information   250–251, 260–261,
    306
personal safety   132–134, 144, 313
piecework system for salaries   373
platform economy   47, 374
PMI indicator   50
political fairness   165
political participation   171–174, 177
Political trust   209, 212
pollution prevention and control   18–19,
    335, 352–353
poor households transferred into cities   271
popularity   205, 246, 256, 297
population   2, 6–7, 9–10, 12–15, 19–21, 23–24,
    27, 32, 44, 52, 63, 69–70, 72, 75, 77, 80,
    86, 91–92, 96, 115, 118, 123, 125–131, 145,
    150, 153–154, 182, 215–216, 237, 241–242,
    270–276, 279–280, 282, 286–291,
    293–294, 297, 300, 319, 332, 338, 359,
    381, 425–428, 430–431
population aging   20–21, 75
Population structure   21, 215, 271–272

INDEX 443

population whose registered residence did not match their actual residences 427
Post-unit communities 132, 144–145, 149–150
post-unit community safety 132–133, 143–144, 150
poverty 1–3, 5, 7, 14–15, 18–20, 26, 33, 43–44, 71, 78–79, 81, 83–86, 91, 94, 106–108, 115, 125–127, 129, 131, 269–270, 272, 276–277, 280–283, 288, 290, 292, 430–431
Poverty Caused by Diseases 115, 125–126, 282
Poverty incidence 288
poverty reduction system through vocational education 108
precise poverty-reduction 71
preferential treatment 84–85
premium rate of unemployment insurance 76
Preschool education 11, 29, 96–97, 284–285
pre-supervision fines 370
primary industry 47, 378, 428
private education 100–101, 109
private enterprises 22, 28, 30, 68, 196, 218–219, 372, 377, 406, 408, 410
private kitchen sharing services 186
private-owned businesses 408
productive fixed assets 403–404
professional annuity fund 74
professional inspector system 332
promotional rate 96
property safety 132–134
public awareness 183
public hospitals 118–122, 124
public management 297, 301
Public Opinion 5, 68, 111, 158, 204–205, 208, 296–297, 300–301, 303–308, 311–317, 319, 332, 356, 420–421
public opinion guidance 313
Public Opinion on Education 111
public opinion pressure 297, 300–303
Public participation 133, 189, 352
public safety 132–134, 136–139, 141–143, 145–146, 150, 168, 297, 301
public sector 30, 218–222, 238, 305, 377–378
public services 15, 19, 23, 37, 41, 87, 128, 185, 321, 373, 381, 418
pyramid selling 94, 112–113, 132, 143–144, 148–149, 299–300

Quality indicators 327
quality of teachers 108

random checks 320, 322–323, 328
random sampling 182
reading contact rate 297
Real-Name System 296
reduced inter-class mobility 296, 305, 313
reemployed laid-off workers 414, 429
reemployed people with difficulties in finding jobs 429
reform by streamlining administration, delegating power, combining management and delegation, and optimizing services for education 98
reform of education related to innovation and start-ups 101
reform of public hospitals 121, 124
reform of separating school administration, establishment, and evaluation 99
reform of talent cultivation modes 101
reform of the commercial affairs system 406–408, 419
reform of the system of examination enrollment 99
reform of the system of running private schools 100
reform on health care insurance payment 122
regular assistance programs 290–291
reimbursement 127, 282–283, 292–294
reimbursement ratio for major diseases 282
relative level of graduates' salaries 62
Resident Consumption 33
resident housing renting services 186
resident income 6, 8, 15, 32–33, 36, 38, 429
Residue of veterinary drugs 328, 331
resource-oriented regions 54
retirees of enterprises 35
risk exchanges 331
road traffic noise 346
robbery cases 133–134
rural and urban households 36
rural collective property rights system 43
rural extremely impoverished population 288–289
Rural Household 386–387, 391, 395
Rural household differentiation 391

rural households   16–17, 33–34, 43, 271–287, 289–295, 386–396, 398–405, 429
rural households with combined occupations   387, 391–396, 398–405
rural labor force working in cities   366
rural poverty reduction standard   288
rural revitalization strategy   3, 23, 359
rural subsistence allowance population   288–289

salaries   11, 62–65, 156–157, 222–223, 364, 368, 372–373, 381, 429
salary distribution   99
sampling inspection   320, 330–331
sampling inspections   330–331
school bullying and violence   111
school district housing   112, 298, 304
school safety   112
secondary industry   47, 54, 365, 377–378, 428
section ratio   342
self-evaluated value   154
self-identity   234–235
senior citizens   116, 240–268, 270, 319, 425
Senior high school education   97, 284–285, 404
sense of identity   236, 238–239
Service consumption   40
service practitioners   376
Shanghai Urban Neighborhood Survey (suns)   213, 215, 217
sharing economy   4, 9, 47, 179–192, 318, 364–366, 372–374, 376, 380–381
site inspections   325–326, 330
Small and Micro-Enterprises   406–409, 411–417, 419–421
smartphones   207–209, 212, 241–246, 248, 263–267, 296, 381
Smuggling crimes   132, 134
social and economic status   215, 240–241, 259–260, 263, 268
Social assistance   71, 77–78, 80, 83–85, 93, 270, 290–291, 294–295, 434
social assistance system   77–78, 295
social attitudes   193–195, 209, 211–215, 230, 232, 239

Social Classes   179, 189, 214, 239, 314–315
Social Cohesion   151–152, 157–159, 177
Social Conditions   1, 45, 139, 141, 177, 204, 213–214, 421
social conflicts   143, 210–212, 316
social contradictions   31, 210, 297, 300–303
social credit system   192, 306
Social Development   1–3, 8, 12, 14–16, 18, 22, 24–26, 29–30, 38, 44, 77, 86, 113, 119, 143, 151–154, 157–159, 161, 163, 171, 178–180, 194, 213, 238, 290, 361, 422
social distance   234
Social Empowerment   151–152, 167–168, 177
Social Fairness   1–2, 7, 22, 116, 151, 153, 166–167, 177, 191, 269
social fairness and justice   1, 22, 116, 151, 153, 164–165, 177, 269
social governance   23, 31, 113, 133, 136, 138, 145, 150, 161, 171, 174–175, 177, 216, 239, 313
social governance system   133
social groups   168–171
Social Inclusion   163–164, 177, 234, 238–239
social insurance   7, 10, 76, 224, 292, 368–369, 372, 380, 405, 433
Social interactions   228, 238–239, 364, 377
socialism with Chinese characteristics   1, 21–22, 30, 90, 92, 94, 113, 133, 158, 178, 214, 239, 316, 334, 364, 376
socialist core values   157–159, 161, 177
socialist values   151
Social Lives   213, 225
social morality   159, 306
Social network activities   203–205
Social Network Participation   202
social participation   80, 88, 90, 171–174, 252–253
social pension insurance + enterprise annuity + commercial insurance + personal savings   295
Social Poverty   269, 280
social public opinion   297
social security   1, 3, 5, 12–13, 19, 21, 23, 32–33, 43–44, 46, 48–50, 52, 55, 69, 71–77, 82–85, 90, 92–93, 98, 102, 112–113, 125, 127, 151, 154–155, 165–166, 168, 177, 198, 222, 224–225, 269, 288, 291, 293–295,

INDEX

364, 366–369, 371, 376, 385, 431–432, 436

social security fairness   165
social security funds   73, 92
Social Security Policies   288, 291, 295
social security system   12–13, 21, 32–33, 43–44, 55, 69, 71–72, 77, 82, 84, 90, 125, 293–295, 364, 368, 376
social security systems   293, 295
social stratum   313–314
social structure   24, 181, 213
social tolerance   163
Social Trust   161, 177, 179, 186–189, 191, 209
Social welfare   71, 86, 93, 158, 173, 178
soil environment   344, 353, 360–361
soil pollution   330, 335, 344–345, 349, 353, 357, 360–361, 363
Solid waste   347–348, 363
special children   97, 110
special education   11, 96–97, 110
speech boundaries   308
splintering of Internet public opinion   313–316
spot over-limit rate   343–345
Structural transformation   350
subsistence allowance   78–79, 84, 270–271, 288–289, 291–292, 294
subsistence allowance households   270–271, 288
subsistence allowances   35, 78–80, 83, 85, 270, 288, 290–292, 295, 434
survival rate of businesses started by graduates   58
sustainable development   114, 157, 337, 339–340

tailored taxi service/ride sharing service/fast vehicle service   186
Targeted poverty reduction for education   94, 106
teaching team   108
Temporary assistance   78, 83–84, 126, 291
terrorist attacks   139–142
tertiary industry   4, 9, 47, 365–366, 377–379, 428
the Belt and Road Initiative Education Action   94, 105–106

the disabled   71, 80, 86–89, 91, 110, 114, 171, 173, 288
the elderly   20–21, 44, 74–75, 80, 86–88, 91, 128, 171, 173, 288, 425
The environmental issue   337
the public's right to know   354, 356
the reform of delegating powers, streamlining administration, and optimizing services   371, 406–407, 417, 419–420
The Zero Marginal Cost Society   180
three-dimensional prevention and control system of public safety   132–133, 137–139, 143
total health expenditure   116, 121
total household expenditures   282, 285, 390, 396–399
total retail sales of consumer goods   422–424
transfer income   16, 34–35, 74, 278–279, 429
trust   159–163, 177, 179, 186–189, 191, 209–210, 212, 236, 256–257
two-invoice system   121, 125

unclear labor relationship   374
unemployment   3–4, 8–9, 12–13, 23, 28, 44, 46, 48–49, 51–54, 64, 72–74, 76, 154–156, 222, 224–225, 291, 364–365, 368, 380, 428–429, 433
unemployment insurance   12–13, 72–74, 76, 154, 222, 224–225, 368, 433
unemployment insurance benefits   73–74
unemployment rate   3–4, 9, 48–49, 51–53, 155, 364–365, 429
unpaid wages   366–368, 380
urban and rural residents   1, 3, 6–8, 13, 36–37, 41–43, 73, 116, 119, 126, 130, 152–154, 269–270, 276, 295, 369, 429
Urban and Rural Residents Living Under Economic and Material Hardship   269–270, 276
urban households   36, 63, 271–281, 283–286, 290, 293–294, 429
urban registered unemployment rate   48–49, 155, 365, 429
urban resident health care insurance   293
urban-rural income gap   37

urban-rural income ratio 37
urban subsistence allowance
    population 288
urban survey 49, 213, 216, 365
urban worker health care insurance 293

values 92, 113, 151, 157–159, 161, 177, 193–194,
    203, 209–212, 232, 239, 309, 314–315,
    318, 323, 374, 378, 381, 404, 409
village (neighborhood) committees 28, 145,
    152, 172, 175, 236, 436
violent terrorism 132, 138–139
virtual currencies 132, 143–144, 147–148
vitality 30–31, 49–50, 98, 109, 136, 182, 339,
    371, 406–407, 409, 419, 421
Vitality Survey 406
Volunteer service 91–92
volunteer services 71, 91–92

vulnerable group 129, 232–233

WeChat 204–208, 212, 242, 244–245, 248,
    251, 253–254, 257, 261, 265, 296–298,
    303–304, 307, 309, 314, 316, 319, 381
We Media 205, 296, 303, 308–309, 311, 421
"White collar" 214
Willingness 21, 54, 169–172, 179, 186–188, 191,
    198, 236, 361
worker resettlement 365
working hours 221, 223, 374–376, 379
workplace 54, 364, 370, 375
work-related injury insurance 12–13, 72–73,
    76, 433
world-class universities and first-class
    disciplines 102, 104, 114

zero addition of grassroots drug prices 282